The Autobiography of

Eleanor
Roosevelt

The Autobiography of
Eleanor
Roosevelt

G.K. HALL & CO.
Boston, Massachusetts
1984

This G. K. Hall paperback edition is reprinted by arrangement
with Harper & Row, Publishers, Inc.

First G. K. Hall printing 1984.

Library of Congress Cataloging in Publication Data

Roosevelt, Eleanor, 1884-1962.
 The autobiography of Eleanor Roosevelt.

 Reprint. Originally published: New York : Harper,
1961.
 1. Roosevelt, Eleanor, 1884-1962. 2. Roosevelt,
Franklin D. (Franklin Delano), 1882-1945. 3. Presidents
—United States—Wives—Biography. I. Title.
E807.1.R36 1984   973.917'092'2 [B]   84-9093
ISBN 0-8398-2851-9

I DEDICATE THIS BOOK
to all those who will be spared reading the three volumes of my autobiography and who may find this easier and pleasanter to read.

As I look through it, I think it gives some insight into the life and times in which my husband and I lived, and anything which adds to future understanding I hope will have value.

E.R.

Contents

PART III   On My Own

PART IV   The Search for Understanding

Illustrations

ix

I WANT TO SAY IN THIS BOOK a special word of thanks to Miss Elinore Denniston. I could not have done, alone, the long and tedious job of cutting that was necessary to abbreviate the three volumes into one nor have added the parts which seemed necessary for a better understanding and for bringing the volume up to date.

Miss Denniston is a most patient, capable, and helpful co-worker. Without her this volume could never have been produced. I thank her warmly and express here my deep appreciation and pleasure in working with her at all times.

E.R.

Preface

THIS IS BOTH an abbreviated and an augmented edition of my autobiography. Abbreviated because, as far as possible, material of only passing interest has been eliminated; augmented by the addition of new material that brings the book up to date. When I first embarked on the story of my life the chief problem I faced was to decide what to put in. Now, in preparing this shorter version, I have had to decide what to leave out. In both cases, the major difficulty lay in trying to see myself and my activities and what happened to me within the framework of a larger picture. It is not easy to attain this kind of perspective because, for me, as for almost everyone, I think, the things that mattered most have not been the big important things but the small personal things.

No one, it seems to me, can really see his own life clearly any more than he can see himself, as his friends or enemies can, from all sides. It is a moral as well as a physical impossibility. The most one can achieve is to try to be as honest as possible.

What my purpose has been I indicated at the end of *This Is My Story*.

It occurs to me to wonder why anyone should have the courage or, as so many people probably think, the vanity to write an autobiography.

In analyzing my own reasons I think I had two objectives: One was to give a picture, if possible, of the world in which I grew up and which today is changed in many ways. The other, to give as truthful a picture as possible of a human being. A real picture of any human being is interesting in itself, and it is especially interesting when we can follow the play of other personalities upon that human being and perhaps get a picture of a group of people and of the influence on them of the period in which they lived. The great difference between the world of the 1880's and today seems to me to be in the extraordinary speeding up of our physical surroundings.

I was for many years a sounding board for the teachings and influence of my immediate surroundings. The ability to think for myself did not develop until I was well on in life and therefore no real personality developed in my early youth. This will not be so of young people of today; they must become individuals responsible for themselves at a much earlier age because of the conditions in which they find themselves in their everyday lives. The world of my grandmother was a world of well-ordered custom and habit, more or less slow to change. The world of today accepts something new overnight and in two years it has become the old and established custom and we have almost forgotten it was ever new.

The reason that fiction is more interesting than any other form of literature to those of us who like to study people is that in fiction the author can really tell the truth without hurting anyone and without humiliating himself too much. He can reveal what he has learned through observation and experience of the inner workings of the souls of men. In an autobiography this is hard to do, try as you will. The more honest you are about yourself and others, however, the more valuable what you have written will be in the future as a picture of the people and their problems during the period covered by the autobiography.

Every individual as he goes through life has different problems and reacts differently to the same circumstances. Different individuals see and feel the same things in different ways, something in them colors the world and their lives. Their experiences and their lessons will be different in each individual case.

To me, who dreamed so much as a child, who made a dreamworld in which I was the heroine of an unending story, the lives of the people around me have continued to have a certain storybook quality. I learned something which has stood me in good stead many times—the most important thing in any relationship is not what you get but what you give.

My Hall family were typical, I think, of the early 1900's. Somewhere in the background there were people who had worked with their hands and with their heads and worked hard, but the need was no longer there and at that time the material conditions of life seemed stable.

My grandfather Hall typified the group, in his generation, that had reached a goal. He was a gentleman of leisure and enjoyed using his brains. He liked to have the stimulation of intelligent companionship but he did not feel the need to work. In his children many of the qualities of the hardfisted, hardheaded ancestors had faded away, but their world was not so stable as they thought and their money began to slip through their fingers. Today, two generations later, the world has changed so much that many of the younger members of the family have to begin again at scratch and it is interesting to see that, with necessity, many of them develop the same abilities that existed in the working forebears.

This cycle, which I have watched in my family, is one reason why, in our country, it always amuses me when any one group of people take it for granted that, because they have been privileged for a generation or two, they are set apart in any way from the man or woman who is working in order to keep the wolf from the door. It is only luck and a little temporary veneer and before long the wheels may turn and one and all must fall back on whatever basic quality they have.

This idea would never have occurred to my grandmother, for to her the world seemed more or less permanently fixed, but to us today it is a mere platitude and our children and grandchildren accept it without turning a hair.

On the other side of my family, of course, many people whom I have mentioned will be described far better and more fully by other people, except in the case of my father, whose short and happy early life was so tragically ended. With him I have a curious feeling that as long as he remains to me the vivid, living person that he is, he will, after the manner of the people in *The Blue Bird*, be alive and continue to exert his influence, which was always a gentle, kindly one.

The more the world speeds up the more it seems necessary that we should learn to pick out of the past the things that we feel were important and beautiful then. One of these things was a quality of tranquillity in people, which you rarely meet today. Perhaps one must have certain periods of life lived in more or less tranquil surroundings in order to attain that particular quality. I read not long ago in David Grayson's *The Countryman's Year* these words: "Back of tranquillity lies always conquered unhappiness." That may be so, but perhaps these grandparents of ours found it a little easier to conquer unhappiness because their lives were not lived at high tension so constantly. Certainly all of us must conquer some unhappiness in our lives.

Autobiographies are, after all, useful only as the lives you read about and analyze may suggest to you something that you may find useful in your own journey through life. I do not expect, of course, that anyone will find exactly the same experiences or the same mistakes or the same gratifications that I have found, but perhaps my very foolishness may be helpful! The mistakes I made when my children were young may give some help or some consolation to some troubled and groping mother. Because of one's timidity one sometimes is more severe with the children, or more irritated at trifles, and one feels the necessity to prove one's power over the only defenseless thing in sight.

We all of us owe, I imagine, far more than we realize to our friends as well as to the members of our family. I know that in my own case my friends are responsible for much that I have become and without them there are many things which would have remained closed books to me.

From the time of my marriage, the life I lived seems more closely allied with the life that all of us know today. It was colorful, active and interesting. The lessons learned were those of adaptability and adjustment and finally of self-reliance and developing into an individual as every human being must.

I have sketched briefly the short trip to Europe after World War I, and yet I think that trip had far-reaching consequences for me. I had known Europe and particularly France, with its neat and patterned countryside, fairly well. The picture of desolation fostered in me an undying hate of war which was not definitely formulated before that time. The conviction of the uselessness of war as a means of finding any final solution to international difficulties grew stronger and stronger as I listened to people talk. I said little about it at the time but the impression was so strong that instead of fading out of my memory it has become more deeply etched upon it year by year.

In *This Is My Story* I covered my early years, the vanishing world in which I grew up, the influences and the values that dominated that era.

In *This I Remember* I dealt with a broader and more vital period, concerned for the most part with my husband's political life during one of the most dramatic and eventful times in history, and with the gradual broadening of my own activities.

In *On My Own* I tried to give some picture of the changing world as I have seen it during recent years and of the various jobs into which I plunged in the hope that, by building international understanding and co-operation, we could hold at bay the ugly stupidity of war and learn to substitute for it, however slowly or painfully—or reluctantly—an era of brotherhood.

In the final part of this book, *The Search for Understanding*, I have added new material, covering the past few years. They have been busy years, with every half hour of every day filled and with my working day often extending from eight in the morning until well past midnight. These crowded hours have been interesting and stimulating. They have, I hope, been useful. They have, at least, been lived to the hilt.

In the long run an autobiography is valuable only if it accomplishes one of two things, or preferably both. It may help to preserve, through the eyes of an individual, a record of a way of life that has vanished, or of people who were historically important in their own era, and so add, even minutely, to our understanding of the background. Or, in a more personal way, it may help other people to solve their problems. There is nothing particularly interesting about one's life story unless people can say as they read it, "Why, this is like what I have been through. Perhaps, after all, there is a way to work it out."

Let me hasten to say that I do not suggest that my solutions should or could prove a guide to anyone. About the only value the story of my life may have is to show that one can, even without any particular gifts, overcome obstacles that seem insurmountable if one is willing to face the fact that they must be overcome; that, in spite of timidity and fear, in spite of a lack of special talents, one can find a way to live widely and fully.

Perhaps the most important thing that has come out of my life is the discovery that if you prepare yourself at every point as well as you can, with whatever means you may have, however meager they may seem, you will be able to grasp opportunity for broader experience when it appears. Without preparation you cannot do it. The fatal thing is the rejection. Life was meant to be lived, and curiosity must be kept alive. One must never, for whatever reason, turn his back on life.

E. R.

Hyde Park
December, 1960

INTRODUCTION

by John Roosevelt Boettiger

THIS IS THE story, in Eleanor Roosevelt's own clear and candid words, of a lifetime of hard-won commitment to the dignity and promise of the human spirit. Although she never held public office, she was in the largest and most honorable sense a public servant. For six decades—from her early, tenatative teaching at the Riverton Street Settlement House in New York City; through the years of her husband's presidency, during which she transformed and vitalized the role of "First Lady" as thoroughly as Franklin Roosevelt did the office of President; to her labor for peace and human rights at the United Nations in the decade and a half following World War II—Eleanor Roosevent built a career of unexampled public accomplishment.

Here is also an intensely and often movingly personal story: an account, in its early pages, of deep and repeated loss, whose pain reverbrated through her life and exacted a formidable self-discipline; an account, above all, of determined personal growth, from the constraining timidity and convention of her class- and family-bound youth to an adult life of enormous energy and profound integrity. Indeed, there is a particularly intimate connection, in Eleanor Roosevelt's life, between the public domain and the personal. The distinctive character and accomplishment of her public service had deeply to do with her finding essential meaning and value in what she called, in the preface to this book, "the small personal things." It was not only that she had a persistently keen eye for the basic human needs whose service is so often lost in the tangle and distraction of public affairs. It was more: the care and love of individual people were the central and sustaining facts of her life, shaping her work and her experience of the world and its issues. "One curious thing," she wrote shortly before her death, "is that I have always seen life personally; that is, my interest or sympathy or indignation is not aroused by an abstract cause but by the plight of a single person whom I have seen with my own eyes." How many dozens of times has someone described to me an encounter with her on some public occasion in virtually the same words: "I had the strongest sense that she was speaking to *me*."

And how many stories are there like that of a young woman named Bertha Brodsky who, among the many who wrote to wish Eleanor well as the White House years began, mentioned that she had difficulty writing with a crooked back. Eleanor's reply was immediate and sympathetic. She arranged for orthopedic consultation and the surgery that followed, visited Bertha in the hospital and called a friend to find a job for her when she had recovered. And that was not the end; it was the beginning of a caringly tended relationship with Bertha and her family.

Eleanor Roosevelt died in her New York City home on November 7, 1962, at the age of 78. Three days later she was buried beside her husband Franklin in the hemlock-bordered rose garden of his family estate at Hyde Park. Three American presidents and one president-to-be[1] were among those who came to mourn and pay homage to the most honored woman of their century. She had recently written, "when you cease to make a contribution you begin to die. Therefore, I think it a necessity to be doing something which you feel is helpful in order to grow old gracefully and contentedly." Virtually to the end, she continued her manifold work for peace, and for the oppressed and dispossessed. In 1961 John F. Kennedy appointed her to the American delegation to the United Nations, where she had earlier served with such distinction; and she chaired, until her final illness made it impossible, the President's Commission on the Status of Women. Nine months before her death President Kennedy, calling her "a living symbol of world understanding and peace," nominated her for the Nobel Peace Prize.

The formative years of Eleanor Roosevelt's life are a striking study in privilege and deprivation. Eleanor's mother, Anna Hall, was a much admired belle of New York society, but one gathers from these pages

---

[1] Harry S. Truman, Dwight D. Eisenhower, John F. Kennedy, and Lyndon B. Johnson.

that her love for her daughter was chilled by a reserved religious
stringency and rigidly conventional standards of conduct. Eleanor's
father, Elliott Roosevelt, stood to his daughter in high contrast:
Charming, spontaneous, full of love—but plagued since childhood
with emotional and physical distress that led, early in his marriage,
to increasingly severe alcoholism. The child Eleanor emerges, in her
self-portrayal, as sensitive, fearful, hungry for affection and praise,
really happy only in the vivid but undependable love of her volatile
father. By the time she was ten both of her parents were dead: her
mother (and little brother Ellie) of diphtheria, her father of an alcohol-
induced fall.

The lonely unhappiness, the manifold fear and anxiety, the sense
of rejection, desertion, and personal shortcoming: all that could well
have crippled Eleanor's development. She did feel the pain for the
rest of her life; and, as she admits in these pages, it was not without
emotional cost to those around her, especially during the early years
of her marriage and motherhood. "Because of one's timidity one sometimes is more severe with the children, or more irritated at trifles,
and one feels the necessity to prove one's power over the only defenseless thing in sight." Her capacity for love, so large in fact, was
in those early adult years constrained, caught in a cage of duty and
reserve. "Duty," she wrote poignantly, "was perhaps the motivating
force of my life, often excluding what might have been joy or pleasure.
I looked at everything from the point of view of what I ought to do,
rarely from the standpoint of what I wanted to do. There were times
when I almost forgot that there was such a thing as wanting anything."
Small wonder that she often seemed stern and withdrawn to her young
children. For her whole life, but more intensely and helplessly in its
first half, Eleanor suffered from recurrent melancholy that she called
her "Griselda moods": "a bad tendency to shut up like a clam" when
she was hurt, "not telling anyone what is the matter, and being much
too obviously humble and meek, feeling like a martyr and acting like
one."

In retrospect, she saw her beloved father's losing fight for his life
as a struggle to recover an essential power of self-control. Later, her
alcoholic Hall uncles offered another frightening example of the costly
loss of that power. And since self-discipline was a central aspect of
her mother's legacy, that quality became a doubly powerful imperative in Eleanor's life. She was able, increasingly in midlife and after,

to put her discipline to wonderfully productive use: her energy and capacity for sustained work became legendary among those who knew her (and were often left in her wake). She also recognized its darker side, from which she struggled progressively but was never wholly free: its sternness, its inhibition of enjoyment, its tendency "to make you draw away from other people and into yourself." The lingering potency of her early experiences of loss and insecurity offer one measure of the remarkable accomplishments of her later years: her insight and compassion, her humor, her tireless work on others' behalf, her passionate devotion to—and need of—those she loved.

Autobiographies intrigue us for many reasons. Other people's gifts and accomplishments feed our dreams. Other people's suffering offers perspective and relief from our own. Our kinship with exemplary lives—those lives whose stories most deeply touch our sense of what we are and what we would become—is often unexpected and sometimes disquieting. Their very differences in scope and circumstance enlarge our vision and stir our recognition. For many who have read this book, in an earlier edition or in its original three volumes, the most absorbing and affecting theme has been that of a woman's finding and making her own life: the slow, often unbidden movement from a dutiful, derivitive existence to thinking and acting for herself, in service to her own humane ends, and thus more freely and truly in service to others.

Her own insecurity and the assumptions of her time and class about women's place dictated a life defined by her husband's needs and interests and dominated by the conventional domestic tasks of wife and mother. "I was not developing any individual taste or initiative. I was simply absorbing the personalities of those about me and letting their tastes and interests dominate me." The seeds of change, of challenge to that pattern, were deeply sown: the strength of what she aptly called her "self-will" was from early childhood an uneasy companion to her desire to please. But those seeds required appropriate circumstances to germinate and grow, circumstances dramatically gathered in the years of midlife.

Eleanor was thirty-two when the United States entered World War I in April, 1917. Her last child had been born a year before. ("For ten years I was always just getting over having a baby or about to have one.") Her wartime activity with the Red Cross and at St. Elizabeth's Hospital, in filling and giving new meaning to her days, broke the circle of domestic dependency: "I was learning to have a certain confidence in myself and in my ability to meet emergencies and deal with them. . . . I had gained some assurance about my ability to run things and the knowledge that there is joy in accomplishing a good job. I knew more about the human heart." It was a critical turning. "She would never again," wrote a biographer, "be content with purely private satisfactions, and for the rest of her life she would look at the injustice of the world, feel pity for the human condition, and ask what she could do about it."[2]

In those same midlife years, redirected by the demands and the terrible human waste of war, she faced two more personal trials by fire. Both, in different ways, confirmed and strengthened her self-assurance and her determination to be herself. The first, unrecorded in this book, was her devastating discovery, in September, 1918, of an affair between her husband and her social secretary, Lucy Mercer. She wrote long after, "The bottom dropped out of my own particular world, and I faced myself, my surroundings, my world, honestly for the first time. I really grew up that year." The second crisis was Franklin's contracting polio in the summer of 1921. Meeting the challenges of that illness, she said, "finally made me stand on my own two feet in regard to my husband's life, my own life, and my children's training. The alternative would have been to become a completely colorless echo of my husband and mother-in-law and torn between them. I might have stayed a weak character forever if I had not found that out." It was very likely those critical years of her mid-thirties that Eleanor had in mind when she wrote a younger friend two decades later, "Somewhere along the line of development we discover what we really are, and then we make our real decision for which we are responsible. Make that decision primarily for yourself because you can never really live anyone else's life, not even your child's. The influence you exert is through your own life and what you become yourself."

However much it will be debated and reassessed, Eleanor Roosevelt's influence on her own and succeeding generations is something for which we may be grateful. At its heart, I suspect, are some of her simplest words: "Life was meant to be lived. . . . One must never, for whatever reason, turn his back on life." She knew deeply, in herself and others, the pain that tempts such a turning; but as her friend Adlai Stevenson said, "She never did, and we are the richer."

---

[2]Joseph P. Lash, *Eleanor and Franklin* (New York: W.W. Norton & Co., 1971).

PART I

This Is My Story

Memories of My Childhood

MY MOTHER WAS one of the most beautiful women I have ever seen. Her father, my grandfather Hall, never engaged in business. He lived on what his father and mother gave him.

He had a house in New York City at 11 West Thirty-seventh Street, and he built another on the Hudson River about five miles above the village of Tivoli, on land which was part of the old Chancellor Livingston estate. My grandmother's mother was a Miss Livingston, and so we were related to the Livingstons, the Clarksons, the DePeysters, who lived in the various houses up and down the River Road.

My grandfather Hall's great interest was in the study of theology, and in his library were a number of books dealing with religion. Most of them were of little interest to me as a child, but the Bible, illustrated by Doré, occupied many hours—and gave me many nightmares!

My grandmother Hall, who had been a Miss Ludlow, a beauty and a belle, was treated like a cherished but somewhat spoiled child. She was expected to bring children into the world and seven children were born, but she was not expected to bring them up. My grandfather told her nothing about business, not even how to draw a check, and died without a will, leaving her with six children under seventeen years of age, a responsibility for which she was totally unprepared.

The two eldest children, my mother and Tissie—whose real name was Elizabeth and who later became Mrs. Stanley Mortimer—bore the marks of their father's upbringing. They were deeply religious; they had been taught to use their minds in the ways that my grandfather thought suitable for girls. He disciplined them well. In the country they walked several times a day from the house to the main road with a stick across their backs in the crook of their elbows to improve their carriage. He was a severe judge of what they read and wrote and how they expressed themselves, and held them to the highest standards of conduct. The result was strength of character, with definite ideas of right and wrong, and a certain rigidity in conforming to a conventional pattern, which had been put before them as the only proper existence for a lady.

Suddenly the strong hand was removed, and the two boys and the two younger girls knew no discipline, for how could a woman who had never been treated as anything but a grown-up child suddenly assume the burden of training a family?

I have been told that my mother, for the first year or so after my grandfather died, was the guiding spirit of the household, but at nineteen she was married to my father.

My mother belonged to that New York City society which thought itself all-important. Old Mr. Peter Marié, who gave choice parties and whose approval stamped young girls and young matrons a success, called my mother a queen, and bowed before her charm and beauty, and to her this was important.

In that society you were kind to the poor, you did not neglect your philanthropic duties, you assisted the hospitals and did something for the needy. You accepted invitations to dine and to dance with the right people only, you lived where you would be in their midst. You thought seriously about your children's education, you read the books that everybody read, you were familiar with good literature. In short, you conformed to the conventional pattern.

My father, Elliott Roosevelt, charming, good-looking, loved by all who came in contact with him, had a background and upbringing which were alien to my mother's pattern. He had a physical weakness which he himself probably never quite understood. As a boy of about fifteen he left St. Paul's School after one year, because of illness, and went out to Texas. He made friends with the officers at Fort McKavit, a frontier fort, and stayed with them, hunting game and scouting in search of hostile Indians. He loved the life and was a natural sportsman, a good shot and a good rider. I think the life left an indelible impression on him. The illness left its mark on him too, on those inner reserves of strength which we all have to call on at times in our lives. He returned to his family in New York apparently well and strong.

My grandfather Roosevelt died before my father was twenty-one and while his older brother, Theodore, later to be President of the United States, fought his way to health from an asthmatic childhood and went to Harvard College, Elliott, with the consent of an indulgent mother and two adoring sisters, took part of his inheritance and went around the world. He hunted in India when few people from this country had done anything of the kind.

My father returned from his trip for the wedding of his little sister, Corinne, to his friend, Douglas Robinson. Then he married Anna Hall, and tragedy and happiness came walking on each other's heels.

He adored my mother and she was devoted to him, but always in a more reserved and less spontaneous way. I doubt that the background of their respective family lives could have been more different. His family was not so much concerned with Society (spelled with a big S) as with people, and these people included the newsboys from the streets of New York and the cripples whom Dr. Schaefer, one of the most noted early orthopedic surgeons, was trying to cure.

My father's mother and his brother Theodore's young wife, Alice Lee, died within a few days of each other. The latter left only a little Alice to console the sorrowing young father. My father felt these losses deeply. Very soon, however, in October, 1884, I came into the world, and from all accounts I must have been a more wrinkled and less attractive baby than the average—but to him I was a miracle from Heaven.

I was a shy, solemn child even at the age of two, and I am sure that even when I danced I never smiled. My earliest recollections are of being dressed up and allowed to come down to dance for a group of gentlemen who applauded and laughed as I pirouetted before them. Finally, my father would pick me up and hold me high in the air. He dominated my life as long as he lived, and was the love of my life for many years after he died.

With my father I was perfectly happy. There is still a woodeny painting of a solemn child, a straight bang across her forehead, with an uplifted finger and an admonishing attitude, which he always enjoyed and referred to as "Little Nell scolding Elliott." We had a country house at Hempstead, Long Island, so that he could hunt and play polo. He loved horses and dogs, and we always had both. During this time he was in business, and, added to the work and the sports, the gay and popular young couple lived a busy social life. He was the center of my world and all around him loved him.

Whether it was some weakness from his early years which the strain of the life he was living accentuated, whether it was the pain he endured from a broken leg which had to be set, rebroken and reset, I do not know. My father began to drink, and for my mother and his brother Theodore and his sisters began the period of harrowing anxiety which was to last until his death in 1894.

My father and mother, my little brother and I went to Italy for the winter of 1890 as the first step in the fight for his health and power of self-control. I remember my father acting as gondolier, taking me out on the Venice canals, singing with the other boatmen, to my intense joy. I loved his voice and, above all, I loved the way he treated me. He called me "Little Nell," after the Little Nell in Dickens' *Old Curiosity Shop*, and I never doubted that I stood first in his heart.

He could, however, be annoyed with me, particularly when I disappointed him in such things as physical courage, and this, unfortunately, I did quite often. We went to Sorrento and I was given a donkey so I could ride over the beautiful roads. One day the others overtook me and offered to let me go with them, but at the first steep descent which they slid down I turned pale, and preferred to stay on the high road. I can remember still the tone of disapproval in my father's voice, though his words of reproof have long since faded away.

I remember my trip to Vesuvius with my father and the throwing of pennies, which were returned to us encased in lava, and then the endless trip down. I suppose there was some block in the traffic, but I can remember only my utter weariness and my effort to bear it without tears so that my father would not be displeased.

My mother took a house in Neuilly, outside of Paris, and settled down for several months, as another baby was expected the end of June. My father entered a sanitarium while his older sister, Anna, our Auntie Bye, came to stay with my mother. It was decided to send me to a convent to learn French and to have me out of the way when the baby arrived.

The convent experience was an unhappy one. I was not yet six years old, and I must have been very sensitive, with an inordinate desire for affection and praise, perhaps brought on by the fact that I was conscious of my plain looks and lack of manners. My mother was troubled by my lack of beauty, and I knew it as a child senses these things. She tried hard to bring me up well so that my manners would compensate for my looks, but her efforts only made me more keenly conscious of my shortcomings.

The little girls of my age in the convent could hardly be expected to take much interest in a child who did not speak their language and did not belong to their religion. They had a little shrine of their own and often worked hard beautifying it. I longed to be allowed to join them, but was always kept on the outside and wandered by myself in the walled-in garden.

Finally, I fell a prey to temptation. One of the girls swallowed a penny. Every attention was given her, she was the center of everybody's interest. I longed to be in her place. One day I went to one of the sisters and told her that I had swallowed a penny. It must have been evident that my story was not true, so they sent for my mother. She took me away in disgrace. Understanding as I do now my mother's character, I realize how terrible it must have seemed to her to have a child who would lie.

I remember the drive home as one of utter misery, for I could bear swift punishment far better than long scoldings. I could cheerfully lie any time to escape a scolding, whereas if I had known that I would simply be put to bed or be spanked I probably would have told the truth.

This habit of lying stayed with me for years. My mother did not understand that a child may lie from fear; I myself never understood it until I reached the age when I realized that there was nothing to fear.

My father had come home for the baby's arrival, and I am sorry to say he was causing a great deal of anxiety, but he was the only person who did not treat me as a criminal!

The baby, my brother Hall, was several weeks old when we sailed for home, leaving my father in a sanitarium in France, where his brother, Theodore, had to go and get him later on.

We lived that winter without my father. I slept in my mother's room, and remember the thrill of watching her dress to go out in the evenings. She looked so beautiful I was grateful to be allowed to touch her dress or her jewels or anything that was part of the vision which I admired inordinately.

Those summers, while my father was away trying to rehabilitate himself, we spent largely with my grandmother at her Tivoli house, which later was to become home to both my brother Hall and me.

My father sent us one of his horses, an old hunter which my mother used to drive, and I remember driving with her. Even more vividly do I remember the times when I was sent down to visit my great-aunt, Mrs. Ludlow, whose house was next to ours but nearer the river and quite out of sight, for no house along that part of the river was really close to any other.

Mrs. Ludlow was handsome, sure of herself, and an excellent house-keeper. On one memorable occasion she set to work to find out what I knew. Alas and alack, I could not even read! The next day and every day that summer she sent her companion, Madeleine, to give me lessons in reading. Then she found out that I could not sew or cook and knew nothing of the things a girl should know. I think I was six.

I surmise that my mother was roundly taken to task, for after that Madeleine became a great factor in my life and began to teach me to sew.

I still slept in my mother's room, and every morning I had to repeat to her some verses which I had learned in the Old or the New Testament. I wish I could remember today all the verses I learned by heart that summer.

Sometimes I woke up when my mother and her sisters were talking at bedtime, and many a conversation not meant for my ears was listened to with great avidity. I acquired a strange and garbled idea of the troubles around me. Something was wrong with my father and from my point of view nothing could be wrong with him.

If people only realized what a war goes on in a child's mind and heart in a situation of this kind, I think they would try to explain more than they do, but nobody told me anything.

We moved back to New York, the autumn that I was seven, to a house which my mother had bought and put in order on East 61st Street, two blocks from Auntie Bye, who lived at Madison Avenue and East 62nd Street. She had Uncle Ted's little girl, Alice, with her a great deal, and that winter our first real acquaintance began. Already she seemed much older and cleverer, and while I admired her I was always a little afraid of her, and this was so even when we were grown and she was the "Princess Alice" in the White House.

That winter we began a friendship with young Robert Munro-Ferguson, a young man sent over from England by an elder brother to make his way in the world. My father and mother had known the elder brother, Ronald (later Lord Novar), and so had Auntie Bye. The boy was taken into her house, given a start in Douglas Robinson's office, and became a dear and close friend to the entire family.

My mother always had the three children with her for a time in the late afternoon. My little brother Ellie adored her, and was so good he never had to be reproved. The baby Hall was always called Josh and was too small to do anything but sit upon her lap contentedly. I felt a curious barrier between myself and these three. My mother made a great effort; she would read to me and have me read to her, she would have me recite my poems, she would keep me after the boys had gone to bed, and still I can remember standing in the door, often with my finger in my mouth, and I can see the look in her eyes and hear the tone of her voice as she said, "Come in, Granny." If a visitor was there she might turn and say, "She is such a funny child, so old-fashioned that we always call her 'Granny.'" I wanted to sink through the floor in shame.

Suddenly everything was changed! We children were sent out of the house. I went to stay with my godmother, Mrs. Henry Parish, and the boys went to my mother's aunt, Mrs. Ludlow. My grandmother left her own house and family to nurse my mother, for she had diphtheria and there was then no antitoxin. My father was sent for, but came too late from his exile in Virginia. Diphtheria went fast in those days.

I can remember standing by a window when Cousin Susie (Mrs. Parish) told me that my mother was dead. This was on December 7, 1892. Death meant nothing to me, and one fact wiped out everything else. My father was back and I would see him soon.

Later I knew what a tragedy of utter defeat this meant for him. No hope now of ever wiping out the sorrowful years he had brought upon my mother —and she had left her mother as guardian for her children. He had no wife, no children, no hope.

Finally it was arranged that we children were to live with my grandmother Hall. I realize now what that must have meant in dislocation of her household, and I marvel at the sweetness of my two uncles and the two aunts who were still at home, for never by word or deed did any of them make us feel that we were not in our own house.

After we were installed, my father came to see me, and I remember going down into the high-ceilinged, dim library on the first floor of the house in West 37th Street. He sat in a big chair. He was dressed all in black, looking very sad. He held out his arms and gathered me to him. In a little while he began to talk, to explain to me that my mother was gone, that she had been all the world to him, and now he had only my brothers and myself, that my brothers were very young and that he and I must keep close together. Someday I would make a home for him again, we would travel together and do many things which he painted as interesting and pleasant, to be looked forward to in the future.

Somehow it was always he and I. I did not understand whether my brothers were to be our children or whether he felt that they would be going to a school and later be independent.

There started that day a feeling which never left me, that he and I were very close and someday would have a life of our own together. He told me to write to him often, to be a good girl, not to give any trouble, to study hard, to grow up into a woman he could be proud of, and he would come to see me whenever it was possible.

When he left I was all alone to keep our secret of mutual understanding and to adjust myself to my new existence.

The two little boys had a room with Madeleine and I had a little hall bedroom next to them. I was old enough to look after myself, except that my hair had to be brushed at night. Of course, someone had to be engaged to take me out, to and from classes, and to whatever I did in the afternoons. I had governesses, French maids, German maids. I walked them all off their feet. They always tried to talk to me, and I wished to be left alone to live in a dreamworld in which I was the heroine and my father the hero. Into this world I withdrew as soon as I went to bed and as soon as I woke in the morning, and all the time I was walking or when anyone bored me.

I was a healthy child, but now and then in winter I would have a sore throat and tonsillitis, so cold baths were decreed as a daily morning routine —and how I cheated on those baths! Madeleine could not always follow me up, and more hot water went into them than would have been considered beneficial had anyone supervised me.

My grandmother laid great stress on certain things in education. I must learn French. My father wished me to be musical. I worked at music until I was eighteen, but no one ever trained my ear! Through listening to my aunt Pussie play I did gain an emotional appreciation of music. She was a fascinating and lovely creature and her playing was one of the unforgettable joys of my childhood.

I would have given anything to be a singer. I felt that one could give a great deal of pleasure and, yes, receive attention and admiration! Attention and admiration were the things through all my childhood which I wanted, because I was made to feel so conscious of the fact that nothing about me would attract attention or would bring me admiration.

As I look back on that household in the 37th Street house, I realize how differently life was lived in the New York of those days, both in its houses and in its streets. There were a number of large and beautiful homes, most of them on Fifth Avenue. Madison Square was still almost entirely residential, and from 14th Street to 23rd Street was the shopping district.

In the streets there were no motorcars. Beautiful horses and smart carriages took their place. Horse-drawn stages labored up Fifth Avenue and horse-drawn streetcars ran on other avenues and crosstown streets; cabs and hansoms were the taxis of those days.

Our old-fashioned, brownstone house was much like all the other houses in the side streets, fairly large and comfortable, with high ceilings, a dark basement, and inadequate servants' quarters with working conditions which no one with any social conscience would tolerate today. The laundry had one little window opening on the back yard and, of course, we had no electric light. We were modern in that we had gas!

The servants' room lacked ventilation and comfortable furnishings. Their bathroom was in the cellar, so each one had a basin and a pitcher in a tiny bedroom.

Our household consisted of a cook, a butler, a housemaid—who was maid as well to my young aunts—and a laundress. The family consisted of my grandmother, Pussie and Maude, who had been the baby of the family until our arrival, Vallie, my older uncle, and, for brief periods, Eddie, who was some two years younger. Eddie had a roving foot and took at least one long trip to Africa which I remember.

Into this household I moved with my two little brothers and their nurse.

My grandmother seemed to me a very old lady, though I realize now that she was still quite young. She was relegated almost entirely to her own bedroom. She came downstairs when she had visitors of her own, but the drawing room, with its massive gilt furniture covered with blue damask, was the room in which she saw her guests. Her daughters took possession of the library, which was a large front room where the piano stood and where a large bow window on the street gave more light.

The dining room, in the extension at the back, was quite a bright room, having three windows on the side. Back of that was the pantry, where I spent considerable time, for the butler, Victor, was kind to me and taught me how to wash dishes and wipe them, though when I broke one he was much displeased. Sometimes when I was in disgrace and sent supperless to bed, he or Kitty, the chambermaid, would smuggle me up something to eat.

The years had changed my grandmother. With her own children she had been chiefly concerned in loving them. Discipline had been my grandfather's part. When he died she still wanted to surround them with the tenderest love, but later on she found that she could not control Vallie or

Eddie or Pussie or Maude. She was determined that the grandchildren who were now under her care should have the discipline that her own children had lacked, and we were brought up on the principle that "no" was easier to say than "yes."

Looking back I see that I was always afraid of something: of the dark, of displeasing people, of failure. Anything I accomplished had to be done across a barrier of fear. I remember an incident when I was about thirteen. Pussie was ill with a bad sore throat and she liked me to do things for her, which made me very proud. One night she called me. Everything was dark, and I groped my way to her room. She asked if I would go to the basement and get some ice from the icebox. That meant three flights of stairs; the last one would mean closing the door at the foot of the stairs and being alone in the basement, making my way in pitch-black darkness to that icebox in the back yard!

My knees were trembling, but as between the fear of going and the fear of not being allowed to minister to Pussie when she was ill, and thereby losing an opportunity to be important, I had no choice. I went and returned with the ice, demonstrating again the fact that children value above everything else the opportunity to be really useful to those around them.

Very early I became conscious of the fact that there were people around me who suffered in one way or another. I was five or six when my father took me to help serve Thanksgiving dinner in one of the newsboys' club-houses which my grandfather, Theodore Roosevelt, had started. He was also a trustee of the Children's Aid Society for many years. My father explained that many of these ragged little boys had no homes and lived in little wooden shanties in empty lots, or slept in vestibules of houses or public buildings or any place where they could be moderately warm, yet they were independent and earned their own livings.

Every Christmas I was taken by my grandmother to help dress the Christmas tree for the babies' ward in the Post-Graduate Hospital. She was particularly interested in this charity.

Auntie Gracie took us to the Orthopedic Hospital which my grandfather Roosevelt had been instrumental in helping Dr. Newton Schaefer to start and in which the family was deeply interested. There I saw innumerable little children in casts and splints. Some of them lay patiently for months in strange and curious positions. I was particularly interested in them because I had a curvature myself and wore for some time a steel brace which was vastly uncomfortable and prevented my bending over.

Even my uncle Vallie, who at this time was in business in New York, a champion tennis player and a popular young man in society, took me to help dress a Christmas tree for a group of children in a part of New York City which was called "Hell's Kitchen." For many years this was one of New York's poorest and worst sections. I also went with Maude and Pussie to sing at the Bowery Mission, so I was not in ignorance that there were sharp contrasts, even though our lives were blessed with plenty.

Though he was so little with us, my father dominated all this period of my life. Subconsciously I must always have been waiting for his visits. They were irregular, and he rarely sent word before he arrived, but never was I in the house, even in my room two long flights of stairs above the entrance door, that I did not hear his voice the minute he entered the front door. Walking downstairs was far too slow. I slid down the banisters and usually catapulted into his arms before his hat was hung up.

My father never missed an opportunity for giving us presents, so Christmas was a great day and I still remember one memorable Christmas when I had two stockings, for my grandmother had filled one and my father, who was in New York, brought one on Christmas morning.

One more sorrow came to my father the winter that my mother died. My little brother Ellie never seemed to thrive after my mother's death. Both he and the baby, Josh, got scarlet fever, and I was returned to my cousin Susie and, of course, quarantined.

The baby got well without any complications, but Ellie developed diphtheria and died. My father came to take me out occasionally, but the anxiety over the little boys was too great for him to give me a good deal of his time.

On August 14, 1894, just before I was ten years old, word came that my father had died. My aunts told me, but I simply refused to believe it, and while I wept long and went to bed still weeping I finally went to sleep and began the next day living in my dreamworld as usual.

My grandmother decided that we children should not go to the funeral, and so I had no tangible thing to make death real to me. From that time on I knew in my mind that my father was dead, and yet I lived with him more closely, probably, than I had when he was alive.

My father and mother both liked us to see a great deal of Aunt Gracie. She was beloved by all her great-nephews and -nieces. As I remember her now, she was of medium height, slender, with clear-cut features, but always looked fragile and dainty. Ladies wore long dresses in those days, which trailed in the dust unless they were held up, and I seem to remember her generally in the rather tight-fitting bodices of the day, high in the back, square-cut in front and always with an immaculate frill of white lace or plaited linen around the neck.

Often her hands would lie folded in her lap as she told us a story and I, who loved to look at hands even as a child, remember watching them with pleasure. My Saturdays were frequently spent with this sweet and gracious great-aunt. Alice Roosevelt, Teddy Robinson, and I were the three who enjoyed those days the most.

After my father died, these Saturdays with Aunt Gracie were not allowed. My grandmother felt we should be at home as much as possible, and perhaps she feared we might slip away from her control if we were too much with our dynamic Roosevelt relatives.

The next few years were uneventful for me. New York City in winter, with classes and private lessons, and for entertainment occasionally, on a Saturday afternoon, a child or two for supper and play. My grandmother believed in keeping me young and my aunts believed in dressing me in a way which was appropriate to my age but not to my size. I was very tall, very thin and very shy. They dressed me for dancing class and for parties in dresses that were above my knees, when most of the girls my size had them halfway down their legs. All my clothes seem to me now to have been incredibly uncomfortable.

I wore flannels from the 1st of November until the 1st of April, regardless of the temperature, and the flannels went from my neck to my ankles. Of course, the attire included a flannel petticoat and long black stockings. How hot they were! And the high-button or high-laced shoes that went with them and were supposed to keep your ankles slim.

We children stayed at Tivoli in summer now with a nurse and governess, even if the others were away, and there were hot, breathless days when my fingers stuck to the keys as I practiced on the piano but I never left off any garments and, even in summer, we children wore a good many. I would roll my stockings down and then be told that ladies did not show their legs and promptly have to fasten them up again!

The house at Tivoli was big, with high ceilings and a good many rooms,

green. I went to my grandmother before I went to Madeleine, knowing that my grandmother would scold less severely.

I was not supposed to read in bed before breakfast, but as I woke at five practically every morning in summer and was, I am afraid, a self-willed child I used to hide a book under the mattress. Woe to me when Madeleine caught me reading!

I have no recollection now of why she frightened me. As I look back it seems perfectly ludicrous, but I did not even tell my grandmother how much afraid I was until I was nearly fourteen years old, and then I confessed, between sobs, as we were walking in the woods. How silly it all seems today.

A few things I wanted desperately to do in those days. I remember that when I was about twelve Mr. Henry Sloane asked me to go west with his daughter, Jessie. I do not think I ever wanted to do anything so much in all my life, for I was fond of her and longed to travel. My grandmother was adamant and would not allow me to go. She gave me no reasons. It was sufficient that she did not think it wise. She so often said "no" that I built up a defense of saying I did not want to do things in order to forestall her refusals and keep down my disappointments.

She felt I should learn to dance, and I joined a dancing class at Mr. Dodsworth's. These classes were an institution for many years, and many little boys and girls learned the polka and the waltz standing carefully on the diamond squares of the polished hardwood floor.

My grandmother decided that because of my being tall and probably awkward I should have ballet lessons besides, so I went once a week to a regular ballet teacher on Broadway and learned toe dancing with four or five other girls who were going on the stage and looked forward to the chance of being in the chorus and talked of little else, making me very envious.

I loved it and practiced assiduously, and can still appreciate how much work lies behind some of the dances which look so easy as they are done on the stage.

Two

Adolescence

I HAD GROWN fond of the theater and Pussie took me to see Duse, the great Italian actress, when she first came to this country. Then she took me to meet her, a thrill which I have never forgotten. Her charm and beauty were all that I had imagined! I was also allowed to see some of Shakespeare's plays and occasionally to go to the opera, but my young aunts and their friends talked all the time of plays which I never went to see. As a result, one winter I committed a crime which weighed heavily on my conscience for a long time.

My grandmother told me to go to a charity bazaar with a friend. To escape my maid, I told her my friend would have her maid with her and that she would bring me home. Instead of going to the bazaar we went to see a play, *Tess of the D'Urbervilles*, which was being discussed by my elders and which I, at least, did not understand at all. We sat in the peanut gallery and were miserable for fear of seeing someone we knew. We left before the end because we knew we would be late in reaching home. I had to lie and could never confess, which I would gladly have done because of my sense of guilt, but I would have involved the other girl in my trouble.

My grandmother, after my father's death, allowed me less and less contact with his family, the Roosevelts of Oyster Bay, so I saw little of those cousins. I did, however, pay one or two short visits to Aunt Edith and Uncle Ted in summer.

Alice Roosevelt, who was nearest my age, was so much more sophisticated and grown-up that I was in great awe of her. She was better at sports, and my having so few companions of my own age put me at a great disadvantage with other young people.

18

I remember the first time we went swimming at Oyster Bay. I couldn't swim, and Uncle Ted told me to jump off the dock and try. I was a good deal of a physical coward then, but I did it and came up spluttering and was good-naturedly ducked and became very frightened. Never again would I go out of my depth.

A favorite Sunday afternoon occupation was to go to Cooper's Bluff, a high sandy bluff with a beach below. At high tide the water came almost to its base. Uncle Ted would line us up and take the lead and we would go down holding on to each other until someone fell or the speed became so great that the line broke. In some way we reached the bottom, rolling or running.

I was desperately afraid the first time we did it, but found it was not so bad as I thought, and then we clambered up again, taking a long time to get there as we slid back one foot for every two we went up.

In some ways I remember these visits as a great joy, for I loved chasing through the haystacks in the barn with Uncle Ted after us, and going up to the gunroom on the top floor of the Sagamore House where he would read aloud, chiefly poetry.

Occasionally he took us on a picnic or a camping trip and taught us many valuable lessons. The chief one was to remember that camping was a good way to find out people's characters. Those who were selfish showed it very soon, in that they wanted the best bed or the best food and did not want to do their share of the work.

My brother did more of this than I did, for he was just Quentin Roosevelt's age, and after I went abroad my grandmother let him visit Uncle Ted and Aunt Edith more frequently. My only other contact with my Roosevelt family was during an annual Christmas holiday visit, when my grandmother permitted me to spend a few days with Auntie Corinne.

This was the only time in the year when I ever saw any boys of my own age. To me these parties were more pain than pleasure. The others all knew each other and saw each other often. They were all much better at winter sports. I rarely coasted and never skated, for my ankles were so weak that when I did get out on the pond my skating was chiefly on those ankles.

I was a poor dancer, and the climax of the party was a dance. What inappropriate dresses I wore—and, worst of all, they were above my knees. I knew, of course, that I was different from all the other girls and if I had not known they were frank in telling me so! I still remember my gratitude at one of these parties to my cousin Franklin Roosevelt when he came and asked me to dance with him.

I must have been a great trial and responsibility to Auntie Corinne, who tried so hard to give every one of us a good time. But what could she do with a niece who was never allowed to see boys in the intervals between these parties and who was dressed like a little girl when she looked like a very grown-up one?

Suddenly life was going to change for me. My grandmother decided that the household had too much gaiety for a girl of fifteen. She remembered that my mother had wanted to send me to Europe for a part of my education. Thus the second period of my life began.

In the autumn of 1899, when I was fifteen, I sailed for England with my aunt, Mrs. Stanley Mortimer, and her family. She took me in her cabin and told me that she was a poor sailor and always went to bed immediately on getting on the boat. I thought this was the proper procedure and followed suit. As a result, I did not enjoy that trip at all, as most of it was spent in my berth, and I arrived in England distinctly wobbly, never having stayed indoors so long before!

I did not know my beautiful Auntie Tissie as well as I knew my two younger aunts, but I was fond of her and she was always kindness itself to me. I think, even then, she felt more at home in Europe and in England than she did in the United States. She had many friends in that little London coterie known as "The Souls." She was one of the people whom the word "exquisite" describes best.

It was decided to send me to Mlle. Souvestre's school, "Allenswood," at a little place called South Fields, not far from Wimbledon Common and a short distance from London. The school was chosen because my father's sister, Mrs. Cowles, had gone to Mlle. Souvestre's school at Les Ruches, outside of Paris, before the Franco-Prussian War. The siege of Paris had been such an ordeal that Mlle. Souvestre left France and moved to England.

The family felt that, as I was to be left alone, it would be pleasanter to know that the headmistress had a personal interest in me. Tissie took me out to see Mlle. Souvestre, and I was left there with the promise that I would spend Christmas with her in London. When she drove away I felt lost and very lonely.

There were a great many rules and the first one was that all had to talk

French, and if they used an English word they had to report themselves at the end of the day.

As my first nurse had been a Frenchwoman and I spoke French before I spoke English, it was quite easy for me, but for many of the English girls who had had little French beforehand it was a terrible effort.

On the inside of each bathroom door were pasted the bath rules and I was appalled to find that we had to fight for three baths a week and were limited to ten minutes unless we happened to have the last period, and then perhaps we could sneak another five minutes before "lights out" was sounded!

We had to make our own beds before leaving the room in the morning. When we got out of bed we had to take the bedclothes off and put them on a chair to air. Our rooms were inspected after breakfast and we were marked on neatness and the way we made our beds. Frequently our bureau drawers and closets were examined, and any girl whose bureau drawers were out of order might return to her room to find the entire contents of the drawers dumped on her bed for rearranging. I also saw beds completely stripped and left to be made over again.

The day began with an early breakfast, café au lait, chocolate or milk, rolls and butter. I think eggs were given to those who wanted them.

Mlle. Souvestre, older and white-haired and obliged to take a certain amount of care of her health, never came to breakfast, but we were well watched over by Mlle. Samaia, a dynamic little woman who adored Mlle. Souvestre and waited on her hand and foot, ran all the business end of the school, and gave Italian lessons.

To be in Mlle. Samaia's good graces you had to show practical qualities. The girls who were singled out by her to hold positions of trust were dependable, could usually do almost anything with their hands, and had the ability to manage and lead their fellow students.

It took me a long time to get into her good graces, for I was a good deal of a dreamer and an American, which to her was an unknown quantity.

Mlle. Souvestre, on the contrary, had a soft spot for Americans and liked them as pupils. A number of her pupils became outstanding women. Auntie Bye, for instance, was one of the most interesting women I have ever known.

My grandfather Roosevelt's interest in cripples had first been aroused by the fact that he had consulted many doctors in trying to do something for his eldest daughter, Auntie Bye. She was not exactly a hunchback but she had a curious figure, thick through the shoulders, evidently caused by a curvature of the spine. Her hair was lovely, soft and wavy. Her eyes were deep-set and really beautiful, making you forget the rest of the face.

Auntie Bye had a mind that worked as an able man's mind works. She was full of animation, was always the center of any group she was with, and carried the burden of conversation. When she reached middle age she was already deaf and the arthritis which was finally to cripple her completely was causing her great pain, but never for a minute did her infirmities disturb her spirit. As they increased she simply seemed to become more determined to rise above them, and her charm and vivid personality made her house, wherever she lived, the meeting place for people from the four corners of the earth.

She had great executive ability, poise and judgment, and her influence was felt not only by her sister and brothers but by all her friends. To the young people with whom she came in contact she was an inspiration and one of the wisest counselors I ever knew. She listened more than she talked, but what she said was worth listening to!

From the start Mlle. Souvestre was interested in me because of her affection for Anna, and day by day I found myself more interested in her. This grew into a warm affection which lasted until her death.

Mlle. Souvestre was short and rather stout, she had snow-white hair. Her head was beautiful, with clear-cut, strong features, a strong face and broad forehead. Her hair grew to a peak in front and waved back in natural waves to a twist at the back of her head. Her eyes looked through you, and she always knew more than she was told.

After breakfast we were all taken for a walk on the common—and you had to have a good excuse to escape that walk! From about November it was cold and fairly foggy, and the fog rose from the ground and penetrated the very marrow of your bones—but still we walked!

At home I had begun to shed some of the underclothes which my grandmother had started me out with in my early youth, but here in England in winter I took to warm flannels again, and while we had central heat, which was unusual, one had positively to sit on the radiator to feel any warmth. There were only a few of us who had grates in our bedrooms, and those of us who had open fires were envied by all the others.

I can remember crowding into the dining room in order to get as near the radiator as possible before we had to sit down. Nearly all the English girls had chilblains on their hands and feet throughout most of the winter.

Classes began immediately on our return from the walks, and each of us had a schedule that ran through the whole day—classes, hours for practice, time for preparation—no idle moments were left to anyone. Immediately after lunch we had two hours for exercises, and most of us played field hockey during the winter months.

I was as awkward as ever at games, and had never seen a game of hockey, but I had to play something, and in time made the first team. I think that day was one of the proudest moments of my life. I realize now it would have been better to have devoted the time which I gave to hockey to learning to play tennis, which would have been more useful to me later on.

When we came in at four o'clock we found on the schoolroom table big slices of bread about half an inch thick, sometimes spread with raspberry jam, more often with plain butter. Those who were delicate were given a glass of milk.

Then we studied until the bell rang, which sent us scurrying to dress for dinner. Fifteen minutes were allowed to change shoes and stockings and dress.

One day a week we did our mending in the period after four P.M.— under supervision, of course—in the school room.

In the evenings we worked again, though occasionally we were allowed to go down to the gym and dance. Most of our lessons were in French, though Miss Strachey, a member of the well-known literary family, gave us classes in Shakespeare; and of course we had German, Latin and music.

Mlle. Souvestre held her history classes in her library, a charming and comfortable room lined with books and filled with flowers, looking out on a wide expanse of lawn, where really beautiful trees gave shade in summer and formed good perches for the rooks and crows in winter.

We sat on little chairs on either side of the fireplace. Mlle. Souvestre carried a long pointer in her hand, and usually a map hung on the wall. She would walk up and down, lecturing to us. We took notes, but were expected to do a good deal of independent reading and research. We wrote papers on the subjects assigned and labored hard over them. This was the class we enjoyed beyond any other.

A few of us were occasionally invited in the evening to Mlle. Souvestre's study, and those were red-letter days. She had a great gift for reading aloud and she read to us, always in French, poems, plays and stories. If the poems were those she liked, occasionally she read them over two or three times and then demanded that we recite them to her in turn. Here my memory trained at home stood me in good stead, and I found this an exhilarating way to spend an evening.

I did not know that my grandmother and my aunts had written about me before I arrived, so I felt that I was starting a new life, free from all my former sins. This was the first time in my life that my fears left me. If I lived up to the rules and told the truth, there was nothing to fear.

I had a bad habit of biting my nails. In short order that was noticed by Mlle. Samaia, who set out to cure me. It seemed a hopeless task, but one day I was rereading some letters of my father's, which I always carried with me, and I came across one in which he spoke of making the most of one's personal appearance, and from that day forward my nails were allowed to grow.

By the first Christmas holidays I was quite at home and happy in school. Christmas Eve and Christmas Day were spent with my Mortimer family at Claridge's Hotel in London. It did not seem right to have a small tree on a table in a hotel. We had always had a big one at home, but Auntie Tissie saw to it that I had a stocking and many gifts, and the day was a happy one, on the whole.

I had been invited to spend a few days with Mrs. Woolryche-Whittemore and her family in the north of England. Her husband was rector of a church at Bridgenorth, in Shropshire, and she had five little girls, one or two about my own age. She was Douglas Robinson's sister and held closely to her American ties, so that, though I could only be considered a connection by marriage, I was made to feel like a real relative and taken into the family and treated like one of the children. I enjoyed every minute of that visit, which was my first glimpse of English family life.

For breakfast there was food on one of the sideboards in covered dishes with lamps under them to keep the food warm, and everyone helped himself to whatever he found. High tea was served in the schoolroom about four-thirty in the afternoon, and the children's father joined us sometimes and shared our bread and jam and tea and cake. Those who were very hungry could have an egg. Long walks and drives, endless games, and books on hand for any unoccupied moments made life full for the days I stayed there.

I had traveled up alone and was going back alone. There had been a good deal of discussion as to how I was to get over to Paris to see Auntie

Tissie once more before she left for Biarritz. I was to live with a French family for the rest of my holiday, in order to study French.

It was finally decided to engage one of the English inventions, a visiting maid, with good references, to travel from London to Paris with me. I had never seen her but I picked her out without any difficulty in the station and went on to Paris.

I really marvel now at my confidence and independence, for I was totally without fear in this new phase of my life. The trip across the Channel was short, and I managed to find myself a windy corner to keep from being ill, but I was glad enough, once through the customs and on French soil, to curl up in the compartment of the train, and drink café au lait poured out of those big cans that were carried up and down the platforms.

We reached Paris in the early hours of the morning. The maid went with me as far as my aunt's hotel. I spent a few hours with her and was then taken over by Mlle. Bertaux. Actually, there were two Mlles. Bertaux and their mother. They had a simple but comfortable apartment in one of the less fashionable parts of Paris, and this was to be my first glimpse of French family life.

The furniture was stuffed, as I remember it, and was of an entirely non-descript period. There was, of course, no bathroom, but hot water was brought by the *bonne à tout faire* mornings and evenings, and a little round tin tub was available if you felt you must have it.

Meals were good, but different from anything I had known. Soups were delicious, and inferior cuts of meat were so well cooked that they were as palatable as our more expensive cuts. A vegetable was a course in itself, and at each place at the table were little glass rests for your knife and fork, which were not taken out with your plate as you finished each course. The household was run with extreme frugality, and yet they lived well. The two Mlles. Bertaux were excellent guides and charming, cultivated women.

The wide avenues, beautiful public buildings and churches, everything combined to make Paris for me the most exciting city I had ever been in. I saw much of it with Mlle. Bertaux on that first visit, but chiefly we did the things that a visitor should do, not the things which, later, came to mean to me the real charm of Paris.

Mlle. Souvestre had arranged that I should go back to England under Mlle. Samaia's care, and after a delightful holiday I went back to school, hoping that I should have another chance to stay with the Bertaux family.

School life itself was uneventful, but in the world outside great excitement reigned. I had hardly been conscious of our Spanish War in 1898, though I had heard a great deal about the sinking of the *Maine* and about Uncle Ted and his Rough Riders. My grandmother and her family lived completely outside the political circles of the day and took little interest in public affairs. But I remember the joy and excitement when Uncle Ted came back and went to Albany as governor of New York.

One read in the papers of scandals and of battles but it was all on a small scale. This war of ours had hardly touched my daily life.

In England, however, the Boer War, which lasted from 1899 to 1902, was of a more serious nature, and the tremendous feeling in the country at large was soon reflected in the school. At first there was great confidence in rapid victory, then months of anxiety and dogged "carrying on" in the face of unexpected and successful resistance from the Boers.

There was a considerable group in England and in other countries that did not believe in the righteousness of the English cause, and Mlle. Souvestre was among this group. She was, however, always fair and she realized that it would be most unfair to the English girls to try to make them think as she did. With them she never discussed the rights and wrongs of the war. Victories were celebrated in the gym and holidays were allowed, but Mlle. Souvestre never took part in any of the demonstrations. She remained in her library, and there she gathered around her the Americans and the other foreign girls. To them she expounded her theories on the rights of the Boers or of small nations in general. Those long talks were interesting, and echoes of them still live in my mind.

I was beginning to make a place for myself in the school, and before long Mlle. Souvestre made me sit opposite her at table. The girl who occupied this place received her nod at the end of the meal and gave the signal, by rising, for the rest of the girls to rise and leave the dining room. This girl was under close supervision, so I acquired certain habits which I have never quite been able to shake off.

Mlle. Souvestre used to say that you need never take more than you wanted, but you had to eat what you took on your plate, and so, sitting opposite her day after day, I learned to eat everything that I took on my plate. There were certain English dishes that I disliked very much; for instance, a dessert called suet pudding. I disliked its looks as much as anything, for it had an uncooked, cold, clammy expression as it sat upon the dish. We had treacle to pour over it and my only association with treacle had been through *Nicholas Nickleby,* which did not make the pudding any more attractive. Mlle. Souvestre thought that we should get over such squeamishness and eat a little of everything, so I choked it down when she was at the table and refused it when she was not.

It was a great advantage in one way, however, to sit opposite Mlle. Souvestre, for sometimes she had special dishes and shared them with three or four of us who sat close by. When she had guests they sat on either side of her, and it was easy to overhear the conversation, which was usually interesting.

I think that I started at this period of my life a bad habit that has stayed with me ever since. Frequently I would use, in talking to Mlle. Souvestre, things which I had overheard in her conversation with her friends and which had passed through my rather quick mind, giving me some new ideas; but if anyone had asked me any questions he would soon have discovered that I had no real knowledge of the thing I was talking about. Mlle. Souvestre was usually so pleased that I was interested in the subject that she did the talking, and I never had to show up my ignorance.

More and more, as I grew older, I used the quickness of my mind to pick the minds of other people and use their knowledge as my own. A dinner companion, a casual acquaintance, provided me with information which I could use in conversation, and few people were aware how little I actually knew on a variety of subjects that I talked on with apparent ease.

This is a bad habit, and one which is such a temptation that I hope few children will acquire it. But it does have one great advantage; it gives you a facility in picking up information about a great variety of subjects and adds immeasurably to your interests as you go through life.

Of course, later on I discovered that when I really wanted to know something I had to dig in.

As the summer holidays came nearer my excitement grew for I was to travel to Saint-Moritz in Switzerland to spend my holiday with the Mortimers.

My first view of these beautiful mountains was breath-taking, for I had never seen any high mountains. I lived opposite the Catskill Mountains in summer and loved them, but how much more majestic were these great snow-capped peaks all around us as we drove into the Engadine. The little Swiss chalets, built into the sides of the hills and with places under them for all the livestock that did not actually wander into the kitchen, were picturesque, but strange to my eyes with their fretwork decoration.

However, I was totally unprepared for Saint-Moritz itself, with its streets of grand hotels tapering off into the more modest *pensions* and little houses dotted around for such patients as had to live there for long periods of time.

The hotels all bordered the lake, and the thing that I remember best about my time there was the fact that Tissie and I got up every morning early enough to walk to a little café that perched out above the lake on a promontory at one end. There we drank coffee or cocoa and ate rolls with fresh butter and honey, the sun just peeping over the mountains and touching us with its warm rays. I can still remember how utterly contented I was!

Toward the end of the summer Tissie told me that she had decided to make a trip by carriage from Saint-Moritz through the Austrian Tyrol to Oberammergau, where the Passion Play was being given. She was taking a friend with her, and I could go along if I were willing to sit either with the coachman on the box or on the little seat facing the two ladies. I would have agreed to sit on top of the bags, I was so excited at the prospect of seeing the Passion Play and all this new country.

We had only a one-horse victoria, and much of the country we drove through was mountainous, and when we climbed I got out and walked, so our progress was not rapid and we had plenty of time to enjoy the scenery.

I still think the Austrian Tyrol is one of the loveliest places in the world. We spent a night in a little inn which had housed the mad King Ludwig of Bavaria, when he went to fish in the rushing brook we saw below us. We visited his castles, and finally arrived in Oberammergau.

It was the night before the play, and because of the crowds our rooms were separated from each other in simple little village houses. We walked the whole length of the village and found the people whom we should see the next day in the holy play sitting in their little shops, selling the carved figures which they made during the winter.

The Passion Play adjourned only when people had to eat, so we sat throughout long hours of the day. I loved it, though I realize now that I must have been a tired child, for I had to go to sleep after lunch and could not get back until the end of the second period, because no one is allowed to move or make a noise during the acting.

From there we went to Munich, back to Paris, and then I returned to school.

Christmas of 1899, I was to have my wish and, with a classmate, spend the holiday entirely in Paris with the Mlles. Bertaux.

As the Mlles. Bertaux had charge of us, and as we were supposed to take French lessons every day as well as do a great deal of sightseeing, we were chaperoned and our days were carefully planned. I was getting to know Paris and to feel able to find my way about and to decide what I should like to do if I ever were free to plan my own days.

The last few days of our stay, Mlle. Souvestre was back in Paris and we went to see her. She quizzed us about what we had learned. At this time she told me frankly what she thought of my clothes, many of which were made-over dresses of my young aunts, and commanded me to go out with Mlle. Samaia and have at least one dress made.

I was always worried about my allowance, for my grandmother felt that we children should never know until we were grown what money might be ours, and that we ought to feel that money was something to be carefully spent, as she might not be able to send us any more. However, I decided that if Mlle. Souvestre thought I should buy a dress I could have it. I still remember my joy in that dark-red dress, made for me by a small dressmaker in Paris, but, as far as I was concerned, it might have been made by Worth, for it had all the glamour of being my first French dress.

I wore it on Sundays and as an everyday evening dress at school and probably got more satisfaction out of it than from any dress I have had since.

The one great event that I remember in the winter of 1901 was the death of Queen Victoria. Some of my Robinson connections had arranged for me to see the funeral procession from the windows of a house belonging to one of them. It was an exciting day, beginning with the crowds in the streets and the difficulty of arriving at our destination, and finally the long wait for the funeral procession itself. I remember little of the many carriages which must have comprised that procession, but I shall never forget the genuine feeling shown by the crowds in the streets or the hush that fell as the gun carriage bearing the smallest coffin I had ever seen came within our range of vision. Hardly anyone had dry eyes as that slow-moving procession passed by, and I have never forgotten the great emotional force that seemed to stir all about us as Queen Victoria, so small of stature and yet so great in devotion to her people, passed out of their lives forever.

By the following Easter Mlle. Souvestre had decided that she would take me traveling with her. This was one of the most momentous things that happened in my education. The plan was to go to Marseilles, along the Mediterranean coast, to stop at Pisa and then spend some time in Florence, not staying in the city in a hotel, but living with an artist friend of Mlle. Souvestre's in his villa in Fiesole, on a hill which overlooked Florence.

Traveling with Mlle. Souvestre was a revelation. She did all the things that in a vague way you had always felt you wanted to do. In Marseilles we walked upon the Quai, looked at the boats that came from foreign ports, saw some of the small fishing boats with their colored sails, and went up to a little church where offerings were made to the Blessed Virgin for the preservation of those at sea. There is a shrine in this church where people have prayed for the granting of some particular wishes, the crippled have hung their crutches there, and people have made offerings of gold and silver and jewels.

We ended by dining in a café overlooking the Mediterranean and ate the dish for which Marseilles is famous, bouillabaisse, a kind of soup in which every possible kind of fish that can be found in nearby waters is used. With it we had *vin rouge du pays*, because Mlle. Souvestre believed in the theory that, water being uncertain, wine was safer to drink, and if you diluted it with water, in some way the germs were killed by the wine.

The next day we started our trip along the shores of the Mediterranean. I wanted to get out at almost every place the name of which was familiar to me, but our destination was Pisa and it never occurred to me, the child of regular trips from New York to Tivoli and back, that one could change one's plans en route.

Suddenly, toward evening, the guard called out "Alassio." Mlle. Souvestre was galvanized into action; breathlessly she leaned out the window and said, "I am going to get off." She directed me to get the bags, which were stored on the rack over our heads, and we simply fell off onto the platform, bag and baggage, just before the train started on its way. I was aghast. Here we stood, our trunks going on in the luggage van and we without rooms and, as far as I knew, in a strange place with no reason for the sudden whim.

When we recovered our breath Mlle. Souvestre said, "My friend Mrs. Humphry Ward lives here, and I decided that I would like to see her; besides, the Mediterranean is a lovely blue at night and the sky with the stars coming out is nice to watch from the beach."

Alas, we found that Mrs. Ward was away, but we spent a wonderful hour down on the beach watching the sky and sea, and though Mlle. Souvestre had a cold the next day, she did not regret her hasty decision and I had learned a valuable lesson. Never again would I be the rigid little person I had been theretofore.

As I think back over my trips with Mlle. Souvestre, I realize she taught me how to enjoy traveling. She liked to be comfortable, she enjoyed good food, but she always tried to go where you would see the people of the country you were visiting, not your own compatriots.

She always ate native dishes and drank native wines. She felt it was just as important to enjoy good Italian food as it was to enjoy Italian art, and it all served to make you a citizen of the world, at home wherever you might go, knowing what to see and what to enjoy. She used to impress on my mind the necessity for acquiring languages, primarily because of the enjoyment you missed in a country when you were both deaf and dumb.

Mlle. Souvestre taught me also on these journeys that the way to make young people responsible is to throw real responsibility on them. She was an old lady and I was sixteen. The packing and unpacking for both of us was up to me, once we were on the road. I looked up trains, got the tickets, made all the detailed arrangements necessary for comfortable traveling. Though I was to lose some of my self-confidence and ability to look after myself in the early days of my marriage, it came back to me later more easily because of these trips with Mlle. Souvestre.

In Florence, we settled down for a long visit. Spring is a lovely time in Florence and I thought it had more flavor of antiquity than any city I had ever seen. I was reading Dante laboriously and had plenty of imagination to draw upon as I walked about the city. Here again Mlle. Souvestre's belief that Americans could be trusted made my trip unique. The morningafter our arrival she took out the Baedeker, opened it at the description of the Campanile, and said, "My dear, I should be exhausted if I walked with you, but the only way to know a city really is to walk its streets. Florence is worth it. Take your Baedeker and go and see it. Later we will discuss what you have seen."

So, sixteen years old, keener than I have probably ever been since and more alive to beauty, I sallied forth to see Florence alone. Innocence is its own protection. Mlle. Souvestre's judgment was entirely vindicated. Perhaps she realized that I had not the beauty which appeals to foreign men and that I would be safe from their advances. In any case, everyone was most helpful. Even when I got lost in the narrow little streets and had to inquire my way I was always treated with the utmost respect and deference.

From Florence we went to Milan and then to Paris, where again I did my sightseeing alone. One day I met the entire Thomas Newbold family in the Luxembourg, and they wrote home that I was unchaperoned in Paris!

Back in school again for a time, and then in the early summer great excitement, for Pussie had come to Europe with the Mortimers, and she and I were to sail for home together.

I stayed with her in lodgings in London two nights before we sailed, and had my first taste of an emotional crisis on her part. I was to know many similar ones in the years to come. She always had men who were in love with her, not always wisely but always deeply!

At this particular moment she thought she was casting away her happiness forever because she was being separated from the gentleman of the moment. I stayed up anxiously most of the night listening to her sobs and protestations that she would never reach home, that she would jump overboard. Being young and romantic, I spent most of the trip home wondering when she would make the effort and watching her as closely as I could. We were on a slow Atlantic Transport Line boat and shared a cabin. Her moods were anything but placid, but by the time we reached home she was somewhat calmer.

Three

Home Again

THAT SUMMER was a stormy one. One day Pussie was annoyed with me. She told me frankly that I probably would never have the beaux that the rest of the women in the family had had because I was the ugly duckling. At the same time she told me some of the painful and distressing facts about my father's last years. The combination made me very unhappy, and Mrs. Henry Parish, Jr., with whom I was spending the summer in Northeast Harbor, had her hands full trying to console me. She tried hard to give me a good time but I knew no one and had no gift for getting on with the younger people in Northeast, where they lived a life totally different from the English school life that I was then completely absorbed in.

I wanted to get back to England to school and more traveling in Europe. After much begging and insistence I was finally told I might go if I found someone to take me over.

I went to New York, where Pussie and Maude helped me to get my first long, tailor-made suit. The skirt trailed on the ground and was oxford gray. I was enormously proud of it.

I engaged a deaconess to take the trip to London with me and return by the next boat. As I look back on it, it was one of the funniest and craziest things I ever did, for my family never set eyes on her until they came to see me off on the steamer. She looked respectable enough and I am sure she was, but I might just as well have crossed alone, for we had a rough crossing, and I never saw her till the day we landed.

In the little Cunard ships of those days (I think we were on the *Umbria*), a rough crossing meant that the steamer chairs, if they were out at all, were lashed to the railing. There were racks on the table, and when you tried to walk you felt you were walking up a mountain or down one.

33

I had learned something since my first trip, and in spite of continually feeling ill I always got on deck and sat for hours watching the horizon rise and fall, and ate most of my meals up there.

My deaconess and I proceeded to London to a large caravanserai of a hotel. The next day I went to school, carefully handed over the return ticket and enough money for her hotel bill to my companion whom I had taken care of and had rarely seen. But she had served the purpose of giving my family the satisfaction of knowing I was well chaperoned.

School was as interesting as ever. Mlle. Souvestre was glad to see me back, and I had the added interest of a young cousin at school that year. Mr. and Mrs. Douglas Robinson brought over their daughter, Corinne, and left her with Mlle. Souvestre. She was younger than I, very intelligent, and soon won her way to Mlle. Souvestre's interest and respect. In athletics she was far better than I was, and established her place with the girls more quickly than I had done.

Having Auntie Corinne and Uncle Douglas in London was a joy for me, as we were allowed an occasional weekend away and frequent Saturday afternoons if we had a relative near enough to take us out, and I know that I went up to London once or twice at least to see Auntie Corinne; later Auntie Bye was there, too.

I was only sorry that I had to go home before the coronation of King Edward VII, as they were all staying in London, where Uncle Ted would join them to act as special ambassador from our government.

During the Christmas holiday of the year 1902 Mlle. Souvestre took me to Rome. We went to a *pension* in one of the old palaces where the rooms were enormous, with high ceilings, and though we rejoiced in their beauty we nearly froze to death trying to warm ourselves over a little portable stove which had a few red coals glowing in its center.

We visited the Forum many times. Mlle. Souvestre sat on a stone in the sun and talked of history and how the men of Rome had wandered here in their togas; pointed out the place where Julius Caesar may have been assassinated and made us live in ancient history. We watched the people on their knees climbing up the "Scala Santa," and, silly little Anglo-Saxon that I was, I felt self-conscious for them!

One day we journeyed to Tivoli, with its beautiful gardens and the little loophole in the hedge through which you get a view of the city of Rome in the distance.

St. Peter's was a terrible disappointment to me, for I had remembered as a little girl kissing the toe of an enormous and heroic statue. In fact, my nurse had held me up so I might accomplish this act of reverence; but when I went back to look at the statue it was so small that I would have had to bend over considerably to kiss the toe.

When Easter came around, Mlle. Souvestre again asked me to travel with her. This time we crossed the Channel and went to stay not far from Calais with her friends, the Ribots, who lived in a house entered by a door set in a wall. You pulled a long, iron bell handle and a cheerful little tinkle ran through the house. In a few minutes you were let into a spacious and comfortable garden surrounded by a wall high above your head, making it possible to have complete privacy, which is one of the things French people strive for even in their city homes.

I do not remember the name of this small town, but I do remember sallying forth alone to look at the churches and to see what could be seen. I felt somewhat awed by our two dignified and very kindly hosts. Later I was to discover in a premier of France my host of this visit.

From there we went to Belgium and visited some other friends of Mlle. Souvestre's, taking a long trip in their coach. Then we went up the Rhine to Frankfort.

The summer was now approaching, and I knew that I must go home for good. Mlle. Souvestre had become one of the people whom I cared most for in the world, and the thought of the long separation seemed hard to bear. I would have given a good deal to have spent another year on my education, but to my grandmother the age of eighteen was the time when you "came out," and not to "come out" was unthinkable.

When I left I felt quite sure that I would return before long, but I realize now that Mlle. Souvestre, knowing her infirmities, had little hope of seeing me again. She wrote me lovely letters, which I still cherish. They show the kind of relationship that had grown up between us and give an idea of the fine person who exerted the greatest influence, after my father, on this period of my life.

I returned to Tivoli, my grandmother's country place, and spent the whole summer there. This was not a happy summer, for while I had been away my uncle Vallie, who had been so kind to me when I was a child, had been slipping rapidly into the habits of the habitual drinker. My grandmother would never believe that he was not going to give it up as he promised after each spree, but the younger members of the family realized that the situation was serious. He made life for them distinctly difficult.

Pussie was away a great deal. Maude was married to Larry Waterbury, Eddie to Josie Zabriskie and was proving himself just as weak as his brother, Vallie. This was my first real contact with anyone who had completely lost the power of self-control, and it began to develop in me an almost exaggerated idea of the necessity for keeping all one's desires under complete subjugation.

I had been a solemn little girl, my years in England had given me my first taste of being carefree and irresponsible, but my return home to the United States accentuated almost immediately the serious side of life, and that first summer was not good preparation for being a gay and joyous debutante.

My grandmother had cut herself off almost entirely from contact with her neighbors, and while Vallie, when he met anyone, would behave with braggadocio, we really lived an isolated life. No one who was not so intimate that he knew the entire situation was ever invited to come for a meal or to stay with us.

That autumn my little brother went off to boarding school. My grandmother and I took him up to Groton. She seemed quite old and the real responsibility for this young brother was slipping rapidly from her hands into mine. She never again went to see him at school and I began to go up every term for a weekend, which was what all good parents were expected to do. I kept this up through the six years he was there, just as I was to do later for my own sons.

That autumn I moved to the old house on West 37th Street. Theoretically, my grandmother lived there too, but as a matter of fact she lived at Tivoli in a vain attempt to keep Vallie there and keep him sober as much as possible.

Pussie, my only unmarried aunt, and I lived together. She was no less beautiful than she had been when I was a child. She was just as popular, with just as many beaux, and several love affairs always devastating her emotions. She went the round of social dinners and dances as hard as any debutante.

Of course, my grandmother could do nothing about my "coming out," but automatically my name was placed on everybody's list. I was asked to all kinds of parties, but the first one I attended was an Assembly Ball, and I was taken by my cousins, Mr. and Mrs. Henry Parish, Jr.

My aunt, Mrs. Mortimer, had bought my clothes in Paris, and I imagine that I was well dressed, but there was absolutely nothing about me to attract anybody's attention. I was tall, but I did not dance well. I had lost touch with the girls whom I had known before I went abroad, though afterwards I picked up some of my old relationships. I went into that ballroom not knowing one single man except Bob Ferguson, whom I had rarely seen since I went abroad, and Forbes Morgan, who was one of Pussie's most ardent admirers.

I do not think I quite realized beforehand what utter agony it was going to be or I would never have had the courage to go. Bob Ferguson introduced a number of his friends but by no stretch of the imagination could I fool myself into thinking that I was a popular debutante!

I went home early, thankful to get away, having learned that before I went to any party or to any dance I should have two partners, one for supper and one for the cotillion. Any girl who was a success would be asked by many men and accepted the one whom she preferred at the moment. These partners were prerequisites, but you must also be chosen to dance every figure in the cotillion, and your popularity was gauged by the number of favors you took home. Pussie always had far more than I had! I knew I was the first girl in my mother's family who was not a belle and, though I never acknowledged it to any of them at that time, I was deeply ashamed.

Later on, Mr. and Mrs. Mortimer gave a large theater party and supper, with dancing afterwards, for me at Sherry's, which was the most fashionable restaurant in those days. This helped to give me a sense that I had done my share of entertaining, and for one night I stood and received with my aunt and had no anxieties. Pussie and I together gave a few luncheons and dinners that winter at the 37th Street house.

Gradually I acquired a few friends, and finally going out lost some of its terrors; but that first winter, when my sole object in life was society, nearly brought me to a state of nervous collapse. I had other things, however, on my mind. I ran the house as far as it was run by anyone, for Pussie was even more temperamental than she had been as a young girl, and her love affairs were becoming more serious. There would be days when she would shut herself in her room, refusing to eat and spending hours weeping.

Occasionally Vallie would come to the house for one purpose and one alone: to go on a real spree. Pussie was no better equipped to cope with this difficulty than I was. In fact, not having any other vital interests, I had more time to handle this situation and a certain kind of strength and determination which underlay my timidity must have begun to make itself felt, for I think I was better able to handle many difficulties that arose during this strange winter than was Pussie, who was some fourteen years my senior.

A number of pleasant things happened that winter, however. Pussie's musical talent kept her in touch with a certain number of artistic people, and I enjoyed listening to her play and going to the theater, concerts and the opera with her. Bob Ferguson, who lived a pleasant bachelor existence in New York and had many friends, introduced me that year to Bay Emmett, the painter, and some of her friends, and I rejoiced that Bob and I had re-established our old friendship. He felt that he was entitled to bring me home after parties we might both attend, which was a great relief to me, as otherwise I had to have a maid wait for me—that was one of the rules my grandmother had laid down. The rule amuses me when I realize how gaily I went around European cities all by myself. However, she accepted Bob as escort, though she would not hear of anyone else having the same privilege.

He took me to several parties in Bay Emmett's studio and gave me my first taste of informally meeting people whose names I recognized as having accomplished things in the sphere of art and letters. I liked this much better than the dinners and dances I was struggling through in formal society each night, and yet I would not have wanted at that age to be left out, for I was still haunted by my upbringing and believed that what was known as New York Society was really important.

During this time I had begun to see occasionally my cousin Franklin Roosevelt, who was at college, and also his cousin, Lyman Delano, and various other members of his family and some of his college friends. His mother, Mrs. James Roosevelt, was sorry for me, I think.

Mrs. Roosevelt and her husband, who died in 1900, had been fond of my mother and, particularly, of my father, who had crossed on the steamer with them when he was starting his trip around the world. They were so fond of him that when their son, Franklin, was born they asked my father to be his godfather.

When I was two years old my father and mother took me to stay at

Hyde Park with them. My mother-in-law later told me that she remembered my standing in the door with my finger in my mouth and being addressed as "Granny" by my mother, and that Franklin rode me around the nursery on his back. My first recollection of Franklin is at one of the Orange Christmas parties, later a glimpse of him the summer I came home from school when I was going up to Tivoli in the coach of a New York Central train. He spied me and took me to speak to his mother, who was in the Pullman car. I never saw him again until he began to come to occasional dances the winter I came out and I was asked to a house party at Hyde Park where the other guests were mostly his cousins.

I did not stay so much in Tivoli the summer after I came out. I was there part of the time but paid a great many visits, for by that time I had made many friends and Mrs. Parish was kind to me as always. In the autumn when I was nineteen my grandmother decided that she could not afford to open the New York house, and the question came up of where Pussie and I were going to live. Mrs. Ludlow invited Pussie to stay with her and Mrs. Parish offered me a home.

I had grown up considerably during the past year and had come to the conclusion that I would not spend another year just doing the social rounds, particularly as I knew that my cousin's house would mean less ease in casual entertainment than I had known in the 37th Street house. She still lived with a great deal of formality and punctuality and the latter was now not one of my strong points.

Cousin Susie (Mrs. Parish) told me that I might occasionally have guests for tea down in a little reception room on the first floor, but there was no feeling that I could ask people in casually for meals. I had my maid, however, and everything was arranged so that I could go out as much as I wished, and she was more than kind in entertaining at formal lunches and dinners for me.

One thing I remember vividly. I had run over my allowance considerably and had many overdue bills, and finally Mr. Parish took me in hand and painstakingly showed me how to keep books. He would not allow me to ask my grandmother to pay these bills, but he made me pay them myself gradually over a period of time. This was probably my only lesson in handling money, and I have been eternally grateful for it.

He was tall and thin and distinguished looking, with a mustache, and while rather formal in manner he was the kindest person I have ever known.

That winter I began to work in the Junior League. It was in its early stages. Mary Harriman, afterwards Mrs. Charles Cary Rumsey, was the moving spirit. There was no clubhouse; we were just a group of girls anxious to do something helpful in the city in which we lived. When we joined we agreed to do certain pieces of work, and Jean Reid, daughter of Mrs. and Mr. Whitelaw Reid, and I undertook to take classes of youngsters in the Rivington Street Settlement House. Jean was to play the piano and I was to keep the children entertained by teaching calisthenics and fancy dancing.

As I remember it, we arrived there as school came out in the afternoon and it was dark when we left. Jean often came and went in her carriage, but I took the elevated railway or the Fourth Avenue streetcar and walked across from the Bowery. The dirty streets, crowded with foreign-looking people, filled me with terror, and I often waited on a corner for a car, watching, with a great deal of trepidation, men come out of the saloons or shabby hotels nearby, but the children interested me enormously. I still remember the glow of pride that ran through me when one of the little girls said her father wanted me to come home with her, as he wanted to give me something because she enjoyed her classes so much. That invitation bolstered me up whenever I had any difficulty in disciplining my brood!

Once I remember allowing my cousin, Franklin Roosevelt, at that time a senior at Harvard, to come down to meet me. All the little girls were tremendously interested.

I think it must have been this same winter that I became interested in the Consumers League, of which Mrs. Maud Nathan was the president. Luckily, I went with an experienced, older woman to do some investigation of garment factories and department stores. It had never occurred to me that the girls might get tired standing behind counters all day long, or that no seats were provided for them if they had time to sit down and rest. I did not know what the sanitary requirements should be in the dress factories, either for air or for lavatory facilities. This was my introduction to anything of this kind and I imagine that by spring I was ready to drop all this good work and go up to the country and spend the summer in idleness and recreation!

As I try to sum up my own development in the autumn of 1903 I think I was a curious mixture of extreme innocence and unworldliness with a great deal of knowledge of some of the less agreeable sides of life—which, however, did not seem to make me any more sophisticated or less innocent.

It would be difficult for anyone in these days to have any idea of the formality with which girls of my generation were trained. I cannot believe that I was the only one brought up in this way, though I imagine that I was more strictly kept to the formalities than were many of my friends.

It was understood that no girl was interested in a man or showed any liking for him until he had made all the advances. You knew a man very well before you wrote or received a letter from him, and those letters make me smile when I see some of the correspondence today. There were few men who would have dared to use my first name, and to have signed oneself in any other way than "very sincerely yours" would have been not only a breach of good manners but an admission of feeling which was entirely inadmissible.

You never allowed a man to give you a present except flowers or candy or possibly a book. To receive a piece of jewelry from a man to whom you were not engaged was a sign of being a fast woman, and the idea that you would permit any man to kiss you before you were engaged to him never even crossed my mind.

I had painfully high ideals and a tremendous sense of duty entirely unrelieved by any sense of humor or any appreciation of the weaknesses of human nature. Things were either right or wrong to me, and I had had too little experience to know how fallible human judgments are.

I had a great curiosity about life and a desire to participate in every experience that might be the lot of a woman. There seemed to me to be a necessity for hurry; without rhyme or reason I felt the urge to be a part of the stream of life, and so in the autumn of 1903, when Franklin Roosevelt, my fifth cousin once removed, asked me to marry him, though I was only nineteen, it seemed entirely natural and I never even thought that we were both young and inexperienced. I came back from Groton, where I had spent the weekend, and asked Cousin Susie whether she thought I cared enough, and my grandmother, when I told her, asked me if I was sure I was really in love. I solemnly answered "yes," and yet I know now that it was years later before I understood what being in love or what loving really meant.

I had high standards of what a wife and mother should be and not the faintest notion of what it meant to be either a wife or a mother, and none of my elders enlightened me. I marvel now at my husband's patience, for I realize how trying I must have been in many ways. I can see today how funny were some of the tragedies of our early married life.

My mother-in-law had sense enough to realize that both of us were young and undeveloped, and she decided to try to make her son think this matter over—which, at the time, of course, I resented. As he was well ahead in his studies, she took him with his friend and roommate, Lathrop Brown, on a cruise to the West Indies that winter, while I lived in New York with Mrs. Parish.

Franklin's feelings did not change, however.

My first experience with the complications that surround the attendance of a president at any kind of family gathering, such as a wedding or a funeral, came when my great-uncle, James King Gracie, whose wife was our beloved Auntie Gracie, died on November 22, 1903, and Uncle Ted came to New York for the funeral.

The streets were lined with police, and only such people as had identification cards could get in and out of Mrs. Douglas Robinson's house, where Uncle Ted stayed. We all drove down in a procession to the church, but Uncle Ted went in by a special door through the clergyman's house, which had a connecting passageway, and left the same way.

Only afterwards did we hear with horror that, in spite of all the precautions, an unknown man stepped up to Uncle Ted in the passageway and handed him a petition. No one could imagine how the man got in or why he had not been seen by the police. Fortunately, he had no bad intentions, but he gave everyone a shock, for had he wanted to attack Uncle Ted he could have done so easily.

In the winters of 1903 and 1904, Auntie Bye, with whom I had already stayed in Farmington, Connecticut, asked me to come to Washington to stay with her. By this time I had gained a little self-confidence and so I really enjoyed meeting the younger diplomats and the few young American men who were to be found in the social circles of Washington. I was invited to the White House to stay for a night, but I was always awed by the White House and therefore preferred to stay with Auntie Bye, where one felt more at ease. She arranged everything so well for me that I did not feel responsible for myself.

I went with Auntie Bye on her rounds of afternoon calls, and though I was aghast at this obligation, I found it entertaining. The dinners, luncheons and teas were interesting, and people of importance, with charm and wit and *savoir-faire*, filled my days with unusual and exciting experiences.

The chief excitement of the winter of 1904-05 was the marriage of

Pussie to W. Forbes Morgan, Jr. It took place on February 16, in Mrs. Ludlow's house, where Pussie was staying. Pussie looked beautiful but no one was happy. Forbes was a number of years younger than Pussie, and we knew she was temperamental and wondered how they would adjust themselves to the complicated business of married life.

Uncle Ted's campaign and re-election had meant little to me except in general interest, for again I lived in a totally unpolitical atmosphere. In Washington, however, I gradually acquired a faint conception of the political world, very different from my New York world. I also acquired little by little the social ease which I sorely needed.

Uncle Ted came occasionally to Auntie Bye's house informally, and those visits were interesting events. She went, now and then, to walk with Aunt Edith, or perhaps Uncle Ted would send for her to talk over something, showing that he considered her advice well worth having. He was devoted to both his sisters, and Auntie Corinne (Mrs. Douglas Robinson) came down to see him or he went to see her in New York or in the country. They all talked on political questions, literature or art, and his wife and his sisters, all in their own ways, made their contributions to what was always stimulating talk.

Auntie Bye had a great gift for homemaking. Some of her furniture was ugly, but wherever she lived there was an atmosphere of comfort. The talk was always lively, and there was friendliness in her unstinted hospitality. The unexpected guest was always welcome, and young or old, you really felt Auntie Bye's interest in you.

This may have been why I loved to be with her, for I was still shy and she gave me reassurance. She once gave me a piece of advice which must have come from her own philosophy. I was asking her how I could be sure that I was doing the right thing if someone criticized me. Her answer was, "No matter what you do, some people will criticize you, and if you are entirely sure that you would not be ashamed to explain your action to someone whom you loved and who loved you, and you are satisfied in your own mind that you are doing right, then you need not worry about criticism nor need you ever explain what you do."

She had lived for many years according to this principle herself. When J. R. ("Rosy") Roosevelt's wife died while he was first secretary to our embassy in London, she went over to be his hostess and take care of his children. There she met and was married to Captain William Sheffield Cowles, who was our naval attaché, and on her return to this country

William Sheffield Cowles, Jr., was born. Because of her deformity and her age, everyone was anxious about her, but courage will carry one through a great deal and the baby arrived perfect in every way and both mother and baby progressed normally to health and strength.

Uncle Will, Auntie Bye's husband, was now an admiral in the Navy, and I began to learn something about the services and to realize that these men who are our officers in the Army and Navy, while they receive little financial compensation, are enormously proud to serve their country. They and their wives have a position which is their right by virtue of their service, regardless of birth or of income. Quite a new idea to a provincial little miss from New York!

In June of 1904 I went with Franklin's mother and most of his cousins to his commencement at Harvard, the first commencement I had ever attended. That summer I paid my aunt, Mrs. Douglas Robinson, a long visit in Islesboro, Maine, where she had a cottage, and then I went up to stay with Franklin and his mother at Campobello Island, New Brunswick, Canada. Franklin came down to get me, and we made the long trip by train, changing at least twice and getting there in the evening. Of course, I had to have my maid with me, for I could not have gone with him alone!

Once there, however, we walked together, drove around the island, sailed on a small schooner with his mother and other friends, and got to know each other better than ever before. This yacht seemed to me, who was not much accustomed to any of the luxuries of life, the last word in extravagance.

In the autumn of 1904 the engagement was announced. I was asked by Franklin's aunt and uncle, Mr. and Mrs. Warren Delano, to spend Thanksgiving at Fairhaven, Massachusetts, with the entire Delano family. It was an ordeal, but I knew so many of them already and they were so kind and warm in their welcome that I began to feel I was part of the clan—and a clan it was.

My mother-in-law's grandfather, Warren Delano, had been a sea captain, sailing from New Bedford. When returning from a trip to Sweden in 1814, his boat was captured by the British and he was taken to Halifax. Finally the men were sent home, but the ship was taken from them. My mother-in-law's father, Warren Delano, remembered as a little boy the occupation of Fairhaven by the British in this same War of 1812. He and his little brothers were hurried to safety up the Acushnet River.

On retiring, Captain Delano built himself a dignified, rambling house with stone walls enclosing the lawn and garden. There was a stable in the rear. When his son, Warren Delano, my mother-in-law's father, was seventeen, Captain Delano drove him up to Boston and put him in the counting-house of his friend, Mr. Forbes. The eldest of a large family must begin early to earn his own living, and before the lad was nineteen he was sailing as supercargo on a ship which went to South America and China. This son helped to start his brothers in life and took care of his sisters and various other relatives.

He was comfortably well off when he married Catherine Lyman, whose father and mother, Judge and Mrs. Lyman, were important people in Northampton, Massachusetts. He had a house in Lafayette Place in New York, and later he built a house called Algonac at Newburgh, New York, on the Hudson River. He lived in China for many years, and was a member of the firm of Russell and Company.

After Warren Delano, the sea captain, died, the Fairhaven house belonged to all the brothers and sisters then living. Their descendants happened to be children of Warren Delano, for the other brothers and sisters had had no children.

Warren Delano, the third in line, was my mother-in-law's oldest brother, and the head of the family when I became engaged to Franklin. He managed the Fairhaven property and the trust fund that went with it. All the family went there whenever they wished.

I grew fond of some of the older members of my husband's family. Mr. and Mrs. Warren Delano were always kindness itself to me, as were Mrs. Forbes, Mrs. Hitch, Mrs. Price Collier and Mr. and Mrs. Frederic Delano.

Mrs. Hitch was the most philanthropic and civic-minded of my husband's relations. She was not only a moving spirit in Newburgh, where she lived in the old family house, but she reached out to New York City and belonged to many of the early state-wide and national movements for the bettering of human conditions. After my husband went into politics she took a tremendous interest in him and wrote him long letters about the local political situation.

Mr. Frederic Delano was still in business in those early years, but later, when he came to live in Washington, he devoted himself entirely to public affairs and became one of the leading citizens not only of his community but of the country, putting into public work the ability that had gained him a place of prominence in the business world and working as hard on his unpaid civic jobs as he had worked in the things he did which had brought him a substantial income.

All the members of my husband's family had business ability, imagination and good sense. That does not mean that they never made mistakes, but standing together as they did in a clan they usually retrieved their mistakes, and the whole family profited.

The Fairhaven house was roomy and had been added to from time to time. In it there were many interesting things. The coat of arms of Jehan de Lannoy, Knight of the Golden Fleece, and ancestor of the original Philippe de Lannoy who came to this country in November, 1621, hung over the door on a painted shield. Some shelves over the old-fashioned desks were filled with interesting little trinkets, and there were some beautiful Chinese vases.

Up in the attic were some ivory carvings done by men on the long whaling voyages. Many of these things are now in the New Bedford museum, but certain trunks held old ships' logs and family diaries, and these Franklin, in particular, reveled in.

Large family reunions had not taken place in my Hall family for many years, perhaps due to the fact that life at Tivoli, where my grandmother lived with Vallie, was not pleasant, or it may have been because we were scattered and had no mutual interests, being held together only by personal affection for each other as individuals.

Therefore, this first big family party at Fairhaven was to me something of a revelation. There was a sense of security which I had never known before. Without realizing it, it was a relief to me, who sensed in those years a certain feeling of insecurity in most of the relationships of my Hall family. Maude, for instance, was in love with her attractive husband, but financial difficulties were always lurking in the background. They seemed the gayest, most carefree of young people, and when they had come to England while I was at school, because Larry Waterbury (Maude's husband) was a member of the American international championship polo team, I watched with awe and envy the clothes that Maude wore and the constant gaiety. Theirs was a world in which pleasure dominated. Under the excitement and gaiety, however, lurked a constant sense of insecurity.

By 1902 I was already beginning to realize that debts sometimes hung over people's heads, that both Eddie and Vallie had squandered what money was left to them, that Pussie had trusted much of hers to gentlemen with good intentions but little business judgment who lost more than they made for her, so that by this time her income was considerably lessened.

My grandmother, as the children came of age, had less and less money because, as there had been no will, she had only her dower right in her husband's estate. She was barely able to meet her expenses and help her somewhat extravagant children.

Tissie's husband was well off and Tissie herself for years spent practically every penny she had on members of her family. Every one of them was conscious of financial strain, primarily because each one was "keeping up with the Joneses" in some way.

The Delanos were the first people I met who were able to do what they wanted to do without wondering where to obtain the money, and it was not long before I learned the reason for this. My mother-in-law taught me, but I am sure that any member of her family could have taught me just as well. They watched their pennies, which I had always seen squandered. They were generous and could afford to be in big things, because so little was ever wasted or spent in inconsequential ways.

If misfortune befell one of them, the others rallied at once. My Hall family would have rallied too, but they had so much less to rally with. The Delanos might disapprove of one another, and if so, they were not slow to express their disapproval, but let someone outside so much as hint at criticism, and the clan was ready to tear him limb from limb!

Before Franklin went to Harvard he had wanted to go into the Navy. His father felt that an only son should not choose a profession which would take him so much away from home. He wanted Franklin to study law as a preparation for any kind of business or profession he might enter later.

After graduating from Harvard, Franklin went to law school at Columbia University. His mother took a house at 200 Madison Avenue, and we had many gay times during the winter of 1905. Parties were given for us, wedding presents began to come, and my cousin Susie helped me to buy my trousseau and my linens. It was exciting and the wedding plans were complicated by the fact that Uncle Ted, at that time president of the United States, was coming to New York to give me away, and our date had to fit in with his plans. Finally, it was decided that we would be married on St. Patrick's day, March 17, 1905, because Uncle Ted was coming on for the parade that day.

Franklin and I were thrilled to be asked to stay with Auntie Bye for Uncle Ted's inauguration on March 4, 1905. Once at the Capitol, only the immediate family went inside. Franklin and I went to our seats on the steps just back of Uncle Ted and his family. I was interested and excited, but politics still meant little to me, for though I can remember the forceful manner in which Uncle Ted delivered his speech, I have no recollection of what he said! We went back to the White House for lunch, and then saw the parade and back to New York. I told myself I had seen a historical event—and I never expected to see another inauguration in the family!

Four

Early Days of Our Marriage

TWO WEEKS before our wedding all was frantic haste. Some of my brides-maids came to help me write notes of thanks for wedding presents, of course signing my name. One day we discovered to our horror that Isabella Selmes was writing "Franklin and I are so pleased with your gift," etc. and then signing her own name instead of mine!

The bridesmaids were dressed in cream taffeta with three feathers in their hair, and had tulle veils floating down their backs. Franklin had a number of ushers, and Lathrop Brown was his best man. My own dress was heavy stiff satin, with shirred tulle in the neck, and long sleeves. My grandmother Hall's rose-point Brussels lace covered the dress, and a veil of the same lace fell from my head over my long train.

The three feathers worn by the bridesmaids were reminiscent of the Roosevelt crest, and Franklin had designed a tiepin for his ushers, with three little feathers in diamonds. He also designed and gave me a gold watch, with my initials in diamonds and a pin to wear it on with the three feathers, which I still wear, though watches dangling from pins are not the fashion today.

My mother-in-law had given me a dog collar of pearls which I wore, feeling decked out beyond description. I carried a large bouquet of lilies of the valley.

The date chosen had an added significance for all my Hall family, as it was my mother's birthday. March 17 arrived. Uncle Ted came to New York from Washington, he reviewed the parade, and then came to Cousin Susie's house, where Franklin and I were married.

Many of our guests had difficulty in reaching the house because of the parade that blocked the streets. No one could enter from Fifth Avenue, and the police guarded Uncle Ted so carefully that it was difficult for anyone to come in from Madison Avenue. A few irate guests arrived after the ceremony was over!

The ceremony was performed by the Reverend Endicott Peabody, the head of Groton School. My cousin Susie's drawing room opened into her mother's house, so it gave us two large rooms. We were actually married in Mrs. Ludlow's house, where an altar had been arranged in front of the fireplace, just as had been done for Pussie's wedding the year before.

After the ceremony we turned around to receive congratulations from the various members of our families and from our friends. In the meantime, Uncle Ted went into the library, where refreshments were served. Those closest to us did take time to wish us well, but the great majority of the guests were more interested in being able to see and listen to the President —and in a short time this young married couple were standing alone! The room in which the President was holding forth was filled with people laughing at his stories. I do not remember being particularly surprised at this, and I cannot remember that even Franklin seemed to mind. We simply followed the crowd and listened with the rest. Later we gathered together enough ushers and bridesmaids to cut the wedding cake, and I imagine we made Uncle Ted attend this ceremony. Then we went upstairs to dress. By this time the lion of the afternoon had gone.

We left amidst the usual shower of rice. One old friend of mine had not been able to be at the wedding. Bob Ferguson was laid up with a fever, which ever since the Spanish War, when he had been one of Uncle Ted's Rough Riders, came back at intervals, so before we went to our train we stopped in to see him and then took the train for Hyde Park, where we spent our first honeymoon. It is not customary to have two honeymoons, but we did, because my husband had to finish out his year at law school.

Our first home was a small apartment in a hotel in the West Forties in New York City for the remainder of the spring while Franklin continued his study of law.

It was lucky that my first housekeeping was so simple. I had a tiny room for Hall, so he could spend his Easter holiday with us, and he seemed to fill the entire apartment. Mending was all that was really required of me in the way of housewifely duties in those first few weeks and I was able to do that. But I knew less than nothing about ordering meals, and what little I had learned at Tivoli before I went abroad to school had completely slipped out of my mind.

When my mother-in-law went to Hyde Park for the summer we moved into her house, so I still did not have to display the depths of my ignorance as a housewife.

As soon as law school was over for the summer we went abroad—and with what qualms did I embark! How terrible to be seasick with a husband to take note of your suffering, particularly one who seemed to think that sailing was a joy! Luckily for me, the trip was calm, and all I remember about it is that we played a great many games of piquet and I invariably lost. I was not wise enough at that time to know that if one played cards with Franklin one must be prepared to win rarely. I claimed he had phenomenal luck. He claimed it was all due to skill!

For the first time we did things that I had always longed to do. We went first to London, and were horrified to find that in some way we had been identified with Uncle Ted and were given the royal suite at Brown's Hotel, with a sitting room so large that I could not find anything that I put down. We had to explain that our pocketbook was not equal to so much grandeur, but that made no difference. We lived in it for those first few days in London.

This is a city that my husband loved and I learned to like it better than I ever had before, because we poked into strange corners while he looked for books and prints, with clothes thrown in. But it was when we crossed the Channel that I was really excited.

In Paris we dined in strange places, ordering the specialties of any particular restaurant, whatever they might be. We wandered along the Seine and looked in all the secondhand stands. I bought clothes and some prints, but Franklin bought books, books, everywhere he went.

His French was good, so in Paris he did the bargaining, but when we reached Italy I spoke better Italian than he did. However, after a few days he gave up taking me when he was going to bargain, becuase he said he did better without me, that I accepted whatever the man said and believed it to be the gospel truth. He got along with his poor Italian, made up largely from the Latin which he had learned in school.

We went to Milan, and then to Venice in July. We spent the Fourth of July there. We had a delightful gondolier who looked like a benevolent bandit and kept us out on the canals a good part of the nights. He and I could understand each other moderately well. Occasionally, when we went on long trips he had a friend to help him, and then the Venetian dialect would fly back and forth, and he had to translate what his friend was saying.

We saw churches until my husband would look at no more, but he was never tired of sitting in the sun at one of the little tables around the piazza and recalling the history of Venice.

We went by gondola out to Murano and saw the glass blown, and ordered a set of glasses with the Roosevelt crest, and some Venetian glass dolphins for table decorations, both of which I still have.

From Venice we went north through the Dolomites and then we took a large, lumbering victoria drawn by two horses. It was a beautiful trip to Cortina, where we spent several days. My husband climbed the mountains with a charming lady, Miss Kitty Gandy. She was a few years his senior and he did not know her well at that time, but she could climb and I could not, and though I never said a word I was jealous beyond description and perfectly delighted when we started off again and drove out of the mountains. Perhaps I should add that Miss Gandy later became one of my good friends!

We stopped at Augsburg and Ulm, two quaint German cities, where we managed to find more interesting prints. Then we drove through the Alps to Saint-Moritz, where Auntie Tissie and her family were staying.

The fact that we drove meant that our luggage had to be light and I had one simple evening dress with me, which by this time was not in its first freshness. We arrived at the Palace Hotel to find a suite reserved for us, and the price appalled us both. We decided that as it was only for a few days our pocketbook would stand the strain. We forgot how much dressing went on in such hotels as this, and we soon found that our clothes were suitable only for one particular dining place, a balcony overlooking the lake, and the food seemed to be even more expensive here than it was elsewhere. We were much relieved when we started off again and drove out of Switzerland by way of Strasbourg and Nancy.

Franklin took pictures of this whole trip, some of them at the tops of passes where we were surrounded only by white peaks covered with snow. When we got home he never had a moment's hesitation as to exactly where they were taken. That extraordinarily photographic mind of his never forgot anything he had once seen.

Back in Paris, I collected my clothes, and we had some gay times, as some of Franklin's cousins were there also, and his Aunt Dora (Mrs. Forbes). She took us to see many places, and her apartment, which was always the center for the entire family when they went to Paris, was a most hospitable home to us.

In England we paid what was to me a terrifying visit to Mr. and Mrs.

Foljambe, who had a beautiful place called "Osberion in Workshop." It is in a part of England known as "the Dukeries," because of its many fine estates belonging to great titled families.

The most marvelous oak tree I have ever seen stood near this place, and we visited a castle which had a little railroad track running from the kitchen to the butler's pantry through endless corridors. We were shown the special rooms in which the plate was kept, more like the vault of a silversmith than a safe in a private house. The library had real charm. You entered it through a doorway from which a divided staircase led down several steps into a long room. A fireplace at the end held some blazing logs. On either side stacks came out into the room, and between them were arranged tables and chairs and maps, everything to make reading or study easy and delightful.

In this tremendous household there was only one bathroom. We had comfortable rooms with open fireplaces, and our tin tubs were placed before the fires in the morning, our cans of hot water beside them. The food was excellent but typically English. Dinner was formal and to my horror there were no introductions. We were guests in the house and that was considered sufficient.

I suffered tortures, and when after dinner I had to play bridge, which I played badly, my horror was increased by the fact that we were to play for money. My principles would not allow me to do this, so I was carried by my partner, but this scarcely eased my conscience. I felt like an animal in a trap, which could not get out and did not know how to act.

Soon after we left the United States, Isabelle Selmes's mother had cabled us that Isabelle was going to marry Bob Ferguson. They came over on their honeymoon to visit his family in Scotland. We were invited to his mother's house, in order that we might have a chance to see them. They were staying at a little watering place not far from Novar, the old family home in the north of Scotland. Up there the head of the house is known to the people as "the Novar," and for many years the present Lord Novar would take no title because he considered that "the Novar" was higher than anything the Crown could give him.

The dower house, where old Mrs. Ferguson lived, was a revelation to me, with its glorious view and the lovely gardens covering the side of the hill. I knew the Ferguson family well and they had been friends of our family for a long time.

Franklin tramped the moors with Hector, and one night, after a long day of exercise and many visits to crofters' cottages, I was awakened by wild shrieks from the neighboring bed. Mrs. Ferguson was delicate and I woke with a "Hush!" on my lips, for I did not want to have her disturbed. I had already discovered that my husband suffered from nightmares. On the steamer coming over he had started to walk out of the cabin in his sleep. He was docile, however, when asleep, and at my suggestion returned quietly to bed.

This time he pointed straight to the ceiling and remarked most irritably to me, "Don't you see that revolving beam?" I assured him that no such thing was there and had great difficulty in persuading him not to get out of bed and awaken the household.

When our early-morning tea with thin slices of bread and butter was brought in, I inquired if he remembered his dream. He said he did, and that he remembered being annoyed with me because I insisted on remaining in the path of the beam which threatened to fall off.

I was asked to open a bazaar while I was there. Any young English girl would have been able to do it easily, but I was quite certain I could never utter a word aloud in a public place. Finally, Franklin was induced to make a speech to the tenantry, and for years we teased him because he told the Scottish crofters that vegetables should be cooked in milk—an extravagance hardly within their means!

From there we went down to stay with the older brother, who was head of the house, Sir Ronald Ferguson, and his wife, Lady Helen, at their other house, Raith, on the Firth of Forth, just across from Edinburgh. This was a beautiful place, with wonderful woods and rhododendrons. My husband was tremendously interested because of the scientific forestry work which made these woods financially valuable and brought in revenue year by year.

I was fascinated by the prints which hung everywhere, even on the walls along the little back stairs which led to our rooms. My final thrill came when we went to dinner and I found the walls hung with Raeburn portraits of all the Ferguson ancestors. The first one I saw, "The Boy with the Open Shirt," I had known in reproductions since childhood but had never expected to see the original hanging in a friend's home.

This was also my first sight of a Scotsman in his dress kilts at dinner. Hector had worn them out on the moor, but I had really not had a chance to take them in, in all their glory, until this occasion.

One afternoon at tea I was alone with Lady Helen, when she suddenly asked me a devastating question: "Do tell me, my dear, how do you explain the difference between your national and state governments? It seems to us so confusing."

I had never realized that there were any differences to explain. I knew that we had state governments, because Uncle Ted had been governor of New York State. Luckily, Sir Ronald and my husband appeared at that moment for tea and I could ask Franklin to answer her question. He was adequate, and I registered a vow that once safely back in the United States I would find out something about my own government.

We had to be home for the opening of Columbia Law School, so our holiday, or second honeymoon, had come to an end. My mother-in-law had taken a house for us within three blocks of her own home, at 125 East 36th Street. She had furnished it and engaged our servants. We were to spend the first few days with her on landing until we could put the finishing touches on our house.

I was beginning to be an entirely dependent person—no tickets to buy, no plans to make, someone always to decide everything for me. A pleasant contrast to my former life, and I slipped into it with the greatest of ease.

The edge of my shyness was gradually wearing off through enforced contact with many people. I still suffered but not so acutely.

Either Maude or Pussie once told me that if I were stuck for conversation I should take the alphabet and start right through it. "A—Apple. Do you like apples, Mr. Smith? B—Bears. Are you afraid of bears, Mr. Jones? C—Cats. Do you have the usual feeling, Mrs. Jellyfish, about cats? Do they give you the creeps even when you do not see them?" And so forth all the way down the line, but some time had passed since anything as desperate as this had had to be done for conversational purposes. As young women go, I suppose I was fitting pretty well into the pattern of a conventional, quiet young society matron.

Five

A Woman

THE TRIP HOME was not pleasant, and I landed in New York feeling miserable. I soon found that there was a good reason, and it was quite a relief —for, little idiot that I was, I had been seriously troubled for fear I would never have any children and my husband would be much disappointed.

I had always been a particularly healthy person, and I think it was a good thing for me to be perfectly miserable for three months before every one of my six babies arrived, as it made me a little more understanding and sympathetic of the general illnesses human beings are subject to. Otherwise, I am afraid I would have been more insufferable than I am—for I always think we can do something to conquer our physical ailments.

Little by little I learned to make even these months bearable. In any case, I never let anything physical prevent my doing whatever had to be done. This is hard discipline, and I do not recommend it either as training for those around one or as a means of building character in oneself. What it really does is to kill a certain amount of the power of enjoyment. It makes one a stoic, but too much of a thing is as bad as too little, and I think it tends to make you draw away from other people and into yourself.

For the first year of my married life I was completely taken care of. My mother-in-law did everything for me. Like many other young women waiting for a first baby, I was sometimes nervous. A girlhood friend of mine said, "When I am a little afraid of the future I look around and see all the people there are and think they had to be born, and so nothing very extraordinary is happening to me."

Some emergencies of this period I remember vividly. We had invited some friends for dinner, and the cook departed the day before. It seemed impossible to get another one. I was simply petrified, because I knew nothing about preparing a meal, and I spent the day going from employment office to employment office until finally I corralled someone to cook the dinner, and worried all the way through for fear the results would be disgraceful.

One would think that this might have suggested to me the wisdom of learning to cook, and though I remember I did take myself all the way up to Columbia University for some cooking lessons one winter I got little good out of it, for the school used gas ranges, and I learned to make special, fancy dishes only. What I needed to know was how to manage an old-fashioned coal range and how to cook a whole meal.

That winter my cousin Alice Roosevelt was married to Nicholas Longworth. Franklin had to go alone to the wedding because I was expecting my first child. On May 3, 1906, a girl whom we named Anna Eleanor after my mother and myself was born. Our trained nurse, a lovely person, Blanche Spring, played an important part in my life for many years. I had never had any interest in dolls or little children, and I knew absolutely nothing about handling or feeding a baby. I acquired a young and inexperienced baby's nurse from the Babies' Hospital, who knew about babies' diseases, but her inexperience made this knowledge almost a menace, for she was constantly looking for obscure illnesses and never expected that a well-fed and well-cared-for baby would move along in a normal manner.

During the next few years we observed much the same summer routine. We visited my mother-in-law at Hyde Park for a time and then went up to stay with her at Campobello. My mother-in-law was abroad for a part of that summer of 1906, and we had her house at Campobello. Ordinarily my husband sailed up or down the coast in the little schooner *Half Moon*, taking some friends with him, and took perhaps one or two short cruises during the summer across to Nova Scotia or to various places along the coast. He was a good sailor and pilot, and nearly always calculated his time so well that rarely do I remember his causing us any anxiety by being delayed. As a rule, he sailed into the harbor ahead of his schedule.

If they were going on a cruise from Campobello, I had to stock the boat up with food for the first few days, and after their return they always told me what delicious things they had had to eat on the boat. Apparently their idea of perfection was a combination of sausages, syrup and pancakes for every meal, varied occasionally by lobsters or scrambled eggs. My husband was the cook as well as the captain and was proud of his prowess.

One evening the next winter, we were having some people in to dinner, the nurse was out, and about six-thirty, after having her bottle and being put to bed, instead of placidly going to sleep, Anna began to howl, and she howled without stopping while I dressed for dinner. Our guests began to arrive. I called the doctor. He asked me if I thought she might have a little wind, and was I sure I had gotten up all the bubbles after her last bottle? I did not dare tell him I had completely forgotten to put her over my shoulder and had no idea whether the bubbles had come up or not. He suggested that I turn her on her tummy and rub her back, so, with my guests arriving downstairs, I told Franklin he would have to start dinner without me. I picked up my howling baby, put her over my knee on her tummy, and in a few minutes she smiled and gurgled. After I had rubbed her back for some time she got rid of her troubles and, when put back to bed, went to sleep like a lamb. I went down to dinner, but was so wrought up by this time that I felt I had to go and look at her several times during the evening, and finally succeeded in waking her up before the nurse came home. I was obliged to leave my guests again before they departed. After this experience I registered a vow that never again would I have a dinner on the nurse's day out.

I know now that what we should have done was to have no servants those first few years; so I could have acquired knowledge and self-confidence and other people could not fool me about either the housework or the children. However, my bringing up had been such that this never occurred to me, nor did it occur to any of the older people who were closest to me. Had I done this, my subsequent troubles would have been avoided and my children would have had far happier childhoods. As it was, for years I was afraid of my nurses, who from this time on were usually trained English nurses who ordered me around quite as much as they ordered the children.

As a rule, they kept the children in pretty good health and I think were really fond of them, but I had a silly theory that you should trust the people with your children and back up their discipline. As a result, my children were frequently unjustly punished, because I was unprepared to be a practical housekeeper, wife or mother.

In the winter of 1907 I had a rather severe operation and was successful in getting Miss Spring to come back to me. Dr. Albert H. Ely, who was our family doctor, performed this operation in our own house, and I was found to be considerably weaker than anyone had dreamed. As a result, they thought I was not coming out of the ether, and I returned to consciousness to hear a doctor say, "Is she gone? Can you feel her pulse?"

The pain was considerable, but as my own impulse was never to say how I felt I do not think I mentioned this until some time later on. I simply refused to speak to those who approached me, and they probably thought that I was far more ill than I really was.

During the time my husband was at law school he had long summer holidays which made it possible for us to be at Campobello. In the summer of 1907 Mr. and Mrs. Henry Parish came to stay with us. I went with my husband to meet them on their arrival on the evening train. A thick fog made crossing the bay blind sailing, but my husband prided himself that with the engine he could do it and strike the exact spot he was headed for. We reached Eastport, Maine, without any mishap, and got our cousins aboard.

On the return trip the compass light went out. Someone brought my husband a lantern and hung it on the main boom so he could see his course. He rang his bell for slow speed at the proper moment, but no buoy appeared for us to pick up, no land was in sight. After proceeding cautiously for some little time, the man on the bowsprit called out, "Hard aport," and there, above us, loomed the Lubec docks, with just enough room to sheer off. Much annoyed and completely mystified, my husband reset his course for Campobello, realizing we had come through a narrow passageway and just by luck had not found ourselves in the tide running through the Narrows. About three minutes later "Hard over" came from the bowsprit, and we just missed a tiny island with one tree on it, which was entirely off our course.

It dawned on my husband that the lantern swinging from the boom was of iron and had been attracting the compass! From there on we used matches, and found our way through the narrow pass and back to our buoy without any further difficulties. Mr. and Mrs. Parish had an uncomfortable time and I think were relieved that five days of solid fog made further sailing impossible for the rest of their stay.

I was having difficulty that summer with my brother. I nagged and expected too much of him. In my most exasperating Griseldaish mood I refused to take any further responsibility. One of my most maddening habits, which must infuriate all those who know me, is this habit, when my feelings are hurt or when I am annoyed, of simply shutting

up like a clam, not telling anyone what is the matter, and being much too
obviously humble and meek, feeling like a martyr and acting like one.
Years later a much older friend of mine pointed this out to me and said
that my Griselda moods were the most maddening things in the world. I
think they have improved since I have been able to live more lightly and
have a certain amount of humor about myself. They were just a case of
being sorry for myself and letting myself enjoy my misery.

But those first years I was serious and a certain kind of orthodox good-
ness was my ideal and ambition. I fully expected that my young husband
would have these same ideas, ideals and ambitions. What a tragedy it was
if in any way he offended against these ideals of mine—and, amusingly
enough, I do not think I ever told him what I expected!

On December 23, 1907, our first boy, James, was born, and with what
relief and joy I welcomed him, for again I had been worried for fear I would
never have a son, knowing that both my mother-in-law and my husband
wanted a boy to name after my husband's father.

This winter of 1907-08 I still think of as one of the times in my life which
I would rather not live over again. We could not find any food that would
agree with the new baby. Miss Spring was pressed into service, and we
turned one of our living rooms into a bedroom, for we had meant to put
the two babies together, but when the younger one cried every night all
night that was not practicable.

I had a curious arrangement out of one of my back windows for airing the
children, a kind of box with wire on the sides and top. Anna was put out
there for her morning nap. On several occasions she wept loudly, and finally
one of my neighbors called up and said I was treating my children inhu-
manly and that she would report me to the S.P.C.C. if I did not take her
in at once! This was a shock to me, for I thought I was being a most modern
mother. I knew fresh air was necessary, but I learned later that the sun is
more important than the air, and I had her on the shady side of the house!

I also learned that healthy babies do not cry long, and that it is wise to
look for the reason when a baby does any amount of prolonged crying.

My mother-in-law thought that our house was too small, and that year
she bought a plot and built in East 65th Street two houses, Nos. 47 and 49.
Charles A. Platt, an architect of great taste, did a remarkable piece of work.
The houses were narrow, but he made the most of every inch of space and

built them so that the dining rooms and drawing rooms could be thrown together and made practically one big room.

My early dislike of any kind of scolding had developed now into a dislike for any kind of discussion and so, instead of taking an interest in these houses, one of which I was to live in, I left everything to my mother-in-law and my husband. I was growing dependent on my mother-in-law, requiring her help on almost every subject, and never thought of asking for anything that I thought would not meet with her approval.

She was a very strong character, but because of her marriage to an older man she had disciplined herself into living his life and enjoying his belongings, and as a result she felt that young people should cater to older people. She gave great devotion to her own family and longed for their love and affection in return. She was somewhat jealous of anything that might mean a really deep attachment outside the family circle. She had warm friends of her own, but she did not believe that friendship could be on the same par with family relations.

Her husband had told her never to live with her children, that it was one thing to have children dependent upon you but intolerable to be dependent on them. This she repeated to me often, but I doubt if she realized that with certain natures it is advisable to force independence and responsibility upon them young.

In the autumn of 1908 I did not know what was the matter with me, but I remember that a few weeks after we moved into the new house on East 65th Street I sat in front of my dressing table and wept, and when my bewildered young husband asked me what on earth was the matter with me, I said I did not like to live in a house which was not in any way mine, one that I had done nothing about and which did not represent the way I wanted to live. Being an eminently reasonable person, he thought I was quite mad and told me so gently, and said I would feel different in a little while and left me alone until I should become calmer.

I pulled myself together and realized that I was acting like a little fool, but there was a good deal of truth in what I had said, for I was not developing any individual taste or initiative. I was simply absorbing the personalities of those about me and letting their tastes and interests dominate me.

Because my husband played golf I made a valiant effort at Campobello one year to practice every day, trying to learn how to play. After days of practice I went out with my husband, and after watching me for a few minutes he remarked that he thought I might as well give it up! My old sensitiveness about my inability to play games made me give it up then and there. I never attempted anything but walking with my husband for many years to come.

For ten years I was always just getting over having a baby or about to have one, and so my occupations were considerably restricted during this period. I did, however, take lessons rather intermittently, in an effort to keep up my French, German and Italian. I did a great deal of embroidery during these years, a great deal of knitting, and an amount of reading which seems incredible to me today when other things take up so much of my time. I doubt that there was a novel or a biography or any book that was widely discussed in the circles in which we moved which I did not read. This does not mean, of course, that I read in a wide field, for we moved still with a restricted group of friends.

On March 18, 1909, another baby was born to us, the biggest and most beautiful of all the babies—the first baby Franklin. Because of all the trouble I had had with James, I was worried about his food and kept Miss Spring with us for several months. The baby seemed to be getting on well, but I loved having her with us and insisted on keeping her until after we had been in Campobello for some time. She did not leave until sometime around the early part of August.

I had an English nurse then for the other two children. I also had a young German girl, and together they took charge of the three children.

In the autumn we moved back to Hyde Park, and I was beginning to go up and down between New York and Hyde Park. All of a sudden they notified me that all the children had the flu and that baby Franklin was very ill. No one knew how serious it might be. I dashed back, taking Miss Spring and a New York doctor with me. We spent a few harrowing days there, moved the baby to New York, but his heart seemed affected and, in spite of all we could do, he died on November 8, not quite eight months old. We took him to Hyde Park to bury him and, to this day, so many years later, I can stand by his tiny stone in the churchyard and see the little group of people gathered around his tiny coffin, and remember how cruel it seemed to leave him out there alone in the cold.

I was young and morbid and reproached myself bitterly for having done so little about the care of this baby. I felt he had been left too much to the nurse, and I knew too little about him, and that in some way I must be to blame. I even felt that I had not cared enough about him, and I made myself and all those around me most unhappy during that winter. I was even a little bitter against my poor young husband who occasionally tried to make me see how idiotically I was behaving.

My next child, Elliott Roosevelt, was born at 49 East 65th Street on September 23, 1910. I left Campobello early that summer to await his arrival in New York City. The other children returned to Hyde Park with my mother-in-law. She was in and out of New York and so was my husband, who was making his first campaign for state senator.

After my husband graduated from law school and was admitted to the bar, he worked in the firm of Carter, Ledyard and Milburn, a much-respected and old-established firm in New York City. He was doing well and Mr. Ledyard liked him, but Franklin had a desire for public service, partly encouraged by Uncle Ted's advice to all young men and partly by the glamour of Uncle Ted's example. Mr. Ledyard was genuinely disturbed but my husband decided to accept the nomination in his district, which for thirty-two years had never elected a Democrat.

My husband's branch and many of the Roosevelt family had been Democrats until the Civil War, when they became Abraham Lincoln Republicans. Later most of them returned to their Democratic allegiance, but some remained Republicans.

I listened to all his plans with great interest. It never occurred to me that I had any part to play. I felt I must acquiesce in whatever he might decide and be willing to go to Albany. My part was to make the necessary household plans and to do this as easily as possible if he should be elected. I was having a baby, and for a time at least that was my only mission in life.

Franklin was conducting a novel campaign, for no one had ever before tried to visit every small four-corners store, every village and every town. He talked to practically every farmer and when the votes were counted that election day my husband was the first Democrat to win in thirty-two years. At the same time, through that firsthand contact with the people, he had learned much of their thinking and of their needs.

I went with Franklin to one meeting before the end of the campaign. It was the first political speech I had ever heard him make. He spoke slowly, and every now and then there would be a long pause and I would be worried for fear he would never go on. What a long time ago that seems!

He looked thin, then, tall, high-strung, and at times nervous. White skin and fair hair, deep-set blue eyes and clear-cut features. No lines as yet in his face, but at times a set look of his jaw denoted that this apparently pliable youth had strength and Dutch obstinacy in his make-up.

Franklin made a good many friends in that campaign; one of them, Thomas Lynch, of Poughkeepsie, was to be a close and warm friend and follower from then on. He believed firmly that Franklin would someday be president, and showed it by buying two bottles of champagne before Prohibition, putting them away and bringing them out in Chicago in 1932 just after Franklin's nomination. Everybody at headquarters had a sip from a paper cup to toast future success.

We rented our house in New York City, and I suppose I must have gone to Albany and looked at the house which we took on State Street, though I have no recollection of doing so. I had a new English nurse with the children, Anna, James, and Baby Elliott. I was so nervous about this new baby that we took a wet nurse to be sure of having him properly fed, as it had been suggested that the first baby Franklin, who had always been a bottle-baby, might have been stronger and better able to stand his illness if he had been breast-fed.

That autumn it was also discovered that James had a murmur in his heart, and in order to take proper care of him he must not be allowed to walk up and down stairs. He was a fairly tall though thin little boy, and quite a load to carry. However, up and down steps we carried him all the rest of that winter.

Six

My Introduction to Politics

WE ARRANGED for a reception to be held in our Albany house on the afternoon of January 1 for as many of Franklin's constituents as wished to come. We arrived in the morning, and naturally we were not very well settled. I brought three servants besides the nurses, and caterers were in the house arranging for the reception, which went on interminably. People from the three counties wandered in and out for three solid hours. When it was all over and some of the debris had been removed and the caterers were out of the house, my mother-in-law and I started to move the furniture around and make the house more homelike.

I have always had a passion for being completely settled as quickly as possible, wherever I lived. I want all my photographs hung, all my ornaments out, and everything in order within the first twenty-four hours. Dirt and disorder make me positively uncomfortable.

I sallied forth that next morning to do my marketing. I received my first shock when a lady stopped me on the street with, "You must be Mrs. Roosevelt, for your children are the only ones I do not know." All my life I had lived in big cities, rarely knowing my neighbors. The realization that everybody up and down the street would know what we were doing and would pay attention to us was a great surprise.

For the first time I was going to live on my own: neither my mother-in-law nor Mrs. Paris was going to be within call. I wrote my mother-in-law almost every day, as I had for many years when away from her, but I had to stand on my own feet now and I wanted to be independent. I was beginning to realize that something within me craved to be an individual.

People were kind and I soon made friends and was very busy that year. Occasionally I went to the gallery in the Capitol and listened to whatever

65

might be the order of business. I came to identify interesting figures. Senator Tom Grady could make a better speech than many people who are considered great orators today. Bob Wagner, "Big Tim" Sullivan, Christy Sullivan, Senator Sage, old Senator Brackett, who looked like a church deacon and was probably as wily a politician as ever paced the Senate floor, all stood out as individuals on the floor of the Senate. In the Assembly I had my first glimpse of Al Smith.

I was at home every afternoon and had tea with the children. I read to them or played with them till they went to bed. I tried having little Anna lunch with us, but after spending a solid hour over the meal on our first attempt I returned her to the nursery. Anna and James and the younger nurse had their room over the big library at the back of the house. The baby and his nurse were in the room next to ours.

Anna was fair-skinned like her father, with good features, blue eyes and straight hair which was bleached almost white by the sun. James was darker as to both hair and complexion, looking in this particular more like me. Luckily for them all, the children inherited their looks from their father's side of the family. One or two of them have eyes like my side of the Roosevelts, but eyes happen to have been rather good in that branch of the family. I had prominent front teeth, not a very good mouth and chin, but these were not handed down to any of my children.

Here in Albany began for the first time a dual existence for me, which was to last all the rest of my life. Public service, whether my husband was in or out of office, was to be a part of our daily life from now on. To him it was a career in which he was completely absorbed. He probably could not have formulated his political philosophy at that time as he could later, but the science of government was interesting—and people, the ability to understand them, the play of his own personality on theirs, was a fascinating study to him.

I still lived under the compulsion of my early training; duty was perhaps the motivating force of my life, often excluding what might have been joy or pleasure. I looked at everything from the point of view of what I ought to do, rarely from the standpoint of what I wanted to do. There were times when I almost forgot that there was such a thing as wanting anything. So I took an interest in politics. It was a wife's duty to be interested in whatever interested her husband, whether it was politics, books or a particular dish for dinner. This was the attitude with which I approached that first winter in Albany.

Here, for the first time, a man who was to become a very close friend of my husband's came upon the scene. I hardly remember meeting him. He was a newspaper correspondent, an old hand in the Albany political game, Louis McHenry Howe by name. He lived in Albany with his wife and daughter, but his home for years had been in Saratoga, so he knew the countryside and had many old friends. I saw little or nothing of the Howes that first year. I still felt myself a good deal of a stranger.

The fate of an insurgent group who stood with my husband in an early senatorial fight against Tammany influence was my first introduction into the grimmer side of machine politics. One man had a little country newspaper and depended largely on government printing of notices for his financial success. The year after, he was given none, as punishment for opposing the Democratic machine, and his paper failed. Similar stories came to us from various sources, and my blood boiled. My husband was not vulnerable but many of his friends were not in so independent a position. I realized that you might be a slave and not a public servant if your bread and butter could be taken from you; and, if you grew too fond of public life, it might exact compromises even if finances were not involved.

After the legislature adjourned I took the children to Hyde Park as usual and later to Campobello, pursuing our usual routine. My husband again had a good deal of time in summer to be with us, though he did have to spend some time in his district, and the legislature met again in August for a short session.

When I had first gone to Campobello there lived next to my mother-in-law a charming woman, a Mrs. Kuhn from Boston. When she died it was found that in her will she suggested Mrs. Roosevelt might want to buy her property, including a little point of land on the Bay of Fundy side of the island, and her house with all its furnishings, even china and glass and linen. She asked that it be offered to Mrs. Roosevelt at a nominal price in case she wanted it for her son.

My mother-in-law bought it and gave it to us, and this house became a great source of joy to me and a place with which I think my children have many happy associations.

The winter of 1912 found us back in Albany in a house on Elk Street. My first cousin, Theodore Douglas Robinson, was elected to the Assembly and came to take his seat that winter. His wife, Helen, was my husband's half niece—J. R. ("Rosy") Roosevelt's daughter—and so our relationship was extremely close and complicated.

Of course, Teddy and Franklin were on opposite sides politically, and one was in the Senate and the other in the Assembly. Both Teddy and Helen had a few close friends who were not great friends of ours, and they moved in a gayer and younger group, on the whole.

I was always more comfortable with older people, and when I found myself with groups of young people I still felt inadequate to meet them on their own gay, light terms. I think I must have spoiled a good deal of fun for Franklin because of this inability to feel at ease with a gay group, though I do not remember that I ever made much objection to his being with them so long as I was allowed to stay at home.

I remember feeling a little responsible that year for the wives of some of the new assemblymen and for the wives of some of the newspapermen, who, I had been told, were very lonely. I religiously called on them and tried to have them occasionally at my house.

I remember little of what my husband did in the legislature, except that he came out for woman suffrage. He always insisted that Inez Mulholland sitting on his desk had converted him but as a matter of fact he came out for woman suffrage two months before that memorable visit.

I was shocked, as I had never given the question serious thought, for I took it for granted that men were superior creatures and knew more about politics than women did, and while I realized that if my husband was a suffragist I probably must be, too, I cannot claim to have been a feminist in those early days.

I had lost a good deal of my crusading spirit where the poor were concerned, because I had been told I had no right to go into the slums or into the hospitals, for fear of bringing diseases home to my children, so I had fallen into the easier way of sitting on boards and giving small sums to this or that charity and thinking the whole of my duty to my neighbor was done.

I was not a snob, largely because I never really thought about why you asked people to your house or claimed them as friends. Anyone who came was grist to my mill, because I was beginning to get interested in human beings, and I found that almost everyone had something interesting to contribute to my education.

In 1909 my brother Hall had entered Harvard College. He was ready for graduation in 1912 and won his Phi Beta Kappa key, though he belonged to the class of 1913. In the spring of 1912 the authorities allowed him to go with my husband on a trip to Panama. Never having been fond of the sea, and also being anxious whenever I went away from the children for a long period of time, I did not accompany them on the first part of their trip. Another member of the legisture, Mayhew Wainwright, joined them, and they had, from all accounts, a delightful time.

In June of 1912 my brother was married to Margaret Richardson of Boston. Hall was not quite twenty-one and she was twenty when they started off on their honeymoon to Europe.

In the latter part of the month, my husband took me to my first political convention. We had taken a house in Baltimore with Mr. and Mrs. Montgomery Hare and Mr. and Mrs. James Byrnes.

That convention was an exciting one. In front of me in the convention hall sat Mrs. August Belmont, who registered righteous indignation and said she would go out and fight the party when William Jennings Bryan practically read her husband out of it.

I understood nothing of what was going on, but I watched with keen interest the demonstration for Champ Clark, and was appalled when his daughter was carried around the room. The demonstrations all seemed senseless to me, and my opinion of conventions changed little for a number of years.

It was extremely hot. I understood little about the fight for Woodrow Wilson's nomination, though my husband was deeply interested and was spending a great deal of time trying to bring it about. Finally, I decided my husband would hardly miss my company, as I rarely laid eyes on him anyway and the children should go to Campobello, so I went home and took them up there and waited to hear the result. I received a wild telegram of triumph when Mr. Wilson was finally nominated. It read:

MRS. F. D. ROOSEVELT
CAMPOBELLO EASTPORT MAINE
WILSON NOMINATED THIS AFTERNOON   ALL MY PLANS VAGUE   SPLENDID
TRIUMPH   FRANKLIN.

We came down early from Campobello, because my husband had another campaign on hand. We traveled by boat, and neither of us gave much thought to the fact that we brushed our teeth with the water in the stateroom pitchers. We settled the children at Hyde Park. Franklin laid his plans for the campaign, and then we went down to an entirely "put up" house in New York City, which we had taken back from the people who had rented it the winter before. We were to spend only one night and our old friend, Ronald Ferguson, who was over from Scotland, was to dine with us. The evening came but my husband was too ill to go out to dinner. He had a low fever and was feeling miserable. I did all I could for him, and took Ronald out to a restaurant by myself.

My husband was still miserable the next morning, so I got a strange doctor, as our regular doctor was out of town. He could not explain the fever. No one could understand what was the matter with him. I was taking complete care of him. We had a caretaker in the house who did what cooking was necessary, and I ran up and down stairs with trays, made his bed, gave him his medicine, and all went well except for the fact that at certain times of the day I felt peculiar. My husband had to take a nap after lunch every day, and I was glad enough to do the same, for the back of my head ached and I was hardly able to drag myself around. It never occurred to me that I, too, might be ill.

After this had gone on for about ten days my mother-in-law came to town one evening, having grown anxious about her son, and I told her that, as she was there, I would have my hair curled and go to bed, because I felt miserable. She kissed me and exclaimed, "You must have a fever!" She insisted that I take my temperature and we found that it was 102. The doctor came and I went to bed, and the next day tests were taken and it was discovered that I had typhoid fever. Franklin had had it when he was a little boy, so he was running only a low temperature, but they now thought he had it also. I proceeded to have a perfectly normal case, and with my usual ability to come back quickly I was up and on my feet while Franklin was still in bed and feeling miserable and looking like Robert Louis Stevenson at Vailima.

In the meantime the campaign was on, and now Louis Howe, the quiet, even then rather gnomelike little newspaper man from Albany, came to the rescue. He had grown interested in my husband at the time of the senatorial fight, and when Franklin asked him to run the campaign he accepted. Going to Dutchess County, he laid his plans and carried the district for a man who was flat on his back at the time.

Louis was an astute politician, a wise reader of newspapers and of human beings, but he was somewhat impractical, in spots. A checkbook was one of the things Louis did not understand. My husband gave him a checkbook and a certain amount of money in the bank. Each time Louis came to see my husband he still insisted that he had money in the bank. Finally, my husband was notified that the account was overdrawn. Louis still insisted he had money on hand, and when Franklin looked over the checkbook he found that Louis always added the amount of the check to the balance instead of deducting it, so of course the amount went up instead of down.

I was not favorably impressed with Louis at this time because he smoked a great many cigarettes! Remember, I was still a Puritan. I felt that his smoking spoiled the fresh air that my husband should have in his bedroom, and I was very disapproving whenever he came down to report on the campaign. I lost sight entirely of the fact that he was winning the campaign and that without him my husband would have worried himself to more of a wreck than he was and probably lost the election. I simply made a nuisance of myself over those visits and his cigarettes. I often wonder now how they bore with me in those days. I had no sense of values whatever and was still rigid in my standard of conduct.

My husband was re-elected, thanks to Louis Howe. I put the New York house in order and moved the children there, as it was too late to rent it and we had decided not to take a house in Albany for the winter, but to live in two rooms at the Ten Eyck Hotel. We commuted between New York and Albany. I went to Albany every Monday afternoon and returned to New York every Thursday morning to be with the children.

During the winter there was some talk of the possibility of my husband's being invited to join the administration in Washington but I was too much taken up with the family to give it much thought.

Seven

Washington

IN APRIL, Franklin was sent for by the President, and I stayed in New York
waiting to hear what would be our fate. In a short time we got word that
my husband had been appointed assistant secretary of the navy. He resigned from the state Senate and took up the work in Washington. There
was an epidemic of smallpox at the time, so we were both vaccinated.

My husband had taken rooms at the Powhatan Hotel in Washington,
and wanted me to come down for a time that spring. I dashed to Auntie
Bye, who was in Farmington, Connecticut, to ask her what were the duties
of an assistant secretary's wife. My heart sank as she gave me careful instructions on my calls. This enormous burden is no longer carried by the
wives of government officials. It became impracticable during the war.

One thing Auntie Bye impressed on me was that as the wife of the
assistant secretary of the navy my duty was first, last and all the time to
the Navy itself. She said, "you will find that many of the young officers'
wives have a hard time because they must keep up their position on very
small pay. You can do a great deal to make life pleasant for them when
they are in Washington, and that is what you should do."

I had come a long way since I moved up to Albany, for then I never
could have paid those first calls and repeated that formula, "I am Mrs.
Franklin D. Roosevelt. My husband has just come as assistant secretary
of the navy." House after house I visited and explained myself in this
way. My shyness was wearing off rapidly.

The autumn of 1913 we took Auntie Bye's house at 1733 N Street. It
was a comfortable old-fashioned house, and the two old colored servants,
Millie and Francis, who had taken care of Uncle Will when Auntie Bye

was away, agreed to take care of it in summer and look after Franklin when he was there alone.

There was a little garden at the back with a lovely rose arbor on the side where one could have breakfast in the late spring or summer days, and even dine on summer evenings. This little garden was kept in order by a delightful man, William Reeves, whom I got to know well. His reticence was really remarkable. We lived in that house four years, and though I talked with him often it was not until I came to the White House in 1933 that I discovered that Mr. Reeves was the head gardener there and that it had been because of his position there that he had gone to Auntie Bye during Uncle Ted's administration. He had kept it up because of his affection for her and his interest in her garden.

When we moved down to Washington my mother-in-law, as usual, helped us to get settled. We had bought a car and brought a young chauffeur with us from Hyde Park, and I had to begin in earnest to pay my calls.

My husband had asked Louis Howe to come down as his assistant in the Navy Department; Louis moved his wife and two children, one of them a fairly well-grown girl and the other a baby boy, into an apartment not far from us.

Anna was going to school with the Misses Eastman, and James began his schooling that autumn in the little Potomac School. I remember that winter primarily as one in which I spent every afternoon paying calls. We lived a kind of social life I had never known before, dining out night after night and having people dine with us about once a week.

We discovered early that unless we made some attempt to see a few people at regular intervals we would never see anyone informally, and so once every two weeks or thereabouts a few of us dined together regularly. This group consisted of Secretary of the Interior Franklin K. Lane and Mrs. Lane, a charming couple who appealed to young and old; Mr. and Mrs. Adolph Miller, old friends of the Lanes; Mr. and Mrs. William Phillips, and ourselves. William Phillips was in the State Department, and he and Caroline were old friends of ours. We put formality behind us for these evenings, and did not even seat the secretary of the interior according to rank. Franklin and I still stayed home on Sunday evenings and continued the informal Sunday evening suppers which we had always had since our marriage. I cooked eggs on the table in a chafing dish, served cold meat and salad, a cold dessert and cocoa.

I tried at first to do without a secretary, but found that it took me such endless hours to arrange my calling list, and answer and send invitations, that I finally engaged one for three mornings a week.

When I was first married I discovered that my husband was a collector. In every other respect he was both careful and economical. I never knew him in those early days to take a cab when he could take a streetcar. I have often seen him carry his bag down the street and board a car at the corner. He took great care of his clothes, never spent a great deal on himself, and there were many things that we felt we could not afford. After our first little car, we went without one for some time; and when we moved to Washington the first two cars that we had were second-hand, until I finally persuaded my husband that we spent more on repairs and had less use out of them than we would have out of a new car. The new car that we finally bought lasted until we left Washington, when he again decided that we did not need a car and sold it.

As a collector he was careful, too, and much of his collection was acquired at reasonable prices, because not many people were interested, at that time, in his field. He really knew about everything he bid for at auctions or acquired after spending hours in old bookstores or print shops.

His interest was in the American Navy and he collected books and letters and prints and models of ships. The collection was fairly sizable and interesting when he went to Washington as assistant secretary of the navy, but those years in the Navy Department gave him great opportunity to add to it. He was offered and acquired an entire trunkful of letters which included the love letters of one of our early naval officers. He also acquired a letter written by a captain to his wife describing receipt of the news of George Washington's death and his subsequent action on passing Mount Vernon. He is said to have instituted a custom which every navy ship has followed from that day to this, and which varies only according to the personnel carried by the ship. All the ships lower the flag to half mast, man the rail, toll the bell and, if a bugler is on board, blow taps.

Franklin also acquired a good model of the old *Constitution*, and his collection grew apace. At different times he collected other things. For instance, there was a period when he was fond of small chapbooks, children's books and classics published in diminutive editions, and first editions of every kind always attracted him, though he never followed any one line. Stamps were also an interest of long standing.

I have often wondered why he never handed down this love of collecting to any of our children. My only explanation is that living in the house with a collector may give everyone else the feeling that only one person in a household can indulge this taste, and even then it is a question of whether the family will have to move out in order to keep the collection intact and properly housed!

With the autumn of 1913 my life in Washington as the wife of a minor official really began. I could have learned much about politics and government, for I had plenty of opportunity to meet and talk with interesting men and women. As I look back upon it, however, I think the whole of my life remained centered in the family. The children were still small, two more were to be born during this period, and outside of the exclusively personal life there was the social aspect, which then seemed to me most important.

Nearly all the women at that time were the slaves of the Washington social system. There were two women who broke loose. One was Martha Peters, wife of Congressman Andrew J. Peters, of Massachusetts, and a sister of William Phillips. She did not care for large social functions and did not think it was her duty to her husband's career to spend every afternoon of her life paying calls on the wives of other public men.

The other woman was Alice Longworth, quite frankly too much interested in the political questions of the day to waste her time calling on women who were, after all, not important to her scheme of life. She liked the social side, but she liked her own particular kind of social life. She wanted to know the interesting people but did not want to be bored doing uninteresting things. Her house was a center of gaiety and of interesting gatherings. Everyone who came to Washington coveted an introduction to her and an invitation to her house.

I was appalled by the independence and courage displayed by these two ladies. I was perfectly certain that I had nothing to offer of an individual nature and that my only chance of doing my duty as the wife of a public official was to do exactly as the majority of women were doing.

My calls began the winter of 1914 under poor auspices, for I was feeling miserable again, as another baby was coming along the following August. Somehow or other I made my rounds every afternoon, and from ten to thirty calls were checked off my list day after day. Mondays the wives of the justices of the Supreme Court; Tuesdays the members of Congress. How many times I have wondered why my New York congressmen moved from place to place so frequently! They rarely had houses, their wives seldom came down, and to leave cards on them I had to climb up stairs in rooming houses and search every large and small hotel! Wednesdays the Cabinet, and here was a problem to be met. If Mrs. Daniels invited me to be with her on that afternoon I could not be calling on the other members of the Cabinet. Thursdays the wives of senators, and Fridays the diplomats. Miscellaneous people were wedged in on whatever days were printed on their cards or, if they had no days, on any days you happened to be near their homes. Saturdays and Sundays were free for the children.

Just as Mr. Daniels was a kind and understanding chief, Mrs. Daniels was a kind and understanding wife, and did not expect me to be with her every Wednesday. Later in the winter I tried to stay at home on Wednesdays and receive anyone who came to call on me. I had my first experience then of entertaining ladies who spoke in three different languages and of being the only person able to interpret what was being said by one to the other!

My husband frequently came home for luncheon and brought some men with him, more often after the war began than in the first years, when he had more time for the Metropolitan Club and games of golf. This was the game he enjoyed above all others. However, when he did come home he wanted a short lunch and no time wasted. They must be able to talk freely, so I developed a habit which I have always retained. I have a little silver bell put beside my place at every meal. It belonged to my mother and is part of the recollection of my earliest days—Old Mother Hubbard with her dog under her arm. It is never far from my hand at meals. When I ring, the servants come in and take the plates away, pass the next course, and then withdraw to the pantry and stay there until I ring again. This was made the rule in Washington and has been continued wherever I am, for conversation can flow more freely. It was necessary during World War I, when conversations were frequently held which must not go beyond the people seated at the table; and I have found it always relieves a certain restraint at the table not to have someone standing behind a chair or hovering in the room.

Here, as in Albany, I tried to get in from my calls by five o'clock so as to have tea at home, and the children were always with me for an hour before their own supper and bedtime.

Somewhere around the middle of that winter—I think in early March —my husband was sent on an inspection trip to the West Coast and I accompanied him.

When we arrived in each place, a naval aide appeared and told us what we should do, for which I was thankful. I was still new at getting on and off naval ships, with all the ceremony attached thereto.

The first time Anna was with us when we bobbed up and down in a little boat, and my husband received the seventeen-gun salute fired for the assistant secretary of the navy, she buried her head in my lap because she was sensitive to noises. Afterwards she carried cotton to put in her ears. I was totally unprepared the first time the salute came, but, as I was somewhat deaf even then, the noise did not bother me.

When it came to boarding a battleship I had to wait to be told whether I went ahead of my husband or whether he went ahead of me. What did I do while he stood at salute, whom did I shake hands with, and what parts of the ship should I not visit; and when we came to leave, did I go first or last? All these questions and many more worried me during these first inspection trips. But gradually I learned. Somehow my husband seemed to know all this without coaching, and I have always wondered how he absorbed knowledge where I had to struggle and ask innumerable questions. Perhaps he grew curious earlier in life. In any case, he was able to answer most of the questions we asked him; and when we thought on occasion we had him trapped and went to an encyclopedia to prove him wrong, almost invariably he was right.

On this trip, as on most other official trips, our engagements began at nine or ten o'clock in the morning and ended somewhere around midnight. After that I wrote my letters and packed my bags.

On all these trips I started out with a great deal of apprehension, in spite of the fact that I loved seeing new places. I hated to leave my children; but once out, my fears were quiescent until we were about two days from home, and then they revived in full force, and the last night I usually imagined all the terrible things that might happen to the children before we saw them again. They might fall out of a window, or into the fire, or be run over! My mother-in-law always had an eye to the children when we were away, so there was really no cause for anxiety, but during those years they had the usual runs of colds and earaches and tonsils which are the lot of children, and, in addition, many of the less serious childish illnesses.

Any woman with children knows that she must be prepared for all kinds of vicissitudes, but it takes time to accustom yourself to these things. At first you feel that you or someone else should have prevented whatever goes wrong. Later you learn that no amount of care will ward off the accidents and all you can do is to meet them, as they come along, with a calm and steadfast spirit.

That summer of 1914 the children and I went to Campobello, as usual, but war clouds were gathering over Europe and Washington was full of anxiety. My baby was due to arrive in August and plans had been made for the doctor who had taken care of me and my four other children to fly up and be with me for the event. Miss Spring, the same nurse who was always with me on these occasions and who managed to come as often as possible when the children had any ailments, came up to keep me company. My husband came for a short holiday, my mother-in-law was in her own cottage nearby. But, instead of waiting until the right time, I woke my husband on the night of August 16, to tell him I thought he had better go to Lubec and get our old friend, Dr. Bennett. My mother-in-law heard my husband call down to the men on the *Half Moon* to bring in the little boat so he could sail over, so she came running over from her cottage to find out what was wrong.

I made everyone wait around for the whole of the next day, and the baby did not arrive until early evening on August 17. I felt guilty, for I knew Dr. Bennett had many other patients, probably much more in need of his care than I was, and I tried to make him leave, but he felt responsible and insisted on sitting around. At last it was all over and he remarked to Miss Spring, "Why, she is just like one of us. I never took care of summer people before."

Franklin Junior, the second baby to be given this name, progressed satisfactorily and I never had a pleasanter convalescence.

Franklin had arrived on July 25, but on the 29th he had a telegram to return to Washington because war seemed imminent. He wired me from there the various events as they occurred before he returned to Campobello. None of us quite realized the years of war that lay ahead. This is best illustrated by the fact that a young banker, who was married to my husband's cousin, said reassuringly to us that summer that this war could not last long; the bankers of the world could control it by refusing credits. When my husband remarked that people had always been able to find money with which to carry on war, more than one man in the financial world smiled knowingly and said it could only be a question of a few months before Europe would be at peace again.

While I was still in bed, one of the destroyers came up and spent a few days cruising around the coast. My husband gave all the young officers heart failure by insisting on taking the ship through a place that looked to them extremely dangerous, but which his intimate knowledge of the waters made safe for navigation.

I remember one occasion when he brought a destroyer through the Narrows. This is a passage running between the mainland at Lubec, Maine, and the island of Campobello. The tide runs through at great speed, except when it is slack, and at low water it would be entirely impossible to take a destroyer or any big ship through; but at high tide, if you know the passage, it can be done. My husband did it on a number of occasions, though the officers with him thought he would surely scrape the bottom.

That autumn, though he did not resign as assistant secretary of the navy, my husband ran in the September primaries against James W. Gerard for United States senator and was defeated. I remember little about the campaign. I had to stay in Campobello until September was well on, and had such a small baby that most of my attention was focused on him at the time. I do not think that my husband ever had any idea that he was going to win, and I have often heard him say that he did not think himself suited to serve in the United States Senate; and it was probably a great relief to find himself back at his desk in the Navy Department.

Eight

Growing Independence

IN THE SPRING of 1915 President Wilson appointed as commissioners to the San Francisco Fair Mr. William Phillips, who was assistant secretary of state, and my husband. Mr. Phillips went out ahead of us. I was to go with my husband and we were to accompany Vice-President and Mrs. Marshall, who were the personal representatives of the President at the fair. Much to our joy, the secretary of the interior and Mrs. Franklin K. Lane and Mr. and Mrs. Adolph Miller decided to go out at the same time.

Vice-President and Mrs. Marshall were to join us in Chicago; and, as I had never known either of them well, and the vice-president had the reputation of being extremely silent, I looked forward with some trepidation of being thrown with them on what must be rather intimate terms. I liked them both very much, and while I struggled through a number of meals with rather a silent gentleman, I discovered that he had a fund of dry humor and there was no pretentiousness about him. When he did not know a thing he said so. When he did not like a thing he said so, and usually had some amusing remark to make. We were on the back platform of the train when we crossed the Great Salt Lake. Everyone was exclaiming at the beauty around us. He removed the cigar which was rarely out of his mouth and remarked, "I never did like scenery."

I was beginning to acquire considerable independence again because my husband's duties made it impossible for him to travel with us at all times, and I was accustomed to managing quite a small army on moves from Washington to Hyde Park and to Campobello and back.

In the summer of 1915 I had not been long in Campobello when a wire came telling me that Franklin had been operated on for appendicitis in Washington. I was on my way to him when one of the men on the train came through calling my name. He handed me a telegram which said, "Franklin doing well, your mother-in-law with him. Louis Howe."

I could cheerfully have slain poor Louis because I had to claim that wire and eyes were turned on me from all over the car. So my shyness was not entirely cured. In fact, it never has been. I remember Louis Howe, years later, taking me out to dinner at a restaurant, sitting at a table he did not like, and eating food he did not like, simply because he knew I would be uncomfortable if he made me conspicuous by getting up and changing to another table or complaining about the food.

I don't suppose that kind of shyness ever really leaves one and to this day it sweeps over me occasionally when I face a crowd, and I wish the ground would open and swallow me. Habit has a great deal to do with what one actually does on these occasions, and the next years were going to give me a very intensive education along many lines.

I found Franklin's mother in Washington at his bedside and we spent some time there together. She finally felt her son was well enough for her to leave and I stayed on alone until Franklin was able to leave the naval hospital and go on board the *Dolphin* for a trip up the coast.

Ever since the beginning of World War I in Europe our country had been becoming the battleground of opposing ideas, and our family was being torn by the differences between Theodore Roosevelt's philosophy and that of President Wilson and his administration in general. I had a tremendous respect for this uncle of mine and for all his opinions. I knew that he felt we should take sides in the European war.

Woodrow Wilson, on the other hand, was determined that our nation should not be dragged into the war if it could possibly be kept out, and above everything else he did not wish our country to go in until the nation itself felt the urge to take a stand that would undoubtedly cost it much in men and money. No one had any realization of how much, and few saw far enough into the future to visualize the results that would come years later.

We had already begun to send ambulances and food to European nations. Mr. Herbert Hoover was feeding the Belgians. My husband was conscious of the pull of varying ideas and standards, and I think, being young, there were times when he wished a final decision could be reached more quickly. I often thought in later years, when he waited while younger advisors champed at the bit for action, of those early days when he played the role of a youthful and fiery adviser.

William Jennings Bryan, secretary of state, was a well-known pacifist. I was always fond of Mrs. Bryan, but in spite of my admiration for Mr. Bryan's powers of oratory there were certain things that did not appeal to me at this time.

Antiwar germs must have been in me even then, however, for I had an instinctive belief in his stand on peace. I remember Mr. Bryan had miniature plowshares made from old guns and given to many people in the government. These were greeted by some with ridicule but to me they were not in the least ridiculous. I thought them an excellent reminder that our swords should be made into plowshares and should continue in this useful occupation.

Many people were already making fortunes out of the war; those who made munitions, for instance; the growers of cotton and of wheat were finding a ready market in the nations that required more raw materials and foodstuffs than they could grow themselves, with most of their men at the front and much of their land out of cultivation.

Distinguished groups came from foreign nations to look after the interests of their own countries over here, and the social life of Washington became busier and more interesting.

In the winter of 1915-16, a large economic conference for South and Central American commerce was held in Washington, and the State Department arranged for every government official to entertain some of the delegates and their wives at different times.

The dinner that we gave I remember vividly because we never could find out how many people were going to dine with us or what their names were. A list was furnished us, but, as the people arrived, many of the names were quite different from the ones on the list. However, we finally sat down and had enough places at table.

I was getting on very well because the men on either side of me spoke English and French. I looked toward the other end of the table and saw that my husband was having a difficult time making conversation with the lady on his right. On his left he had a man who seemed able to talk to him. Later that evening I inquired how he had enjoyed his dinner companions and he answered that they were charming; the lady had been difficult to talk to as she could speak only Spanish and all he could say was: "How many children have you, madam?" to which she always responded smilingly with the number and nothing more!

The German ambassador was conscious, I think, of the general antagonism growing around him, particularly after the sinking of the *Lusitania,* but he had a few warm friends and went his way serenely enough in Washington society. The French and English ambassadors were under great pressure; many people wanted them to undertake the same kind of propaganda that the German ambassador was carrying on. The French ambassador, M. Jules Jusserand, had been so many years in this country that he had a great knowledge of the United States and its people, and the same was true of Sir Cecil Spring-Rice, the English ambassador, and neither of them would consent to much active propaganda. Perhaps they felt that there was enough interest among certain United States citizens to bring about all the propaganda that was really needed, and events later vindicated their judgment!

Sir Cecil Spring-Rice had been in this country as a young man; he had become a great friend of Theodore Roosevelt's family, and retained that friendship through the years, so that when we went to Washington one of the first houses that opened to us was the British embassy. He was a great reader and student of American history; one of the things he asked me the first time I sat beside him at dinner was which of the American histories I felt was the best. When I hesitated he remarked how strange it seemed that we citizens of the United States read so little of our own history. Sir Eustace Percy, one of the younger members of the embassy staff, was making an exhaustive study of our Civil War and had visited all the battlefields. Few young Americans do as much.

Stories of "Springy," as he was called by his intimates, and his peculiarities were current in Washington. They said that one day he came in from a long walk in the rain, went upstairs and dressed for dinner, came back to his study and sat down to read by the fire. In a short time the dressing bell rang and he arose and went back and put on all the wet clothes and came down thus dressed for dinner!

Without Lady Spring-Rice many official engagements would not have been met on time. I have been at the embassy when she has gone into his sitting room and said, "Your appointment with the French ambassador is in ten minutes and the car is at the door," and a reluctant Springy would get up from his book and his wife, put on his hat, and go to meet the French ambassador or the Secretary of State or whoever it might be.

The French ambassador and his charming wife had many friends. M. Jusserand had been one of Theodore Roosevelt's "walking Cabinet." He was a small man and had grown up in the mountains of France and was an expert climber. All his life he had taken walking trips, so he was not daunted by Theodore Roosevelt's excursions through Rock Creek Park, even when they required crossing the brook in some deep spot.

One other person stands out among the people we knew in these first years in Washington. While I cannot say I knew him well, the few opportunities we did have to be with him left a great impression upon us. The Theodore Roosevelts and Mrs. Cowles had known Mr. Henry Adams well and were constant visitors at his house on Lafayette Square. We knew some of the people who were his intimate friends and so occasionally we received one of the much-coveted invitations to lunch or dine at his house.

My first picture of this supposedly stern, rather biting Mr. Adams is of an old gentleman in a victoria outside our house on N Street. Mr. Adams never paid calls. He did, however, request that the children of the house come out and join him in the victoria; and they not only did join him, but they brought their Scottie dog, and the entire group sat and chatted and played all over the victoria.

One day after lunch with him, my husband mentioned something which at the time was causing him deep concern in the government. Mr. Adams looked at him rather fiercely and said: "Young man, I have lived in this house many years and seen the occupants of the White House across the square come and go, and nothing that you minor officials or the occupant of that house can do will affect the history of the world for long!" True, perhaps, but not a good doctrine to preach to a young man in political life!

Henry Adams loved to shock his hearers, and I think he knew that those who were worth their salt would understand him and pick out of the knowledge that flowed from his lips the things that might be useful, and discard the cynicism as an old man's defense against his own urge to be an active factor in the world of politics, a role that Henry Adams rejected in his youth.

Nine

A Changing Existence

IN MARCH, 1916, our last child was born. We named him John Aspinwell, after Franklin's uncle.

That winter of 1916 had been rather hard on my husband, because of a throat infection. He had had such a bad time with it that he had to go to Atlantic City, where his mother met him. He was supposed to take a two-week vacation, but the inactivity was more than he could bear, and in a week he was at work again. I hoped we were through with serious illness.

However, the baby was scarcely two days old when Elliott developed a bad cold and swollen glands. I thought this would amount to very little but in another day he was worse. Anything more trying than to be in bed and have a child ill in a room on the floor above I do not know, so I look back on this spring as a difficult experience. Finally we sent for an old friend of Miss Spring's, who came down from New York to take charge of Elliott and gradually nurse him back to comparative health.

From that day until he went to boarding school at the age of twelve he was a delicate small boy whom we had to watch carefully. Sometimes when I look at the strong man he has grown to be it is hard to realize the years of anxiety that went into his upbringing. From the spring of 1916 he seemed to have everything more seriously than the others, and spent days and weeks in bed. This gave him a taste for books; and I think of all the children he had the greatest pleasure in reading and developed a real appreciation of literature.

The summer of 1916 I went up, as usual, with the children to Campobello. Franklin came occasionally. That summer there was a bad infantile paralysis epidemic among children. I had never stayed in

Campobello late into September, but there I was entirely alone with my children, marooned on the island, and apparently I was going to be there for some time. Finally Franklin was allowed to use the *Dolphin* again, and in early October he came up, put the entire family on board and landed us on our own dock in the Hudson River.

There were beginning to be wild rumors of German submarines crossing the ocean and being seen at different places along the coast, and on the one stop we made on the way down we heard that a German submarine had been sighted and its officers had landed.

The children remained at Hyde Park until it was safe for them to travel, and I went back to Washington. From a life centered entirely in my family I became conscious, on returning to the seat of government in Washington, that there was a sense of impending disaster hanging over all of us.

The various attacks on our shipping were straining our relations with Germany and more and more the temper of the country was turning against the Germans. Stories of the atrocities in Belgium drifted in and were believed, but in spite of an increasing tenseness we had not actually broken off diplomatic relations with Germany. That winter my husband went to Haiti. The marines were in control. Franklin took with him the president of the Civil Service Commission, John McIlhenny, an old friend of Theodore Roosevelt and one of his Rough Riders. Later he was made financial adviser to Haiti and managed his difficult job extremely well, with the result that we later returned to the Haitian government the control of their own financial affairs.

This trip of my husband's was extremely interesting and took him on horseback through a good part of the island. He was far away from the coast of Santo Domingo, up in the mountains, when a cable came from the secretary of the navy announcing that political conditions required his immediate return to Washington, and that a destroyer would meet him at the nearest port. We had severed diplomatic connections with Germany and the ambassador had been given his papers and asked to leave the United States. The German naval attaché, Captain Boy-Ed, and others had finally succeeded in thoroughly arousing the antagonism of the American people by spying into American affairs. This, however, my husband did not know. When he went to the dinner given him by the Marine officers in charge of this station, he showed the decoded telegram, which he had just received, to the lady who sat next to him. She had lived so long in the parts of the world where revolutions were uppermost in people's minds that she promptly said: "Political conditions! Why, that must mean that Charles Evans Hughes has led a revolution against President Wilson."

Back in Washington, my husband plunged into intensive work, for the possibility that the United States would be drawn into the war seemed imminent. The Navy must be ready for action immediately on the declaration of war.

We found it necessary to move in the autumn of 1916 because five children were more than Auntie Bye's house on N Street was designed to hold comfortably. No. 2131 R Street was a pleasant house with a small garden at the back.

All too soon we were to find ourselves actually in the war, and during those spring months of 1917 my husband and I were less and less concerned with social life except where it could be termed useful or necessary to the work that had to be done. Again my husband frequently brought people home for luncheon because he had to talk to them, and we often entertained particular people who came from other nations because it was necessary that they should know the people with whom they were dealing.

After weeks of tension, I heard that the President was going to address Congress as a preliminary to a declaration of war. Everyone wanted to hear this historic address and it was with the greatest difficulty that Franklin got me a seat. I listened breathlessly and returned home half dazed by the sense of impending change.

War was declared on April 6, 1917, and from then on the men in the government worked from morning until late into the night. The women in Washington paid no more calls. They began to organize at once to meet the unusual demands of wartime. Mrs. J. Borden Harriman called a meeting to form a motor corps for Red Cross work. I attended the meeting but at that time I could not drive a car, so I decided that that was not my field of work.

No work was fully organized until the next autumn, but I joined the Red Cross canteen, helped Mrs. Daniels to organize the Navy Red Cross, and began to distribute free wool for knitting, provided by the Navy League.

I found myself very busy that spring, entertaining members of foreign missions who continued to come to this country to talk over the type of co-operation that we were to give the Allies. Mr. Balfour came over with a mission from England, arriving three days before the French mission. This was a quiet, unspectacular mission, but he had with him men who had served at the front and been wounded. They found their way at times to our home.

In the first French mission were Marshal Joffre and former Premier Viviani, who arrived in this country on April 25, 1917.

Franklin's cousin, Warren Robbins, was at that time attached to the State Department and was given the responsibility of accompanying the French mission and making their trip in the country as comfortable and pleasant as possible. A great crowd greeted them in Washington, and Joffre, who had been the hero of the stand at the Marne, was received everywhere with the greatest enthusiasm. People knew that his soldiers had called him "Papa Joffre" and his appearance suited this name so well that the crowd over here would often hail him in this way.

Viviani was not an agreeable personality, but he was a brilliant speaker. There were, of course, a number of people in the party, and the man who appealed to me most was Lieutenant Colonel Fabry, known as the Blue Devil of France. Before and after the war he was a newspaper editor, a gentle, quiet person to whom this nickname seemed hardly appropriate. Badly wounded many times, he was in constant pain while he was in Washington.

Before our entry into the war, many foolish people like myself said that only our financial resources would be needed and that the only branch of the service which would be called upon to fight would be the Navy. However, on our entry into the war both services were called into action, and the first plea made by the French mission was that some American soldiers be sent to France in July instead of in October, as our government had planned. The argument was that the Allies were tired and that the sight of a new uniform and of fresh men at the front would restore their morale, which was being subjected to such a long strain.

I remember most vividly the trips from Washington down to Mount Vernon on the *Sylph*, especially the first one with Mr. Balfour, Marshal Joffre and Premier Viviani. Secretary and Mrs. Daniels and my husband and I, with other members of the Cabinet, accompanied them, and their first duty was to lay a wreath on the tomb of George Washington. It was a ceremonious occasion, and as we gathered around the open iron grille at the tomb each man made a speech. How odd it must seem to Mr. Balfour to be paying honor to the memory of the man who had severed from the mother country some rather profitable colonies, but he was graceful and adequate in this rather peculiar situation.

Only when someone on the lawn at Mount Vernon told him the story of George Washington's throwing a silver dollar across the Potomac to the other shore, did his eyes twinkle as he responded, "My dear sir, he accomplished an even greater feat than that. He threw a sovereign across the ocean!"

Immediately after the declaration of war, Uncle Ted came to Washington to offer his services to the President. He had a large group of men who wished to go to the front with him. He felt he could easily raise a division and in it would be many of the best officers in the Army who wished to serve under him, such as General Wood, and many of the old Rough Riders and probably the pick of American youth. Uncle Ted could not bear the thought that his boys should go and he be left behind. He was strong and able enough, he contended, to fight in this war as he had in the Spanish War, and as he had urged the people to enter on the side of the Allies he wanted to be among the first to enlist.

On this visit he stayed with his daughter, Alice Longworth, and I went with Franklin to see him. Though he was kind to us, as he always was, he was completely preoccupied with the war; and after he had been to see President Wilson and the President had not immediately accepted his offer, Uncle Ted returned in a very unhappy mood. I think he knew from the noncommittal manner in which he had been received that his proposal was not going to be accepted.

I hated to have him disappointed and yet I was loyal to President Wilson, and was much relieved later on, when I learned that Uncle Ted's offer had been submitted to General Pershing and the War Department and that the consensus had been that it would be a grave mistake to allow one division to attract so many of the men who would be needed as officers in many divisions. Uncle Ted certainly did his best to go overseas, but it was felt that the prominence of his position and his age made it unwise for him to be in Europe. I think the decision was a bitter blow from which he never quite recovered.

I did little war work that summer beyond the inevitable knitting which every woman undertook and which became a constant habit. No one moved without her knitting.

The Navy Department was co-operating so closely with England and France that my husband hardly left Washington, but I went back and forth. He came for short periods of time to the coast of Maine. It was decided that we had no right to keep the boat which we had always used at

Campobello, and so the *Half Moon* was sold, much to the regret of both my husband and my mother-in-law. The latter had a sentimental attachment for it on account of the pleasure her husband had had in sailing her.

My brother, Hall, who was at this time working for the General Electric Company in Schenectady, was forbidden to enlist, under the rules which barred a man from everything but aviation if he was responsible for the production of war materials in the General Electric Company plant. He had been so close to Uncle Ted and his family that when all those boys enlisted he felt he must join also. He slipped away from work on the plea that he wanted to visit his uncle, and he and Quentin Roosevelt went together on July 14 and enlisted in the only branch of the service which was permissible for Hall under the circumstances—aviation.

I think both Hall and Quentin must have memorized the card for the eye test, because neither of them could have passed otherwise. Hall was called to the first school of aviation in Ithaca in late July or August. My grandmother felt strongly that he should not leave his wife and little children, and I remember my feeling of utter horror when I went to see her one day and she demanded to know why he did not buy a substitute! I had never heard of buying a substitute and said that no one did such a thing. Her old eyes looked at me curiously and she said: "In the Civil War many gentlemen bought substitutes. It was the thing to do." I hotly responded that a gentleman was no different from any other kind of citizen in the United States and that it would be a disgrace to pay anyone to risk his life for you, particularly when Hall could leave his wife and children with the assurance that at least they would have money enough to live on.

This was my first really outspoken declaration against the accepted standards of the surroundings in which I had spent my childhood, and marked the fact that either my husband or an increasing ability to think for myself was changing my point of view.

That autumn, back in Washington, real work began, and all my executive ability, which had been more or less dormant up to this time, was called into play. The house must run more smoothly than ever, we must entertain, and I must be able to give less attention to it. The children must lead normal lives; Anne must go to the Eastman School every day, and James and Elliott must go to the Cathedral School, which was in the opposite direction. All this required organization.

My mother-in-law used to laugh at me and say I could provide my chauffeur with more orders to be carried out during the day than anyone else she had ever listened to, but this was just a symptom of developing executive ability. My time was now completely filled with a variety of war activities, and I was learning to have a certain confidence in myself and in my ability to meet emergencies and deal with them.

Two or three shifts a week I spent in the Red Cross canteen in the railroad yards. During the winter I took chiefly day shifts in the canteen, for I was obliged to be at home, if possible, to see my children before they went to bed, and I frequently had guests for dinner. I can remember one or two occasions when I got home in my uniform as my guests arrived, and I think it was during this period that I learned to dress with rapidity, a habit which has stayed with me ever since.

Everyone in the canteen was expected to do any work that was necessary, even mopping the floor, and no one remained long a member of this Red Cross unit who could not do anything that was asked of her. I remember one lady who came down escorted by her husband to put in one afternoon. I doubt if she had ever done any manual labor in her life, and she was no longer young. The mere suggestion that she might have to scrub the floor filled her with horror and we never again saw her on a shift.

Once a week I visited the naval hospital and took flowers, cigarettes and any little thing that might cheer the men who had come back from overseas.

The naval hospital filled up rapidly and we finally took over one building in St. Elizabeth's Hospital for the so-called shell-shocked patients. The doctors explained that these were men who had been submitted to great strain and cracked under it. Some of them regained sanity, others remained permanently in our veterans' hospitals for mental care.

St. Elizabeth's was the one federal hospital for the insane in the country. A fine man was at the head of it, but he always had been obliged to run his institution on an inadequate appropriation, and as yet the benefits of occupational therapy were little understood in the treatment of the insane, though I knew that in some hospitals this work was being done with a measure of success.

I visited our naval unit there and had my first experience of going into a ward of people who, while they were not violent, were more or less incalculable because they were not themselves. Those who were not under control were kept in padded cells or in some kind of confinement.

When the doctor and I went into the long general ward where the majority of men were allowed to move about during the daytime, he unlocked the door and locked it again after us. We started down that long room, speaking to different men on the way. Quite at the other end stood a young boy with fair hair. The sun in the window placed high up, well above the patients' heads, touched his hair and seemed almost like a halo. He was talking to himself incessantly and I inquired what he was saying. "He is giving the orders," said the doctor, "which were given every night at Dunkirk, where he was stationed." I remembered my husband's telling me that he had been in Dunkirk and that every evening the enemy planes came over the town and bombed it and the entire population was ordered down into the cellars. This boy had stood the strain of the nightly bombing until he could stand it no longer; then he went insane and repeated the orders without stopping, not being able to get out of his mind the thing which had become an obsession.

I asked what chances he had for recovery and was told that it was fifty-fifty, but that in all probability he would never again be able to stand as much strain as before he became ill.

The doctor told me that many of our men in the naval hospital unit were well enough to go out every day, play games and get air and exercise, and that we had enough attendants to make this possible in the rest of the hospital; however, they had been so short of attendants since the war started that the other patients practically never got out. The doctor also told me that in spite of the fact that wages had gone skyrocketing during this period, the hospital had never been able to pay its attendants more than $30 a month and their board, which was low in comparison with what men were getting in other occupations.

I drove through the grounds and was horrified to see poor demented creatures with apparently little attention being paid them, gazing from behind bars or walking up and down on enclosed porches.

This hospital was under the Department of the Interior, so I could hardly wait to reach Secretary Lane, to tell him that I thought an investigation was in order and that he had better go over and see for himself. He appointed a committee which later appeared before Congress and asked for and obtained an increased appropriation. I believe this action of the secretary's enabled Dr. White to make the hospital what every federal institution in Washington should be, a model of its kind which can be visited with profit by interested people from various parts of our country.

In the meantime I was so anxious that our men should have a meeting place that I went to the Red Cross and begged them to build one of their recreation rooms, which they did. Then, through Mrs. Barker, I obtained $500 from the Colonial Dames, which started the occupational therapy work, and in a short time the men were able to sell what they produced and to buy new materials for themselves.

I was seeing many tragedies enacted in that hospital. There was a woman who sat for days by the bed of her son who had been gassed and had tuberculosis. There was a chance that he might be saved if he could get out west. She could not afford to go with him but we finally obtained permission to send a nurse.

Another boy from Texas, with one leg gone, wanted so much to get home; finally, with the help of the Daughters of the Confederacy, some of whom were our most faithful workers, he achieved his desire and I think became self-supporting.

These are just examples of the many things touching the lives of individuals which came to all of us in those days; and so far as I was concerned, they were a liberal education. Some of the stories were sordid, all of them filled with a mixture of the heroism in human nature and its accompanying frailties.

Out of these contacts with human beings during the war I became a more tolerant person, far less sure of my own beliefs and methods of action but more determined to try for certain ultimate objectives. I had gained some assurance about my ability to run things and the knowledge that there is joy in accomplishing a good job. I knew more about the human heart.

One by one, all of Uncle Ted's boys sailed. Auntie Corinne's two boys enlisted, and Monroe Robinson went overseas, as did another cousin, James Alfred Roosevelt. Harry Hooker, one of my husband's former law partners in New York City, sailed with his division.

Over and over again my brother tried to be assigned to work overseas. Over and over again he was refused, with the admonition that his value was greater where he was. He pulled every wire possible, besought my husband to use his influence, got Uncle Ted to use his, and ate his heart out because he could not get to the other side. In spite of the fact that we pointed out to him that he took his life in his hands more frequently in instructing novices than he would at the front, he was never satisfied. He always felt that if some of us had just tried a little harder we could have put him on a transport and given him his heart's desire.

All the time I knitted incessantly and worked in various ways. I wished that I might offer my services to go overseas. I was very envious of another Eleanor Roosevelt, Colonel Theodore Roosevelt's wife, who had gone over before her husband and, in spite of the regulations against wives of officers going to France, was serving there in a canteen.

My husband was engaged in naval operations and of necessity had to keep in close touch with the members of the English and French embassies. Gradually the foreign offices of England and France began to feel that their representatives were not being active enough, and Sir Cecil Spring-Rice was recalled by his government, much to the regret of his many friends in this country, who realized that he and his wife were rendering a great service to the Allied cause.

They were succeeded, in January, 1918, by Lord and Lady Reading. Everyone in Washington recognized this diplomat's great ability and liked them both.

M. Jusserand remained French ambassador until after the war was over, but a special envoy, M. Andre Tardieu, was sent over in 1918 to take up certain financial questions. My recollection is that this was not an entirely happy arrangement. M. Tardieu was an able man, but he had not, perhaps, the temperament that appealed to the French ambassador. However, the mission was successful in carrying through its business and M. Tardieu returned to France.

The winter of 1917-18 wore away and remains to me a kaleidoscope of work and entertaining and home duties, so crowded that sometimes I wondered if I could live that way another day. Strength came, however, with the thought of Europe and a little sleep, and you could sleep, and you could always begin a new day. When summer came I decided that I would spend most of it in Washington to help out at the canteen, for so many people had to be away.

Hot though the Hudson River was, I felt the children were old enough to stand it, particularly as my mother-in-law had built a large addition to the old house and the rooms that the children occupied were less hot than they had been because of the new insulation. I took the children with their nurse to Hyde Park for the summer and stayed with them awhile to get them settled.

I was making preparations to return to Washington, for I had promised to be on duty during the month of July. In June my husband got word that he was to go to Europe. Franklin had spoken and written to various people ever since we had entered the war, seeking to get into uniform. He stated that, "Even though this means doing far less important work for the Navy than if I continue the organization and operations' supervision, not only in the department itself, but also in the patron bases, in the transport service and in many shipyards, I will be in active service."

Then came orders to go overseas and report on the operations and needs of the many American naval and aviation bases and ships in European waters. He obtained a promise that when this was done he would be permitted to return to Europe as a lieutenant commander.

He sailed on the destroyer *Dyer* on July 9, 1918. The *Dyer* was convoying a number of transports taking troops to France. Franklin was naturally much excited at the prospect of this trip, and it gave him great satisfaction to feel that he was going to the front.

Neither his mother nor I could see him off, because they sailed under secret orders; and I realized at the time that it was for her a fearful ordeal, for he was the center of her existence. Luckily, she had the grandchildren to keep her busy, and there were numerous activities in which she took her full share in Hyde Park and Poughkeepsie.

I went back to Washington and spent all day and most of the night at the canteen. I had nothing else to do. Many of the members were away, and in the heat, to which I was quite unaccustomed, I was anxious to keep busy. No place could have been hotter than the little corrugated-tin shack with the tin roof and the fire burning in the old army kitchen. We certainly were kept busy, for we were sending troops over just as fast as we could train them, and we knew now that it was manpower that the Allies wanted as much as our financial resources or the assistance of the Navy.

It was not an unusual thing for me to work from nine in the morning until one or two the next morning, and be back again by ten. The nights were hot and it was possible to sleep only if you were exhausted. When my month was up and others came to take my place, I went to Hyde Park to be with the children and my mother-in-law.

In early September we began to expect to hear of my husband's start for home; but before that news came I received word, on September 12, 1918, that my uncle, Douglas Robinson, had died.

We finally heard that my husband had sailed from Brest to return to this country. A day or so before the ship was due, my mother-in-law and I received word through the Navy Department that Franklin had pneumonia and that we were to meet him on arrival with a doctor and an ambulance. We left the children at Hyde Park and went to my mother-in-law's house in New York, for our own house was rented. The flu had been raging in Brest and Franklin and his party had attended a funeral in the rain. The ship on which they returned was a floating hospital. Men and officers died on the way home and were buried at sea.

When the boat docked and we went on board I remember visiting several of the men who were still in bed. My husband did not seem to me so seriously ill as the doctors implied, but we soon had him settled in his mother's house.

All but one member of my husband's party were seriously ill. Fortunately, they all recovered. With them on the boat, coming to this country for a visit, were Prince Axel of Denmark and his aides. When they felt the flu coming on they consulted no doctor but took to their berths with a quart of whisky each. In the course of a day or two, whether because of the efficacy of the whisky or because of their own resistance, they were practically recovered.

The question of the children's schooling was beginning to weigh heavily upon my mind, so soon after Franklin was better I moved the children who had to be in school back to Washington and commenced commuting back and forth until the whole family was together again.

Franklin improved steadily but he required good nursing and care for some time, for the pneumonia left him very weak. He went to Hyde Park for two weeks, and about the middle of October was well enough to return to Washington and turn in his official reports, firsthand observations of naval activities in the North Sea, the Irish and English channels, and some of the Belgian, British and French ports. He was preparing to resign and join the naval battery in France when word came late in October that Germany had suggested to President Wilson that peace would be discussed.

As soon as we returned to Washington the flu epidemic, which had been raging in various parts of the country, struck us with full force. The city was fearfully overcrowded, the departments had had to expand and take on great numbers of clerical workers. New bureaus had been set up, girls were living two and three in a room all over the city, and when the flu hit there were naturally not enough hospitals to accommodate those who were stricken. The Red Cross organized temporary hospitals in every available building, and those of us who could were asked to bring food to these various units, which often had no kitchen space at all.

Before I knew it, all my five children and my husband were down with the flu, and three of the servants. We succeeded in getting one trained nurse from New York, as Miss Spring was not available. This nurse was put in charge of Elliott, who had double pneumonia. My husband was moved into a little room next to mine, and John, the baby, had his crib in my bedroom, for he had bronchial pneumonia. There was little difference between day and night for me, and Dr. Hardin, who worked as hard as he possibly could every minute of the time, came in once or twice a day and looked over all my patients. He remarked that we were lucky that some of us were still on our feet, for he had families with nobody able to stand up.

In the intervals of cooking for this galaxy of invalids, my cook prepared food to go out, as we had pledged ourselves to send it every afternoon. If all the children were asleep, I went in the car and visited the Red Cross unit I had been assigned to supply and tried to say a word of cheer to the poor girls lying in the long rows of beds. Like all other things, the flu epidemic finally came to an end.

These emergencies of domestic and family life were extremely good training. Gradually I was learning that what one has to do usually can be done, and my long association with Miss Spring had made me a fairly practical nurse. Fear of being left alone to care for my children had vanished. In fact, I had had sense enough in the past few years to send my nurse away in the summer for short vacations and take charge of my last two babies myself. At least I was no longer the inexperienced, timid mother, and the older children say that in consequence the younger ones were never so well disciplined as they were! Of course, the truth of the matter was that I had gained a sense of values and no longer fussed about nonessentials nor allowed myself to be stampeded by the likes and dislikes of a nurse or governess.

The feeling was growing everywhere that the end of the war was in sight. President Wilson's messages to the people of other nations made a deep impression. Ever since the Allied armies had been under the supreme command of Marshal Foch a turn had come for the better in the military affairs of the Allies. Suddenly, on November 7, we got word that an armistice had been signed and pandemonium broke loose, but a few hours later it was declared a mistake and everybody's spirits sank.

Four days later, on November 11, 1918, the real Armistice was signed and the city of Washington, like every other city in the United States, went completely mad. The feeling of relief and thankfulness was beyond description.

Ten

Readjustment

SOON AFTER the Armistice my husband heard that he would have to go abroad after the New Year to wind up naval affairs in Europe, dispose of what could be sold and ship home what could be used here again.

It was so soon after his recovery from pneumonia that it was dangerous for him to be subjected to the winter climate of either France or England, so it seemed wise for me to sail with him, which I could do, now that the war was over.

As we were not to sail until early January, we were at home for Christmas with the family. My mother-in-law usually came to spend Christmas with us if we did not go to her. Our only other guests as a rule were Louis Howe and his family.

Uncle Ted was ill in the hospital when we sailed, but none of us dreamed that it was anything very serious. On the way over we were saddened to receive by radio on January 6 the news of his death. I knew what his loss would mean to his close family, but I realized even more keenly that a great personality had gone from active participation in the life of his people. The loss of his influence and example was what I seemed to feel most keenly.

Admiral Wilson, in command at Brest, came aboard with Admiral Moreau when we arrived. Admiral Wilson boasted that he had the best apartment to be obtained in Brest, with the only bathtub in the town, but the water ran only during certain hours of the day. Most of the people of the town carried all their water from taps placed at intervals along the streets.

Admiral Wilson took me to see something of the country while Franklin worked. General Smedley Butler had finally succeeded in lifting the camp

98

a little out of the mud by building duckboard paths everywhere, but constant rain still made it no paradise.

My husband's business completed, we went to Paris where he spent some busy days. My first duty was to call on all our superiors. Luckily, they all lived in the same hotel except, of course, President and Mrs. Wilson. Franklin and I went together to call on the President of France and sign his book. Later we went again to be received formally and pay our respects.

We were staying at the Ritz Hotel and I was thrilled one day to see at luncheon Lady Diana Manners, for she had always been to me a character in a storybook. She was very beautiful, but some of the glamour of my storybook princess was gone after I had actually seen her.

A great effort was being made to revive the beautiful gay city Paris had once been. The city itself was unchanged but practically every Frenchwoman was dressed in black, and, though the tradition of long black mourning veils was forbidden, the older women could not be prevented from wearing them.

I went with my husband's aunt, Mrs. Forbes, to the oldest military hospital in Paris, the Val de Grâce, where remarkable plastic surgery was being done. I dreaded this but it was not quite so bad as I feared, though I saw all I cared to see of people whose faces were being made over by one operation after another.

We also visited what is known as the Phare, the hospital for the blind where the patients were being taught to manage for themselves and acquire a skill that would enable them to earn a living or at least keep their hands busy.

We dined one night with Belle and Kermit Roosevelt, and Teddy Roosevelt, who was a colonel in the Army, left their apartment that night to go to the American hospital to have an operation on his leg. This hospital I visited later with Mrs. Woodrow Wilson. She left a few flowers at each boy's bed, and I was lost in admiration because she found something to say to each one.

Few people came to France at this period without picking up some kind of germ and the day before we left for London I realized that I was running a temperature, with considerable pain in my side. We were to be on our way the next day, driving over the front where our soldiers had fought with the British and nothing, if I could help it, was going to prevent me from taking that trip.

I got up the next morning at six-thirty, dressed and left, sitting on the back seat of a car, feeling, whenever the road was rough, that a knife was stabbing my side, but the rest of the time, on the whole, I was fairly comfortable.

We made a number of stops, one at the Saint-Quentin Canal. They wished to show us what our troops had done and so we walked to the bottom where the canal runs between steep banks. The cut is about sixty feet deep and the sides were lined with dugouts. I wondered if the state of my feelings would give me an approximate idea of the way the soldiers felt on the cold, gray, foggy morning when they, with full packs on their backs and rifles in their hands, plunged down one side of the canal and climbed up the other. The enemy was afraid to fire until they were well under their guns for fear the approaching army might be their own men. In that way, while armored tanks plowed the plain, the canal itself with its high banks, was taken.

We drove along the straight military roads with churned mud on either side of us, and deep shell holes here and there. Along the road there were occasional piles of stones with a stick stuck into them bearing the name of a vanished village. On the hillsides stumps showed that once there had been a forest.

When we reached Amiens that night I had to confide in my husband that I had a pain and thought I might have caught cold. After dinner I obtained a hot-water bottle and managed to sleep fairly well and was up and able to be interested in the cathedral when we started out at eight o'clock the next morning. The bags of sand which had been placed around the cathedral to protect it made it difficult for us to appreciate its beauty.

Commander Royes met us at Folkestone and when we reached London we were met by Admiral Sims and naval constructor Smith, who took us to the Ritz Hotel. The next day an English doctor came and looked me over. I had pleurisy and was told to stay in bed. I attempted to obey his orders for one day, but as the men all had to be about their business and the telephone and doorbell rang incessantly, I was in and out of bed so often that I decided, even if I could not go out, it was better to be up and dressed.

In the course of a few days I began to feel better. The doctor shook his head gloomily and was convinced I was going into a rapid decline. In fact, he told me to be examined for tuberculosis as soon as I reached home. I was quite sure, however, that I was recovering, and Major Kilgore and Commander Hancock did everything possible to make me comfortable.

Finally, his work was done and Franklin with his aide left for Belgium and then to go down to see the Marines stationed at Coblenz on the Rhine. I moved from the hotel to Muriel Martineau's house and spent four days there.

We were to sail for home with President and Mrs. Wilson, and on February 4 we left by train for Brest. I remember our great excitement when Mr. Grasty, the *New York Times* correspondent, brought us a copy of the charter of League of Nations. What hopes we had that this League would really prove the instrument for the prevention of future wars, and how eagerly we read it through!

President Wilson had been acclaimed by the French people as a savior; his position in his own country seemed impregnable. No organized opposition had as yet developed. His trip had been a triumphant one, and now the people of France stood everywhere to watch for his train in the hope of getting a glimpse of him.

Our first glimpse of the President and Mrs. Wilson and their party was when they came on board the *George Washington*. We were already on the ship and stood behind the captain to welcome them. One funny incident occurred which threw the naval officers into quite a bustle of excitement. Instead of following the prescribed procedure, the President refused to go ahead of his wife and Miss Benham, her secretary, and they boarded the battleship first, a situation unheard of in naval regulations. Nothing happened, however, and when the President came over the side, ruffles rolled out from the drums and "The Star-Spangled Banner" was played and nothing really essential was left out of his welcome.

We lunched one day with the President and Mrs. Wilson. At the table was Ambassador Francis, returning from his post in Russia, a kindly humorous man, giving one a feeling of latent strength. The other guests were Captain McCauley, Dr. Grayson and Miss Benham. In my diary I noted that the talk was, as usual on such occasions, an exchange of stories, but the President spoke of the League of Nations, saying: "The United States must go in or it will break the heart of the world, for she is the only nation that all feel is disinterested and all trust." Later he said he had read no papers since the beginning of the war, that Mr. Tumulty clipped them all for him, giving him only important news and editorials. My diary comment was: "This is too much to leave to any man."

It was, I learned later when my husband became president, a problem of allotting time. Franklin reserved certain periods for his study of the press, particularly the opposition press, and, at least while Louis Howe was with him, he was always closely informed on all shades of opinion in the country. This firsthand awareness of what people are doing and thinking and saying is essential to a president. When this information is filtered through other people, or selected with a view to what a few individuals think the President should know, the inevitable result is that this source of information is dangerously curtailed or misleadingly slanted. This is fatal in the formulation of far-reaching decisions.

We landed in Boston and went through the streets in a long procession. We could see the President and Mrs. Wilson ahead of us, the President standing up and waving his hat at intervals to the crowds that lined the streets. Everyone was wildly enthusiastic and he never sat down until we reached the Copley Plaza Hotel.

At the hotel word was brought that Governor and Mrs. Calvin Coolidge would be glad to have us lunch with them and Mayor and Mrs. Andrew Peters. The President was to make a speech after luncheon and he and Mrs. Wilson did not feel that they could attend a social gathering beforehand.

Thus it fell to my lot to meet a future president of the United States and to know perhaps before the rest of the country how silent the gentleman could be! I regarded his silence on that occasion as a sign of the disappointment he felt at not having Mrs. Wilson to talk to, but I have since decided that even Mrs. Wilson could not have brought forth a flow of conversation!

Immediately after lunch we went to Mechanics Hall and the mayor in greeting the President came out for the League. We were all very much stirred by the President's speech, which was one of the best I ever heard him make. Strange as it may seem, the governor of Massachusetts, Mr. Calvin Coolidge, committed himself to "feeling sure the people would back the President."

We went on to Washington. At every station cheering crowds greeted the President until long after dusk. This was my first experience of the kind and very moving, because the people seemed to have grasped his ideals and to want to back them.

We had been gone not quite two months but it was a great relief to be back with the children.

My household soon functioned as smoothly as ever and my life was not so filled with war work, though much of the hospital work continued unabated and the pathetic funerals in Arlington were frequent in the spring. The government brought back the bodies of many of our men from the battlefields or hospitals in Europe. Sometimes men died on the transports. The funerals were held in Arlington Cemetery if the family desired, and some members of the family usually attended. The Red Cross would detail some of its members to attend and take flowers, and I can never go to a military funeral today without the vision of those scenes and the pictures of certain faces rising before me.

That spring of 1919, on the side of my official duties, I had my first personal contact with the cause of woman suffrage. Back in the Albany days my husband had been for it. Through the years courageous women carried on a constant fight for ratification of woman suffrage by the different states. It looked as though their fight was nearing a successful end and therefore the opposition rallied its forces.

Coming down on the train one day to Washington from New York, I happened to meet Alice Wadsworth, wife of Senator James Wadsworth, who, with her husband, had always been much opposed to woman suffrage. We lunched together and she spent the time trying to persuade me to come out against the ratification. I was noncommittal, for I considered any stand at that time was outside my field of work. I think she had hopes that she might make a convert of me. Before she could succeed, the amendment was ratified, and soon after I undertook work which proved to me the value of a vote. I became a much more ardent citizen and feminist than anyone about me in the intermediate years would have dreamed possible. I had learned that if you wanted to institute any kind of reform you could get far more attention if you had a vote than if you lacked one.

The Navy Department was, of course, busy liquidating the war setup as rapidly as possible. Secretary and Mrs. Daniels went abroad in March, which left my husband in charge during their short trip. Any absence on the part of the secretary made the assistant secretary acting head and gave him opportunity for closer contact with the President.

The President, after presenting his plan to Congress, was having a very hard fight. Senator Lodge felt that Congress should have been consulted sooner; in fact, should have had representatives on the European delegation. He became the leader of the criticism of the President's plan. The fight went on all through the spring.

President Wilson went back to Europe on March 6, 1919, to sign the Treaty of Versailles, feeling sure that the people were with him. The tension between the President and Congress during this period was great, and thoughtful people both here and abroad were wondering about a situation in which the Executive, charged with the duty of dealing with foreign nations, might come to an agreement and the agreement be turned down by the Senate, as had been done before.

Perhaps the answer is that these agreements should be worked out in conjunction with the leaders of Congress instead of by the Executive alone, but one cannot always be sure that even the leaders of Congress can carry all their followers with them. It is interesting, however, to find out how often Congress has not agreed with the Executive and has refused to ratify treaties negotiated by the President and the secretary of state; it leads one to wonder if some more satisfactory means should not be found.

President Wilson returned July 8, 1918, and on September 3 started out on a campaign to take the cause of the League of Nations to the American people. The President was taken ill on this trip, but recovered enough to walk off the train and into his car and into the White House when he returned on September 28.

This same year many of us realized that my grandmother Hall was failing, and on August 14 word came that she had died at her home in Tivoli, where she would have wished to be. I was in Washington, and Franklin and I went on to Tivoli to help my aunts with the last few things that could be done.

I wondered then and I wonder now whether, if her life had been less centered in her family group, that family group might not have been a great deal better off. If she had had some kind of life of her own, what would have been the result? When she was young she painted rather well. Could she have developed that talent? I know that when she was young she might have had friends of her own, might even have married again. Would she have been happier, and would her children have been better off? She was not the kind of person who would have made a career independently; she was the kind of woman who needed a man's protection. Her willingness to be subservient to her children isolated her, and it might have been far better, for her boys at least, had she insisted on bringing more discipline into their lives simply by having a life of her own.

My grandmother's life had a considerable effect on me, for even when

I was young I determined that I would never be dependent on my children by allowing all my interests to center in them. This conviction has grown through the years, and in watching the lives of those around her I have felt that it might have been well in their youth if they had not been able to count on her devotion and her presence whenever they needed her.

Up to a certain point it is good for us to know that there are people in the world who will give us love and unquestioned loyalty to the limit of their ability. I doubt, however, if it is good for us to feel assured of this without the accompanying obligation of having to justify this devotion by our behavior.

It is hard sometimes to realize what factors in our experience have influenced our development, but I am sure that my grandmother's life has been a great factor in determining some of my reactions to life.

On October 28 I went to the House of Representatives when the King and Queen of the Belgians and the crown prince were received there. It was an interesting occasion, and I was impressed by the soldierly bearing of the King and by the Queen's graciousness.

My husband arrived back from a hunting trip in time to take the usual trip down the Potomac with the royal party. Franklin had visited them at the front and again on his trip in 1919 and felt great admiration for them. He had been much drawn to their daughter, the Princess Marie José, who reminded him of his own daughter, Anna.

I could not help feeling a little sorry for Crown Prince Leopold. He was so carefully watched and his constant companion was an army officer many years older than himself. If he was out of his parents' sight for a few minutes, they were sure to inquire where he was. There were no "off the record" trips or entertainments for this young prince, and we had glimpses of what it meant to be trained to be a king.

In October, also, I had my first contact with women's organizations interested in working conditions for women. The International Congress for Women Workers, with representatives from nineteen nations, met in Washington. Because of the number of foreign delegates to be present, they tried to find wives of government officials who could speak foreign languages to attend various social functions, and so Lily Polk and I went to tea one afternoon. I liked all the women very much indeed, but I had no idea how much more I was going to see of them in the future.

On November 10, 1919, the prince of Wales, later King Edward VIII,

arrived in this country and there was again the usual wreath-laying at
Mount Vernon, and we met the young prince at several formal dinners. I
marveled at the ease with which he conversed with older people. His usual
neighbors at dinner were the vice-president's wife, Mrs. Marshall, and Mrs.
Lansing, wife of the secretary of state. He did, however, manage to break
away and go to some dances with younger people when formal official affairs
were over.

Sir Edward Grey had come over that autumn to take up the work at the
British embassy for a short time. He was almost blind and was being treated
by Dr. Wilmer, our great eye doctor. Sir Edward had insisted that he could
not take over the responsibility of this office unless his old friend and colleague, Sir William Tyrrell, came with him, and so this delightful pair
spent a few months in this country. Because of Sir Edward Grey's affection
for Uncle Ted, the name of Roosevelt was a key to his affections and we
saw a great deal of him.

We invited Sir Edward and Sir William to have their Christmas dinner
with us and attend our Christmas tree, our only other guests being my
husband's mother and, as usual, Louis Howe and his family. They accepted,
much to our joy.

Alice Longworth, Mrs. Leavitt, my grandmother Roosevelt's old friend,
and Miss Spring, who was now with her most of the time, came over to
join our Christmas party.

Eleven

The 1920 Campaign
and Back to New York

IN JUNE, 1920, my husband went out to the San Francisco National Convention of the Democratic party and I took the children to Campobello, where I received a telegram from Secretary Daniels, saying that my husband had been nominated as candidate for vice-president to run with Mr. James M. Cox, who was the Democratic nominee for president. The message read:

IT WOULD HAVE DONE YOUR HEART GOOD TO HAVE SEEN THE SPONTANEOUS AND ENTHUSIASTIC TRIBUTE PAID WHEN FRANKLIN WAS NOMINATED UNANIMOUSLY FOR VICE-PRESIDENT TODAY STOP ACCEPT MY CONGRATULATIONS AND GREETINGS STOP WILL YOU BE GOOD ENOUGH TO SEND MY CONGRATULATIONS AND GREETINGS ALSO TO HIS MOTHER AS I DO NOT KNOW HER ADDRESS.

JOSEPHUS DANIELS

I was glad for my husband, but it never occurred to me to be much excited. I had come to accept the fact that public service was my husband's great interest and I always tried to make the necessary family adjustments easy. I carried on the children's lives and my own as calmly as could be, and while I was always a part of the public aspect of our lives, still I felt detached and objective, as though I were looking at someone else's life.

My husband stopped to see Mr. Cox on the way home. Both of them later visited President Woodrow Wilson, preparatory to laying plans for the issues that would be fought out in the campaign. It was decided that the League of Nations should be the main issue.

My husband sent me word that his notification would take place at

Hyde Park and to bring Anna and James back from Campobello for the occasion, and to arrange to go back to Washington for a few days and then start west to attend Mr. Cox's notification at Dayton, Ohio. I was to take Anna on this trip and send James back to Campobello with his grandmother.

This notification meeting was the first really mammoth meeting to be held at Hyde Park. The gathering was the predecessor of many others, but I sympathized with my mother-in-law when I saw her lawn being trampled by hordes of people. My admiration for her grew through the years as I realized how many political guests she had to entertain in her house, where for so many years only family and friends had been received. The friends were chosen with great discrimination and invitations were never lightly given by my husband's father and mother. Mrs. Roosevelt was quite remarkable about this plunge into the national political picture and made the necessary adjustments in her life in a remarkable way.

Mr. Henry Morgenthau, Jr., and the committee of Hyde Park and Poughkeepsie friends arranged the details of Franklin's homecoming and his notification. Anna and I went with Franklin to Washington for a few days of terrible heat. While there I made the arrangements for giving up the house and Franklin resigned as assistant secretary of the navy, and that period of our life in Washington was over.

Franklin returned with us to Campobello for a brief rest and then started a strenuous campaign. I stayed with the children, got James ready for school and took him to Groton in late September. He seemed to me very young and lonely when I left him, but it was a tradition in the family that boys must go to boarding school when they reached the age of twelve, and James would be thirteen the following December, so of course we had to send him. I never thought to rebel then, but now it seems ludicrous to have been bound by so many conventions. I unpacked his trunk, saw his cubicle was in order, met some of the masters, said good-by to Mr. and Mrs. Endicott Peabody, the heads of the school, and went back to Hyde Park.

I did not stay there, however, but started immediately on the last campaign trip with my husband, a four-week trip which took us as far as Colorado. I was the only woman on the car. Franklin had a private car attached to different trains and on it were his secretary, Mr. Camellier; a young man who did general secretarial work, James Sullivan; Louis Howe; Marvin McIntyre, who was in charge of the train, the working out of

Anna Hall Roosevelt, the author's mother, in 1886. *Franklin D. Roosevelt Library*

Eleanor Roosevelt with her brother Elliott in 1891, and (below) about a year later with her father, Elliott Roosevelt, and her brothers, Elliott and Hall. *Franklin D. Roosevelt Library*

Eleanor Roosevelt with her horse (far left) at her grandmother Hall's country home at Tivoli, New York. *UPI*

Franklin Roosevelt at Fairhaven, Massachusetts, en route to Groton, autumn, 1897. *Franklin D. Roosevelt Library*

The author in her wedding gown, March 17, 1905. *Franklin D. Roosevelt Library*

On their honeymoon Eleanor and Franklin Roosevelt visited friends in Strathpeffer, Scotland. *Franklin D. Roosevelt Library*

In a gondola in Venice, photographed by her husband. *Franklin D. Roosevelt Library*

The young Roosevelts (left) at Hyde Park in 1913, with Mr. and Mrs. Henry Parrish, *Culver Service;* (right), with Anna in 1907; and (below), the Roosevelt family at Campobello, N.B., in 1920. *Franklin D. Roosevelt Library*

As wife of the Assistant Secretary of the Navy, Eleanor Roosevelt accompanies her husband on an inspection tour, *UPI;* (below), the Democratic candidate for Governor with his family at Hyde Park in 1928: (l. to r., standing) Curtis Dall, James Roosevelt; (seated) Elliott, Mrs. Roosevelt, Anna, F.D.R., his mother; (in front) John and Franklin, Jr. *Wide World*

In the Monroe Room at the White House (right). Portrait above the mantel is of Theodore Roosevelt I, father of President Theodore Roosevelt. *Bradford Bachrach*

Reading the congratulatory telegram from Herbert Hoover, conceding his defeat in the 1932 presidential election. *N.Y. Daily News Photo*

Greeting the Easter egg rollers, with Buzzie, Sistie and Anna Roosevelt Dall, April, 1933. *UPI*

The First Lady at the inaugural ball, March, 1933, with (l. to r.) Mrs. Cary T. Grayson, Ray Stannard Baker, James Roosevelt, Rear Admiral Cary T. Grayson, retired, and Brigadier General William T. Horton, retired. *Wide World*

A descent into a coal mine in Ohio, 1935. *UPI*

An inspection trip to Puerto Rico in 1934. *N.Y. Daily News Photo*

On a bridle path in Rock Creek Park, Washington, in 1933. *UPI*

Mrs. Roosevelt with her grandchildren, Sistie and Buzzie Dall, on the White House lawn where she had slides, sandboxes and swings built for them. *UPI*

On the *Amberjack II* at Southeast Harbor, Maine; (l. to r.) the author, F.D.R., James; (directly behind) Franklin, Jr., and John; (extreme left) Nancy Cook. *UPI*

The President and Mrs. Roosevelt stop at Fremont, Nebraska, September, 1935, during a western tour, *Franklin D. Roosevelt Library;* and (below), F.D.R., his wife, and Franklin, Jr., on the porch of their Hyde Park home on election night, 1936. *UPI*

President and Mrs. Roosevelt with their thirteen grandchildren in the White House on the occasion of his fourth inauguration, January, 1945. (Front, l. to r.) Christopher Roosevelt, son of Franklin, Jr.; Anne Sturges Roosevelt, John's daughter; back of her, Haven Clark Roosevelt, John's son; John Roosevelt Boettiger, Anna's son; Elliott Roosevelt, Jr.; Kate and Sara Roosevelt, James's daughters. (Back, l. to r.) Buzz Boettiger, Anna's son; Sistie Boettiger, Anna's daughter; William Donner Roosevelt, Elliott's son; Chandler Roosevelt, Elliott's daughter; David Boynton Roosevelt, Elliott's son, and Franklin D. Roosevelt, III. *Franklin D. Roosevelt Library*

The coffin bearing the body of the President is carried into the White House. Mrs. Roosevelt is escorted by Vice Admiral Wilson Brown, the President's naval aide, on her right and White House usher Charles Claunch at her left. *Wide World*

With General Charles de Gaulle (right) in the rose garden at Hyde Park after he placed a wreath on the late President's grave in August, 1945. *Wide World*

Mrs. Roosevelt with President and Mrs. Truman at the commissioning of the aircraft carrier *Franklin D. Roosevelt,* October, 1945. *UPI*

With Queen Elizabeth in Washington, D.C., during the state visit of the royal couple in June, 1938. *UPI*

At a dinner given by the Netherland-American Foundation in January, 1944, with (l. to r.) Crown Prince Olaf of Norway, Princess Juliana of Holland, Crown Princess Marta of Norway and Thomas J. Watson. *Wide World*

Gathered at the White House for Christmas, 1938: (l. to r.) Mrs. James R. Roosevelt, the President's sister-in-law, Eleanor Roosevelt, Mrs. James Roosevelt, the President's mother, the President, James Roosevelt and his wife, Franklin, Jr., and Harry L. Hopkins, then Secretary of Commerce; in front, Sara Roosevelt, James's daughter, and Diana Hopkins. *Wide World*

Arriving in London during October, 1942, Mrs. Roosevelt is met by General Dwight D. Eisenhower, King George, Queen Elizabeth and Ambassador John Winant, *Wide World;* and (below), the First Lady visits the troops in the Southwest Pacific in the fall of 1943. *Franklin D. Roosevelt Library*

As a delegate to the United Nations: (upper left) at the General Assembly opening at Flushing Meadows, October, 1946, with Senator Tom Connally and Senator Arthur H. Vandenburg; (upper right) in Paris, September, 1948, with John Foster Dulles, Warren Austin, U.S. Ambassador to the UN, and General George C. Marshall, Secretary of State; (below) in New York, October, 1952, with (front, l. to r.) Sen. Alexander Wiley, Sen. Theodore Green, Ambassador Warren Austin, Secretary of State Dean Acheson, (rear, l. to r.) Mrs. Edith F. Sampson, Benjamin V. Cohen, Philip C. Jessup and Ernest Gross. *Wide World*

Mrs. Roosevelt leaving the London home of Sir Winsto Churchill after lunching wi him and Mrs. Churchill in April, 1948. *Wide World*

Talking with President Tit of Yugoslavia at his summe estate on the Island of Brior in July, 1953. *Wide World*

itineraries, and so on; Tom Lynch, our old friend from Poughkeepsie, who acted as disbursing officer, paying all bills, and so on; and Stanley Prenosil, who was the only newspaperman assigned continuously to covering the vice-presidential candidate.

I had never had any contact with newspaper people before. My grandmother had taught me that a woman's place was not in the public eye, and that idea had clung to me all through the Washington years. It never occurred to me to do more than answer through my secretary any questions that the reporters asked about social events. I gave as little information as possible, feeling that that was the only right attitude toward any newspaper people where a woman and her home were concerned.

But the years had taught me a certain adaptability to circumstances and I did receive an intensive education on this trip, and Louis Howe played a great part in this education from that time on. Ever since the Albany days he had been an intimate friend and coworker of my husband's. At times I resented this intimacy, and at this time I was very sure of my own judgment about people. I frequently tried to influence those about me, and there were occasions when I thought that Louis Howe's influence and mine, where my husband was concerned, had clashed; and I was, of course, sure that I was right.

Louis was entirely indifferent to his appearance; he not only neglected his clothes but gave the impression at times that cleanliness was not of particular interest to him. The fact that he had rather extraordinary eyes and a fine mind I was fool enough not to have discovered as yet, and it was by externals alone that I had judged him in our association prior to this trip.

In later years I learned that he had always liked me and thought I was worth educating, and for that reason he made an effort on this trip to get to know me. He did it cleverly. He knew that I was bewildered by some of the things expected of me as a candidate's wife. I never before had spent my days going on and off platforms, listening apparently with rapt attention to much the same speech, looking pleased at seeing people no matter how tired I was or greeting complete strangers with effusion.

Being a sensitive person, Louis knew that I was interested in the new sights and the new scenery, but that being the only woman was embarrassing. The newspaper fraternity was not so familiar to me at that time as it was to become in later years, and I was a little afraid of it. Largely because of Louis Howe's early interpretation of the standards and ethics of the newspaper business, I came to look with interest and confidence on the writing fraternity and gained a liking for it which I have never lost.

My husband was busy most of the day, when not actually out on the platform of the car, or at meetings in the various cities where we stopped. He had speeches to write, letters to answer, and policies to discuss. In the evenings, after they got back to the train, all the men sat together in the end of the car and discussed the experiences of the day from their various points of view and the campaign in general from the point of view of what news might be coming in from newspapers and dispatches.

Frequently for relaxation they started to play a card game, which went on until late. I was still a Puritan, thought they were an extremely bad example, and was at times much annoyed with my husband for not conserving his strength by going to bed. I did not realize how much he received through these contacts and how impossible it would have been, after the kind of days he was putting in, to go placidly to sleep.

Louis Howe began to break down my antagonism by knocking at my stateroom door and asking if he might discuss a speech with me. I was flattered and before long I found myself discussing a wide range of subjects.

Stephen Early had been borrowed from the Associated Press and acted in a personal capacity as advance man for this trip and went ahead of us for publicity purposes. He only now and then joined us on the train but was always in close touch. All these men were to become good friends of mine in the future.

That trip had many amusing incidents, and as the newspapermen and I became more friendly, they helped me to see the humorous side. They would stand at the back of the hall when Franklin was making the same speech for the umpty-umpth time and make faces at me, trying to break up the apparent interest with which I was listening. When I followed my husband down the aisle and the ladies crowded around him and exclaimed over his looks and charm, they would get behind me and ask if I wasn't jealous.

On this trip I saw a great deal of our country that I had never seen before; though I had not begun to look at the countryside or the people with the same keenness which the knowledge of many social problems brought me in the future, still I was thrilled by new scenery, and the size of my own country, with its potential power, was gradually dawning upon me.

We ended this trip very weary, for four weeks is a long time to be on the road, but when we reached Buffalo, New York, I who had never seen Niagara Falls insisted on seeing them. Though my husband went to Jamestown, New York, for political meetings, I took the day off and Louis Howe went with me to Niagara Falls.

One of the standing jokes of that campaign was a reference to the day in Jamestown and certain photographs which were taken of lovely ladies who served luncheon for my husband and who worshiped at his shrine. He had to stand much teasing from the rest of the party about this particular day.

It was impossible, of course, to make any arrangements for the children. Our house in New York was rented for another year to Mr. and Mrs. Thomas W. Lamont, and so we decided it would be better for Anna and Elliott to spend the winter at Hyde Park. I went to Vassar College to find a tutor to take over their schooling. A charming girl, Jean Sherwood, was recommended and we all liked her so much that she came to us that autumn and spent the entire winter with the two children at Hyde Park.

It still remained a question what would happen to the rest of us in case of either election or defeat, but most of us were fairly sure that defeat was in store. Even then I was beginning to wonder what was the point of these long campaign trips, where the majority of people who came to hear you were adherents of your own party. Only now and then would a heckler appear in the audience, and he was usually the type who could never be changed from the opposition point of view.

I still think campaign trips by anyone except the presidential candidates themselves are of little value. In 1920, however, the kind of campaign my husband made was considered reasonable.

Come what might, we had to live somewhere and my husband would probably go to work somewhere. He had already made arrangements to resume the practice of law. The old firm of Marvin, Booker and Roosevelt had ended with the war and he decided to form a partnership with Grenville Emmet and Langdon Marvin, under the firm name of Emmet, Marvin and Roosevelt.

The election was an overwhelming defeat, accepted philosophically by my husband, who had been prepared for the result. In this campaign I had taken no active part in the work at headquarters, but I had been in once or twice and had met my husband's office manager, Charles McCarthy. He had a young secretary during the campaign, Miss Marguerite

LeHand. It was through this association that she first came to my husband as a secretary and she remained with him as his private secretary until her last illness.

I did not look forward to a winter of four days a week in New York with nothing but teas and luncheons and dinners to take up my time. The war had made that seem an impossible mode of living, so I mapped out a schedule for myself. I decided that I would learn to cook and I found an ex-cook, now married, who had an apartment of her own, and I went twice a week and cooked an entire meal which I left with her for her family to criticize. I also attended a business school, and took a course in type-writing and shorthand every day while I was in New York.

Before I had been in New York many days I was visited by Mrs. Frank Vanderlip, who was at that time chairman of the League of Women Voters for New York State. She asked if I would join the board and be responsible for reports on national legislation. I explained that I had had little or no contact with national legislation in Washington, that I had listened a great deal to the talk that went on around me, and that I would be interested but doubted my ability to do this work. Mrs. Vanderlip said she was sure I had absorbed more than most of the New York members of the board knew and that I would have the assistance of an able woman lawyer, Miss Elizabeth Read. She would take the Congressional Record, go through it and mark the bills that she thought were of interest to the league, send for them and even assist me to understand them if I required any assistance.

With this assurance, I finally agreed that I would attempt to do the work. I decided that I would go to Miss Read's office one morning a week and devote that time to the study of legislation and bring home the bills that needed further study before I wrote my monthly reports.

I felt humble and inadequate when I first presented myself to Elizabeth Read, but I liked her at once and she gave me a sense of confidence. It was the beginning of a friendship with her and with her friend, Miss Esther Lape, which was to be lasting and warm. Esther had a brilliant mind and a driving force, a kind of nervous power. Elizabeth seemed calmer, more practical and domestic, but I came to see that hers was a keen and analytical mind and in its way as brilliant as Esther's.

My husband was working hard; he went occasionally to men's dinners, and I remember many pleasant evenings spent with Elizabeth and Esther in their little apartment. Their standards of work and their interests played a great part in what might be called the "intensive education of Eleanor Roosevelt" during the next few years.

My mother-in-law was distressed because I was not always available, as I had been when I lived in New York before. I had long since ceased to be dependent on my mother-in-law, and the fact that my cousin Mrs. Parish suffered from a long illness, lasting several years, had made me less dependent on her. I wrote fewer letters and asked fewer questions and gave fewer confidences, for I had begun to realize that in my development I was drifting far afield from the old influences.

I do not mean that I was the better for this, but I was thinking things out for myself and becoming an individual. Had I never done this, perhaps I might have been saved some difficult experiences, but I have never regretted even my mistakes. They all added to my understanding of other human beings, and I came out in the end a more tolerant, understanding and charitable person. It has made life and the study of people more interesting than it could have been if I had remained in the conventional pattern.

I was back on one or two boards for charities, such as the Bryson Day Nursery, but I had developed an aversion to serving on boards and having no personal contact with actual work. I tried to seize whatever opportunities for actual contact with people the nursery presented, but it was not very satisfactory.

Twelve

Trial by Fire

THE SUMMER of 1921 found us all going to Campobello again and various visitors coming up for short or long periods. There was a certain amount of infantile paralysis in some places again that summer, but it was not an epidemic, particularly among children, as it had been a few years before.

My husband did not go up with us, but came early in August, after we were settled, bringing quite a party with him. He did a great deal of navigating on Mr. Van Lear Black's boat, which he had joined on his way up the coast.

While Mr. Black and his party were with us, we were busy and spent days on the water, fishing and doing all we could to give them a pleasant time. My husband loved these waters and always wanted everybody who came up to appreciate the fact that they were ideal for sailing and fishing. The fishing is deep-sea fishing and rather uninteresting unless you go outside and into the Bay of Fundy or have the luck to do some casting into schools of fish as they came in.

Mr. Black had left and we were out sailing one afternoon in the little *Vireo* which my husband had bought after giving up the *Half Moon*, in order that the boys might learn to sail. On our return trip we spied a forest fire, and of course we had to make for shore at once and go fight the fire. We reached home around four o'clock and my husband, who had been complaining of feeling logy and tired for several days, decided it would do him good to go in for a dip in the land-locked lake called Lake Glen Severn, inside the beach on the other side of the island. The children were delighted and they started away. After their swim Franklin took a dip in the Bay of Fundy and ran home.

When they came in, a good deal of mail had arrived and my husband sat around in his bathing suit, which was completely dry, and looked at his mail. In a little while he began to complain that he felt a chill and decided he would not eat supper with us but would go to bed and get thoroughly warm. He wanted to avoid catching cold.

In retrospect I realize he had had no real rest since the war. A hunting trip after the campaign had been strenuous, and plunging back into business had not given him any opportunity to relax and he had been going on his nerves.

We had Mrs. Louis Howe and her small boy, Hartley, staying in the house with us. Mr. Howe arrived a little later. He had stayed in the Navy Department after my husband left, to look after his papers and be of any assistance he could to the incoming assistant secretary, who happened to be Colonel Theodore Roosevelt. When Louis finally left the Navy Department he was considering an offer to go into business on a rather lucrative salary, and decided to take his holiday at Campobello before he made up his mind.

The next day my husband felt less well. He had quite a temperature and I sent for our faithful friend, Dr. Bennett, in Lubec. Dr. Bennett thought my husband had just an ordinary cold and I decided that the best thing to do was to get everybody else off on a camping trip, though I was sufficiently worried not to consider going myself.

The trip lasted three days, and by the time the campers were back it was evident that my husband's legs were getting badly paralyzed. Dr. Bennett wanted a consultation and we found that Dr. Keen was in Bar Harbor, Maine. By now Mr. Howe had arrived and he went with Captain Calder to meet Dr. Keen. Dr. Keen decided that it was some form of paralysis but could not explain it. By this time my husband's lower legs were paralyzed.

For a little while he showed no improvement. The days dragged on and the doctors kept saying he must have a nurse, but it was hard to get one, so I kept on taking care of him and slept on a couch in his room at night. His temperature at times was very high. It required a certain amount of skilled nursing and I was thankful for every bit of training Miss Spring had given me.

Finally my husband's uncle, Frederic Delano, begged us to have the well-known infantile paralysis doctor, Dr. Lovett, come up from Newport. He examined my husband carefully and after consultation told me it was infantile paralysis.

I was in a panic because, besides my own children, we had Mr. Howe's little boy with us. I asked Dr. Lovett what the chances were that some of the children would come down with it. He said that probably none of them would do so since they had not already become ill.

After Dr. Lovett's visit, we finally got a nurse from New York, called Miss Rockey, but Dr. Lovett had been so flattering as to certain aspects of my husband's care, not knowing that I had been the only nurse on the case, that it was decided I should continue to do a certain amount of the nursing. This I did until we were finally able to move him back to New York.

My mother-in-law returned from abroad and came up to see my husband and then returned to New York to get things ready for us. When it was considered safe, we obtained a private car in which to move my husband. Dr. Bennett agreed to go down with us, and it was arranged that the car was to be switched around in Boston so we would be able to go straight into New York without any change. This move required a great deal of planning.

Mr. Howe had made up his mind to give up all idea of taking the position that was open to him and to come back to his old boss, because he saw quite plainly that his help was going to be needed. From that time on he put his whole heart into working for my husband's future. The handling of his mail and the newspapers all fell entirely into Louis's hands.

At first we tried to keep all news out of the papers, not wanting to say anything until we knew something definite about the future. Of course we were anxious to make the trip home as inconspicuous and unsensational as possible. We put Franklin on an improvised stretcher and took him down from the house over the rough ground and stony beach and put him into the small motorboat, chugged two miles across the bay, carried him up the steep gangway, and placed him on one of the drays used for luggage in that northern part of the country. Every jolt was painful, as we walked to the station and the stretcher went into his compartment through the window.

The strain of this trip must have been great for my husband. First of all, a sense of helplessness when you have always been able to look after yourself makes you conscious every minute of the ease with which someone may slip and you may be dropped overboard, in transferring from the dock to the boat. In addition, he had not wanted crowds to witness his departure, and of course there was not only kindly interest in Eastport but there was a certain amount of interest inspired by newspapers in other parts of the country that were trying to find out just what was the matter.

We finally reached New York, and here again my husband was taken out of the car through the window and then by ambulance to the Presbyterian Hospital.

There followed days and weeks at the hospital. Dr. Lovett came occasionally, but his young associate, Dr. George Draper, was in charge most of the time.

The children were all back at school and stopped in to see him every day, with the exception of James, who was in Groton. The time seemed endless but he actually came home before Christmas.

Franklin's mother was really remarkable about this entire illness. It must have been a terrific strain for her, and I am sure that, our of sight, she wept many hours, but with all of us she was very cheerful. She had, however, made up her mind that Franklin was going to be an invalid for the rest of his life and that he would retire to Hyde Park and live there. Her anxiety over his general health was so great that she dreaded his making any effort whatever.

Though Franklin was in bed most of the time, Miss Rockey took charge of him except in the afternoons. Then I had to be at home. He was tall and heavy to lift, but somehow both of us managed to learn to do whatever was necessary. For several weeks that winter his legs were placed in plaster casts in order to stretch the muscles, and every day a little of the cast was chipped out at the back, which stretched the muscles a little bit more. This was torture and he bore it without the slightest complaint, just as he bore his illness from the very beginning. I never but once heard him say anything bordering on discouragement or bitterness. That was some years later, when he was debating whether to do something which would cost considerable money, and he remarked that he supposed it was better to spend the money on the chance that he might not be such a helpless individual.

In many ways this was the most trying winter of my entire life. It was the small personal irritations, as I look back upon them now, that made life so difficult. My mother-in-law thought we were tiring my husband and that he should be kept completely quiet, which made the discussions about his care somewhat acrimonious on occasion. She always thought that she understood what was best, particularly where her child was concerned, regardless of what any doctor might say. I felt that if you placed a patient in a doctor's care you must at least follow out his suggestions and treatment. The house was not overlarge and we were very crowded.

My husband's bedroom was at the back of the house on the third floor, because it was quieter there. I had given my daughter, who was fifteen that winter, the choice of a large room at the front of the third floor, which she would be obliged to share with the nurse during the afternoon and early evening, or a small room on the fourth floor rear, next to Elliott's room. This she would have entirely to herself. She chose the latter.

Mr. Howe took the big room on the third floor, as he had come to live with us during the week, because his wife could find no apartment in New York which was suitable both to their needs and their purse. During the weekends he journeyed to Poughkeepsie, where his wife and little boy were installed in a house and his daughter was at Vassar College. He was downtown most of the day at my husband's office, so the nurse could use his room undisturbed.

We had a connecting door into a room in my mother-in-law's house on the fourth floor, so the two little boys and their nurse had those rooms. This accounted for all the bedrooms and left me with no room. I slept on a bed in one of the little boys' rooms. I dressed in my husband's bathroom. In the daytime I was too busy to need a room.

The boys soon became entirely oblivious of the fact that their father had ever been ill. By spring he would sit on the floor with the little boys in the library, and they would play with him without the slightest idea that he was not able to do anything he wished to do in the way of roughhousing with them.

Anna, however, felt the strain of the overcrowded house and the atmosphere of anxiety. I had put her in Miss Chapin's School. I canvassed several schools and decided that Miss Chapin had the kind of personality which would appeal to me. I hoped the same relationship would grow up between Anna and Miss Chapin as I had had with Mlle. Souvestre. I did not realize how set and rigid New York schools were and that a girl coming in from outside would be looked upon by all the children as an outsider and would hardly be noticed by the teachers. Anna was very unhappy, though I did not realize it. She felt lost, and the different methods of teaching bewildered her. She tried to hide her feelings by being rather devil-may-care about her marks and her association with the other girls.

Someone had suggested to her that it was unfair that she should have a little fourth-floor room and Mr. Howe should have the large room on the third-floor front. Because of constant outside influences, the situation grew in her mind to a point where she felt that I did not care for her and was not giving her any consideration. It never occurred to her that I had far less than she had. There were times at the dinner table when she would annoy her father so much that he would be severe with her and a scene would ensue, then she would burst into tears and go sobbing to her room.

I knew nothing, of course, of what had been said to her and went on rather blindly thinking that girls of fifteen were far more difficult to bring up than boys.

I realize now that my attitude toward her had been wrong. She was an adolescent girl and I still treated her like a child and thought of her as a child. It never occurred to me to take her into my confidence and consult with her about our difficulties or tell her just what her father was going through in getting his nerves back into condition.

I have always had a bad tendency to shut up like a clam, particularly when things are going badly; and that attitude was accentuated, I think, as regards my children. I had done so much for them and planned everything and managed everything, as far as the household was concerned, for so many years that it never occurred to me that the time comes, particularly with a girl, when it is important to make her your confidante. If I had realized this I might have saved Anna and myself several years of real unhappiness. I would have understood her a great deal better because she would have been able to talk to me freely, and she would have understood me and probably understood her father and all he was fighting against.

As it was, I am responsible for having given her a most unhappy time, and we can both be extremely grateful for the fact that finally the entire situation got on my nerves and one afternoon in the spring, when I was trying to read to the two youngest boys, I suddenly found myself sobbing as I read. I could not think why I was sobbing, nor could I stop. Elliott came in from school, dashed in to look at me and fled. Mr. Howe came in and tried to find out what the matter was, but he gave it up as a bad job. The two little boys went off to bed and I sat on the sofa in the sitting room and sobbed and sobbed. I could not go to dinner in this condition. Finally I found an empty room in my mother-in-law's house, as she had moved to the country. I locked the door and poured cold water on a towel and mopped my face. Eventually I pulled myself together, for it requires an audience, as a rule, to keep on these emotional jags. This is the one and only time I remember in my entire life having gone to pieces in this particular manner. From that time on I seemed to have got rid of nerves and uncontrollable tears, for never again has either of them bothered me.

The effect, however, was rather good on Anna, because she began to straighten out, and at last she poured out some of her troubles and told me she had been wrong and she knew that I loved her and from that day to this our mutual understanding has constantly improved.

Today no one could ask for a better friend than I have in Anna or she has in me. Perhaps because it grew slowly, the bond between us is all the stronger. No one can tell either of us anything about the other; and though we may not always think alike or act alike, we always respect each other's motives, and there is a type of sympathetic understanding between us which would make a real misunderstanding quite impossible.

Dr. Draper felt strongly that it was better for Franklin to make the effort to take an active part in life again and lead, as far as possible, a normal life, with the interests that had always been his. Even if it tired him, it was better for his general condition.

The previous January Franklin had accepted an offer made by Mr. Van Lear Black to become vice-president of the Fidelity and Deposit Company of Baltimore, in charge of the New York office, and he had worked there until his illness. Mr. Black was a warm friend and kept his place for him until he was well enough to resume his work.

Mr. Howe felt that the one way to get my husband's interest aroused was to keep him as much as possible in contact with politics. This seemed to me an almost hopeless task. However, in order to accomplish his ends Mr. Howe began to urge me to do some political work again. I could think of nothing I could do but during the spring I was thrown on two or three occasions with a young woman who interested me considerably. Her name was Marion Dickerman. She was interested in working conditions for women and she taught in a school. I, too, was interested in working conditions for women, harking back to the interests of my girlhood. Mrs. James Lees Laidlaw asked me to attend a luncheon of the Women's Trade Union League and become an associate member. I joined the organization and have been a member ever since. This luncheon was my second contact with some of the women whom I had first met in Washington at the International Conference for Working Women and this resulted in a long association. I have never lost touch with this group. Many of them were interested in politics, and I soon found that Marion Dickerman also was interested.

Through my acquaintance with Miss Dickerman I met her friend Nancy Cook. Miss Cook invited me to preside at a luncheon to raise funds for the women's division of the Democratic State Committee. I had been carrying on to a limited extent my work for the League of Women Voters, but I had never done anything for a political organization before nor had I ever made a speech in any sizable gathering. Here I found myself presiding at a luncheon, without the faintest idea of what I was going to say or what work the organization was really doing. That was the beginning of a warm and lasting friendship with both Miss Dickerman and Miss Cook, and through them I met Miss Harriet May Mills and Mrs. Caroline O'Day and went to work with the Democratic women of New York State.

We moved to Hyde Park, bag and baggage, and spent the whole summer there except for a short time when I took the younger children to Fairhaven for a change of air and some sea bathing. I did not even stay with them all the time, but there I became conscious of the fact that I had two young boys who had to learn to do the things that boys must do— swim and ride and camp. I had never done any of these things. I had ridden when I was a child, and up to the age of twenty, but that was far behind me. I had no confidence in my ability to do physical things at this time. I could go into the water with the boys but I could not swim. It began to dawn upon me that if these two youngest boys were going to have a normal existence without a father to do these things with them, I would have to become a good deal more companionable and more of an all-round person than I had ever been before.

All that summer at Hyde Park my husband struggled to do a great number of things which would make it possible for him to be more active. He learned to use crutches and walked every day to gain confidence. Each new thing he did took not only determination but great physical effort.

That autumn of 1922 I took Elliott to Groton School. I drove him up myself, unpacked for him and left a much more miserable little boy than even James had been. I felt that he would settle down as James had done. He was far better prepared in his work, for he had had one year at the Buckley School, where he had done very well. He passed his examinations without any conditions. My hopes were vain, however; he never really loved the school as James did.

When we went back to New York, and when my husband was there, he followed an ordinary businessman's routine. He now had a chauffeur to take him back and forth between his office and our house every day.

Through my interest in the League of Women Voters, the Women's Trade Union League and the Democratic State Committee, where now I had become finance chairman, I was beginning to find the political contacts that Louis wanted. I drove a car on election day and brought people to the polls. I began to learn a good deal about party politics in a small place. It was rather sordid in spots. I worked with our county committee and our associate county chairwoman. I saw how people took money or its equivalent on election day for their votes and how much of the party machinery was geared to crooked business. On the other hand, I saw hard work and unselfish public service and fine people in unexpected places. I learned again that human beings are seldom all good or all bad and that few human beings are incapable of rising to the heights now and then.

We were rid of a trained nurse and we never treated my husband as an invalid. Anna had graduated to the large room and we were much less crowded with James and Elliott at school. In the holidays we usually went to Hyde Park. The whole family relationship was simpler. Anna continued to tell me about things which upset her, and her trials and tribulations away from home, and I was able more intelligently to manage the various elements of our existence.

The boys at school had on the average one accident each autumn during the football season which would necessitate my bringing them home or taking them to a hospital for a short time. We had, of course, a certain amount of illness among the children at home, but my husband's general health was good and I had not been ill since John was born. There was really no time for me to think of being ill.

In winter my husband had to go south, so for two winters we had a houseboat and cruised around the Florida waters. I went down and spent short periods with him; this was my first glimpse of the South in winter. I had never considered holidays in winter or escape from cold weather an essential part of living, and I looked upon it now as a necessity and not a pleasure. I tried fishing but had no skill and no luck. When we anchored at night and the wind blew, it all seemed eerie and menacing to me. The beauty of the moon and the stars only added to the strangeness of the dark waters and the tropic vegetation, and on occasion it could be colder and more uncomfortable than tales of the sunny South led me to believe was possible. Key West was the one place I remember as having real charm.

In New York I had begun to do a fairly regular job for the women's division of the Democratic State Committee and was finding work very satisfactory and acquiring pride in doing a semiprofessional job. We started a small mimeographed paper with which Mr. Howe gave me considerable help. We finally had it printed, and in an effort to make it pay for itself I learned a great deal about advertising, circulation, and make-up. From Mr. Howe I learned how to make a dummy for the printer, and though he never considered I was really capable of writing the headlines, I became quite proficient in planning, pasting, and so on.

Miss Cook and Miss Dickerman and I had become friends in just the way that Miss Lape and Miss Read and I had been first drawn together through the work we were doing. This is one of the most satisfactory ways of making and keeping friends.

Many of my old friends I saw very little, because they led more or less social lives. I had dropped out of what is known as society entirely, as we never went out. Now and then I would go to the theater with a friend, but my free hours were few. Ever since the war my interest had been in doing real work, not in being a dilettante. I gradually found myself more and more interested in workers, less and less interested in my old associates, who were busy doing a variety of things but were doing no job in a professional way.

Slowly a friendship grew with a young couple who lived in Dutchess County, New York, not far from us—Mr. and Mrs. Henry Morgenthau, Jr. They were younger and perhaps for that reason we did not at first see so much of one another. We had many interests in common in the county, and Mr. Morgenthau and my husband were thrown more and more together. Mrs. Morgenthau came eventually to work in the women's division of the Democratic State Committee, and she and I grew gradually to have a warm affection for each other. Good things are all the better for ripening slowly, but today this friendship with Elinor and Henry Morgenthau is one of the things I prize most highly.

During these years I also came to know Mrs. Carrie Chapman Catt, Mrs. Raymond Brown, Mrs. Louis Slade, Mrs. Henry Goddard Leach, Lillian Wald, Mary Simkovitch and many other women who had a great influence on me. To all of them I shall be deeply grateful always for opening up so many new avenues of thought and work.

I was beginning to make occasional speeches and on various occasions Louis Howe went with me and sat at the back of the audience and gave me pointers on what I should say and how I should say it. I had a bad habit, because I was nervous, of laughing when there was nothing to laugh at. He broke me of that by showing me how inane it sounded. His advice was: "Have something you want to say, say it, and sit down."

Under Mrs. O'Day, who was vice-chairman of the Democratic State Committee, I did a certain amount of organization work each summer among the Democratic women of the state. I usually went with either Miss Dickerman or Miss Cook. I paid my own traveling expenses and so did Mrs. O'Day; because money-raising was hard for women we felt every expense must be kept down. Miss Cook did wonders of economical management. All the work among the women had been started by Miss Harriet May Mills, who for many years was the outstanding Democratic woman leader of New York State. Even after her retirement as vice-chairman of the state committee, she responded to every call for assistance. I was always glad of this experience because I came to know my state, the people who lived in it, and rural and urban conditions extremely well.

Since his illness my husband had undertaken the presidency of the Boy Scout Foundation, the presidency of the American Construction Council, the chairmanship of the American Legion campaign, and a number of other nonpolitical activities. His only political effort during those years was in the summer of 1922 when he helped to persuade Al Smith to run again for the governorship.

He was entirely well and lived a normal life, restricted only by his inability to walk. On the whole, his general physical condition improved year by year, until he was stronger in some ways than before his illness. He always went away in the winter for a time and in summer for a long vacation, trying in each case either to take treatment or at least to keep up exercises which would improve his ability to get about. In the spring of 1924, before the National Democratic Convention met in New York, Al Smith, who was a candidate for the presidential nomination, asked him to manage his preconvention campaign. This was the first time that my husband was to be in the public eye since his illness. A thousand and one little arrangements had to be made and Louis carefully planned each step of the way.

I had been asked to take charge of the committee to present to the resolutions committee of the convention some of the planks of interest to women. This was to be a new step in my education. I knew a little now about local politics, a good deal through the League of Women Voters and, through my Democratic organization work, about my state legislature and state politics, and I was to see for the first time where women stood when it came to a national convention. They stood outside the door of all important meetings and waited. I did get my resolutions in, but how much consideration they got was veiled in mystery.

I heard rumors of all kinds of maneuvers and all the different things that the men were talking about drifted my way, but most of the time at the convention I sat and knitted, suffered with the heat, and wished it would end.

At this convention I caught my first glimpse of Will Rogers when he wandered by the box one day and asked, "Knitting in the names of the future victims of the guillotine?" I felt like saying that I was almost ready to call any punishment down on the heads of those who could not bring the convention to a close.

Finally, in spite of all that could be done, in spite of a really fine nominating speech by my husband and the persuasion and influence of many other people in the convention, Al Smith lost the nomination. My husband stepped gracefully out of the political picture, though he did make one or two speeches for John W. Davis.

And so ended the early phases of the education of Eleanor Roosevelt, both in life and in politics.

PART II

This I Remember

Thirteen

The Private Lives
of Public Servants

AS I BEGIN this book it seems to me an infinitely more difficult task than the previous volume. In the first place, it can no longer be only my autobiography. Most people will be interested primarily in what I may have to tell about my husband.

Perhaps I shall be able to give some impressions which may help in the understanding of the stream of history during those complicated years. What I have to say, if it is to contribute anything to the understanding of his life and character and objectives, must be about him as an individual.

I do not claim that I can be entirely objective about him, but there are some things I know that I feel sure nobody else can know. Although no human being ever completely knows another, one cannot live for many years with a person without learning something about him. Other people may know certain sides of Franklin's character or particular facets of his personality better than I; but if I can contribute what I learned and what I believe to be true I may help to fill in the true picture for future historians.

The books that have already been written about Franklin show quite plainly that everyone writes from his own point of view, and that a man like my husband, who was particularly susceptible to people, took color from whomever he was with, giving to each one something different of himself. Because he disliked being disagreeable, he made an effort to give each person who came in contact with him the feeling that he understood what his particular interest was.

Often people have told me that they were misled by Franklin. Even when they have not said it in so many words, I have sometimes felt that he left them, after an interview, with the idea that he was in entire agreement with them. I would know that he was not, but they would be surprised when, later, his actions were in complete contradiction to what they thought they would be.

This misunderstanding arose not only from his dislike of being disagreeable but from the interest that he always had in somebody else's point of view and his willingness to listen to it. If he thought it was well expressed and clear, he nodded his head and frequently said, "I see," or something of the sort. This did not mean that he was convinced of the truth of the argument, or even that he entirely understood it, but only that he appreciated the way in which it was presented.

There is another fact which few people realize: the President of the United States gets more all-round information than most of the people who come to see him, though any one of them may know his own subject better than the President does. The President, however, must have a general outlook which takes in over-all considerations; whereas other people think primarily about their own ideas, plans and responsibilities for the specific thing they hope to accomplish. This circumstance puts on a President the responsibility of gathering all possible points of view, of often hearing conflicting ideas on a given subject, and then of making a final decision. It is one of the most difficult things a President has to do.

In addition, the fact that he can never have a personal loyalty greater than that to the nation sometimes makes it seem as though he were disloyal to his friends; but a man holding the office of President of the United States must think first of what he considers the greatest good of the people and the country.

I know Franklin always gave thought to what people said, but I have never known anyone less influenced by others. Though he asked for advice from a great many people, he simply wanted points of view which might help him to form his final decision, and which he sifted through his own knowledge and feelings. But once he reached a decision, people flattered themselves if they thought they ever changed it.

Franklin often used me to get the reflection of other people's thinking because he knew I made it a point to see and talk with a variety of people. I did not need to go on lecture trips or to inspect projects in different parts of the country, but my husband knew that I would not be satisfied to be merely an official hostess. He often suggested that I interest myself in certain things, such as the homestead projects. For my sake he was glad when he found that for a few weeks in spring and fall I could and did go on paid lecture trips. I would not plan such trips unless I had definite commitments and had signed formal contracts; but when they were an obligation, I arranged my time so they were possible. The trips took me to many places throughout the country to which otherwise I might never have gone.

Naturally, these lecture trips gave me more money for things I wanted to do than my husband could afford to give me. At the same time I felt that Franklin used whatever I brought back to him in the way of observations and information as a check against the many official reports he received.

Often, when some matter was being fought out with his advisers, he would bring up the question at dinner and bait me into giving an opinion by stating as his own a point of view with which he knew I would disagree. He would give me all the arguments that had been advanced to him and I would try vociferously and with heat to refute him.

I remember one occasion when I became extremely vehement and irritated. My husband smiled indulgently and repeated all the things that everyone else had said to him. The next day he asked my secretary, Miss Thompson, if I could have tea in the West Hall in the White House for him and Robert Bingham, who was then our ambassador to London and about to return to his post. I dutifully served them with tea, fully expecting to sit and listen in silence to a discussion of questions with which I would not be in agreement. Instead, to my complete surprise, I heard Franklin telling Ambassador Bingham to act not according to the arguments that he had given me but according to the arguments that I had given him! Without giving me a glance or the satisfaction of batting an eyelash in my direction, he calmly stated as his own the policies and beliefs he had argued against the night before! To this day I have no idea whether he had simply used me as a sounding board, as he so often did, with the idea of getting the reaction of the person on the outside or whether my arguments had been needed to fortify his decision and to clarify his own mind.

After Franklin became president, many people told me they disagreed with him and that they were going in prepared to tell him so in no uncertain terms. They went in for their interview, but if I saw them as they came out, they usually behaved as though they had never disagreed at all. Only now and then was someone honest enough to say he had not been able to put forward his own point of view—a difficulty due partly to the effect of Franklin's personality and partly to the person's awe of the office itself.

Franklin had the gift of being able to draw out the people whom he wished to draw out and to silence those with whom he was bored, and in both cases the people were greatly charmed. When he did not want to hear what somebody had to say he had a way of telling stories and talking about something quite different. Everyone who worked with him had to learn how to handle this technique of his if they were not to find that the questions they wanted to ask or the opinions they wanted to state never got into words because Franklin talked so steadily and so interestingly that they forgot what they had come to say.

Of all his intimates only a few, I think, ever really understood how it was that people sometimes thought he was in agreement with them when he was not or had given his consent when really he had never contemplated giving it. Louis Howe always understood this trait in Franklin, and Frank Walker, Edward J. Flynn, Henry Morgenthau, Jr., and Bernard Baruch came to know it well. With none of these men was his own interest ever paramount. The interest of each was in my husband and in the work to be done and they could be objective even when their own work was involved.

I was often supposed to be a great influence on my husband politically. Over and over again people wrote, crediting me with being responsible for his action and even for some of his appointments. Frances Perkins' appointment to the Cabinet is a case in point. As a matter of fact, I never even suggested her. She had worked with Franklin in New York State and was his own choice, though I was delighted when he named her and glad that he felt a woman should be recognized.

There were times when a list of names suggested for appointment, to serve as individuals or groups, would come out and there would be no woman's name on the list. Then I might go to my husband to say that I was weary of reminding him to remind the members of his Cabinet and his advisers that women were in existence, that they were a factor in the life of the nation and increasingly important politically. He always smiled and said: "Of course. I thought a woman's name had been put on the list. Have someone call up and say I feel a woman should be recognized." As a result, I was sometimes asked for suggestions and would mention two or three names. Sometimes they were considered and sometimes they were not.

The political influence that was attributed to me was nil, where my husband was concerned. If I felt strongly about anything I told him, since he had the power to do things and I did not, but he did not always feel as I did.

I have since discovered that a great many government people to whom I referred letters regarded them as a mandate requiring prompt attention. Evidently they thought that if what I suggested was not done I would complain to my husband. Actually, all I ever expected was that they would be interested in accomplishing the things that should be accomplished, since government is supposed to serve the good of the people. I thought that every government official investigated complaints and gladly tried to correct injustices. I realize now that this was a rather naïve idea, for it is apparent from what people told me that it was often only fear of White House displeasure that set the wheels in motion. This was not true of many departments, but I suppose it is only natural that some of the older departments, where a number of civil service people feel entrenched, should not want to bother with new activities. Both Mr. Woodin and Mr. Morgenthau must have made great changes in the old Treasury Department management. The standards set, particularly after Mr. Morgenthau became secretary of the treasury, must have seemed alarming to some of the old type of civil service officials.

I felt critical of civil service officials at times. When they have been in a department for a long while they can make any change very difficult. Nevertheless, there are an astonishing number of people who want to serve their country and are willing to accept the modest security and low pay of a civil service employee simply because they feel that they are performing a patriotic service.

Consciously, I never tried to exert any political influence on my husband or on anyone else in the government. However, one cannot live in a political atmosphere and study the actions of a good politician, which my husband was, without absorbing some rudimentary facts about politics. From him I learned that a good politician is marked to a great extent by his sense of timing. He says the right thing at the right moment. Though the immediate reaction may be unfavorable, in the long run it turns out that what he said needed to be said at the time he said it.

I do not mean that Franklin never made mistakes; most of the time, however, his judgment was good. He could watch with enormous patience as a situation developed and wait for exactly the right moment to act or speak. The quarantine speech, for instance, was delivered at a time when it was necessary that people be made to think. The meeting with Winston Churchill at Argentia and the announcement of the Atlantic Charter came at a crucial point in the country's life; in the same way, the D-day prayer lifted the morale of the people at a moment when that kind of inspiration was needed.

Franklin was a practical politician. He could always be told why certain actions or appointments were politically advisable. Sometimes he acted on this advice; on the other hand, he did many things and made many appointments against the advice of the party politicians, simply because he believed they would have a good effect on the nation as a whole. And he was almost always right. However, as a practical politician, he knew and accepted the fact that he had to work with the people who were a part of the Democratic party organization. I often heard him discuss the necessity and role of local political organizations, but he recognized that certain of them were a detriment to the party as a whole. He never got over his feeling against Tammany Hall or any boss-ridden organization, though he acknowledged that some were well administered and valuable.

Though Franklin always said I was far too impatient ever to be a good politician, and though my sense of timing is nowhere near so trustworthy as his was, I have grown more patient with age and have learned from my husband that no leader can be too far ahead of his followers. Also I think my observations of conditions and of the feelings of the average people within our country are fairly trustworthy.

During the years of my husband's governorship and presidency, but particularly after we were in the White House, I had many occasions to think seriously about the problem that faces the family of a man in American public life, especially a man who becomes the subject of great controversy— hated wholeheartedly by some and loved equally wholeheartedly by others. Of necessity, the attitude toward him must carry through to the members of his family and have some effect on them all.

For the young the situation is extremely difficult. Special privileges are offered them on every side. If they do not accept, they are considered ungracious and unappreciative. If they do accept, they are accused of being selfish, arrogant and greedy and of thinking themselves important and above other people—in fact, of having all the disagreeable traits that we most dislike in the young.

I remember, for instance, when Franklin Junior, then a young college student, was arrested for speeding between Albany and Boston. His father and I hoped that he would be treated as severely as possible, so that he would learn once and for all the inevitable results of breaking the law, even when the offense is not very serious. Above all, we wanted him to learn that punishment for breaking the law falls inexorably on all alike in a democracy. I can remember our utter dismay on discovering that he had got off without even a fine.

Our trouble, of course, came not only from the way the boys were treated outside the home—given too many privileges, on the one hand, and too much criticism, on the other—but from the fact that my husband's mother adored her grandchildren and thought of them as her own. She often got angry with me because I seldom told them what was right or wrong. The reason I didn't was that I never was sure. However, everything was always black or white to her; she had no doubts and never hesitated to tell the children what she thought. As a result, they often fooled her. The two youngest members of the family particularly always treated her with an affectionate camaraderie which won from her almost anything they desired.

Franklin Junior wrecked the small car we gave him when he graduated from school, and we decided it would be a good thing for him to go without one for a while. Almost before we knew it his grandmother, at his request, had replaced the car with a much more expensive one. When we objected, she looked at us blandly and said she had not realized we disapproved. She never heard anything she did not want to hear.

My husband had some very firm ideas about what children should do once they were educated. Up to that time they shared in the family life and possessions, but he thought that the day the boys graduated they should go to work and live on their earnings.

My mother-in-law differed in only one respect from my husband in these ideas. Although she believed the children should work, she wanted them all at home under her supervision and guidance, for she had a strong feeling about holding the family together in almost matriarchal style. Consequently, she disliked having any of the young members of the family financially independent of their elders; keeping them financially dependent, she thought, was one way of keeping them at home and controlling them.

She always regretted that my husband had money of his own from his father and that I had a small income of my own; and when I began to earn money it was a real grief to her. When Franklin was ill, however, she offered him any money he needed without question and longed to have him return to Hyde Park and never work again.

In spite of my mother-in-law's dejection about my earning money, I think she eventually became reconciled to it, realizing that it enabled me to do many things for which my own income was insufficient and which would have been too great a financial drain on my husband. The money I had inherited from my parents' estate shrank during the depression years, and I ended with a very small yearly income. However, long before leaving New York City in 1933, I had begun to earn money through teaching, writing and radio work. I can remember my pleasure when I first was able to give some substantial help to the Women's Trade Union League in paying off the mortgage on their clubhouse, and to carry through some of our plans on the Val-Kill experiment.

With the first money I earned through commercial radio work, during the bad days of the depression, I established two places where girls who were unemployed and searching for work could have lunch and a place to rest. One was in the Women's Trade Union League clubhouse and the other was in the Girls' Service League headquarters on Madison Avenue. We gave the girls a hot lunch and snacks during the day, and provided facilities for sewing, mending, and the like.

The large sums I was able to earn through radio and writing during those bad times made it possible for me not only to make contributions to organized charities but also to give work or help to individuals who could not be helped through the usual channels. I do not question that I often gave to people who were not worthy; but in those years it seemed better to take that risk than to fail those who were worthy. After a few disillusionments, however, I finally made an arrangement with the American Friends Service Committee whereby they did much of the investigating and I gave them almost all the money I earned through radio. At first I had this money paid directly to them, not receiving any of it myself. Then Hamilton Fish made an attack on me in Congress, claiming that I was evading income taxes by regarding a series of radio talks as benefits. I had, of course, obtained a ruling from the Treasury Department in 1933 that it was legal to turn over the money to a recognized charity, but as long as there was any basis for questioning my right to do this I decided to have the money paid directly to me, deducted part of it toward my income tax, and sent the balance to the American Friends.

The money I earned from all my radio work and some of my writing during the years I was in the White House I felt should be used not simply for charity donations but primarily to help people help themselves. Because that is also the philosophy of the Friends, I chose them to handle the money for me. I never gave a present to any of my children out of that earned money. On some occasions I had to use part of my small principal because I had given away so much I could not meet my income tax otherwise. I did not save a single penny during those years because I thought it was not right to do so, and I left the White House with less cash in my own principal account than I had when I went to Washington.

My husband's income was never large and he had to spend some of his principal every year he was in Albany and in the White House. As he died before his mother's estate was settled, that never was of any help to him.

At the time I married my income varied from $5,000 to $8,000 a year. Franklin knew that I had little knowledge of how to handle money, and he also knew that I had no right to disturb the existing trust arrangements, under which my money was managed largely by older members of my family and I simply received the income at certain intervals.

When I look back on how little we spent in our early married days I appreciate the changes in the cost of living in the past forty years. My husband and I agreed that we would put an equal amount into the house account, and we lived easily and comfortably if not luxuriously on $600 a month.

As our household expenses grew over the years, Franklin assumed more responsibility for running the home, and gave all the children modest allowances up to the time they left school. Before they were old enough to be put on an allowance, I bought their clothes and I always bought my own; however, Franklin thought that once they had an allowance they should buy their own clothes in order to learn how to manage money. Now and then I had to rescue them by giving them useful gifts of underwear, shirts and socks. The habit has persisted and they tease me about it now.

After our daughter Anna was married, both Franklin and his mother gave her a small allowance. However, because of my husband's theory that once a male child of the family was educated he should be on his own, our two older boys, James and Elliott, were not given an allowance after they finished their schooling. They, therefore, had to begin at once to earn a living. That complicated their lives considerably, because instead of being allowed to start at the bottom and work up, they were offered jobs that gave them too high returns. And they were too young and too inexperienced to realize that they were offered these jobs only because of their name and their father's position.

Franklin had a strong feeling that our sons should be allowed to make their own decisions and their own mistakes. Occasionally some of his friends suggested that he could give the boys a little guidance, but he always said they must find things out for themselves. I think his attitude came largely from the fact that his mother had wanted to direct his every thought and deed and that he had had to fight for independence.

She always complained that she never saw Franklin alone, but if they were left together by themselves for long they often disagreed. Those two were too much alike in certain ways to be left long alone. Franklin was as determined as she was, and as the years passed he went ahead and did anything he wanted to do in spite of the fact that he had a great respect and love for his mother. But, though out of her devotion to him she did a great many things that were difficult for her, she never accepted the fact of his independence and continued to the last to try to guide his life.

Nevertheless, I often think of how much she had to put up with. For instance, though she entertained them for his sake, she strongly disapproved of Governor Smith and some of Franklin's other political acquaintances and was unable to believe that they could have any ability. Curiously enough, I think Al Smith respected her in spite of the fact that he must have known how she felt, which only made him more self-assertive in her presence. However, she was always pleasant and one had to know her to appreciate her little barbs.

I remember one time when Huey Long was lunching with me at Hyde Park and Franklin, in order to talk to him about some bill on which he wanted his support, had seated him next to himself. My mother-in-law, who could whisper louder than anyone else I ever knew when she wanted to be heard, was at the opposite end of the table. And suddenly I heard her say to the man on her right, in her piercing whisper, "Who is that dreadful person sitting next to my son?"

As a result of Franklin's long experience with his own parent, he had an almost exaggerated determination that he would not subject his sons to similar interference, and the feeling became a plan of action. As he became busier in his public life he found it impossible to take time for the boys' interests, which kept them from asking for advice they might have sought quite naturally had he been freer to give it. One after the other, James and

Elliott learned through bitter experience and it was a bitter disillusionment as well. Their early marriages came about largely because they were not really rooted in any particular home and were seeking to establish homes of their own.

For the two younger boys things were easier because, as a great concession, my husband continued their allowances until his death. Franklin Junior went to law school after he graduated from Harvard and married, so he couldn't earn money; and John started at the bottom in the merchandising business and needed something to keep him going after his marriage. When they went into the Navy they wanted to keep on paying some share of their home expenses. Having an allowance, these two had less immediate need to earn money, so they were not put through the same experiences that the two older brothers had undergone.

Perhaps it is well at this point to clear up a story that has come back to me at various times: that our youngest son, John, was a conscientious objector and a pacifist and did not want to go into the services. Like every other young man I know, he was not, in the years before we were attacked, eager to go to war. But once we were at war there never was any question for him, any more than there was for any of our other sons. Whatever had to be done for the war had to be done, and none of them dreamed of being a conscientious objector or a pacifist.

As life grew busier at the White House, my husband had less time for family affairs, and I can remember how resentful the boys were when they found they actually had to make an appointment to see their father if they wanted to talk to him privately. On one occasion one of our sons had something he felt it was important to talk over with his father, so he made an appointment. My husband was always kind and gentle, and while our son talked he seemed to be listening, though he was reading a document he held in his hand. The boy asked if he had heard him. His father answered, "Yes," but when there was a pause in the talk, he looked up and handed the boy the paper. "This is a most important document. I should like to have your opinion on it." I imagine that seemed like a slap in the face to the boy, who thought that what he was talking about was more important than anything else in the world. He looked at the paper, commented on it and left the room.

Soon a very indignant young man came to me saying, "Never again will I talk to Father about anything personal." It took me a long while before I could bring him to understand that he had happened to strike the wrong moment and that his father had paid him a compliment in asking his opinion.

It may seem that I have gone into a great deal of frank detail about our family affairs and the personal life of the family. I have done so with a purpose, because I sometimes wonder whether the American public, which encourages the press to delve into the private lives of public servants and their families, realizes how much the family of a public man has to pay in lack of privacy for the fact that he is willing to serve his country in an elective or an appointive office.

Fourteen

Private Interlude: 1921-1927

AFTER LEAVING the law office of Carter, Ledyard and Milburn in 1910 and up to the time of his illness in 1921, Franklin had been more or less continuously in public life.

His job in the Navy Department was, I believe, one of the milestones in his life. It would have been easy for him to have become just a nice young society man who, after his work in the department was over for the day, sat around in the Metropolitan Club for a while and talked with his friends. But Louis Howe decided that this was a period when Franklin had better learn something new. He insisted that Franklin find out something about labor conditions in the navy yards, which were his special province in the department, and come in contact with the men. This was Franklin's first close contact with labor, and it was one of the turning points in his development. Certainly it proved of value to him later, both as governor and as president. In both of those periods he increased enormously in his understanding of people and their needs, and with Louis's help gradually developed a political flair that gave him great confidence.

My friend Esther Lape had become member-in-charge of the Bok Foundation. At Mr. Bok's request I helped her to organize the committee and this work. From our past experience in the League of Women Voters we knew that working together would be easy. We had Esther's friend and partner, Elizabeth Read, who was practicing law in New York City, to count on too, so the thinking and planning proceeded smoothly.

In January of the year following Alfred E. Smith's 1924 state victory, Franklin became a partner in D. Basil O'Connor's law firm. The firm became Roosevelt and O'Connor, an association which continued until March 3, 1933. However, from 1924 to 1928 Franklin devoted a good part

141

of his time to finding out how far he could recover from infantile paralysis. The use of his hands and arms came back completely and he developed, because he used them so constantly, broad shoulders and strong arms; but his legs remained useless.

Little by little, through exercise and wearing braces, he learned to walk, first with crutches and then with a cane, leaning on someone's arm. The first braces were heavy; later, lighter ones were made. However, for the rest of his life he was unable to walk or stand without the braces and some help, though he could still swim and play water polo.

The perfect naturalness with which the children accepted his limitations, though they had always known him as an active person, helped him tremendously in his own acceptance of them. He had so many outside interests that he was always busy, and boredom was something he never experienced in his whole life.

Two things he could still enjoy—swimming and driving his own car, which had special hand controls. He was as good a driver as anyone I have ever known with this specially equipped car.

Franklin's illness proved a blessing in disguise, for it gave him strength and courage he had not had before. He had to think out the fundamentals of living and learn the greatest of all lessons—infinite patience and never-ending persistence.

People have often asked me how I felt about his illness. To tell the truth, I do not think I ever stopped to analyze my feelings. There was so much to do to manage the household and the children and to try to keep things running smoothly that I never had time to think of my own reactions. I simply lived from day to day and got through the best I could.

We had tried so hard to ignore any handicap he labored under that I'm sure the two youngest boys had never even thought about what their father could not do, and much of his gallant joking was merely a way of forcing himself to accept cheerfully what he could not help. I remember, for instance, one night in New York City, during a campaign, when he had to be carried on and off the speaker's platform. It was a difficult ordeal, but he passed it off with a smile and a joke.

Franklin went to Warm Springs for the first time in the autumn of 1924. It was then a run-down southern summer resort which had seen better days. The outdoor swimming pool was the one really fine thing about the place. These springs had been known since the days of the

Indians, who, even when they were at war with one another, maintained peace in that area, believing the waters had medicinal value. There is no claim made now that they have any healing powers, but the buoyancy and warm temperature of the water make it possible for one to swim for long periods without becoming tired or chilled. My husband loved the place.

For a number of years my husband went to Warm Springs every autumn, and I remember with a mixture of joy and sadness the Thanksgiving Day celebrations. There seemed so much happiness in the children's faces, but the complete gallantry of all the patients always brought a choke to my throat. Some of them were on stretchers, some in wheelchairs, some on crutches. Some hoped to get well, many faced permanent handicaps, but all were cheerful that one evening at least.

During those years before Franklin went back actively into politics a number of things I did were undertaken at Louis Howe's suggestion in order to interest Franklin. The organization of state campaigns was primarily my job and, again with Louis Howe's help, I thought up some of the best stunts that were undertaken. For instance, in the campaign of 1924 Alfred E. Smith was running against my cousin, Theodore Roosevelt, Jr., who had previously been Assistant Secretary of the Navy in the Harding administration. The recent Teapot Dome scandal—with which Theodore Roosevelt, Jr., had nothing to do—had created much excitement; so, capitalizing on this, we had a framework resembling a teapot, which spouted steam, built on top of an automobile and it led the procession of cars which toured the state, following the Republican candidate for governor wherever he went!

In the thick of political fights one always feels that all methods of campaigning that are honest are fair, but I do think this was a rough stunt and I never blamed my cousin when he retaliated in later campaigns against my husband.

It was during these years, too, that I became engaged in two enterprises with Nancy Cook and Marion Dickerman. Franklin was particularly interested in one of our undertakings. He helped to design and build a stone cottage beside a brook where we often went to picnic during the first years after he was paralyzed. The brook was called Val-Kill, so we called the cottage Val-Kill Cottage. Franklin was the contractor and the builder and, though Mr. Henry Toombs was the architect, he liked to talk over every detail. We built not only the cottage but a swimming pool in which the children and occasionally Franklin enjoyed much sport. Later we built a more elaborate pool, but by that time Franklin was the President and we had to conform to the regulations set up by his doctor and put in filtration machinery. I do not think we had any more fun, however, in the bigger and more elaborate pool than we had in the original small one, the building of which my husband had supervised.

The cottage was not an end in itself. It was the place in which Nancy Cook and Marion Dickerman lived and from which Miss Cook directed a furniture factory. Nancy Cook was an attractive woman who could do almost anything with her hands. She had long wanted to make reproductions of Early American furniture. We obtained help and co-operation from the Metropolitan Museum, the Hartford Museum, and from many individuals. We produced drawings and went to look at famous pieces of old furniture. Miss Cook had no desire to reproduce worm-eaten antiques; she wanted to use methods employed by our ancestors, and see whether she could find a market for furniture which, though the first processes were done by machinery, would be largely handmade and therefore expensive. Because the finishing was all done by hand, the wood looked and felt as though it had been used and polished for years.

My husband was greatly interested in finding some industry that could be developed in country areas such as ours, and that could perhaps furnish occupation for some of the younger men who would otherwise leave the farms. By giving them work in an industry which would yield them a fairly good income during the slack period on the farms, he thought one could keep the progressive, more active group of young people working steadily and so raise the standard of farm development in our area.

He had a great love for the soil and wanted to see it developed; but he realized that many of the farmers around us had a difficult time holding their young sons on the land, because the return for hard and strenuous work was meager. His interest in our enterprise was therefore in the training and the employment of young men in the vicinity.

Nancy Cook ran the enterprise and I put in most of the capital from my earnings from radio and writing and even used some of the small capital that I had inherited from my mother and father. The others, especially Nancy Cook, contributed what they could afford.

We kept the factory going all through the early depression years, when the employment of people seemed vitally important. At last Miss Cook found that carrying two jobs—she was also executive secretary of the women's division of the Democratic State Committee—was too much for her, so we closed the shop.

My husband's object was not achieved, and I think the idea has been proved impractical on a much larger scale in some of the homesteads which were started during the depression. Some succeeded but few returned much on the original investment. Nevertheless, in the crisis they took people off relief and gave them back self-respect and a sense of security—a considerable achievement.

Although this experiment was a disappointment to Franklin, he accepted the failure philosophically both in our own case and later in the case of the country-wide experiment. I think he felt regret; but, with the same acceptance of the inevitable which he showed in so many other matters, having tried the experiment and become satisfied that it did not work, he gave it up and sought other solutions. He hoped that some day it might work out. He always accepted things as they were and set such experiences aside as something to remember and perhaps use in the future.

I never made any money out of this furniture-making venture. In fact, I was probably one of the best customers the shop had, because I bought various pieces of furniture as wedding presents and as gifts for other occasions.

During the depression I took over the factory building and was able, through my earnings, to turn it into a fairly comfortable if somewhat odd house. Though I did not have any architectural advice, I did have the help of a friend, Henry Osthagen, an engineer. We used local labor entirely. Employing people seemed the best way to spend some of the money I was able to earn during those years. Part of the shop we made into an apartment for my secretary, Malvina Thompson, and I frequently went there to work quietly with her; the rest of the building became a guest cottage, which we used when the big house was overcrowded—something that often happened during the years when my husband was president. Since turning the old Hyde Park house over to the government, I have made the converted shop building my year-round home.

During the early years of my acquaintance with Nancy Cook and Marion Dickerman I became associated in the Todhunter School with Miss Dickerman, who was first the assistant principal and then the principal. It was a private school for girls from the primary grades through high school. Miss Todhunter, who was British, finally sold the school to Marion

Dickerman, Nancy Cook and myself and went back to England. I began
teaching there in 1927. I taught only the older girls because I considered
that it took far less training to teach them than to teach the younger
children. I gave courses in American history and in English and American
literature and later we tried some courses in current events which I hope
were more practical than are many of the courses given to sixteen- and
seventeen-year-old girls. We visited the New York City courts and I think
many young people learned a great deal from sitting in one of the children's courts for an hour. Those whom their parents allowed to go I took to
see the various kinds of tenements that exist in a city like New York, as well
as the big markets and various other places. All this made the government
of the city something real and alive, rather than just words in a textbook.

In spite of my political activities and having to run the Executive Mansion in Albany, after my husband was elected governor, I continued to
teach for two and a half days a week, leaving Albany on Sunday evenings
and returning on Wednesday afternoons. It was rather strenuous when
we were in Albany, but, of course, fairly easy when we were at Hyde Park,
as we were there for longer periods, when the legislature was not in session.
For a while, after we went to Washington, I conducted a class for grad-
uates and their friends, first on a weekly and then on a monthly basis.

Fifteen

The Governorship Years: 1928-1932

IN THE SPRING of 1928, when it looked as though Governor Smith would be the candidate for the Presidency on the Democratic ticket, Mrs. Belle Moskowitz asked me to organize the women's end of the office for the national campaign.

That June my husband went with our son, Elliott, to the Democratic National Convention, which met in Houston, Texas. Elliott was thrilled at the chance to be with his father, but I had no desire to take part in the hurly-burly of a convention—the 1924 convention had given me all I wanted of that type of experience. My husband stood the Texas heat remarkably well and came back to Hyde Park feeling that he had had a great part in bringing about the nomination of Alfred E. Smith.

Franklin and I had long supported Governor Smith politically because of his social program; we believed that he sought the welfare of the average man and woman. Franklin remembered how after the Triangle Fire in 1911 in New York City Governor Smith had worked for better factory laws in our state. This fire had been a shocking disaster, in which a great many girls and women had been burned to death because of the lack of fire exits and fire protection in the factory.

Because Governor Smith had spent the greater part of his life in one state and practically in one city, he had certain shortcomings; nevertheless, we felt that he understood the needs of the people and that he had a genius for government; and we never doubted his integrity. His memory was prodigious and his method of talking to people during the campaigns, particularly in his own state, which he knew so well, was remarkably effective.

Franklin did not feel he could do a great deal of work in the campaign, but he came into the office occasionally, and he headed the Businessmen's Division, sat in on planning meetings and made some speeches. He assigned

147

Louis Howe to represent him at the headquarters full time, working with Governor Smith, John Raskob, Edward J. Flynn and others.

It was not until I began to see the full alignment against us that I became doubtful of success. Governor Smith was a Roman Catholic, and the kind of propaganda that some of the religious groups, aided and abetted by the opposition, put forth in that campaign utterly disgusted me. If I needed anything to show me what prejudice can do to the intelligence of human beings, that campaign was the best lesson I could have had.

In 1928 I was still fairly young and could put in prodigious hours of work, but I sometimes wonder how any of us, particularly Miss Thompson and Miss Tully, lived through that campaign. It proved that work is easier to carry if your heart is involved. Miss Thompson was interested because I was interested; and Miss Tully, who had been Cardinal Hayes's secretary, probably felt a religious interest in the campaign in addition to her admiration for Governor Smith.

Grace Tully was young and very pretty, and had been extremely well trained by Cardinal Hayes. Our work was somewhat different from that to which she had been accustomed, but it was good preparation for her future work with my husband and Miss LeHand.

In the fall, after school began, I did not go into the office until noon on the days I taught, but I stayed until the work was finished at night, often well after midnight. Then I went home to do my school papers and was at school the next morning at half past eight. On the other days I was in the office at nine o'clock in the morning and stayed until late in the evening.

Speaking was still something of an ordeal for me, so it was understood that my part of the work would involve simply organizing the office, handling the mail, greeting women visitors, consulting on requests for speakers; in fact, just being generally useful. Mrs. Mary Norton, congresswoman from New Jersey, as head of the women's speakers' bureau, made the arrangements for women speakers, and all requests were referred to her.

Elinor Morgenthau and Nancy Cook, who were working with the Democratic State Committee, moved with their staff to the General Motors Building for the campaign. Then, in the latter part of the summer of 1928, the vice-chairman of the Democratic National Committee, Mrs. Nellie Tayloe Ross, moved into her office at the national headquarters, with Mrs. James O'Mahoney as her assistant. Mrs. Ross had served as governor of Wyoming after the death of her husband, who had been the previous governor.

Her arrival at headquarters meant that we started to make plans for an extensive speaking trip for her, and she was always in demand for activities at headquarters. We kept her pretty busy. I remember one day I had Miss Tully scurrying everywhere to find her while a tea party waited to greet her. She was found completely exhausted, lying on the floor of our diminutive restroom, trying to regain enough energy to face shaking hands with several hundred people.

Later, she continued in active government work and became director of the mint of the Treasury Department, remaining a popular speaker with women's groups.

In September of that year I motored to Groton with our youngest son, John, to put him in boarding school. By then I had come to feel that once a child went to boarding school there never again could be the strong ties with and the dependence on the family that had existed up to that time. I had never been a convinced advocate for boarding school for the twelve-year-old but my husband, who had not gone to boarding school until he was fourteen, always felt that the loss of those two years was a hardship, because by the time he entered the school the other boys had already formed their friendships and he remained always a little the outsider.

The day I took each boy to school, unpacked his clothes and settled him was always a terrible day for me, and when it came to the last child, it was particularly hard.

Even though I was teaching school and working in the national campaign headquarters in New York City, I attended the New York State Democratic Convention in Rochester that fall. I mention this here to tell the story, as I remember it, of how my husband was finally induced to run for the governorship.

The afternoon before the nominations were made, John J. Raskob, then chairman of the National Democratic Committee, and Governor Smith asked me to come to talk with them. I had heard that Governor Smith wanted my husband to run. However, I knew Franklin felt he should continue his treatment at Warm Springs. They told me how much they wanted him to run, and asked me if I thought it would really injure his health. I said I did not know; that I had been told the doctors felt that if he continued with his exercises and swimming at Warm Springs he might improve. My husband once laughingly said that if he lived long enough he might be able to walk again, but progress was slow and I sometimes wondered how much more could be achieved.

Both Governor Smith and Mr. Raskob insisted that they did not want to urge anything that would injure Franklin's health. If, however, it was not simply his health but other reasons which kept him from consenting, they would like to know it. I said I did not think any other reasons were paramount and that Franklin felt the possibility of making further improvement in his health was worth a try. Also, having undertaken a heavy financial responsibility in Warm Springs, he felt an obligation to try to make it a success.

Finally, after Governor Smith, Mr. Raskob and I talked over the situation, they asked me if I would be willing to get my husband on the telephone and ask him to run for governor. They had been trying all day to reach him and had not been able to do so. I answered that I would not ask him to do anything he felt he should not do, let alone run for office.

They put in a call to my husband for me early in the evening and found that he had gone to Manchester, Georgia, to make a speech and could not be reached until he returned to Warm Springs. I finally succeeded in getting Franklin on the telephone at the Foundation after his return. He told me with evident glee that he had been keeping out of reach all day and would not have answered the telephone if I had not been calling.

I had just time enough to tell him that I had called because Governor Smith and Mr. Raskob begged me to, and that I was leaving him to Governor Smith because I had to catch a train. Then I ran. I can still hear Governor Smith's voice saying, "Hello, Frank," as I hurried from the room to gather up my belongings and catch the train. I did not know until the following morning when I bought a newspaper that my husband had been persuaded to accept the nomination. I never heard him say later whether he regretted his decision or not. Having decided, he put any other possibility out of his mind.

Louis Howe was not happy about Franklin's candidacy. He always thought in terms of the future, and he had planned that Franklin should be a candidate four or eight years later. Louis feared that if Governor Smith lost nationally, it might not be possible for Franklin to carry the state for the governorship, which might spoil any chance he had for future political office.

I used to laugh at Louis and say one could not plan every move in this world, one had to accept circumstances as they developed. Louis hated to do that. He liked to feel that he dominated circumstances and, so far as it was humanly possible, he often did.

Comparatively speaking, I knew very little about the 1928 campaign for the governorship. Since I had started to work in the national office, Franklin felt I was obligated to continue there, and that took the greater part of my time. I did go to hear him speak occasionally, and he made a complete campaign throughout the state. I think he did not expect to carry the state if Governor Smith lost the Presidency, and when we left the state headquarters at a late hour on election night we were still uncertain of the outcome. The next morning, when the final figures were in, my husband was governor-elect by a very narrow margin. He had a feeling that it was a great tribute to have been elected while Governor Smith, who had such a large following in the state, had been defeated.

On that election night I visited the national as well as the state campaign headquarters, and I thought that Governor Smith accepted his defeat very gallantly. It must have been hard for him to have Franklin elected while he himself was defeated, but he never showed it in any way. He went back to work in the state and on January 1, 1929, he received us when we went to Albany.

Many people have suggested to me that when Governor Smith asked my husband to run for the governorship, while he himself was running for the Presidency, he had it in mind that he would still be able to direct the work of the governor.

One of the ways in which he undoubtedly expected to keep his hold on the state government was through Mrs. Belle Moskowitz. He suggested a number of times to my husband that she would be invaluable to him, and each time Franklin replied that while he had great respect for Mrs. Moskowitz's ability and knew what her advice and help had meant to Governor Smith, he felt it would be unwise for him to retain her in his own close administrative circle. He thought it impossible for anyone to transfer loyalty after working so long and so closely with someone else.

Governor Smith had asked Franklin to nominate him for the Presidency and to run on the state ticket as governor because Franklin would bring him needed strength. However, I think that Governor Smith did not have much confidence in the Harvard man who had a different kind of education and who cared about many things which meant little or nothing to Governor Smith.

There are two kinds of snobbishness. One is that of the man who has had a good many opportunities and looks down on those who lack them.

The other kind is rarely understood, that of the self-made man who glories in his success in overcoming difficulties and admires greatly people who have achieved the things he considers of importance. Governor Smith had a great deal of respect for material success, but he tended to look down upon a man like Franklin who was content not to make a great deal of money so long as he had enough to live comfortably.

In those days I think that in some ways I understood Governor Smith better than Franklin did, because during my intensive work with the Democratic State Committee, while Franklin was ill, I had had more opportunity to observe him from different points of view. While he and Franklin had known each other for a long time, they were never really intimate. Franklin thought only of his ability as an administrator, as a campaigner, as a statesman and as a governor, and he had the greatest admiration for his knowledge of government.

I agreed that he had an extraordinary flair for government and that his memory and his knowledge of New York State were phenomenal. Indeed, I believed in him and considered him a great man in many ways, and I worked for him. I thought that had he been elected president, he would have chosen his Cabinet well, even though his knowledge of the country as a whole was slight and his advisers in the state knew little of the nation. However, I never felt he could have handled our foreign relations or gauged what was happening in the world. Also, I thought him less of a humanitarian than most people did, crediting Mrs. Moskowitz with the social welfare plans for which he was generally acclaimed, and which he carried out, I thought, largely because he knew they were politically wise.

It was natural for him to feel that he was responsible for Franklin's success in politics, since he had urged my husband to run for governor. Franklin himself, however, felt the request to run had been made to help Governor Smith, and it was on that basis and that basis alone that the appeal had been considered.

In many ways Governor Smith did not know my husband. One of Franklin's main qualities was that he never assumed any responsibility that he did not intend to carry through. It never occurred to him that he was not going to be the governor of New York with all the responsibility and work that position carried. That ended the close relationship between my husband and Governor Smith, though there was no open break, so far as I ever knew.

Franklin had some clear ideas about state government. He studied the reorganization plans that had been initiated under Governor Smith and he approved practically everything that he had done. Franklin's attitude toward the objectives that later were developed on a national scale were apparent in his approach to questions in the state. For instance, he pushed old-age pensions.

As governor, Franklin also showed his interest in labor and his belief in labor's rights. He felt that workers should receive the same consideration that management's rights received; and when times became hard, the theory that government had a responsibility toward the people was incorporated in the state policies. Franklin had been accused of giving labor too much power, but his effort was simply to equalize the power of labor and capital. As a close student of history, he knew how great and unhampered capital's power had been during some previous administrations.

His particular personal interest was in soil conservation and forestry. However, his interest in the development of water power, in the Indian problem, transportation, education, and finally in relief and general welfare was also stimulated by his experience as the administrator of a state. All these objectives, as well as his understanding of them, were expanded during the presidential years. And because he had traveled so extensively even before he was president, he knew how different the problems were in different areas of the country. All this was excellent preparation for the years ahead.

Once back in public affairs, Franklin's political interests and ambitions reawakened. When he found he could again play an active part in politics he took a satisfaction in the purely political side of the struggle, in achieving new office. It is hard to dissociate his ambition and enjoyment of the science of politics for its own sake from his desire to achieve through political action real gains for the people, first of the state, then of the nation, and finally of the world. The objectives grew as circumstances developed the need for them and the horizons broadened as time went on and we, as a nation, were swept into a position where the world was depending on us.

In Albany he had the experience of working with legislative groups in which his political party was in a minority. Later, in Washington, I often wished that it were possible for him to carry out with the Democratic representatives there the kind of educational work he had done in Albany. There were occasional meetings when all the legislation backed by the administration was talked over and explained and the entire campaign mapped out. My husband always said the group in Congress was too large and he did not see how it was possible to hold the same type of meeting.

The years in Albany cast their shadow before them. Frances Perkins was in the New York State Labor Department, Harry Hopkins was doing a job on relief and welfare, Dr. Thomas Parran was commissioner of public health, Henry Morgenthau, Jr., was conservation commissioner. Many experiments that were later to be incorporated into a national program were being tried out in the state. It was part of Franklin's political philosophy that the great benefit to be derived from having forty-eight states was the possibility of experimenting on a small scale to see how a program worked before trying it out nationally.

My own life during those governorship years was a full one. In my teaching I really had for the first time a job that I did not wish to give up. This led to my planning to spend a few days every week in New York City, except during the school vacations.

My husband, who loved being on the water, found that the state of New York had a small boat used by state officials for canal travel on inspection trips. He decided to use it himself during the summers for the same purpose. During the day we would leave the boat and visit various state institutions. This was valuable training for me. I had paid occasional visits to state prisons, insane asylums or state hospitals for crippled children, but never with the intention of looking into the actual running of any institution or gauging its good and bad points.

The head of the institution that we were visiting usually got into the car with my husband and drove around the grounds, pointing out what new buildings were needed and where they should be built. In this way Franklin gained a personal knowledge of the exterior of the institution which helped him when he met with the legislative appropriations committee.

Walking was so difficult for him that he could not go inside an institution and get a real idea of how it was being run from the point of view of overcrowding, staff, food, and medical care. I was asked to take over this part of the inspection, and at first my reports were highly unsatisfactory to him. I would tell him what was on the menu for the day and he would ask: "Did you look to see whether the inmates were actually getting that food?" I learned to look into the cooking pots on the stove and to find out if the contents corresponded to the menu. I learned to notice whether the beds were too close together, and whether they were folded up and put in

closets or behind doors during the day, which would indicate that they
filled the corridors at night! I learned to watch the patients' attitude toward
the staff, and before the end of our years in Albany I had become a fairly
expert reporter on state institutions.

In the summer of 1929 we made an inspection trip on the canal which
eventually brought us out to a point from which Franklin went down the
St. Lawrence River to discuss the St. Lawrence Waterway with Canadian
and United States officials.

That summer, with the two younger boys, I went to Europe. My husband
had particularly wanted me to show them the fronts over which our men
had fought in World War I, Quentin Roosevelt's grave, and some of the
cemeteries. I had already pointed out to them in the little villages of England the monuments to the men who had been killed in that war. The
cemeteries, with their rows and rows of crosses, made an impression on the
boys, but they were, of course, unable to gather the significance of the new
buildings in the old French villages and towns. To young Americans, new
buildings were not strange, and while I was impressed by the way nature
had covered her scars in the woods and fields, I pointed out to the boys
the whitened stumps and the fact that the trees were young, showing that
whole forests had been mowed down just a few years ago. In the fields I
pointed out the ditches, which had been dug by soldiers for protection, and
the curious holes made by bursting shells, now covered with grass.

My older son said to me one day: "This is a funny country. There are
only boys our age and old men coming out of the fields. There don't seem
to be any men of father's age." That was simply another proof that the war
had taken from France a heavy toll of her young men from 1914 to 1918.

This same sense of the loss of a generation came to me vividly at the first
organizational meeting of the United Nations in London, in 1946. So many
of the Europeans were older men who had made the effort with the League
of Nations and were doubtful about a second international effort to keep
the world at peace. The loss of a generation makes itself felt acutely twenty
to thirty-five years later, when many men who would have been leaders
are not there to lead.

Back in Albany, I became immediately submerged again in the busy
routine of my life as mother, governor's wife and teacher, and there were
few breaks until the state campaign of 1930. That was an easy campaign,
and it was a satisfaction to all of Franklin's supporters that he won the
largest vote cast for any Democrat up to that time in a gubernatorial elec-

tion. This circumstance had the double advantage of making Franklin strong in the state and strong as a potential candidate for the Presidency. This prospect did not interest me particularly but it did interest his political supporters.

During his terms as governor of New York he attended many of the Governors' Conferences, because he felt that they were important. Whenever possible he wanted the advantage of contact with other governors for the discussion of problems. Sometimes I went with him. I remember particularly one of the last Governors' Conferences, at which President Hoover started to make an address. The wind blew away his papers and he was so completely dependent on them that he had to break off his speech.

In the course of that conference, which was at Richmond, Virginia, all the governors were invited to dine at the White House. My husband was already considered one of the strongest possible candidates for the Democratic nomination for president. I was familiar with the way in which guests had to stand in the East Room at a state dinner before they were received by the President and his wife, so I was worried about Franklin, who had to have somebody's arm and a cane. In addition, he became tired if he stood without support for any length of time.

We arrived a little ahead of time, since we knew we should have to walk rather slowly down the main hall to get into line, and then we waited and waited. The President and Mrs. Hoover did not appear. My husband was twice offered a chair, but he thought that if he showed any weakness someone might make an adverse political story out of it, so he refused each time. It seemed as though he was being deliberately put through an endurance test, but he stood the whole evening very well, though the half hour before President and Mrs. Hoover appeared was an ordeal.

This idea may seem preposterous but in political life you grow suspicious. The strategists on both sides weigh how far they can go without awakening in the people a feeling that the rules of fair play have not been observed. You hear a whisper of this or that, but the whispers are never brought to the attention of the candidates and no official recognition is given to them.

I can hardly remember a campaign in which, in our village of Hyde Park, scurrilous things were not said about my husband and his mother and myself, and even about the children. Some of my friends came to me in anxiety because they had heard a story that my husband did not have infantile paralysis but had some other disease which was progressive and would eventually attack the brain.

During the 1932 campaign Louis Howe heard that the Republicans planned to issue a statement claiming that infantile paralysis was a progressive disease which eventually affected the brain. Louis immediately asked Dr. George Draper, a leading authority on polio, who with Dr. Lovett had taken care of Franklin, for a counterstatement which he could use if necessary. Dr. Draper gave him a full statement, from the medical point of view, refuting any such ideas. He noted that Sir Walter Scott had had infantile paralysis when he was a small boy, and no one could point to any impairment in his brain.

My husband's mother was never happy about the gossip and rumors concerning her and her son and her grandsons. Disagreeable letters upset her very much, and the statement that she was paid by the government for the use of her house at Hyde Park as a summer White House distressed her above everything. She was proud of her home and extremely happy when her son and his family and friends could be with her, and nothing would have induced her to accept money from any source. In any case, there was at no time a suggestion of government pay, and after her death my husband continued to pay the expenses of the house and grounds out of his own pocket.

All people in public life are subject to this type of slander. Circumstantial evidence can almost always be produced to make the stories that are circulated about their private lives seem probable to the people who want to believe them. A man who chooses to hold public office must learn to accept the slander as part of the job and to trust that the majority of the people will judge him by his accomplishments in the public service. A man's family also has to learn to accept it. In my husband's case, even his little dog, Fala, came in for his share of false accusations.

Sixteen

I Learn to Be a President's Wife

FRANKLIN DID NOT tell me when he decided to run for the Presidency, but I knew that for a year or more everything that Louis Howe had undertaken for my husband had been with the idea of broadening his acquaintance-ships and knowledge of conditions throughout the country. This little man was really the biggest man from the point of view of imagination and de-termination I have ever known. He made few personal friends and he judged most of those by their loyalty to "the Boss," as he called my hus-band. He was one of the few people who never said "yes" when he meant "no."

It was Louis Howe who mapped out the preconvention campaign. The strategy and the choice of men were left largely to him and, though he talked his plans over with Franklin, he really "masterminded" the whole campaign. He loved the sense of power and, though he wanted a few people to know he had it, on the whole he preferred anonymity. It was he who chose Edward J. Flynn and James Farley to play their important roles, though Franklin liked and trusted them both. Ed Flynn came to understand much that my husband believed in and worked for. Jim Farley believed in the man for whom he worked, but he was not so much concerned with the ideas and ideals for which the man stood. He had a marvelous gift with people; he could do a prodigious amount of work, and he carried his share of the burden as magnificently as did Louis and Ed Flynn.

There were many other devoted and loyal men who believed in my hus-band and who, contributing generously of their time and money, worked directly in the campaign. Among them were Frank Walker, the Henry Morgenthaus, Sr. and Jr., W. Forbes Morgan, and Bernard Baruch. These men gathered about them other men who became active in planning to meet future problems. The men who formed the so-called brain trust were picked chiefly by Louis Howe and Sam Rosenman. They were a group with whom Franklin consulted in laying plans to meet the problems ahead, lawyers, professors, politicians, all gathered together to think out ways and means of doing specific things. The original "brain trust" consisted of Professor Raymond Moley, Professor Rexford G. Tugwell, and Judge Samuel I. Rosenman. Later, Adolf Berle was brought in and on certain occasions Dr. Joseph McGoldrick and General Hugh Johnson were consulted.

Through the whole of Franklin's career there never was any deviation from his original objective—to help make life better for the average man, woman and child. A thousand and one means were used, difficulties arose, changes took place, but this objective always was the motive for whatever had to be done. In the end, in spite of all his efforts to prevent it, a war had to be fought, because the inexorable march of events showed that only by war could fascism be wiped out. The persecution of the Jews was only the beginning of the persecutions that would have been inflicted upon all those who differed from the Fascist leaders. All freedom for the average man would have gone, and with its going, the objectives that Franklin and all other men in democratic nations believed in would have been lost.

While Franklin's desire was to make life happier for people, mixed with it, as I mentioned earlier, was his liking for the mechanics of politics, for politics as a science and as a game which included understanding the mass reactions of people and gambling on one's own judgment.

Franklin always felt that a president should consider himself an instrument chosen by the people to do their bidding, but that he should also consider that as president he had an obligation to enlighten and lead the people.

I have never known a man who gave one a greater sense of security. I never heard him say there was a problem that he thought it was impossible for human beings to solve. He recognized the difficulties and often said that, while he did not know the answer, he was completely confident that there was an answer and that one had to try until one either found it for himself or got it from someone else.

I never knew him to face life or any problem that came up with fear, and I have often wondered if that courageous attitude was not communicated to the people of the country. It may well be what helped them to pull themselves out of the depression in the first years of his administration as president. He knew quite well that he could not pull them out with the best policies in the world unless the people themselves made those policies work. But he believed in the courage and ability of men, and they responded.

From the personal standpoint, I did not want my husband to be president. I realized, however, that it was impossible to keep a man out of public service when that was what he wanted and was undoubtedly well equipped for. It was pure selfishness on my part, and I never mentioned my feelings on the subject to him.

The nominating convention was held in Chicago, with Senator Thomas J. Walsh as permanent chairman. Franklin owed much to his skillful handling of the convention.

Alfred E. Smith also was a candidate for the nomination and had many ardent supporters. I think he felt that gratitude should have compelled Franklin to withdraw in his favor, since he had been instrumental in getting Franklin to re-enter public life previously. My husband believed that he could meet the tremendous crisis the country was facing better than anyone else in the party. A man must have this confidence in himself or he could never undertake the heavy responsibilities of leading a nation. People used to comment to me on the egoism of my uncle, President Theodore Roosevelt. I know many people felt that Franklin D. Roosevelt had the same quality. Undoubtedly he did to a certain extent; a man could not carry the burdens of the Presidency otherwise.

The regular machinery of the Democratic National Committee, which handled the tickets to the convention, was, of course, favorable to Smith, and refused to give a fair proportion of tickets to our convention committee. The day after my husband made his acceptance speech, however, a large carton of convention hall tickets was sent to our suite in the Congress Hotel!

As each state delegation to the convention was pledged to support my husband's nomination, that state was painted red on a large map of the United States which hung just outside the Franklin D. Roosevelt headquarters in the Congress Hotel. One morning it was discovered that during the night someone had pasted a large sign over the map: "It's votes not acres that count!" The Smith supporters were suspected.

The night before my husband was nominated, we sat up until morning in the Executive Mansion. Two days later, my husband, John, Elliott, and I flew to Chicago where Franklin was to accept the nomination.

The plane trip was something no candidate had ever before undertaken and it created considerable excitement. Previously, the candidate had not been notified officially of his nomination until later in the summer.

Mr. Raymond Moley has stated that he wrote that acceptance speech. I feel sure he was never aware of the things that happened in connection with it. There were two versions of the speech. Evidently they were somewhat alike, and thus the confusion must have come about. My husband wrote one speech himself, dictated to a stenographer in Chicago over the long-distance telephone from Albany, Franklin, Miss LeHand, Miss Tully and Judge Rosenman taking turns at dictating.

That speech, together with one that Mr. Moley and Mr. Tugwell wrote as an improvement on it, were brought by Louis Howe when he met us at the Chicago airport. As he started to hand both versions to my husband, Franklin said: "Oh, I've revised it and have a new draft in my pocket. I have been working on it in the plane." The one in his pocket was the one he read at the convention, though he read through the others and consented to include one or two things that Louis felt were especially important and that were not in Franklin's own revised draft.

Governor Smith and his family and supporters did not wait to congratulate Franklin but left Chicago immediately. The other candidates stayed and felt less bitter.

In September Franklin started on a long campaign trip across the country. Some of the children accompanied him but I did not join him until he reached Williams, Arizona, on the way home. Fortunately, one or more of the children were always able to be on all the campaign trips, for he loved having some of the family with him. They not only helped to entertain people on the train but also kept him amused, for we made it a family practice to look for funny incidents to make him laugh.

Exhilarated as always by contact with people, Franklin came home from the 1932 campaign trips with a conviction that the depression could be licked. He had an extraordinarily acute power of observation and could judge conditions in any section from the looks of the countryside as he traveled through. From him I learned how to observe from train windows; he would watch the crops, notice how people dressed, how many cars there were and in what condition, and even look at the washing on the clotheslines. When the CCC was set up, he knew, though he never made a note, exactly where work of various kinds was needed.

On the 1932 campaign trips Franklin was impressed by the evidences of our wastefulness, our lack of conservation, our soil erosion; and on what he saw he based his plans for action. But the thing he felt most strongly was that there was a vitality in the people that could be salvaged. I believe it was from his faith in the people that he drew the words of his first inaugural address: "The only thing we have to fear is fear itself."

The campaign speeches and later the fireside chats, as they came to be known, entailed a great deal of work on Franklin's part. In the campaigns the subjects were carefully chosen, the places and times to speak discussed with many advisers. Then the research began. Franklin expected the people assigned to this to bring him arguments on both sides of the question, and as much information on the subject as it was possible to gather. He went over all their material carefully and picked out the facts that were to go into the speech; then he gave it to those whom he entrusted with the writing of the first draft. When they brought this back to him, he worked over it with them two or three times.

I have known him, even after a draft had been submitted for literary criticism to the best person who had been asked to help from that point of view, to read the final copy over and over again, put in words or take them out, transpose sentences, and polish it until he knew it by heart and it completely represented his own thought.

I have sometimes been asked what role I played in connection with my husband's speeches. The answer is that I played no role at all. It is true that he sometimes used parts of letters or paragraphs from articles I gave him to look at; and I often read his speeches before he actually delivered them. But that was the extent of it.

His voice lent itself remarkably to the radio. It was a natural gift, for in his whole life he never had a lesson in diction or public speaking. His voice unquestionably helped him to make the people of the country feel that they were an intelligent and understanding part of every government undertaking during his administration.

The night of the election we were in New York City, and I circulated between the State Committee headquarters and those of the National Committee.

I was happy for my husband, because I knew that in many ways it would make up for the blow that fate had dealt him when he was stricken with infantile paralysis; and I had implicit confidence in his ability to help the country in a crisis. Naturally he had wanted to win, and he wanted this opportunity to serve his country in public life.

But for myself I was deeply troubled. As I saw it, this meant the end of any personal life of my own. I knew what traditionally should lie before me; I had watched Mrs. Theodore Roosevelt and had seen what it meant to be the wife of a president, and I cannot say that I was pleased at the prospect. By earning my own money, I had recently enjoyed a certain amount of financial independence and had been able to do things in which I was personally interested. The turmoil in my heart and mind was rather great that night, and the next few months were not to make any clearer what the road ahead would be.

Life began to change immediately. As soon as my husband's election was established, the Secret Service assumed responsibility for his protection. Our house in 65th Street was filled with Secret Service agents, and guests were scrutinized and had to be identified when Franklin was in the house.

Herbert H. Lehman had been elected governor. We turned the Executive Mansion over to him and Mrs. Lehman on Inauguration Day, January 1, 1933, and drove to Hyde Park. The work of the governorship was familiar to Mr. Lehman, so he took over with complete confidence.

Soon after the New Year my husband paid a visit to Washington. President Hoover asked him if in the interim before inauguration he would take joint responsibility for certain policies, but Franklin felt that until he had the control he could not share the burdens.

Later in the winter I paid the customary visit to Mrs. Hoover and decided how, on moving in, I was going to use the rooms. She showed me some of the rooms herself, but when I asked to see the kitchen, she turned me over with relief, I am sure, to the housekeeper and to Ike Hoover, the chief usher in the White House, whom I had known in President Theodore Roosevelt's day.

Inauguration of 1933 was not a lighthearted occasion for the man going out of office or for the man coming in or for the people of the country as a whole. President Hoover had been through a trying period. His great anxiety had been reflected in his inability to preserve his equanimity in his daily contacts with the people in the White House. We were told afterwards how difficult it had been for him even to say good morning or smile at the people of his household.

He was a victim of circumstances and of economic and political beliefs that could be changed only by a complete crisis and courageous new actions. He had served the country well during World War I, and there is no question but that during his term of office he wanted to do what was best for the country. He has, since those unhappy days, rendered service to his country and to the world on numerous occasions.

My husband often told me of his drive with Mr. Hoover from the White House to the Capitol and of how he, Franklin, tried to keep up a cheerful conversation in the face of a silent companion. Crowds were cheering and unconsciously my husband responded, until he realized that Mr. Hoover was sitting motionless. There was hope in my husband's heart and mind, but he realized that could not be the state of mind of the man sitting next to him. Finally, as they reached one of the government buildings which had been begun during Mr. Hoover's administration, my husband found himself remarking on the "lovely steel." It must have sounded inane, but it indicates how desperate he was in his search for small talk.

The condition of the country was so serious on that Inauguration Day, March 4, 1933, that little time was given to purely social amenities. Almost at once my husband began calling meetings, and the first thing that happened was the bank holiday. I was concerned because we had been staying at the Mayflower Hotel for two or three days and I had no extra cash. I went to my husband and asked him what would happen if we needed some money, particularly since the boys, some of them, had to leave soon. He smiled and said he thought we should be able to manage whatever was absolutely necessary. I began to realize then that there were certain things one need not worry about in the White House.

In the first days of his administration my husband was too busy finding ways and means of meeting the financial crisis in the country to be bothered with anything else, so I went to work to organize the household and the secretarial side of the office which did the work for the President's wife.

The inauguration was on a Saturday. The following day Miss Thompson and I went over the White House from basement to attic, looking into closets and generally inspecting the entire house. Unconsciously, I did many things that shocked the ushers, especially Ike Hoover. My first act was to insist on running the elevator myself without waiting for one of the doormen to run it for me. That just wasn't done by the President's wife.

Mrs. Hoover had furnished what we called the West Hall as a solarium, with birds, wicker furniture and plants. I decided to use that end of the wide hall as an extra sitting room, and in order to hurry things along I helped with the moving and placing of the furniture, much to the horror of the household staff.

Fortunately for me, Miss Thompson had been willing to go with me to Washington. She had lived in New York while my husband was governor and had made only occasional trips to Albany. Until now Miss Tully had helped me as well as Franklin, but from the time we went to Washington she worked only for him.

Long before Inauguration Day, Mrs. James M. Helm had offered to help us out at the White House on a voluntary basis for a "few days," until we learned our way about. Mrs. Helm, the daughter of an admiral and the widow of an admiral, had lived in Washington for many years and knew all those formidable people called the "cave dwellers," a term applied to the few people who really live in Washington and are not birds of passage. Franklin and I had seen her with the President and the second Mrs. Wilson in Paris, when Mrs. Helm was Mrs. Wilson's secretary. Franklin liked her very much, so we were all equally grateful for her offer of assistance.

The mail kept piling up around Miss Thompson's desk—letters, books, gifts and various other packages. She tried to cope with it singlehanded, because no one had told us we had a staff to help us, until finally Edith Helm could stand it no longer and said: "Why don't you give that mail to Mr. Magee? He is sitting downstairs with nothing to do and he is there with his staff to help you." After that we worked out a system which operated very well, and we were always complimented on the fact that all the mail was answered in a fairly short time after it was received.

Later Edith Helm's volunteer work developed into the permanent position of social secretary. Miss Thompson soon found that handling the mail and doing my personal work was all she could possibly manage, and she had as little interest in mastering the intricacies of Washington social life as I had.

From the beginning I made it a habit to breakfast in the West Hall at eight or half past. My husband breakfasted in bed and I always went to his room as soon as his breakfast tray was brought up. I stopped only to say good morning, for he liked no conversation at this hour, which he devoted to reading all the newspapers.

After breakfast each morning I went to my desk in my sitting room to see in turn the housekeeper, the usher and the social secretary. My grandmother and my mother-in-law had taught me how to run a house and I assumed, in accordance with their teachings, that all good housewives made out their own menus, put away and gave out the household linen, bought the food and gave all the orders for the day. In the White House I learned this was done under the housekeeper's supervision. As far as the house was concerned, I had no work and little responsibility.

I had brought down a housekeeper, Mrs. Henry Nesbitt, who had worked for me at Hyde Park in the League of Women Voters. Her husband came down with her to do the bookkeeping. She herself did the buying, prepared the menus and generally supervised the household. She was the first person who came to see me after breakfast every morning, with her menus prepared for the day. I tried to tell her approximately how many people were expected for meals, but we soon discovered that the number frequently changed at the last minute, so she had to be prepared for any contingency.

I was surprised to find how inadequate the arrangements were for the household help in the White House. A few of them had rooms on the third floor and stayed at night. Most of them came in by the day, as they do in most southern communities, but the arrangements for changing their clothes, as well as their dining-room facilities, were extremely inadequate. I tried to organize things more comfortably but I never was happy about it until extensive changes were made on the basement floor.

Some aspects of housekeeping in the White House might be of general interest. For one thing, I think few people realize what the expenses are of a man who holds a public office such as the Presidency or even a governorship. Both New York State and the federal government pay the wages of the household help, but whatever it cost to feed them came out of my husband's own pocket. In Albany we had eight or ten regular household employees and in the White House usually about thirty. I have always thought that the governments of both the state and the nation should pay for their food.

In the White House the yearly thousands of visitors meant that we had to employ many more people than we should otherwise have needed, simply to keep the public rooms clean. In addition, the Christmas parties that we gave every year for the guards and all the people working in the White House, on the grounds and in the garage were paid for by my husband. Formal parties and state dinners were paid for by the government, but if Franklin and I had any of our children or personal friends at a formal dinner, we had to pay their pro rata share of the cost. Then, of course, the requests for contributions were countless—and a president is always expected to give more generously than anyone else. Every president, I am sure, leaves the White House poorer than he was when he went in.

All this made the bookkeeping and the housekeeping complicated jobs. There were also complications and difficulties about purchases made for the White House. Nothing that is worn out and discarded can disappear. It must be produced when you say you have bought something to replace it. As a result, warehouses are filled with old furniture which is disposed of only when there is no longer a square foot of room left. If the housekeeper has to buy even a new tea strainer, the old one has to be kept in case she is asked to produce it.

Everything is used until it is worn out. Any items no longer usable are destroyed in the presence of witnesses. Anything of historical interest, such as the gold piano and the old elevator cage, is placed in the Smithsonian Institution.

The replenishing of curtains and rugs and the re-covering of walls and furniture in the formal rooms have to be seen to carefully and constantly, because a house that is always on exhibition should look its best at all times. Mrs. Hoover told me that some visitors wrote her that one of the curtains over the large staircase window had a darn in it, not realizing that the height and size of the windows made new curtains a great expense.

Every morning after Mrs. Nesbitt and I finished our discussion of the relevant housekeeping matters the usher would come to my sitting room. His purpose was primarily to check over the comings and goings of guests and members of the family. He also had to have a list of any people who were coming to see us, because otherwise they would not be admitted.

Then Edith Helm would arrive with her list of invitations to public functions, of receptions I should hold, or whatever else she thought I ought to do. These three interviews took comparatively little time. I think Edith Helm often felt I did not take enough interest in the social side of the White House duties, but at that time they seemed to me rather unimportant; indeed, there never came a point when I felt the world was sufficiently stable for us to take time to think very seriously about purely social matters.

Certain duties, however, which I thought at first were useless burdens I later grew to realize had real meaning and value. For instance, the teas. It seemed to me utterly futile to receive anywhere from five hundred to a thousand people of an afternoon, shake hands with them, and then have them pass into the dining room to be given a cup of tea or coffee by Mrs. Helm and Miss Thompson.

I soon discovered that, particularly to people from out of town, the White House has a deep significance. It is a place where the people's hospitality is dispensed to the representatives of other countries; in a way, it is with a sense of ownership that citizens of the United States walk through the simple but dignified and beautiful rooms. To many people the White House symbolizes the government, and though standing and shaking hands for an hour or so, two or three times a week, is not an inspiring occupation, still I think it well worth while. I did it regularly, three times a week, during the winter months.

At the first few receptions of each season my arms ached, my shoulders ached, my back ached, and my knees and feet seemed to belong to someone else.

My husband found the formal receptions tiring, since standing for a long period of time with braces on was something of an ordeal. He tried never to have more than a thousand people to greet, and after the reception was over he went upstairs at once.

All protocol was foreign to me, and until I learned that it was really required for two purposes—protection and orderly procedure—I resented it deeply, as do most Americans. One congressman's secretary, in replying to a formal invitation for him, addressed the envelope to "The Chief of the Proletariat" instead of "The Chief of Protocol," which indicates how little protocol means to the average American.

Washington lives by a rigid schedule. Some of it I think unnecessarily complicated but by and large I know it is necessary. The foreigners living in Washington would understand no other procedure. Also, the importance that most Americans attach to the posts they hold, whether elective or appointive, is probably justified; for in prestige most public servants find their only return. Certainly the financial returns are slight in comparison to what the majority of them could earn in business or in a profession.

Mrs. Helm had the help of the State Department on all questions of protocol. This relieved me of all responsibility. I never had to seat a formal dinner table.

I added a few parties to the social calendar of the White House—a so-called Gridiron Widows' party, and teas and a garden party for the women who held executive or administrative positions in the government. Every year the newspapermen invite the President to the Gridiron dinner. Women are never allowed to attend, not even the women of the press. I decided it would be fun to have an evening party for the women on the same night, not only newspaperwomen but wives of newspapermen, and the Cabinet wives.

As for the teas and the garden party for the women executives, I discovered that a great many women who held rather important positions in the government had never been in the White House or met the wives of the secretaries heading their departments. I had one large garden party in the spring and a series of teas during the winter season for these women, and I invited the wives of the Cabinet members to receive with me.

I include here a sample of my social calendar for one week. I think you will see that a president's wife is not exactly idle.

Monday
1:00 p.m.   Lunch with Mrs. Hull
4:00 p.m.   Tea for 175 guests
5:00 p.m.   Tea for 236 guests

Tuesday
1:00 p.m.   Lunch with Mrs. Garner
4:00 p.m.   Tea for members of Delaware Democratic Club
4:30 p.m.   Tea for foreign diplomats' wives
7:00 p.m.   Dinner for 22
9:00 p.m.   Judicial reception

Wednesday
4:00 p.m.   tea for 266 guests
5:00 p.m.   tea for 256 guests

Thursday
1:00 p.m.   Formal luncheon for 52 guests
4:00 p.m.   Tea, women's division of Infantile Paralysis Foundation
5:00 p.m.   Tea for Executive Board of the Federation of Women's Clubs

Friday
1:00 p.m.   Lunch for wives of cabinet members
8:00 p.m.   Diplomatic dinner—94 guests
            197 additional guests for music after dinner.

I am also giving some figures on the number of people who visited the White House in normal years as well as the number who had tea, lunch or dinner, or evening refreshments in the White House.

During the year of 1939:

    4,729 people came to a meal
      323 people were house guests
    9,211 people came to tea
    14,056 people were received at teas, receptions, etc.; all of them had
some light refreshments
    1,320,300 people visited the public rooms of which 264,060 had special
passes from their Congressmen to see the state dining room, the Red
Room, the Blue Room and the Green Room.

The average attendance at the Easter Egg Rolling was 53,108. The
record shows that 180 children were lost and found; two people were sent
to the emergency hospital; six people fainted and twenty-two had to be
treated for small abrasions.

After I finished the morning routine of seeing the three people I have
already mentioned—Mrs. Nesbitt, Mrs. Helm and the usher—Miss Thompson came into my sitting room to begin work on the mail. We had to work
out a completely new system for handling the correspondence. We found
that most of the mail in former administrations had been answered by
form letters; Ralph Magee, head of the correspondence bureau, had copies
of forms used in President Cleveland's administration!

After I had fulfilled my obligations to my guests, whether at formal or
informal parties, I signed the mail and read such letters as I had not seen
before, wrote on other letters an outline of what I wanted said in reply
and laid aside those that I had to dictate answers to. This often kept me
busy far into the night. Before I went to bed I returned these baskets to
Miss Thompson's desk so she could work on them in the morning. As
soon as she came to my desk in the morning we attended to the letters
that had to be dictated.

Personal work, such as my column, articles, books, radio scripts and the
like, was always done on overtime for which I personally compensated
Miss Thompson so that there could be no question of her using time that
belonged to the government for work that was purely personal. This work
was done in the evenings and on Saturdays and Sundays. In all the years
we were in Washington I could never drive Miss Thompson away for a
holiday, so she had much accumulated leave which she never used and

which, under civil service rules, she could not claim when we left Washington.

From March, 1933, to the end of the year I received 301,000 pieces of mail. The year before the 1940 election I received about 100,000 letters. The campaign for a third term, the draft, and various other administration measures caused it to increase. During the war it assumed large proportions but was, of course, of an entirely different character than it had been during the depression years.

The variety of the requests and the apparent confidence that I would be able to make almost anything possible always worried me. Many of the requests, of course, were not honest. I tried from the beginning to find people in various communities to whom I could refer letters that sounded desperate. Miss Thompson was always accusing me of being too soft-hearted, but I caught her once about to send money for a dress and shoes and underclothes to a young girl who wrote that she was going to be graduated from high school, was to be the valedictorian of her class, and had only her brother's overalls and shoes to wear. She, too thoughtfully, I felt, included a page from a mail-order catalogue with sizes, colors, prices, and so on, all carefully written in. I was suspicious and asked someone to investigate and we found the whole story was untrue. The child's parents were fairly comfortably off, and she was not the valedictorian of her class—she wasn't even graduating. She simply wanted some new clothes.

In addition to the regular duties I have already mentioned, there were my press conferences. I soon discovered that the women reporters in Washington were living precariously. People were losing their jobs on every hand, and unless the women reporters could find something new to write about, the chances were that some of them would hold their jobs a very short time.

Miss Lorena Hickok, who had been assigned by the AP to "cover" me, pointed out many of these things, because she felt a sense of responsibility for the other women writers. My press conferences were her suggestion. I consulted Louis Howe and he agreed that I should hold them regularly for women reporters.

I realized that I must not trespass on my husband's prerogatives, that national and international news must be handled by him, but it seemed to me there were many things in my own activities that might be useful. It was new and untried ground and I was feeling my way with some trepidation.

Louis Howe was responsible for my confidence in newspaper reporters. He had a high regard for his own craft and insisted that newspaper people were the most honorable group in the world. I took it for granted that the women would be as honorable as the men, and my confidence was seldom betrayed.

Every press conference was a battle of wits, and at times it was not easy for me, nor, I imagine, for them. For instance, when they were trying to find out whether Franklin would run for a third term, they asked all sorts of trick questions, such as: "Will the social season next winter be the same as usual?" Or: "Where would you hang all these prints in Hyde Park?" Usually I was able to detect the implications of the questions and avoid any direct answer, for Louis Howe had trained me well. My press conferences did not bother me or my husband as much as they seemed to worry other people. I believe the reporters and I came through with mutual respect.

Seventeen

The First Year: 1933

DURING THE EARLY White House days when I was busy with organizing my side of the household, my husband was meeting one problem after another. It had a most exhilarating effect on him. Decisions were being made, new ideas were being tried, people were going to work and businessmen who ordinarily would have scorned government assistance were begging the government to find solutions for their problems.

What was interesting to me about the administration of those days was the willingness of everyone to co-operate with everyone else. As conditions grew better, of course, people's attitudes changed, but fundamentally it was that spirit of co-operation that pulled us out of the depression. Congress, which traditionally never has a long honeymoon with a new president, even when the political majority is of his party, went along during those first few months, delegating powers to the President and passing legislation that it would never have passed except during a crisis.

Soon after the inauguration of 1933 we began to have a succession of visitors whom after dinner Franklin would take upstairs to his study. There were two reasons why these particular people were invited to the White House those first years. One was that the economic and political situation in the world made it necessary for him to establish contacts with the leaders of other countries; the other was his desire to build new contacts for better understanding on this continent and abroad.

For the heads of nations, Franklin worked out a reception which he thought made them feel that the United States recognized the importance of their governments. If the guests arrived in the afternoon we had tea for the entire party; afterwards, all but the most important guests went to a hotel or to their own embassy. Later Blair House, across Pennsyl-

173

vania Avenue, was acquired by the government and arranged for the use of important visitors. The head of a government spent one night in the White House, accompanied by his wife if she was with him. There usually was a state dinner with conversation or music afterwards. The following morning Franklin and his guest would often have another talk before the guest went over to Blair House or to his embassy.

One of our first guests in 1933 was Ramsay MacDonald, who came with his daughter, Ishbel. We enjoyed meeting him, but even then we sensed in him a certain weariness. The loss of his wife had been a great blow to him. In many ways his daughter was a more vivid and vital person than he.

I think Franklin believed even then that it was most important for the English-speaking nations of the world to understand one another, whether the crisis was economic or, as later, military. This did not mean that he always agreed with the policies of these other countries; but he recognized the importance to us and to them of good feeling and understanding and co-operation.

The prime minister of Canada also came to stay with us that first spring, so that he and my husband and the prime minister of Great Britain could more or less co-ordinate their common interests.

In the same period Edouard Herriot, the French statesman, also arrived in Washington. As I look over the lists of what seem to be an unbelievable number of guests that first year, I find that we received an Italian mission, a German mission, and a Chinese mission, and even a Japanese envoy who came to lunch. Other guests included the governor general of the Philippines, Frank Murphy, later on the Supreme Court, who brought with him Manuel Quezon; the prime minister of New Zealand, who came with his wife to lunch; and His Highness Prince Ras Desta Dember, special ambassador of the Emperor of Ethiopia.

The President of Panama also paid us a visit. He was not the only guest from our own hemisphere. There was a stag dinner for the Brazilian delegation; we received a special ambassador from the Argentine; the Mexican envoy came to lunch; and the Brazilian envoy returned, after a trip through the country, to report on his travels.

Franklin had a deep conviction that we must learn to understand and to get on with our neighbors in this hemisphere. He believed it was up to us, who had been to blame in many ways for a big brother attitude which was not acceptable to our neighbors, to make the first effort. So even at that early date he was beginning to lay down through personal contacts the policy of the Good Neighbor, which was to become of increasing importance.

From the time we moved to Washington in 1933, Louis Howe became more and more of an invalid. At first he was able to be in his office and to keep his finger on much that was going on, and the second bonus march on Washington by the veterans of World War I he handled personally.

The first march, which had taken place in Mr. Hoover's administration, was still fresh in everybody's mind. I shall never forget my feeling of horror when I learned that the Army had actually been ordered to evict the veterans from their encampment. In the chaos that followed, the veterans' camp on the Anacostia flats was burned and many people were injured, some of them seriously. This one incident shows what fear can make people do, for Mr. Hoover was a Quaker, who abhorred violence, and General MacArthur, his chief of staff, must have known how many veterans would resent the order and never forget it. They must have known, too, the effect it would have on public opinion.

When the second bonus march took place in March of 1933 I was greatly worried for fear nothing would be done to prevent a similar tragedy. However, after talking the situation over with Louis Howe, Franklin immediately decided that the veterans should be housed in an old camp and provided with food through the relief administration. Louis spent hours talking with the leaders. I think they held their meetings in a government auditorium and were heard by the proper people in Congress. As a result, everything was orderly.

Although Louis often asked me to take him for a drive in the afternoon, I was rather surprised one day when he insisted that I drive him out to the veterans' camp just off Potomac Drive. When we arrived he announced that he was going to sit in the car but that I was to walk around among the veterans and see just how things were. Hesitatingly I got out and walked over to where I saw a line-up of men waiting for food. They looked at me curiously and one of them asked my name and what I wanted. When I said I just wanted to see how they were getting on, they asked me to join them.

After their bowls were filled with food, I followed them into the big eating hall. I was invited to say a few words to them—I think I mentioned having gone over the battle fronts in 1919—and then they sang for me some of the old army songs. After lunch I was asked to look into several other buildings, and finally we came to the hospital that had been set up for them.

I did not spend as much as an hour there; then I got into the car and drove away. Everyone waved and I called, "Good luck," and they answered, "Good-by and good luck to you." There had been no excitement, and my only protection had been a weary gentleman, Louis Howe, who had slept in the car during my entire visit.

Most of us who watched Louis could tell that he was failing. He sat a good deal of the time in his room, surrounded by newspapers, but up to the last few months his advice was still valuable. He died on April 18, 1936, at the naval hospital in Washington. He had lived in the White House until a short time before his death.

I always felt that the loss of Louis's influence and knowledge and companionship was a great blow to my husband. Louis had seemed to have an acute sense of the need for keeping a balance in Franklin's appointments, making sure that my husband saw a cross section of people and heard a variety of points of view. While Louis was alive, I had fewer complaints from various groups that they had been excluded than ever again. Considering how many people want to see the President and how hard it is to keep some semblance of balance, I think Louis did a remarkable job. He tried to see that all points of view reached Franklin so that he would make no decision without full consideration.

The President's wife does not go out informally except on rare occasions to old friends. Now and then, in the spring, Elinor Morgenthau and I stole away in my car or hers, and stopped in at some little place for lunch or tea. Driving my own car was one of the issues the Secret Service people and I had a battle about at the very start. The Secret Service prefers to have an agent go with the President's wife, but I did not want either a chauffeur or a Secret Service agent always with me; I never did consent to having a Secret Service agent.

After the head of the Secret Service found I was not going to allow an agent to accompany me everywhere, he went one day to Louis Howe, plunked a revolver down on the table and said, "Well, all right, if Mrs. Roosevelt is going to drive around the country alone, at least ask her to carry this in the car." I carried it religiously and during the summer I asked a friend, a man who had been one of Franklin's bodyguards in New York

State, to give me some practice in target shooting so that if the need arose I would know how to use the gun. After considerable practice, I finally learned to hit a target. I would never have used it on a human being, but I thought I ought to know how to handle a revolver if I had to have one in my possession.

Always, when my husband and I met after a trip that either of us had taken, we tried to arrange for an uninterrupted meal so that we could hear the whole story while it was fresh and not dulled by repetition. That I became, as the years went by, a better reporter and a better observer was largely owing to the fact that Franklin's questions covered such a wide range. I found myself obliged to notice everything. For instance, when I returned from a trip around the Gaspé, he wanted to know not only what kind of fishing and hunting was possible in that area but what the life of the fisherman was, what he had to eat, how he lived, what the farms were like, how the houses were built, what type of education was available, and whether it was completely church-controlled like the rest of the life in the village.

When I spoke of Maine, he wanted to know about everything I had seen on the farms I visited, the kinds of homes and the types of people, how the Indians seemed to be getting on and where they came from.

Franklin never told me I was a good reporter nor, in the early days, were any of my trips made at his request. I realized, however, that he would not question me so closely if he were not interested, and I decided this was the only way I could help him, outside of running the house, which was soon organized and running itself under Mrs. Nesbitt.

In the autumn I was invited by the Quakers to investigate the conditions that they were making an effort to remedy in the coal-mining areas of West Virginia. My husband agreed that it would be a good thing to do, so the visit was arranged. I had not been photographed often enough then to be recognized, so I was able to spend a whole day going about the area near Morgantown, West Virginia, without anyone's discovering who I was.

The conditions I saw convinced me that with a little leadership there could develop in the mining areas, if not a people's revolution, at least a people's party patterned after some of the previous parties born of bad economic conditions. There were men in that area who had been on relief for from three to five years and who had almost forgotten what it was like to have a job at which they could work for more than one or two days a week. There were children who did not know what it was to sit down at a table and eat a proper meal.

One story which I brought home from that trip I recounted at the dinner table one night. In a company house I visited, where the people had evidently seen better days, the man showed me his weekly pay slips. A small amount had been deducted toward his bill at the company store and for his rent and for oil for his mine lamp. These deductions left him less than a dollar in cash each week. There were six children in the family, and they acted as though they were afraid of strangers. I noticed a bowl on the table filled with scraps, the kind that you or I might give to a dog, and I saw children, evidently looking for their noonday meal, take a handful out of that bowl and go out munching. That was all they had to eat.

As I went out, two of the children had gathered enough courage to stand by the door, the little boy holding a white rabbit in his arms. It was evident that it was a most cherished pet. The little girl was thin and scrawny, and had a gleam in her eyes as she looked at her brother. She said, "He thinks we are not going to eat it, but we are," and at that the small boy fled down the road clutching the rabbit closer than ever.

It happened that William C. Bullitt was at dinner that night and I have always been grateful to him for the check he sent me the next day, saying he hoped it might help to keep the rabbit alive.

This trip to the mining areas was my first contact with the work being done by the Quakers. I liked the theory of trying to put people to work to help themselves. The men were started on projects and taught to use their abilities to develop new skills. The women were encouraged to revive any household arts they might once have known but which they had neglected in the drab life of the mining village.

This was only the first of many trips into the mining districts but it was the one that started the homestead idea. The University of West Virginia, in Morgantown, had already created a committee to help the miners on the Quaker agricultural project. With that committee and its experience as a nucleus, the government obtained the loan of one of the university's people, Mr. Bushrod Grimes, and established the Resettlement Administration. Louis Howe created a small advisory committee on which I, Mr. Pickett, and others served. It was all experimental work, but it was designed to get people off relief, to put them to work building their own homes and to give them enough land to start growing food.

It was hoped that business would help by starting on each of these projects an industry in which some of the people could find regular work. A few small industries were started but they were not often successful. Only a few of the resettlement projects had any measure of success; nevertheless, I have always felt that the good they did was incalculable. Conditions were so nearly the kind that breed revolution that the men and women needed to be made to feel their government's interest and concern.

I began to hear very serious reports of conditions in Logan County, West Virginia, where for many years whole families had been living in tents because they had been evicted from company houses after a strike. All the men had been blacklisted and could not get work anywhere; they were existing on the meager allowance that the State of West Virginia provided for the unemployed. Now the tents were worn out, illness was rampant, and no one had any medical care. Finally Mrs. Leonard Elmhirst and I established a clinic to take care of the children. When I told my husband of the conditions there he said to talk to Harry Hopkins and to tell him that these families must be out of tents by Christmas. It was done, and for two years, out of my radio money and Mrs. Elmhirst's generosity, we tried to remedy among the children the effects of conditions which had existed for many years.

I came to know very well a stream near Morgantown called Scott's Run, or Bloody Run, because of the violent strikes that once occurred in the mines there. Some of the company houses, perched on hills on either side of the run, seemed scarcely fit for human habitation. The homestead project started near Morgantown was called Arthurdale and took in people from all the nearby mining villages.

One of the first people to go to Arthurdale was Bernard M. Baruch, who helped me to establish the original school and always took a great interest in the project, even visiting it without me on some occasions. I have always hoped that he got as much satisfaction as I did out of the change in the children after they had been living on the project for six months.

The homestead projects were attacked in Congress, for the most part by men who had never seen for themselves the plight of the miners or what we were trying to do for them. There is no question that much money was spent, perhaps some of it unwisely. The projects were all experimental. In Arthurdale, for instance, though the University of West Virginia recommended the site, apparently nobody knew what was afterwards discovered—that there was a substratum of porous rock which finally caused great expense in making the water supply safe. Nevertheless, I have always felt that many human beings who might have cost us thousands of dollars in tuberculosis sanitariums, insane asylums, and jails were restored to usefulness and given confidence in themselves. Later, when during World War II, I met boys from that area I could not help thinking that a great many of them were able to serve their country only because of the things that had been done to help their parents through the depression period.

Nothing we learn in this world is ever wasted and I have come to the conclusion that practically nothing we do ever stands by itself. If it is good, it will serve some good purpose in the future. If it is evil, it may haunt us and handicap our efforts in unimagined ways.

Years later, after the Social Security Act was passed, I saw how it worked in individual cases in this area. There was a mine accident in which several men were killed, and my husband asked me to go down and find out what the people were saying. One man received the Carnegie medal posthumously because he had gone back into the mine to help rescue other men. His widow had several children, so her social security benefits would make her comfortable. In talking to another widow who had three children and a fourth about to be born, I asked how she was going to manage. She seemed quite confident and told me: "My sister and her two children will come to live with us. I am going to get social security benefits of nearly sixty-five dollars a month. I pay fifteen dollars a month on my house and land, and I shall raise vegetables and have chickens and with the money from the government I will get along very well. In the past probably the mine company might have given me a small check and often the other miners took up a collection if they could afford it, but this income from the government I can count on until my children are grown."

Two other events of that first autumn in Washington stand out in my mind. On November 17, 1933, Henry Morgenthau, Jr., was sworn in as undersecretary of the treasury in the Oval Room in the White House, thus starting on his long and arduous labors in the Treasury Department. When Secretary Woodin resigned, Henry Morgenthau succeeded him and held the office until shortly after my husband's death, when he also resigned and left Washington.

On that same day my husband and Mr. Litvinov held the final conversations on the recognition of the Soviet Union. There was considerable excitement over the first telephone conversation between the two countries which took place between Mr. Litvinov in the White House and his wife and son in Russia. The ushers noted it in their daily record book because, while there had been overseas conversations with many other European countries, this was the opening of diplomatic relations with Russia.

Needless to say, among some of my husband's old friends there was considerable opposition to the recognition of Russia. His mother came to him before the announcement was made to tell him she had heard rumors that he was about to recognize Russia, but that she felt this would be a disastrous move and widely misunderstood by the great majority of their old friends.

Not only his old friends but with various other people my husband had frequent run-ins over the new theory that government had a responsibility to the people. I remember that when Senator Carter Glass insisted that Virginia needed no relief, Franklin suggested that he take a drive with him to see some of the bad spots. The senator never accepted his invitation.

The opening of diplomatic relations with Russia and our relations in this hemisphere were the administration's first points of attack in our foreign policy, but the major emphasis in those early years was and had to be on questions of domestic policy and our internal economic recovery.

As I look back over the actual measures undertaken in this first year I realize that the one in which my husband took the greatest pleasure was the establishment on April 5, 1933, of the Civilian Conservation Corps camps. The teen-age youngster, the boy finishing high school, the boy who had struggled to get through college, were all at loose ends. There was no organization except the Army that had the tents and other supplies essential for a setup of this kind, which was why part of the program was promptly put under its jurisdiction.

Franklin realized that the boys should be given some other kind of education as well, but it had to be subordinate to the day's labor required of them. The Civilian Conservation Corps had a triple value: it gave the boys a chance to see different parts of their own country, and to learn to do a good day's work in the open, which benefited them physically; also it gave them a cash income, part of which went home to their families. This helped the morale both of the boys themselves and of the people at home. The idea was his own contribution to the vast scheme of relief rehabilitation planning.

This was followed on June 16 by the National Recovery Act, with General Hugh Johnson in charge. The basic importance of the NRA was that it made it easier for the industrialist who wanted to do the right thing. The chiseler and the man who was willing to profit by beating down his labor could no longer compete unfairly with the man who wanted to earn a decent profit but to treat his employees fairly. The NRA was declared unconstitutional almost two years later. I thought this was unfortunate, for it seemed a simple way to keep bad employers doing what was right.

The Public Works Administration, which came into being on the same day, made it possible for the government to plan and undertake public works during this period of depression. It helped to take up the slack of unemployment by lending money to the states for projects that they could not finance by themselves.

Five months later, in November, 1933, the Civil Works Administration was set up and in time put four million unemployed to work.

In my travels around the country I saw many things built both by PWA and by CWA. I also saw the results of the work done by CCC. The achievements of these agencies began to dot city and rural areas alike. Soil conservation and forestry work went forward, recreation areas were built, and innumerable bridges, schools, hospitals and sanitation projects were constructed—lasting monuments to the good work done under these agencies. It is true they cost the people of the country vast sums of money, but they did a collective good and left tangible results which are evident today. They pulled the country out of the depression and made it possible for us to fight the greatest and most expensive war in our history.

Perhaps the most far-reaching project was the Tennessee Valley Authority. That was Senator George Norris' greatest dream and no one who witnessed the development of the Authority will ever forget the fight he put up for something that many people ridiculed. The development had been begun during World War I, but at the end of that war most of the work was stopped. Nothing further was done until my husband, who understood Senator Norris' vision, supplied the impetus at a time when it could accomplish the maximum results for the country. With the demands of a possible war in mind, Franklin insisted on pushing work on the TVA as rapidly as possible. He believed even then that under certain circumstances war might come soon, and he knew if that happened we would need everything the TVA could make available.

In the campaign of 1932 my husband and I had gone through some of the TVA area, and he had been deeply impressed by the crowds at the stations. They were so poor; their houses were unpainted, their cars were dilapidated, and many grownups as well as children were without shoes or adequate garments. Scarcely eight years later, after the housing and educational and agricultural experiments had had time to take effect, I went through the same area, and a more prosperous region would have been hard to find. I have always wished that those who oppose authorities to create similar benefits in the valleys of other great rivers could have seen the contrast as I saw it. I realize that such changes must come gradually, but I hate to see nothing done. I wish, as my husband always wished, that year by year we might be making a start on the Missouri River and the headwaters of the Mississippi. Such experiments, changing for the better the life of the people, would be a mighty bulwark against attacks on our democracy.

Eighteen

The Peaceful Years: 1934-1936

THE YEARS from 1934 to 1936 seem to me the least anxious of any we spent in the White House. The reforms instituted were beginning to put the country back on a more even keel; good feeling existed generally between capital and labor and between the President and Congress; and in our family life we had gradually managed to adapt our private traditions and habits to the exigencies of the White House.

In the spring of 1934 Franklin suggested that I make a trip to Puerto Rico. General Blanton Winship, governor of the island at that time, was faced with great difficulties. Labor conditions were bad, and there was not enough food for the constantly increasing population. The sugar companies owned large tracts of land and, because the work was seasonal and the wages pitifully small, the workers practically starved in off-seasons. Rexford Tugwell, who was then in the Department of Agriculture, was going down to make a study of what could be done in that field, and my husband thought if I went, too, it might show the people that he was really interested in conditions there.

Following the careful program laid out for me, I visited a number of rural schools, some of which were trying to improve the quality of education offered the children. I also saw the homework done by the women. Factory wages were low and the amount paid for homework was unbelievably small. Little girls sat all during their lunch hour in school embroidering handkerchiefs in order to add a few pennies to the family income.

The conditions in rural homes were unsanitary enough, but in the towns they were even more shocking. I remember going down a street, looking into the houses of factory workers. Most of them consisted of two rooms; the back room had no light, and practically the only light in the

184

front room came through the doorway. There were no screens and, of course, no plumbing or other modern conveniences. Many of the women cooked out of doors on little stoves.

The real slums were actually worse, in the capital city. Huts made of bits of tin and scrap iron and wood picked up after the last hurricane were built out over the water. We walked on duckboards placed precariously over the piling, and the water came up under every house.

There was one slum which clung precariously to the side of a cliff. Here goats and other animals lived under the houses. Again, there was no sanitation, and typhoid was common. If it had not been for the climate and the diet of rice and beans bought from the United States, there probably would have been a great deal of rickets. Tuberculosis took a heavy toll. Every year more and more children were born, which made the question of population a matter for serious thought.

From Puerto Rico we went to the Virgin Islands where, bad though some of the conditions were, they seemed slightly better than in Puerto Rico. Efforts were being made there as well as in Puerto Rico to put up some new houses, but the people had to be taught how to use them. They did not know how to live decently even under better physical conditions, because the circumstances under which they had been forced to live had made cleanliness almost impossible.

On my return I begged my husband to send down some labor people and industrialists to look over the situation. Some of my friends have since gone there to develop new industries and I think several small industries are going successfully. When Mr. Tugwell later became governor of Puerto Rico, he tried to carry out many of the ideas he had thought, on his first trip, might help, but the islands still remain a difficult problem and one which the United States is far from having solved satisfactorily.

In the summer of 1934 my husband decided to make a trip through the Caribbean and the Panama Canal and out to Hawaii, taking with him our two youngest sons, Franklin Junior and John. The newspapermen traveled on a separate ship, visiting Franklin every now and then. I remember his telling me with gleeful chuckles that he had had to provide the newspapermen with the historical background of most of the places where they stopped. Once they reached Hawaii, he and the boys had a wonderful time. He enjoyed meeting the native Queen and eating poi, which few members of the party really liked.

In the winter of 1936 Louis Howe finally moved from the White House to the hospital. We kept telling him and ourselves that he was going to improve and come back again, but suddenly word came that he had died. It was one of the greatest losses that my husband sustained. He was to have others and all were hard to bear, because in public life you can have no private time for sorrow. Duties must be performed and your own feelings must be suppressed. Louis's death deprived my husband of a close relationship and the satisfaction of having someone near to whom he could talk frankly, whose advice he might not always follow but whose presence was stimulating.

Louis Howe's death left a great gap in my husband's life. I have always felt that if Louis had lived the number of people drawn closely but briefly into the working and social orbits of Franklin's life would have been fewer. For one reason and another, no one quite filled the void which unconsciously he was seeking to fill, and each one in turn disappeared from the scene, occasionally with bitterness which I understood but always regretted. There are not many men whose personal ambition is to accomplish things for someone else, and it was some time before a friendship with Harry Hopkins, somewhat different but similar in certain ways, again brought Franklin some of the satisfaction he had known with Louis.

What worries we had in those two years from 1934 to 1936 were largely such personal ones as this. In fact, we approached the campaign of 1936 with a feeling that the country was getting back on its feet. I did no formal work in that campaign, though I visited the campaign headquarters and went with Franklin on some of his trips. To tell the truth, I never felt it was good taste to go out and electioneer for my husband, so in none of the campaigns did I take any particular part in the political activities unless I was specially asked to for some specific reason.

When the returns came in on election night, Maine and Vermont were found to be still in the Republican fold. My husband said with a wicked twinkle in his eye: "I knew I should have gone to Maine and Vermont, but Jim wouldn't let me."

There was no uncertainty or waiting for the returns this election. As usual we were at Hyde Park, where the dining room on election night was always turned into what seemed to me the nearest thing to a newspaper office. The machines on which news came in were set up in a little room off the dining room. Franklin himself had telephones, long dispatches were handed to him by relays of people, and everybody made out averages. I was expected to show interest in the returns, but also to be with his mother in the library to help entertain the guests and keep them out of the dining room, except for a few favored individuals. The newspaper people would come and be given refreshments, and finally, when the returns came in, the people of the village of Hyde Park would have a torchlight parade and come to greet my husband. We would go out on the porch and listen to a few words from him, usually shivering in the cold.

When we went back to Washington in 1936, Franklin was received with great acclaim, and his second term of office began auspiciously. He had carried with him a big Democrat majority in the Congress, and the party members felt so secure that they began to believe they could do anything they wanted. That is a bad attitude for any group to adopt, particularly when responsible for the smooth running of a country that has only just become stabilized after a great depression.

Throughout all those early years in Washington, one of Franklin's major interests was in changing the bad feeling that existed between us and our Latin-American neighbors. After the November elections he made a personal effort to implement this policy by attending the Inter-American Conference for the Maintenance of Peace, held in Buenos Aires, in 1936. He was deeply touched by the evident enthusiasm that his trip created and particularly happy that he seemed able to inaugurate the good feeling that he so greatly desired to see grow.

This trip and all other trips that had diplomatic significance were planned in consultation with Secretary Hull and the State Department. Sumner Welles, Franklin's able undersecretary of state, was not only particularly well informed about South American affairs but also very much in sympathy with what Franklin was trying to do in Latin America, and he supported the Good Neighbor policy wholeheartedly. Franklin found him an excellent coworker and counted on him for help with detailed background information. I think, however, that Franklin's own good will toward the governments and people of these countries was an important aid to the State Department in making our policy effective.

On the way home Franklin stopped in Uruguay. He always liked to tell the story of his greeting by the President of that country. When they met, he assured Franklin that he need not worry about anything happening to *him*, but since he, the President of Uruguay, had been threatened, Franklin must not be surprised if there were some shots. However, the President of the United States would not be the target. My husband got into the car and drove around, but in telling about it afterwards he said he could not help wondering if he might not get hit by mistake, even though he was not the target. However, no one was shot that day.

From Uruguay they went to Brazil, and Franklin again was much pleased by the enthusiasm that his visit called forth. It was there that he was given the gifts for me that later created so much comment in one of the newspaper columns and in radio broadcasts. For this reason I think it wise to tell the whole story here.

Undersecretary Welles was asked by President Vargas and his wife if they might send some gifts to me, for they knew the rule that no president of the United States or any government official could accept personal gifts from a foreign government while in office. Senhora Vargas sent me a beautiful hammered silver tea set and she and her husband together sent me, from their collection, a large aquamarine, one of the biggest and most perfect stones in the world. My husband presented me with these gifts on his return and I was deeply impressed by them, but realized that only in the White House or at some official gathering could such a large tea set be used. The stone was kept in my safe at the White House.

After Franklin's death I gave the tea set to the airplane carrier, U.S.S. *Franklin D. Roosevelt,* and I hope that the Brazilians were pleased to see it on the ship when she made a good-will visit there shortly after being put into commission.

I gave the aquamarine to Bernard Baruch in order that he might make some inquiries about its value. I had tried to have it appraised, but no jeweler seemed able to tell me its exact value. At that time Drew Pearson, the columnist, announced that I was about to sell this stone, that it had been given to my husband and not to me, and that it was valued at $25,000. I was appalled at the thought that I might be accused of having kept out of my husband's estate something that had actually belonged to him.

I had not wanted to give this stone to the Franklin D. Roosevelt Library because I felt it had little connection with any of my husband's collections. I hoped to do something with it that would in some way benefit the Brazilian people. Fortunately, I discovered that Mr. Welles knew all about the presentation of this gift to my husband for me, and he told me that it would give great pleasure to the Brazilian people if the stone were placed with Franklin's other collections in the Library at Hyde Park. It is there now.

While Franklin was in South America, Miss Thompson and I went on my first real lecture trip. In the spring I had undertaken four lectures in the Middle West and I had not felt happy about them; this was to be my first trip under the W. Colston Leigh Lecture Bureau.

These trips gave me a wonderful opportunity to visit all kinds of places and to see and get to know a good cross section of people. Always during my free time I visited as many government projects as possible, often managing to arrive without advance notice so that they could not be polished up for my inspection. I began to see for myself some of the results of my husband's actions during the first hundred days of his administration, and in meeting and talking with people all over the country I got the full impact of what the new programs had meant to them. It was evident that the home and farm loans, for example, had saved many a family from outright disaster.

Of course, I always reported to Franklin upon my return, but aside from any value my reports may have been to him, I had another, more personal, reason for wanting to make these trips. All the years I lived in Washington I was preparing for the time when we should no longer be there. I did not want to give up my interests in New York City, because I always felt that someday I would go back. I never anticipated that so many years would pass before I left Washington. I kept expecting to leave at the end of every four years.

During those years in Washington we tried to maintain our home traditions as well as those that had been established in the White House, particularly in regard to the celebration of holidays. Christmas Eve in Washington was usually a busy day for me. I started by going to a party for underprivileged children, given by the welfare council at the National Theater. Then I joined my husband to wish all the people in the executive offices a merry Christmas.

Usually at lunchtime I had to be at the Salvation Army headquarters, where we had a service just before the food baskets were given out. I am afraid that during the depression years these services had an unchristian effect upon me, because invariably, before receiving their baskets, the poor wretches were told how grateful they should be. I knew if I were in their shoes I would be anything but grateful. From there I went to the Volunteers of America for the same sort of service and giving of food baskets, returning home in time for the afternoon party in the East Room.

After the party my husband and I and any of the family that were with us went to the lighting of the Community Christmas Tree, where my husband broadcast a Christmas message. Then he would return to the White House while I went on to a Christmas tree in one of the alleys (the slums of Washington), where again we sang carols. As I looked at the poor people about me I could not help wondering what Christmas could mean to those children.

Returning home I would find my husband reading Dickens' *The Christmas Carol* to any of the family that were gathered together. Having a great sense of the dramatic, he always put a good deal of drama into his reading of the parts about the ghosts. Whenever he read anything aloud like this, he acted it out straight through, which was why he held the attention of the little children so well, even before they could understand the meaning of the words. After the stockings had been filled, Miss Thompson and I nearly always went to midnight services at St. Thomas Church.

My husband liked to be in the White House on New Year's Eve. We always gathered a few friends, and at midnight in the oval study the radio was turned on and we waited with the traditional eggnog in hand for midnight to be announced. Franklin always sat in his big chair and, as the President, would raise his glass and say: "To the United States of America." All of us stood and repeated the toast after him. Somehow the words were especially meaningful and impressive in that house and gave a touch of solemnity to the personal greetings that followed.

Nineteen

Second Term: 1936-1937

FRANKLIN DID NOT talk a great deal about the work he was doing, either at meals or in private family conversations. Most of us felt that when he was with his family he should have a respite from the concerns of his office.

When an administration bill was up before Congress, we often found that the number of Congressmen coming to his study in the evenings increased. I learned that I must make an evaluation of the bills on which he had to get support. He calculated votes closely on what was known as the administration policy, and considered "must" legislation.

Only bills that were "must" legislation got full administration support. In the first years these were largely economic measures; later on, they were measures for defense. While I often felt strongly on various subjects, Franklin frequently refrained from supporting causes in which he believed, because of political realities. There were times when this annoyed me very much. In the case of the Spanish Civil War, for instance, we had to remain neutral, though Franklin wanted the democratic government to be success-ful. But he also knew he could not get Congress to go along with him. To justify his action, or lack of action, he explained to me, when I complained, that the League of Nations had asked us to remain neutral. By trying to convince me that our course was correct he was simply trying to salve his own conscience, because he himself was uncertain. It was one of the many times when I felt akin to a hairshirt.

I also remember wanting to get all-out support for the anti-lynching bill and the removal of the poll tax, but though Franklin was in favor of both measures, they never became "must" legislation. When I would protest, he would simply say: "First things first. I can't alienate certain votes I

191

need for measures that are more important at the moment by pushing any measure that would entail a fight." And as the situation in Europe grew worse, preparations for war had to take precedence over everything else. That was always "must" legislation, and Franklin knew it would not pass if there was a party split.

Often people came to me to enlist his support for an idea. Although I might present the situation to him, I never urged on him a specific course of action, no matter how strongly I felt, because I realized that he knew of factors in the picture as a whole of which I might be ignorant.

One of the ideas I agreed to present to Franklin was that of setting up a national youth administration. Harry Hopkins, then head of the WPA, and Aubrey Williams, his deputy administrator and later head of the National Youth Administration, knew how deeply troubled I had been from the beginning about the plight of the country's young people. One day they said: "We have come to you about this because we do not feel we should talk to the President about it as yet. There may be many people against the establishment of such an agency in the government and there may be bad political repercussions. We do not know that the country will accept it. We do not even like to ask the President, because we do not think he should be put in a position where he has to say officially 'yes' or 'no' now."

I agreed to try to find out what Franklin's feelings were and to put before him their opinions and fears. I waited until my usual time for discussing questions with him and went into his room just before he went to sleep. I described the whole idea, which he already knew something of, and then told him of the fears that Harry Hopkins and Aubrey Williams had about such an agency. He looked at me and asked: "Do they think it is right to do this?" I said they thought it might be a great help to the young people, but they did not want him to forget that it might be unwise politically. They felt that a great many people who were worried by the fact that Germany had regimented its youth might feel we were trying to do the same thing in this country. Then Franklin said: "If it is the right thing to do for the young people, then it should be done. I guess we can stand the criticism, and I doubt if our youth can be regimented in this way or in any other way."

I went back to Harry Hopkins and Aubrey Williams the next day with Franklin's message. Shortly after, the NYA came into being and undoubtedly benefited many young people. It offered projects to help high school and college youngsters to finish school, and provided training in both resident and nonresident projects, supplementing the work of the Civilian Conservation Corps in such a way as to aid all youth.

It was one of the occasions on which I was proud that the right thing was done regardless of political considerations. As a matter of fact, however, it turned out to be politically popular and strengthened the administration greatly.

I am reminded here of a story Miss Thompson told about the time I visited one of the prisons in Baltimore with Mr. Maury Maverick, who was in charge of prison industries during the war and wanted me to see the salvage work being done there. In order to fit the trip into my schedule I had to leave the White House early without saying good morning to Franklin. On his way to the office, he called to Tommy and asked where I was. "She's in prison, Mr. President," Tommy said. "I'm not surprised," said Franklin, "but what for?"

As time went by I found that people no longer considered me a mouthpiece for my husband but realized that I had a point of view of my own with which he might not at all agree. Then I felt freer to state my views. However, I always used some care, and sometimes I would send Franklin one of my columns about which I was doubtful. The only change he would ever suggest was occasionally in the use of a word, and that was simply a matter of style. Of course, this hands-off policy had its advantages for him, too; for it meant that my column could sometimes serve as a trial balloon. If some idea I expressed strongly—and with which he might agree —caused a violent reaction, he could honestly say that he had no responsibility in the matter and that the thoughts were my own.

Though Franklin himself never tried to discourage me and was undisturbed by anything I wanted to say or do, other people were frequently less happy about my actions. I knew, for instance, that many of my racial beliefs and activities in the field of social work caused Steve Early and Marvin McIntyre grave concern. They were afraid that I would hurt my husband politically and socially.

One afternoon I gave a garden party at the White House for the girls from the reform school in Washington, most of whom were colored. Steve thought that was unwise, politically, and I did get some bad publicity in the southern papers. Steve felt the same way about my work with the members of the American Youth Congress. Franklin, however, never said anything to me about it. I always felt that if Franklin's re-election depended

on such little things that I or any member of the family did, he could not
be doing the job the people in the country wanted him to do.

I know Franklin felt the same way. Many of his political advisers, as
well as some of the family, were deeply troubled over Elliott and Anna's
divorces, feeling that they would react unfavorably on my husband's
political career. In each case Franklin had done what he could to prevent
the divorce, but when he was convinced that the children had made up
their minds after careful reflection, it never occurred to him to suggest
that they should subordinate their lives to his interests. He said that he
thought a man in politics stood or fell by the results of his policies; that
what the children did or did not do affected their lives, and that he did
not consider that their lives should be tied to his political interests.

Sometimes Franklin carried his disregard of criticism too far. I was
appalled when, in 1937, he asked James to come to Washington as one
of his secretaries. James was delighted, for he had always been interested
in politics and thought the opportunity to help his father a great chance
to learn much and be really useful. I, however, could foresee the attacks
that would be made on his father for appointing him, and on James himself, and I could imagine all kinds of ways in which, through his necessarily political activities, he might get himself and his father into trouble.
I protested vehemently to Franklin and told him he was selfish to bring
James down. I talked to James and tried to persuade him not to come,
but he could see no objections. Finally I was silenced by my husband
saying to me: "Why should I be deprived of my eldest son's help and
the pleasure of having him with me just because I am the President?"
It did seem hard and what he said had a point. Nevertheless, I was unhappy, and I think my fears were justified by what actually happened.

Jimmy did a good job and it meant a great deal to Franklin to have
him, but he was more vulnerable to jealousies and rivalries than were the
other secretaries, and he did get into trouble when he began to work with
people in Congress. As a result of the work and anxiety, he developed
ulcers of the stomach and eventually had to go out to the Mayo Brothers
hospital for an operation. They told James the nervous strain was bad for
him, and he accepted their advice not to return to his duties at the White
House.

In 1937, about the time he brought Jimmy to Washington, Franklin
became much troubled over the decisions that the Supreme Court was
rendering. His advisers were divided, some of them feeling that it was un-

wise to have any change made in the Court. Franklin felt that if it was going to be possible to pass progressive legislation only to have it declared unconstitutional by the Supreme Court, no progress could be made. He also felt that people became too conservative as they grew older and that they should not be allowed to continue indefinitely to wield great power.

The defeat of the Supreme Court bill seemed to me to be a real blow to Franklin, but he spent no time in regrets and simply said, "Well, we'll see what will happen."

Later he was able, little by little, to change the complexion of the court. He remarked one day that he thought the fight had been worth while in spite of the defeat, because it had focused the attention of the public on the Supreme Court and its decisions, and he felt that aroused public interest was always helpful. He had a firm belief in the collective wisdom of the people when their interest was awakened and they really understood the issues at stake.

Though I had been in complete sympathy with what he was trying to do, I used to think that he might have saved himself a good deal of trouble just by waiting awhile, since it was death and resignations that really gave him the opportunity to appoint new people to the Supreme Court. However, if he had not made the fight, perhaps fewer people would have resigned.

As we neared the Congressional election in 1938, I could see that Franklin was again troubled. The way he had felt about the Supreme Court was in line with the way he felt about reactionary legislators. He believed it was essential to have liberal congresssmen if his liberal program was to continue. The fact that the Democratic party had a large majority had not unified it as a fighting group, but rather had divided it into factions; at times it seemed that within the Democratic party there was, to all intents and purposes, a group of people who might work better with the more conservative Republican party. This situation led to a division among the presidential advisers and within the Cabinet, and resulted finally in what was known as "the purge."

If there were political mistakes in this campaign, some of them, I think, might have been avoided if Louis Howe had been alive. After Louis's death, Franklin never had a political adviser who would argue with him, and still give him unquestioned loyalty. Louis gave Franklin the benefit of his sane, reasoned, careful political analysis and even if Franklin disagreed and was annoyed, he listened and respected Louis's political acumen.

Whether he ignored his advice or not, at least all the reasons against the disputed action had been clearly stated and argued.

In Harry Hopkins my husband found some of the companionship and loyalty Louis had given him, but not the political wisdom and careful analysis of each situation. Louis would argue, but Harry would not do this. He gave his opinion honestly, but because he knew Franklin did not like opposition too well—as who does?—he frequently agreed with him regardless of his own opinion, or tried to persuade him in indirect ways.

Louis Howe had been older than Franklin and, because he had helped him so greatly in so many ways during his early political life, could be more independent than Harry Hopkins. Franklin, in turn, shaped Harry; he widened his horizons and taught him many things about domestic politics and foreign affairs. Consequently, Harry's opinion did not carry the weight with Franklin that Louis's had.

Jim Farley would argue with Franklin, but never very effectively, because his reasons for advocating a course were always those of political expediency. Ed Flynn told him the truth as he saw it and argued fearlessly, but he was not always on hand. Consequently, after Louis died, Franklin frequently made his decisions without canvassing all sides of a question.

Much, of course, can be done by the vice-president, the speaker of the House, the party leaders both in the Senate and in the House, and the Cabinet members, if they develop strength in Congress. In the last analysis, however, the President is the one responsible for the action of his followers; when they do not follow, he feels that his leadership has been weakened. Of course, it is impossible to have 100 per cent agreement within a party, particularly when that party has a comfortable majority in Congress, but the larger proportion of it must be united to be effective.

Of course, Franklin did not expect Congress to go down the line on every occasion. From his lifelong study of American history, and from his own experience, he keenly appreciated the value of the checks and balances established in our government by the Founding Fathers. He realized that the willingness of Congress to vote whatever powers were necessary to meet an emergency was not a situation it was desirable to perpetuate in a democracy.

Franklin never resented constructive criticism from the members of Congress. What he did resent was the refusal of certain congressmen to understand the over-all needs of the country, the narrow point of view which let them pit their local interests against the national or international interest. Franklin always said that no leader could get too far ahead of his followers, and it was because he felt that Congress was close to the people that he had a healthy respect for its reaction to any of his proposals.

Franklin's activities in the campaign of 1938 were thought by many people to have been a political mistake. I am not a good enough politician to know, but I have tried here to set forth the reasons that I think actuated him.

Harry Hopkins threw his whole heart and all his abilities into organizing relief on a national scale. He was a man whom I not only admired but came to have a deep trust and confidence in. Later, after the death of his second wife, I began to see a side of him that I had not known before. It is a natural development, I imagine, to seek entertainment and diversion when your life is lonely. What surprised some of us was the fact that Harry seemed to get so much genuine pleasure out of contact with gay but more or less artificial society. People who could give him luxuries and the kind of party in which he probably never before had the slightest interest became important to him. I did not like this side of Harry as much as the side I first knew, but deep down he was a fine person who had the courage to bear pain and who loved his country enough to risk the curtailment of his life in order to be of service, after all chance of fulfilling any personal ambition was over.

My own work had to go on regardless of anything else. When I first went to Washington I had been writing a weekly column and a page in the *Woman's Home Companion,* as well as many articles for other magazines.

The weekly column seemed a dull affair, and finally an enterprising gentleman, Monte Bourjaily of the United Feature Syndicate, had an idea that he thought would vastly increase its interest. He said he felt sure that if I would write a daily column in the form of a diary it would be of great interest to the people of the United States, who were curious about the way anyone who lived in the White House passed his time, day after day. At first I thought it would be the most dreadful chore; but I was so dissatisfied with what I was doing in the way of writing that in January, 1936, I decided to sign a five-year contract with the United Feature Syndicate for a daily column, which would be shorter and perhaps for that reason easier to do. From that time on I wrote a column six days a week, and only once failed to get it in on time. I wrote Sundays through Fridays, which meant that I had Saturdays off. When I went on trips I sometimes had to write a number of columns ahead. Otherwise, I wrote the column during the morning or at noon every day, though occasionally, if the following day looked like a very busy one, I wrote it in the middle of the night before. It had to be in by six P.M. Writing this column became so much of a habit that when people remarked that it must be difficult to do I was always a little surprised.

When I went to the South Pacific in 1943 on a five weeks' trip, I did not take anyone with me to act as secretary. Every night, after a long day of hard work, I painfully typed my own column unless I had been able to do it on a flight during the day. I learned to type many years ago but, not having had much practice, I am slow, and it took me a long time to write about what I had done during the day.

The *Ladies' Home Journal* page, which I wrote from 1941 until the spring of 1949, when I moved over to *McCall's*, was an experience suggested to me by Mr. and Mrs. Bruce Gould and Mr. George Bye, who was then my literary agent. The page turned out to be a successful feature and is something that I really enjoyed, though I was much amused by some of the questions. Occasionally they were rude and personal, but on the whole, they came from people sincerely seeking information or asking for help. At first, unable to believe that people would really ask me some of the questions which were sent me, I accused the editorial staff of making them up. As a result, they always sent me the letters on which the questions were based. Frequently they took a number of letters containing questions on similar subjects and made one composite question.

At least, I have never known what it was to be bored or to have time hang heavily on my hands.

Twenty

The Royal Visitors

THE ARRIVAL of the Swedish crown prince and princess in the United States in the summer of 1938 marked the beginning of a series of visits from members of Europe's royal families. The people of Europe were deeply troubled by the general feeling of unrest and uncertainty on the Continent and were looking for friends in other parts of the world—hence their sudden interest in the United States.

The crown prince and princess were making a trip through the country to visit the various Swedish settlements, and on July 1 came to stay at Hyde Park, where we had a dinner for them. In May, the following year, the day after a dinner and musical for the President of Nicaragua and Señora de Somoza, we entertained the crown prince and princess of Denmark at tea. In June we had another South American guest when the chief of the Brazilian Army paid my husband a visit, and later that same month the crown prince and princess of Norway arrived and came to tea. They, like the other royal guests, visited the settlements of their countrymen here, later coming to Hyde Park for a short time.

In each case we had a few people to meet them at dinner and a picnic at Franklin's newly built stone cottage on top of the hill. There are a number of Norwegians living near us at Hyde Park who asked to put on a show for the crown prince and princess of Norway. I shall always remember that as one of our pleasantest parties.

We were to come to know Princess Marta and Prince Olaf and their children very well, for during the long years of the war, though the prince was here only occasionally, the princess with the children lived in this country.

At the time of his visit our impression was that the Danish prince was

199

more interested in his holiday than in the serious questions of the moment and had perhaps less realization of the menace of Hitler than we had expected of one in his position.

My husband welcomed these visits and encouraged everyone to come here whom he had any chance of persuading. Convinced that bad things were going to happen in Europe, he wanted to make contacts with those who he hoped would preserve and adhere to democracy and prove to be allies against fascism when the conflict came.

That same spring the King and Queen of England decided to visit the Dominion of Canada. They, too, were preparing for the blow that might fall and knew well that they would need the devotion of every subject in their dominions. My husband invited them to come to Washington because, believing that we all might soon be engaged in a life-and-death struggle, in which Great Britain would be our first line of defense, he hoped that their visit would create a bond of friendship between the peoples of the two countries. He knew that, though there is always a certain amount of criticism and superficial ill feeling toward the British in this country, in time of danger we stand firmly together, with confidence in our common heritage and ideas. The visit of the King and Queen, he hoped, would be a reminder of this deep bond. In many ways it proved even more successful than he had expected.

Their visit was carefully prepared for, but Franklin always behaved as though we were simply going to have two nice young people to stay with us. I think he gave some of the protocol people, both in the State Department and in the entourage of the King and Queen, some difficult moments.

There was one person, however, who looked on the visit as a very serious affair—William Bullitt, then our ambassador to France. He sent me a secret memorandum, based on experience gained from the King and Queen's visit to Paris the year before, in which all the smallest details were noted. I still keep that memorandum as one of my most amusing documents. Among other things he listed the furniture which should be in the rooms used by the King and Queen, told me what I should have in the bathrooms and even the way the comfortables on the beds should be folded. He admonished me to have a hot-water bottle in every bed, which I did, though the heat of Washington must have made them unbearable. One thing that was listed and that I was never able to find was a linen blanket for the queen's couch. Nobody I asked on this side of the ocean knew what it might be.

The Scotland Yard people had to stay in the house, of course, and outside the King and Queen's rooms were chairs where messengers always sat. It seemed foolish to me, since the rooms were just across the hall from each other. Not until 1942, when I spent two nights in Buckingham Palace and saw how large it was, did I understand the reason for the messengers. There they wait in the corridors to show guests where to go, and to carry any messages one wishes to send.

One day before the visit I invited Lady Lindsay, wife of the British ambassador, to tea and asked her if she was being given any instructions which might be helpful to me. Lady Lindsay was an American whom I had known a long while, and we looked at things from more or less the same point of view. She looked at me rather wickedly when she said: "Yes, Sir Alan Lascelles has told us that the King must be served at meals thirty seconds ahead of the Queen. The King does not like capers or suet pudding. I told him we did not often have suet pudding in the United States and that I really had not expected the King to like capers."

In the White House there are in the dining room two special, high-backed armchairs, one for the President and one for his wife, and no one else ever sits in them at meals. They presented a great problem for the household on this occasion. Should only the King and the President have the armchairs? That did not seem respectful to the Queen, but we could not take his chair away from the President. Finally Franklin solved the difficulty. "Why don't we buy two more armchairs identical with those we now have?" This was done and all was well.

I told Franklin that British protocol required that the head butler, Fields, stand with a stop watch in his hand and, thirty seconds after he and the King had been served, dispatch a butler to serve the Queen and myself, and I inquired what was to happen about the White House rule that the president was always served first. "We will not require Fields to have a stop watch," he said. "The King and I will be served simultaneously and you and the Queen will be served next."

Then came another serious question: Should the President sit with the King on his right and the Queen on his left and me on the right of the King? Or should we follow our usual custom? Franklin finally decided we would follow the usual custom of the United States. The King would sit on my right and the Queen on Franklin's right. The reason for this decision was that since the King and Queen were going to see a good deal of us, it did not seem quite fair to box the King in between us when he had so little time in which to meet and talk with other people. Franklin later explained this to the King, who accepted every arrangement in the most charming and delightful manner.

The secretary of state and Mrs. Hull with their party had met the members of the royal party at Niagara Falls, and accompanied them on the train to Washington. There was much pageantry about their arrival and the procession to the White House. That was something my husband always enjoyed, for he liked to put on a show. I dreaded it. At the appointed time we went down to the station and, with the government officials who were members of the reception committee, stood waiting in the President's reception room for the train's arrival.

After the presentations were over, my husband and I escorted the King and Queen through the Guard of Honor, which was drawn up in front of the station. The British National Anthem and "The Star-Spangled Banner" were played, and there was a twenty-one gun salute. Then the inevitable photographs were taken and finally my husband and the King and the Queen and I got into our respective cars and started with military escort on the slow drive to the White House. There were crowds all along the way and I was fascinated watching the Queen. She had the most gracious manner and bowed right and left with interest, actually looking at people in the crowd so that I am sure many of them felt that her bow was really for them personally.

In spite of the heat, a light cover had been placed by her footman over her knees when she got into the car. She sat upon a cushion which I afterwards discovered had springs to make it easier for her to keep up the continual bowing. The same arrangements were made for the King.

Immediately on our arrival at the White House, what is known as a Diplomatic Circle was held in the East Room for the heads of all the diplomatic missions and their wives. At that time the British ambassador, Sir Ronald Lindsay, was dean of the diplomatic corps, so he presented the chiefs of missions and their wives to the King while Lady Lindsay presented them to the Queen.

After lunch, the King and my husband in one car and the Queen and I in another drove about Washington. Our route was given out beforehand, so that people could have an opportunity to see Their Majesties. It meant, of course, that we had little chance to talk except when we were driving where people could not line up on the sidewalks. At one point the Queen endeared herself to me by saying suddenly: "I saw in the paper that you were being attacked for having gone to a meeting of the WPA workers. It surprises me that there should be any criticism, for it is so much better to allow people with grievances to air them; and it is particularly valuable if they can do so to someone in whom they feel a sense of sympathy and who may be able to reach the head of the government with their grievances."

While we were out, some amusing things had happened at home. The housekeeper, Mrs. Nesbitt, was harassed and when she was harassed she usually went to Miss Thompson. The fact that the many servants quartered in our servants' rooms were requiring as much attention as she had expected to give to everyone combined was an unexpected burden. The first intimation of any difficulty between our staff and the royal servants came when the housekeeper reported that the King's valet was making unreasonable demands and did not like our food and drink. Even the ushers were not having an easy time, for they were not accustomed to having protocol hold good among the servants. As the Queen's maid was walking down the middle of the second floor hall on her way from the Queen's room to the elevator, one of the ushers asked her if she would tell the lady in waiting that the Queen wanted her to come to her room. The maid drew herself up and said, "I am the Queen's maid," and swept down the hall. The usher, who by this time was exhausted by the heat and the extra work, reported, "Oh, so you're a big shot?"

When finally everyone got to bed that night, they must all, including the King and Queen, have breathed sighs of relief.

The next morning, before Their Majesties left the White House, they walked down a line of newspaperwomen and greeted them, then went to the British embassy, where they received members of the British colony, and from there to the Capitol. At the Capitol they were received by the vice-president and by Speaker Bankhead, and escorted to the rotunda where they received members of the Senate and the House. After that they met us on the U.S.S. *Potomac* and we had lunch on the way down the river. At Mount Vernon the usual ceremony was observed and the King laid a wreath on Washington's tomb. Time was growing short, and some people who had driven out there were presented to the King and Queen as they hurriedly got a glimpse of the old Mount Vernon house and grounds.

On the way home we stopped at Fort Hunt to visit a Civilian Conservation Corps camp. My husband, of course, could not walk with the

King and Queen, but I have a vivid recollection of that visit; it taught me many things.

The King walked with the commandant of the camp toward the boys, who were drawn up in two lines in the broiling sun. A large bulletin board had been put up with pictures of the various camps throughout the country, showing the different kinds of work done by the boys, but he did not stop to look at them.

As we went down the long line, the King stopped at every other boy and asked questions while the Queen spoke to the intervening boys. I, of course, walked with the Queen. At the end of the first line, the commandant was prepared not to go down the second one, but the King turned automatically and started down. He asked really interested questions, such as whether they were satisfied with their food, what they were learning and whether they thought it would help them to obtain work and, lastly, how much they were earning.

He had explained to us beforehand that for a long time he had had a summer camp for boys from the mining areas of Great Britain. He had been deeply troubled to find that many boys had no conception of doing a full day's work, because they had never seen their fathers do a day's work, many of Great Britain's miners having been on the dole for years. This spoke volumes for the conditions of the mining industry in Great Britain, but the King seemed interested chiefly in the effect it had on these young men; he wanted to set up something as useful as the CCC camps in Great Britain.

When we reached the end of the second row of boys, the commandant said: "Your Majesty, the day is so hot that, while the boys have prepared their barracks and mess hall for your inspection, we shall all understand if you do not feel it wise to cross the field in this sun." The King responded: "If they expect me to go, of course I will go." This was a kind of *noblesse oblige* that I had not often seen in our own officials with whom I had inspected CCC camps and NYA activities and other projects.

The Queen and I followed slowly across the field in the hot sun, and I saw one of the most thorough inspections I have ever witnessed. They looked at the shelves where supplies were kept, and when they heard the boys made their own equipment, they had tables turned upside down to see how they were made; they looked into pots and pans on the stove, and at the menu; and when they left there was little they did not know.

In the sleeping barracks the King felt the mattresses and carefully examined shoes and clothes.

My husband had carefully coached me for the tea party that followed this trip, for he said the King had particularly asked to meet the heads of all the agencies which were contributing to the recovery and doing new things in the government. As I introduced each agency head I was supposed, as briefly as possible, to outline the work that person was doing, and then give the man or woman, as the case might be, about three minutes alone with the King, then take him over to the Queen and present the next person to the King. I had rather dreaded trying to engineer this and wondered how I was going to condense the introduction into a brief enough explanation, but I soon found that my explanation could be very short, for the King seemed to know at once, as I spoke the name, what the person was doing, and he started right in with questions. I had expected to have a hard time keeping the line moving; I had watched my husband's secretaries struggling with him and it was impossible, if he got interested, to pry anyone away, but the King proved much more amenable.

The party seemed to go off successfully for all concerned. I was so impressed with the King's knowledge that at the next meal at which I sat beside him I asked him to tell me how he knew what work every person in our government did. He told me that before he came he had made a study of the name and occupation of everyone in the government; that the material had been procured for him, and was only part of his preparation for this trip to Washington.

After they left we took a train to Hyde Park, where we had the day to prepare for the twenty-four hours which the King and Queen were to spend with us there. My husband always loved taking people he liked home with him. He felt he knew them better once they had been to Hyde Park.

The day in New York City was interesting but completely exhausting, for Mayor LaGuardia had filled every minute to overflowing. As the day advanced the King and Queen realized they were going to be late reaching us; but they were not told how late they were until they actually started, whereupon the King insisted on stopping and telephoning at intervals along the way.

We sat in the library in the Hyde Park house waiting for them. Franklin had a tray of cocktails ready in front of him, and his mother sat on the other side of the fireplace looking disapprovingly at the cocktails and telling her son that the King would prefer tea. My husband, who could be as obstinate as his mother, kept his tray in readiness, however. Finally the King and Queen arrived and I met them at the door and took them to their rooms. In a short time they were dressed and down in the library. As the King approached my husband and the cocktail table, my husband said, "My mother does not approve of cocktails and thinks you should have a cup of tea." The King answered, "Neither does my mother," and took a cocktail.

Two startling things happened at dinner. They seem funny now, but they caused my mother-in-law much embarrassment. We had brought up the colored butler from the White House. My mother-in-law had an English butler who, when he heard that the White House butlers were coming up to help him, was so shocked that the King and Queen were to be waited on by colored people that he decided to take his holiday before Their Majesties came, in order not to see them treated in that manner!

Just exactly what happened to our well-trained White House butlers that night I shall never know. My mother-in-law had the extra china that was needed put on a serving table that was not ordinarily used, and suddenly in the middle of dinner the serving table collapsed and the dishes clattered to the floor. Mama tried in the best-bred tradition to ignore it, but her stepdaughter-in-law, Mrs. James Roosevelt Roosevelt, from whom she had borrowed some plates for the occasion, was heard to say, "I hope none of my dishes were among those broken." As a matter of fact, the broken dishes were part of a set my husband had been given; none of the old family china suffered.

One would think that one mishap of this kind would be enough for an evening, but just after we had gone down to the big library after dinner there was a most terrible crash; the butler, carrying a tray of decanters, glasses, bowls of ice, and so on, fell down the two steps leading from the hall and slid right into the library, scattering the contents of the tray over the floor and leaving a large lake of water and ice cubes at the bottom of the steps. I am sure Mama wished that her English butler had stayed. I wrote about this in my column at the time because I thought it was really funny, but my mother-in-law was indignant with me for not keeping it a deep, dark family secret.

Dinner had been so late that the evening was soon over and we all retired, leaving Prime Minister Mackenzie King and the King to talk with Franklin. It seemed so late when they came upstairs that I felt sorry for them, but the next day Mackenzie King told my husband that the King had knocked on his door and asked him to come to his room for a talk; he added that the King had said: "Why don't my ministers talk to me as the President did tonight? I felt exactly as though a father were giving me his most careful and wise advice."

The next day, after we had all been to church, people from far and near came to Franklin's cottage for a picnic. I had corralled two friends to cook hot dogs on an outdoor fireplace, and we had smoked turkey, which Their Majesties had not tasted before, several kinds of ham cured in different ways from different parts of the United States, salads, baked beans, and a strawberry shortcake with strawberries from Henry Morgen-thau's farm in Dutchess County.

When the picnic and the handshaking were over, my husband invited the King to swim with him in the pool. I hoped the Queen would feel she could relax in the same way, but I discovered that if you were a Queen you could not run the risk of looking disheveled, so she and her lady in waiting sat by the side of the pool with me while the men were swimming.

After a quiet dinner we took the King and Queen to join their train at the Hyde Park station. Their luggage and all the rest of their party were on board. Their Majesties had said good-by to everybody and were about to get on the train when the Queen suddenly came back to me and said: "Where is the man who has been driving the King? I want to thank him." I found my husband's chauffeur and the Queen thanked him for the care with which he had driven.

The royal couple stood on the rear platform of the train as it pulled out and the people who were gathered on the banks of the Hudson suddenly began to sing, "Auld Lang Syne." There was something incredibly moving about the scene—the river in the evening light, the voices of many people singing this old song, and the train slowly pulling out with the young couple waving good-by. One thought of the clouds that hung over them and the worries they were going to face, and turned away and left the scene with a heavy heart.

Twenty-one

Second Term: 1939-1940

MANY PEOPLE may have forgotten how worried we were about the young people in our country during the early days of the depression. How deeply troubled these young men and women were was shown by the fact that many of them felt it necessary to leave their homes, because they could not find jobs and could not bear to eat even a small amount of what little food their families had.

I felt that in any efforts they made to help themselves or one another the young people should have all the consideration and assistance their elders could possibly give them. My deep concern led to my association with various youth groups and to my meeting with many young people who either were brought by their elders to Washington or came through an organization of their own.

I believed, of course, that these young people had the right to be heard. They had the right to fight for the things they believed in as citizens of a democracy. It was essential to restore their faith in the power of democracy to meet their needs, or they would take the natural path of looking elsewhere.

One of the most prominent young people's organizations of this unsettled time was the American Youth Congress. It spread all over the country and worked closely with other youth groups, such as the Southern Youth Council and the Negro Youth Congress.

During one of their meetings in Washington the leaders of the AYC came to see me and told me what they were trying to do. In time I came to know some of them quite well. I like all young people and those in the American Youth Congress were an idealistic, hard-working group. Whether they were Communist-inspired from the beginning I have never

208

known. After I had been working for them for a while accusations began to be made, and I had a number of the leaders come to my sitting room in the White House. I told them that since I was actively helping them I must know exactly where they stood politically. I asked each one in turn to tell me honestly what he believed. In every case they said they had no connection with the Communists, had never belonged to any Communist organizations, and had no interest in Communist ideas. I decided to accept their word, realizing that sooner or later the truth would come out.

The first direct contact that Franklin had with the American Youth Congress came after I was fairly sure that they were becoming Communist-dominated. Ordinarily, Franklin had little time to devote to individuals or even to particular groups. On February 10, 1940, the American Youth Congress organized a parade and a meeting in Washington, and I thought it advisable to ask Franklin to speak to them. It rained that day, and a wet group stood out in the south grounds, expecting to be patted on the back. Instead, Franklin told them some truths which, though they might be unpalatable, he thought it wise for them to hear. They were in no mood for warnings, however kindly meant, and they booed the President.

When the leaders of several youth organizations were summoned to appear before the Dies Committee, I sat through most of the hearings, because I had heard that when the members had before them people of little influence or backing, their questions were so hostile as to give the impression that the witness had been haled before a court and prejudged a criminal. If there is one thing I dislike it is intimidating people instead of trying to get at facts. At one point, when the questioning seemed to me to be particularly harsh, I asked to go over and sit at the press table. I took a pencil and a piece of paper, and the tone of the questions changed immediately. Just what the questioner thought I was going to do I do not know, but my action had the effect I desired.

Because I dislike Gestapo methods in this country, I have never liked that kind of Congressional committee. I doubt that they ever harm the really powerful, but they do harm many innocent people who are unable to defend themselves.

On one occasion my husband and I were given a confidential list of organizations which were considered Communist or subversive or un-American, a list compiled by the FBI for the use of the Dies Committee. People who belonged to any group on that list or who had even contributed to any of them were *ipso facto* under suspicion. We found that among those listed as contributors to two or three of these organizations were Secretary Stimson, Secretary Knox and my husband's mother. Franklin and I got particular amusement out of the inclusion of her name; we could picture her horror if she were told that the five or ten dollars she had given to a seemingly innocent relief organization put her among those whom the Dies Committee could easily call before it as belonging to subversive organizations.

I once asked the Dies Committee and the FBI point-blank what evidence they had on any of the young people they were talking so loosely about. They told me they had none. A book written later by a woman in Washington states that Mr. Dies offered me information which I refused to read. The fact of the matter is that I invited Mr. Dies to lunch and asked specifically for information; he never sent it to me.

After my decision to part from them, the young people of the Youth Congress accused me of having been "sold down the river to the capitalists," and some of them picketed the White House with a peace group.

When news was received that Germany had invaded Russia, however, the Youth Congress held another mass meeting and clamored for cooperation with Russia and for greater preparation for war. They even sent me a telegram saying: "Now we can work together again." The war was suddenly no longer an imperialistic war, and the pickets were called off at the White House.

Of course, I never worked with the Youth Congress again. I could not trust them to be honest with me.

I wish to make it clear that I felt a great sympathy for these young people, even though they often annoyed me. It was impossible ever to forget the extraordinary difficulties under which they were growing up. I have never felt the slightest bitterness toward any of them. I learned from them what Communist tactics are. I discovered for myself how infiltration of an organization is accomplished. I was taught how Communists get themselves into positions of importance. I learned their methods of objection and delay, the effort to tire out the rest of the group and carry the vote when all their opponents have gone home. These tactics are now all familiar to me. In fact, I think my work with the American Youth Congress was of infinite value to me in understanding some of the tactics I had to meet later in the United Nations!

During the summer of 1939 we spent a great deal of time at Hyde Park. When the news finally came that Hitler's troops had gone into Poland, Franklin called me at Hyde Park at five o'clock in the morning. All that September day I could not help remembering the good-by to the King and Queen and the lump that had come into my throat as they stood on the back platform of their departing train. Now their people faced the final hour of decision.

As I look back over the whole year of 1939, it seems to me that my husband's major efforts were bent on trying to avert total war in Europe and to awaken us here to the need for preparation. Perhaps he might have saved himself the trouble of these various efforts, yet one would not like to feel that the President of this country had not done all he could to try to change the threatening course of history.

His actions during this year and the next were only a continuation of the line of action he had begun to follow as far back as 1936. Immediately after the failure of the London Naval Conference, he had secured from Congress money to construct additional battleships and airplane carriers. The following year, in his quarantine speech in Chicago, he warned the country of the worsening political situation abroad and of the dangers it held for the United States; and he tried to persuade the people that this country should make a definite and positive effort to preserve the peace. The opposition this speech aroused was so great that Franklin realized the people were not yet ready to go along with any drastic steps toward international co-operation.

All through the Czech crisis in 1938 he continued his attempts to save the peace, through appeals to Hitler and the heads of other countries. After Munich, he blamed Neville Chamberlain for weakness, but said that England had let her defenses go down so much that there was perhaps nothing else the prime minister could do. To ensure that our country would never be found similarly unprepared was now Franklin's greatest concern.

In January he asked Congress for funds to expand our air force and construct new naval air bases. In April he warned the country of the approach of war in Europe and sent a personal message to both Hitler and Mussolini, appealing for a ten-year pledge not to attack or invade other countries. In late August Russia and Germany signed their non-aggression pact. Franklin sent a peace appeal to Hitler, King Victor

Emmanuel of Italy, and President Moscicki of Poland, urging settlement of the Danzig-Polish Corridor issue. On the following day he sent another message to Hitler.

Then Hitler invaded Poland. Convinced that further peace efforts would be unsuccessful, Franklin on September 21 urged Congress to repeal the embargo on the shipment of arms under the Neutrality Act, which he had signed reluctantly in 1937, at the time of the Spanish Civil War. In December Franklin appointed Myron Taylor as his special representative at the Vatican.

The letters between my husband and the Pope seem to indicate that this appointment was one of the wise preliminary steps in the preparation for war, although it created a certain amount of difficulty among some of our Protestant groups. Mr. Taylor was well known and respected, and most people felt that the Pope could be a potent force for peace at this time and that we should have some direct tie with him. I do not think Franklin regarded this appointment as creating a permanent diplomatic post, but he thought it a necessity during a period of emergency.

During this year Franklin had persuaded his mother to deed, with him, to the United States government a piece of their property on the Post Road. Frank Walker headed a committee, made up of a number of other friends, to collect the money to build a library at Hyde Park. The war had its influence in this, too. For a long time Franklin had felt that it would be a great advantage if the important papers and collections of the country were not all crowded together in one building. In case of war, the European countries would have to scatter their collections, since one bomb could completely destroy the historical records of the whole nation. In particular, he realized that Congress was never likely to give the Congressional Library sufficient appropriation for the continuing flow of public papers to be brought rapidly up to date and made available to those who wanted to study them. He also thought it would be easier to deal with a particular period if all the records relating to it were in one place. Intending to give his own papers and many other interesting things to the library, he believed he could persuade other people who had been active in the life of the period to do the same thing.

I shall never forget his pleasure and pride in laying the cornerstone of the library on November 19 of that year. It was a simple but moving occasion. His strong feeling for history added greatly to his pleasure in knowing that here, on his own land, there would be gathered in one building the record of the period of his country's history in which he had had a part.

The next year, 1940, had the disadvantage of all election years; everything that happens seems of necessity to have a political slant. Though the war in Europe was moving inexorably on and Hitler seemed to be sweeping all before him, some people were concerned only with the effect that any move of Franklin's would have on the chances of the Democratic party for success in the next election.

Nevertheless, throughout the year he took additional steps which, though each one in itself seemed unimportant, together tended to prepare the country for the ordeal before it. In February he urged the immediate purchase of strategic war materials; in April the combat areas were defined; and in May he asked for additional appropriations of over one billion dollars for defense. These moves were justified, since Hitler was moving fast.

Dunkirk was a sad and anxious time for us in the White House as well as for the people of Great Britain. When the full story was told, the heroism of the people on that embattled island and the way the Royal Air Force defended the country called forth admiration from everyone in the United States. We understood the kind of courage and tenacity that Winston Churchill was beginning to put into words, words that expressed the spirit of the British people in the months following Dunkirk.

It was this admiration of good sportsmanship that made my husband so bitter again Mussolini when he came into the war against France. The familiar phrase "stab in the back," which some of his advisers begged him to leave out of his Charlottesville, Virginia, speech was largely a tribute to the spirit which he recognized in the people of Great Britain and which he felt the leadership of Mussolini never fostered in the Italian people.

The occasion for that speech was the commencement at the University of Virginia Law School, where Franklin Junior was graduating. It was a curious trip; we were all there; a trip to one's son's commencement is normal; but that was not a normal and happy occasion. The times were fraught with promise of evil. Franklin's address was not just a commencement address; it was a speech to the nation on an event that had brought us one step nearer to total war.

Immediately after the speech I went to Hyde Park, leaving my husband and Franklin Junior in Washington. I knew by that time that those who thought the war inevitable had persuaded Franklin that he could not refuse to run for a third term if he were nominated.

So much has been said about the third term issue that I can contribute only my own impressions. I never questioned Franklin about his political intentions. The fact that I myself had never wanted him to be in Washington made me doubly careful not to intimate that I had the slightest preference.

Although I never asked my husband what he wanted to do, it became clearly evident, from little things he said at different times, that he would really like to be in Hyde Park and that the role of elder statesman appealed to him. He thought he would enjoy being in a position to sit back and offer suggestions and criticism. There were innumerable things that all his life he had meant to do—write on naval subjects, go through his papers, letters, and so on. He had the library at Hyde Park and had even agreed on a job which he would take on leaving the White House. As I remember, he was to write a longish editorial or article at stated intervals for one of the large New York magazines. He had built a small stone cottage to which he could retreat when too many people came to the big house; and while he was furious when people called it his "dream house," nevertheless it was part of his dream.

I had every evidence to believe that he did not want to run again. However, as time went on, more and more people came to me saying that he must run, that the threat of war was just over the horizon and no one else had the prestige and the knowledge to carry on through a crisis.

I had been deeply troubled by the fact that I saw no one being prepared to take Franklin's place, and on several occasions I asked him if he did not think he should make a definite effort to prepare someone. Franklin said he thought people had to prepare themselves, that all he could do was to give them opportunities and see how they worked out. I felt that he, without intending to do so, dominated the people around him and that so long as he was in the picture it was hard for anyone to rise to a position of prominence. Finally, I came to realize that no man could hand another more than opportunity.

I heard many other people discussed as possible candidates, but as the time for the convention drew nearer I could see that it was going to be extremely difficult to have anyone else nominated. First, the Democratic party had not found anyone else it thought could keep it in office and, second, serious-minded people were worried about the war.

Before the convention actually opened it was evident that Franklin was going to be nominated and would run; I think he had been persuaded that if he were nominated he could not refuse. I believe he did not honestly want the nomination. If he had not been nominated, he would have been completely satisfied, and would have lived his life very happily; and yet when you are in the center of world affairs, there is something so fascinating about it that you can hardly see how you are going to live any other way. In his mind, I think, there was a great seesaw; on one end, the weariness that had already begun, and the desire to be at home and his own master; on the other end, the overwhelming interest that was the culmination of a lifetime of preparation and work, and the desire to see and to have a hand in the affairs of the world in that critical period.

Finally I said to Franklin: "You have made up your mind you will not go to the convention even if you are nominated but that you will speak over the radio, and that means, I hope, I do not have to go." He said firmly that it was his definite intention that neither he nor I should go. I told him in that case I would go to Hyde Park and stay at my cottage and get the big house ready, so that when the convention was over he could come up for a rest.

Miss Thompson and I went to Hyde Park. Life was going placidly when one day the telephone rang. Frances Perkins was on the wire. She said: "Things look black here; the temper of the convention is ugly. The President should come to Chicago if he wants Mr. Wallace nominated; but if he won't come, I think you should come." I told her I thought it utter nonsense for me to go, but she ought to tell my husband her feeling and that he ought to go if anyone went. Miss Perkins rang off, saying she would talk to Franklin. When she called him, he told her he was not going to the convention, but that if he were nominated he wanted Henry Wallace as his running mate.

The next day Frances Perkins called me again and said that my husband had told her he would be willing to have me go if she felt it was essential. I said: "Franklin may be willing, but how do I know how Jim Farley feels about it? I certainly am not going out there unless he invites me. I know there is bad feeling because Harry Hopkins has been more or less running things and perhaps has not been very tactful, and I am not going to add to the hard feelings." She then wanted to know whether I would go if Jim asked me to, and I said I should have to ask my husband first. After she had finished talking, I called Franklin and told him what

Frances Perkins had said and asked him what he wanted me to do. He said: "It might be nice for you to go, but I do not think it is in the least necessary." I said: "If Jim Farley asks me to go, do you think it would be wise?" He replied: "Yes, I think it would be."

Then I waited, and later in the morning the telephone rang and Jim Farley asked me to come out. Since he was in rather a hurry, he asked me to talk to Lorena Hickok, who was then working with Charles Michelson on publicity for the Democratic National Committee. She told me she felt it was important for me to come and that Jim Farley really wanted me.

The next day we landed in the late afternoon in Chicago. Jim Farley met me at the airfield. The newspaperwomen were in the airport, and he asked me to see them at once. I told him I had nothing to say, but he thought I had better see them, so I got through the interview as best I could, saying as little as possible.

Then Jim Farley and I drove alone into Chicago. On the way he told me that Franklin had not talked to him since the convention opened and had never told him who was his choice for vice-president. I was horrified to realize that things had come to this pass between the two men, because I always had a feeling of real friendship for Jim Farley. He told me why he thought that Jesse Jones or William B. Bankhead or Paul McNutt or some other candidate should get the nomination. He also told me that Elliott, who was a resident of Texas at that time and a member of the delegation from that state, was planning to second Jesse Jones' nomination.

I said that before anything happened he should talk to my husband. I went directly to the hotel where Jim Farley had his office and called Franklin. I told him what Jim had said. I also told him I had just learned he had not talked to Jim and I suggested that he talk to him and tell him how he felt. I expressed no preference for any candidate; and I think the account of the convention which Jim Farley gave in his book, as far as my part is concerned, was his impression of what I said rather than what I actually said. He quoted me as saying to my husband: "I've been talking to Jim Farley and I agree with him, Henry Wallace won't do. I know, Franklin, but Jesse Jones would bolster up the ticket, win it business support and get the party contributions." Jim Farley had said these things to me and I repeated carefully what he had said, but I never expressed a preference or an opinion on matters of this kind, and I am sure I did not change my habits on this occasion.

When Jim Farley got on the telephone, my husband evidently told him that Mr. Wallace was the person he wanted. Jim argued with him rather halfheartedly and Franklin finally said it must be Wallace. He felt that Wallace could be trusted to carry out our policies on foreign affairs if by chance he, Wallace, found himself hurled into the Presidency. Franklin's feeling then was so strong that he was willing to insist on his running mate and thereby give him a chance to prove his ability. It was then that Jim Farley said: "You're the boss. If you say so, I will do all I can to nominate Wallace, but I will have to work fast." He turned to me and said he would have to get hold of Elliott, because he was about to second the nomination of Jesse Jones, that Paul McNutt was strong too, and we would have to get to the Convention Hall as quickly as possible. We drove there immediately and I could see that Jim was much disturbed.

As soon as we got to the Convention Hall he turned me over to Frances Perkins and Lorena Hickok, and disappeared. I went to my seat immediately, got hold of Franklin Junior and told him to find Elliott, because I was most anxious that he should not nominate anyone and so appear to be in opposition to his father's desires. Elliott came over and we talked for a minute, and I found that Jim Farley had already reached him with the information, so he did no nominating.

I saw Ed Flynn and a number of other people walking about, and many of them spoke to me briefly. Suddenly in the midst of the turmoil and confusion, Frank Walker came over to me and said: "We think now is the time for you to speak."

I made up my mind that what I said would be brief. I had prepared nothing, but I decided to base my short speech on the conversation I had heard in the hotel. If Franklin felt that the strain of a third term might be too much for any man and that Mr. Wallace was the man who could carry on best in times such as we were facing, he was entitled to have his help; no one should think of himself but only of the job that might have to be done.

The only way to accomplish my aim was to persuade the delegations in the convention to sink all personal interests in the interests of the country and to make them realize the potential danger in the situation we were facing. While I spoke there was complete silence. It was striking after the pandemonium that had existed.

Then the balloting began. Franklin Junior and I kept tallies on the roll calls, and for a while Mr. Wallace did not do well. The convention was decidedly out of order; the galleries were packed with special groups favoring different candidates, and confusion was rampant. Word began to get around, however, that Mr. Wallace was to be the candidate. Mrs. Wallace sat beside me. I doubt if she had ever tried to follow a roll call before. She looked very unhappy and asked: "Why do you suppose they are so opposed to Henry?" I did not have time to explain that probably most of the people had been sent in purposely to demonstrate for someone else.

As soon as Henry Wallace's nomination as Franklin's running mate was announced, I left Convention Hall, asking Mrs. Wallace to congratulate her husband for me. I drove directly back to the airfield and got on the plane. As we started to taxi down the field someone waved frantically. We stopped and I was told to come back, that my husband was on the telephone. He told me that he had listened to my speech and that I had done a very good job. Harry Hopkins was on another wire, waiting to speak to me, and he said practically the same thing. Then I dashed back to the plane and we took off.

The next morning my car was waiting for me at LaGuardia Field and I drove straight to Hyde Park, where I found myself in time for a nine-o'clock breakfast. I felt as though it had all been a dream with a somewhat nightmarish tinge. I had to come down to earth quickly, however, and write my daily column just as though the past eighteen hours had not seemed the longest I had ever lived through.

When Franklin and I next met we talked the whole thing over. I told him that he should not leave Jim so uninformed, that I realized that the rift had become deep and that he had simply hated to call him. Franklin always insisted, however, that Harry Hopkins had had no headquarters and no official authority. Harry had simply gone ahead and acted on his own. I believe it was one of those occasions when Franklin kept hands off because to act was so disagreeable to him; only when he was forced to act did he do so. My going out, talking to Jim, and calling Franklin forced him to say definitely what he wanted, but he never told me this in so many words, though on several occasions he said to others, "Her speech was just right."

All this was in July. The campaign really began in September. On

September 2 Franklin spoke at the Chickamauga Dam celebration, near Chattanooga, Tennessee.

The next day he announced the agreement to send Great Britain fifty of our over-age destroyers in exchange for naval and air bases in Newfoundland and the West Indies; and about two weeks later, on September 16, he signed the Selective Service Act.

Then I began to feel that war was close. Elliott had already enlisted. He had had some aviation training and hoped to get into the Air Force. His eyes were bad but a new kind of lens, which he had acquired, enabled him to take off and land an airplane, and he had his civilian pilot's license.

A little while later he was commissioned captain and sent to Wright Field. Inevitably, he was attacked in the 1940 campaign because he had been made a captain. It was one of the many issues used by the opposition in the hope of defeating Franklin. It always seemed unfair to me that Elliott should have to suffer because his father decided to run for a third term, but fairness does not enter into political strategy. Franklin and I had long since learned to accept such personal attacks; but Elliott was bitter, because he saw other people appointed to the same rank in exactly the same way, frequently with less background and fewer qualification than he had.

I resented criticisms of this kind deeply for him and for our other children, but it is useless to resent anything; one must learn to look on whatever happens as part of one's education and make it serve a good purpose. At the same time I could be amused at the attacks on me personally, especially the large campaign buttons announcing "We don't want Eleanor either," which many women wore.

Neither Franklin nor I ever minded the disagreeable things my cousin Alice Longworth used to say during the various campaigns. When the social season started after the third campaign, in which she had been particularly outspoken, she was invited as usual to the diplomatic reception. General Watson, Franklin's aide, wondered if she would have the face to come; in fact, he was sure she would not. Franklin was equally sure that she would be there, so he and Pa Watson made a bet on it. On the night of the reception, when Alice was announced, Franklin looked at Pa with a grin, and said in a loud voice: "Pa, you lose!"

It was during this campaign that the "guru letters" were brought to light and there was great excitement about the chance of their being used against Mr. Wallace. I did not know Henry Wallace well, but my feeling was that he had simply been carried away by his intellectual curiosity. He was not realistic enough to appreciate how these letters would look to people who did not have the same kind of curiosity.

When it came to Mr. Wallace's renomination in 1944, the men who went out through the country to get the feeling of the people reported back that there was a strong belief that Wallace was too impractical to help the ticket. Franklin's faith in Wallace was shaken by that time, anyway; he said that Wallace had had his chance to make his mark, and since he had not been able to convince the party leaders that he was the right person for the job, it was not possible to dictate again who was to be the candidate. Franklin had a fatalistic feeling that if there was work for him to do he would be here to do it. If not, he believed the leaders should have a man of their own choice with whom to carry on.

Franklin had intended to make no speeches in this campaign except over the radio, but he finally was persuaded to make a few. He liked Wendell Willkie very much; he never felt the bitterness toward him that he felt toward some of his other opponents, and I do not remember his ever saying anything derogatory of him in private conversation. I myself thought Mr. Willkie courageous and sincere, and I liked the way he stood for certain principles.

Franklin was always fairly confident of success, though he said one could never be sure until the votes were counted. However, this was the election he was least certain of winning, not only because Mr. Willkie was a strong candidate but because he thought the third term issue would be a greater hurdle than it proved to be. As usual, I wanted him to win, since that was what he wanted, and I would have been sorry for his sake if he had been defeated. I knew, though, that if he lost he would go on living a good and full life, for he was a philosophical person who accepted and made the best of whatever happened.

Twenty-two

The Coming of War: 1941

IN FEBRUARY, 1941, the Grand Duchess of Luxembourg came to stay and we had the customary parties. In that month, too, Harry Hopkins was sent to England to maintain personal contact between Franklin and the British government, for Ambassador Kennedy was about to resign and the new ambassador had not been appointed. I recalled Harry's disgust with some of our career diplomats during a previous trip to observe living conditions in various European countries. He had said to me on his return: "They are so busy socially that they haven't time to find out anything about working or agricultural conditions."

Mr. Willkie came to see my husband one day and the household was so anxious to get a glimpse of him while he sat waiting in Franklin's study on the second floor of the White House that suddenly many people had errands that took them down the hall. I would have gone myself, but I didn't hear of his visit until Franklin told me of it later.

June was a difficult month, because Missy LeHand was taken ill, the beginning of her long, last illness. However, life in the White House had to go on just the same. On the 17th, Crown Princess Juliana of the Netherlands and her husband, Prince Bernhard, came to stay, and through the summer we had a number of other visitors, including, in August, the Duke of Kent and, in October, Lord and Lady Mountbatten. Later, the Duke and Duchess of Windsor came to lunch with my husband, though I had to be away to keep a long-standing engagement.

Early in August my husband, after many mysterious consultations, told me that he was going to take a little trip up through the Cape Cod Canal and that he wished to do some fishing. Then he smiled and I knew he was not telling me all that he was going to do.

221

I had already learned never to ask questions when information was not volunteered, and it became almost an obsession with me as the war went on. Because I saw a great many people I might let something slip that should not be told, so I used to beg my husband to tell me no secrets. Many times it was impossible not to know something was afoot, but if I made no effort to find out what, my knowledge was pretty vague.

Franklin invited some friends to go with him for the first few days of this Cape Cod cruise, and the trip was well covered in the news. He was seen by crowds of people from the shores of the canal and then—blank! Later he loved to tell the story of how he changed from the presidential yacht to the U.S.S. *Augusta*, which steamed up the coast and into the harbor of Argentia, where he met Prime Minister Churchill.

The story of that meeting has been told often and Franklin Junior and Elliott, who were there, could describe their part in it far better than I. To both boys the meeting with their father came as a pleasant surprise. Elliott had been doing exciting work. After he enlisted he had been sent to Wright Field for training and then assigned to a group going to Gander Lake Field. Because he was in that area, he was ordered to Argentia in August when his father and Prime Minister Churchill met to discuss the Atlantic Charter. Elliott had no idea why he was being hauled off the job he was on and sent to Argentia, and when he saw all the ships lying in the harbor he was a most surprised young man.

The same surprise awaited Franklin Junior. Being in the Naval Reserve, he had been called into the Navy before we were in the war and was executive officer on a destroyer, convoying merchant ships to England, and a most unpleasant job it was. It can be very cold in the North Atlantic in late winter and the early spring, so he had been beseeching all the family to send him warm clothes, and told tales of coming into Portland, Maine, practically encased in ice. Because of this duty, however, his ship had the good luck to be assigned to guard the President and the prime minister. Arriving in Argentia, he received word that he was to report to the commander in chief on board such-and-such a ship. He was considerably uneasy and thought to himself: "Now, what have I done?" It never occurred to him that the commander in chief was not Admiral King, so when he walked on board and saw his father it was a pleasant surprise and a great relief.

On his return, Franklin seemed happy that the Atlantic Charter had been agreed upon and announced and that he and Mr. Churchill had had the chance to begin to know and to like each other. He had met Mr. Churchill before, but had not really known him. He felt that this meeting had broken the ice and said he knew now that Churchill, who he thought was typical of John Bull, was a man with whom he could really work.

The fact that he had pulled off the trip without being discovered gave him a keen sense of satisfaction. He used to chuckle as he told of the presidential yacht sailing quietly through the Cape Cod Canal for a whole day with a gentleman more or less like Franklin in size, wearing a cap pulled well down over his eyes, sitting on the deck waving.

As the years went on, I was more and more careful to know as few secrets as possible, and Miss Thompson, whose office was off the main hall near the elevator on the second floor, became practically a recluse, making it a point to tell everybody that she knew nothing about my husband's business.

Even in my press conferences I established the fairly well-understood pattern that affairs of state were not in my bailiwick but were dealt with by my husband in his news conferences. Occasionally, when I was asked for my personal opinion on some matter I would give it, and later I would be told that a good correspondent could not afford to miss my press conferences because I often foreshadowed my husband's point of view. As a matter of fact, Franklin and I would rarely have discussed the subject, and only when it was one on which I felt justified in expressing my own point of view did I answer questions on affairs of state. I suppose long association makes people think along the same lines on certain subjects, so these coincidences were not so very extraordinary.

After he came back from Argentia, Franklin was increasingly busy; but fortunately he decided to go to Hyde Park for the weekend of September 4, because his mother, who had seemed to pick up after her return from Campobello and to be well again except for a slight cold, took a turn for the worse. On September 7 she died. It was a great sorrow to my husband. There was a close bond between them in spite of the fact that he had grown away from her in some ways and that in later years they had often not been in sympathy about policies on public affairs.

Franklin's mother had always wanted to die in her own room at Hyde

Park, and to be buried simply in the churchyard, with the men who had worked for her on the place for many years carrying the casket. Her wishes were carefully observed.

The same night that my mother-in-law was dying, my brother Hall, who had a little house not far from my cottage at Hyde Park, was taken ill. We took him to Vassar Hospital in Poughkeepsie, and the day of my mother-in-law's funeral I had him moved to Walter Reed Hospital in Washington at his insistence. Having been there for treatments made necessary by his service in World War I, he wished to go back to the same doctors.

As soon as we could, after my mother-in-law's funeral was over, we returned to the White House, and the next few weeks I spent watching my brother die. He was so strong that his heart kept him alive long after most people would have peacefully sunk into oblivion, and now and then he would recognize me when I went into his room. On September 25 he died, and the funeral was held in the White House. Franklin and I took his body to Tivoli, New York, to be buried in the Hall family vault there.

The loss of a brother is always a sad breaking of a family tie, but in the case of my brother it was like losing a child. He had come to live with us when we were first married and from then on Franklin and I had been his closest family; whatever happened to him, in spite of his great desire for independence, he always came to us. I had watched with great anxiety a fine mind gradually deteriorate. He had such a strong physique that he was sure he could always regain his self-control, even though he voluntarily relaxed it for a while. You could never convince him that it is hard to shake a habit you have once let get hold of you.

Fundamentally, I think Hall always lacked self-control. He had great energy, great physical strength, and great brilliance of mind but he never learned self-discipline. Whenever his responsibilities became irksome he tended to thrust them aside and to feel that it was unfair that he should be asked to make any concessions to circumstances that he did not wish to make. As a result of this attitude, his first marriage went on the rocks. While there were undoubtedly many contributing factors, I always felt that a major one was his lack of discipline and his unwillingness to compromise or make adjustments in the light of other people's needs. In fact, he saw only with great difficulty any point of view but his own and then only when his respect for a person's strength of character was deeper than his instinctive desire to attain his particular objective.

As I look back on the life of this man whom I dearly loved, who never reached the heights he was capable of reaching, I cannot help having a great sense of sorrow for him, knowing that he must often have felt deeply frustrated and disappointed by his own failure to use the wonderful gifts that were his.

Sorrow in itself and the loss of someone whom you love is hard to bear, but when sorrow is mixed with regret and a consciousness of waste there is added a touch of bitterness which is even more difficult to carry, day in and day out. I think it was in an attempt to numb this feeling that I worked so hard at the Office of Civilian Defense that fall.

On September 22, a few days before Hall died, I agreed to take charge for Mayor LaGuardia of the activities that were not strictly defense activities but allied and necessary for the protection of the civilian population as a whole.

Elinor Morgenthau volunteered to work as my assistant. I soon found that every activity which Mayor LaGuardia did not want in his part of the program was thrust into my division. His work as mayor of New York City prevented him from giving his full time to organizing civilian defense. The few group meetings we had left me with the impression of great hurry and a feeling that decisions were taken which had not been carefully thought out. Frequently heads of divisions, including myself, were unable to discuss with him some of the things we hoped to get settled. The mayor was more interested in the dramatic aspects of civilan defense, such as whether or not cities had good fire-fighting equipment, than in such things as building morale.

One day, while I was staying in my small apartment on 11th Street in New York, I invited Mr. LaGuardia to luncheon with me, for there was something I particularly wanted to talk with him about. I planned a simple lunch, but in the midst of the preparations my maid, who had worked with me off and on for years, went to Miss Thompson completely upset and said she could not cook for the mayor. Miss Thompson reminded her that she had cooked for the President and that the mayor was an easy person to please.

After lunch the mayor, as he was leaving, said: "My wife never asks me where I have been nor whom I have seen, but she always asks me what I have had to eat. Today, I can truthfully say I did not have too much!"

I put in many hours every day at the Office of Civilian Defense, carrying on my own work at home by toiling every night. In the White House someone makes the rounds every hour to see that all is well. One morning my husband said: "What's this I hear? You didn't go to bed at all last night?" I had been working on my mail without regard to time, and when it began to get light, I decided it was not worthwhile going to bed. The man patrolling the house had seen my light under the door, heard me moving about and had reported it to the household, and someone told my husband. I did not do that very often, however.

I soon discovered that the thing I had feared was true! I could not take a government position, even without salary or paid expenses, without giving ample opportunity for faultfinding to some members of the opposition in Congress and even to some of our own party people who disagreed with certain policies. I did not much mind what they said about me, but when I found that anyone I appointed was in trouble merely because I appointed him, I did mind.

I hope that, despite these troubles, at least the trip I made with Mayor LaGuardia the night after Pearl Harbor was helpful. If I was able to give impetus to the work on the West Coast and, by the mere fact of going out there, to quiet many of the rather hysterical fears prevalent at that time, then the country benefited and the trip justified my short term of office in the OCD.

Pearl Harbor day began quietly. We were expecting a large party for luncheon and I was disappointed but not surprised when Franklin sent word a short time before lunch that he did not see how he could join us. He had been increasingly worried and frequently at the last moment would tell me that he could not come to some large gathering that had been arranged. The fact that he carried so many secrets in his head made it necessary for him to watch everything he said, which in itself was exhausting. In addition, anxiety as well as the dampness had made his sinus bad, which necessitated daily treatments of his nose. I always worried about this constant treatment, for I felt that, while it might help temporarily, in the long run it must cause irritation. Sometimes Franklin decided to eat alone in his study, sometimes he had Harry Hopkins or a secretary eat with him, or some person with whom he wished to talk privately.

Harry Hopkins ate with Franklin in the study that day and there were thirty-one of us at lunch. By the time lunch was over the news had come of the attack on Pearl Harbor, but we did not hear it until we went upstairs, when one of the ushers told me. The information was so stunning that there was complete quiet, and we took up our next occupation in a kind of vacuum. I saw my guests off, and waited till Franklin was alone to slip into his study, but I realized he was concentrating on what had to be done and would not talk about what had happened until this first strain was over. So I went back to work.

A few minutes after three o'clock the secretaries of war and navy, Admiral Beardall, my husband's naval aide, secretaries McIntyre and Early, and Grace Tully were all in Franklin's study on the second floor of the White House. They were soon joined by General Marshall and the secretary of state. Later, when my husband and I did have a chance to talk, I thought that in spite of his anxiety Franklin was in a way more serene than he had appeared for a long time. It was steadying to know that the die was cast. One could no longer do anything but face the fact that this country was in a war; from here on, difficult and dangerous as the future looked, it presented a clearer challenge than had the long uncertainty of the past.

The next day was a busy one for us all. I went to the Civilian Defense Office that morning at nine o'clock as usual, but came back to the White House shortly before twelve to go with my husband to the Capitol to hear him deliver his message to a joint session of Congress. I was living through again, it seemed to me, the day when President Wilson addressed the Congress to announce our entry into World War I. Now the President of the United States was my husband, and for the second time in my life I heard a president tell the Congress that this nation was engaged in a war. I was deeply unhappy. I remembered my anxieties about my husband and brother when World War I began; now I had four sons of military age.

It was a very impressive occasion, one of those occasions when a spirit of unity and strength prevailed. There was no criticism—only an acceptance of the fact that something had happened to us which, as a nation, we had to face.

We knew that the Pearl Harbor attack had set us back a long way, that before us stretched endless months of building up our forces. We might have to retreat, because we had been a peace-loving people and as a nation had not wanted to prepare for war. We had been denied the wherewithal to fortify our islands in the Pacific by people who backed their representatives in Congress in the feeling that Japan did not want war with us. Many believed that only our insistence on preparation for war would force Japan to make war on us. The mistakes of those who thought that way are obvious today, but before Pearl Harbor they were not so obvious, and many patriotic people honestly believed that Japan was not planning war on us. The war in China was far away, and they thought that was all the Japanese were interested in. They did not realize that we were an obstacle to the fulfillment of the Japanese schemes for complete domination in the Pacific.

In retrospect, it is easy to see things that were obscure at the time. My husband had long suspected that these Japanese dreams of grandeur and domination existed. I remember his concern about Guam and the other islands of the Pacific as far back as when he was assistant secretary of the navy. His suspicion of Japan was based on his own ideas of what made the Pacific safe for us, and in all the war games in the Pacific Japan was always the enemy. But anyone who dared to voice such suspicion would immediately have been called a warmonger. After Franklin's message to Congress, war was a grim reality to the whole country.

From the Capitol I went straight back to the Civilian Defense Office and stayed there most of the afternoon. I got home at a quarter before six and Miss Thompson and I were at the Washington airport at ten minutes past seven, ready to start with Mayor LaGuardia to the West Coast. As I was leaving, I had a glimpse of Elliott, who arrived to make an overnight stop at the White House. He was taking training in navigation and was on a final flight before graduation. The course had been speeded up because of the war. Immediately after that, Elliot went on patrol duty on the West Coast.

Miss Thompson and I were still working in a small forward compartment on the plane when they brought me a message that had been received by the pilots: a San Francisco paper had announced that the city of San Francisco was being bombed by the Japanese. I was asked to tell Mr. LaGuardia. Just before our next landing I awakened him, and he put his head out of the curtains, looking for all the world like a Kewpie. When I gave him the message, he asked me to get off when we landed and telephone the Washington airport for verification, saying: "If it is true, we will go direct to San Francisco." It was so characteristic of him that I glowed inwardly. One could be exasperated with him at times, but one had to admire his integrity and courage. I telephoned and found that it was a rumor without verification, so I went back to the plane and the mayor decided we should continue to Los Angeles.

As we proceeded we began to receive instructions. First the pilot had orders to land us at Palm Springs, but finally we were allowed to land at an almost completely deserted airport in Los Angeles. There everything was shrouded in mystery, since most airline travel had been stopped.

Mayor LaGuardia had a field day talking to everybody about fire-fighting equipment and defense preparation. As he could not go down to San Diego, I left him in Los Angeles and went without him; it meant that he was ahead of me the rest of the trip, so I got the full impact of his visits on all the officials. His complete courage and lack of fear had a wonderful effect on everyone, but I did not know and never have known how much all our plans, both his and mine, really helped, since so much equipment was lacking that they could not do many of the things that were considered essential. He did get the organizing of doctors and medical supplies started and he did a great deal to spur the reorganizing of fire departments. I talked about the other activities, going up as far as Seattle on this trip. I worked all day and traveled to my next stop by night train since no planes were flying after dark. It was a queer sensation to be on a train with all the lights concealed—even the headlight on the locomotive was dimmed—and no lights to be seen outside.

I was back in Washington on December 15. I had been gone seven days and had traveled and worked unceasingly. That same afternoon Elinor Morgenthau and Justice Justine Polier, Betty Lindley and Anna Rosenberg, all of whom were helping Elinor, came to give me the latest news of the OCD from the office front. We discussed plans and policies and then some gossip, but I was getting hardened to gossip. Never did I have a more unfavorable press than at that time, but I did not give it much thought. I knew someday I would be out of it and if it did Franklin no harm, I had no feelings about it for myself. Franklin stayed serene and untroubled through it all.

There was gossip, too, about Harry living in the White House. Some people felt that since he had not been elected to any office he should not live there at government expense. They never seemed to understand that all the food eaten in the White House is paid for by the President and that therefore Harry was no added expense to the taxpayers.

And Harry did indeed do all—and more—that Franklin expected of him.

Once the war was started and he grasped the seriousness of the situation, he put the running of the war ahead of everything else. As far as he was concerned, war needs were paramount. My husband felt the same. I, however, could not help feeling that it was the New Deal social objectives that had fostered the spirit that would make it possible for us to fight this war, and I believed it was vastly important to give people the feeling that in fighting the war we were still fighting for these same objectives. It was obvious that if the world were ruled by Hitler, freedom and democracy would no longer exist. I felt it was essential both to the prosecution of the war and to the period after the war that the fight for the rights of minorities should continue.

I wanted to see us go on with our medical program not only in the field of military medicine but in the whole area which concerned children and young people. I thought the groundwork should be laid for a wide health program after the war. Harry Hopkins could not be bothered. He felt that money could not be diverted to anything which did not have a direct bearing on the fighting of the war. He was probably right, but I never could entirely agree with him.

After the Pearl Harbor attack, all activity in the White House centered more than ever on preparations for war. The Supply Priorities and Allocation Board began its meetings, and Franklin had more and more appointments with the military people and with people like Mrs. Anna Rosenberg, who was one of his close links with labor. Next to military operations, labor was the most important consideration in our preparation for war.

The Russian ambassador came on two occasions to see my husband; and Crown Princess Marta of Norway, who must have been deeply troubled through all those days, came to gain reassurance and talk over the situation.

Meanwhile I continued working at the Office of Civilian Defense, organizing a youth division. I also tried unsuccessfully to get the Cabinet wives to take some responsibility for the hordes of girls pouring into Washington to work in the various departments.

The whole OCD episode was unfortunate. I had been reluctant to take the job and had done so only at the insistence of Harry Hopkins and another of my husband's advisers. Franklin himself was neutral, though he told me he thought it would help Mayor LaGuardia. When the mayor found what a controversial person I became he was appalled at having me; and I did not blame him for disclaiming any responsibility for the "dreadful" things that some members of Congress felt I had done. After the mayor resigned from the OCD I was instrumental in obtaining his successor. The mounting wave of attack in Congress finally convinced me that I was not going to be able to do a real job in the OCD, so on February 20, I, too, resigned, leaving Judge Landis a prickly problem which he handled well.

It is history that as soon as Prime Minister Winston Churchill heard of the Pearl Harbor attack he made up his mind to come to the United States. His trip was top secret and none of us knew until shortly before he arrived that he was coming.

A few days before his visit, my husband sent for Miss Thompson and asked her whom I had invited to stay in the house over Christmas. He also asked to see the list of people invited to dinner. In all the years that we had been in the White House he had never paid much attention to such details, and this was the first time he had made such a request. He gave no explanation and no hint that anything unusual was going to happen.

When we learned that Mr. Churchill was coming on December 22, everyone scurried around to get ready. The Monroe Room on the second floor had to be turned into a map room and an office for the British delegation, and we shifted beds around to make room for all our Christmas guests.

My husband, on that memorable day of December 22, saw the Russian ambassador, the Chinese ambassador, and the Dutch minister, besides filling innumerable other engagements. He left shortly before six in the evening to meet the British prime minister, and they all arrived at the White House at six-thirty. We had quite a houseful, but it represented only a small quota of those who came over with Mr. Churchill.

I had been asked by Franklin to have tea ready in the West Hall for our British guests, but I found on their arrival that they preferred more stimulating refreshments. We were seventeen at dinner that night. I had come back to Washington that morning on the night train from New York City and had spent a good part of the day at the Office of Civilian Defense. I had gone to the Salvation Army Christmas party, to a Catholic Charities Christmas party, and the Alley Christmas tree programs, so I had added a good deal to the already heavy official program of the day. I still remember that as time wore on that evening I caught myself falling asleep as I tried to talk to my guests.

On this visit of Mr. Churchill's, as on all his subsequent visits, my husband worked long hours every day. The prime minister took a long nap every afternoon, so was refreshed for hard work in the evening and far into the night. While he was sleeping, Franklin had to catch up on his regular work. Even after he finally retired, if important dispatches or messages came in, he was awakened, no matter what the hour, and nearly every meal he was called on the telephone for some urgent matter. It always took him several days to catch up on sleep after Mr. Churchill left.

A number of people have accused me at various times of having no sense of propriety, because frequently I had what they called unimportant people to meet important ones. Throughout the war years the comings and goings of official people was shrouded in mystery, and it was never as simple as it now sounds to make arrangements for them. They arrived and they left suddenly, and none of us were warned beforehand. This often accounted for my having conflicting engagements and for the presence of people whom I might not have invited had I known in advance what was going to happen.

During this first visit of the British prime minister I had invited Mr. and Mrs. Louis Adamic, Monroe Robinson, my cousin, and several others to dinner on January 13. Of course, when I invited them I had no idea that Mr. Churchill would be there. After dinner I took Mr. and Mrs. Adamic, Monroe Robinson and Miss Thompson to the Philadelphia concert, and the evening seemed to me of casual interest.

The reason for asking Mr. and Mrs. Adamic was that I had read a book of his, *Two-Way Passage*, which I thought interesting. Because I was always looking for new points of view to interest my husband, I had given him the book to read.

No one was more surprised than I when Mr. Adamic wrote a book, *Dinner at the White House*, based on this occasion. He seemed to think every smallest detail of the evening had some particular significance or meaning behind it. It was the supreme example of how much can be made of how little. In the book Mr. Adamic repeated a story which was most derogatory to the British prime minister; in fact, the whole book was anti-British and anti-Churchill. Mr. Churchill hotly resented it and sued Mr. Adamic in Great Britain, where the libel laws are somewhat different from ours. Of course, Mr. Adamic to the contrary, the whole evening had been a completely casual affair.

In these first talks which my husband and the prime minister had, they faced the fact that there was a long drawn-out war ahead during which there would be many setbacks, and that both of them, as leaders of their nations, would have to be prepared to bolster the morale of their people. To explain to one's country that there must be a long period while the military forces are being trained and armed, during which production will be one of the most important factors, and that meanwhile people must be patient and hope at best to hold the line is no easy or popular thing to do.

I always had great admiration for the way in which Mr. Churchill did this. In some ways he was more blunt with the people of Great Britain than my husband ever was with us. The British people were closer to the danger and I suppose for that reason could better understand the blunt approach.

Twenty-three

Visit to England

IN RETROSPECT, the thing that strikes me about these days is my triple-barreled effort to work with the OCD, carry out my official engagements, and still keep the home fires burning. I wonder particularly how I ever managed to get in all the trips I took. At the same time my husband was having more and more meetings with the Cabinet, military advisers, foreign diplomats and labor people. In one morning he saw Major General Joseph W. Stilwell, the Greek minister, and David Dubinsky.

The list of White House guests was interestingly varied during the first half of 1942. It seems to me that everyone we were to know well during the next few years began coming at about that time; and all the royal families whose countries had been overrun sooner or later appeared, looking for assistance. Each was given a formal dinner; whatever else they got, of course, I do not know.

One of the most interesting and peculiar visitors was Alexander Woollcott, who came to the White House in January and spent four days with us. I doubt if it would have been possible to have had Mr. Woollcott as one's guest very long in any ordinary household, because he required a good many things that the ordinary household could not easily provide. For instance, he wanted coffee at all hours, and he invited guests for meals in his bedroom or in a sitting room where he could be alone with them. My work and my engagements kept me away from the house a good part of the time, but late one afternoon I returned just as he was leaving for an engagement. As I came in the door he said: "Welcome, Mrs. Roosevelt, come right in. I am delighted to see you. Make yourself at home."

Among our other guests in 1942 were Prime Minister Mackenzie King, President and Señora Quezon. In May Foreign Minister Molotov came, accompanied by his interpreter, Mr. Pavlov. I was not at home when they arrived so he was given a stag dinner, but the following morning Mr. Molotov came into my sitting room with Mr. Pavlov, to have a talk with me. He talked about social reforms in his country and in mine, and he hoped that I would some day visit the U.S.S.R. I had already been told of an incident that had caused much quiet amusement. One of the White House valets was astounded when he unpacked Mr. Molotov's bag to find inside a large chunk of black bread, a roll of sausage and a pistol. The Secret Service men did not like visitors with pistols, but on this occasion nothing was said. Mr. Molotov evidently thought he might have to defend himself, and also that he might be hungry.

I liked him and I was impressed by Mr. Pavlov's English, which, he told me, he had learned from American students in Russia. He must have been gifted with a good ear, for he had no accent. I think Mr. Molotov, too, could understand English, for he often began to answer questions without waiting for the translation.

The King of Greece was with us on June 10, and on the 14th there was an impressive Flag Day ceremony in the state dining room of the White House, at which the secretary of state and the diplomatic representatives of twenty-seven other nations were present.

I spent a good deal of time in New York City that spring, emptying our house and Mrs. James Roosevelt's. We had lived in these houses since 1908 and one can imagine the accumulation of the years. My mother-in-law never threw anything away. It was a tremendous job.

Mr. Churchill was with us again from the 21st to the 25th of June. The friendship and affection between my husband and Mr. Churchill grew with every visit. It was evident that Great Britain and the United States would have to co-operate in any case, but the war could be carried on to better advantage with the two nations closely united through the personal friendship of Mr. Churchill and my husband. The two men had many interests in common, in addition to the paramount issue of the war. They were men who loved the sea and the Navy. They knew a great deal of history and had somewhat similar tastes in literature. Both of them had read much biography. Their companionship grew, I think, with their respect for each other's ability.

I remember the day Tobruk fell. Mr. Churchill was with us when the news came, and though he was stricken, his immediate reaction was to say, "Now what do we do?" To neither of these men was there such a thing as

not being able to meet a new situation. I never heard either of them say
that ultimately we would not win the war. This attitude was contagious,
and no one around either of them would ever have dared to say, "I am
afraid."

Franklin knew and understood Mr. Churchill's background. He seemed
to agree when I said on one occasion that I thought the time that would
be hardest for Mr. Churchill would be after the war. The world that had
existed before the war had been pleasant as far as he was concerned; his
tendency would be to want to go back to it, even though he might realize
that there was no way in which one could go back to a prewar world.

My husband often said he felt sure Mr. Churchill would retire from
office after the war ended, but I gathered that he expected that he and
Mr. Churchill and Mr. Stalin would still be in office for at least a short
time afterward and have something to say about the policies laid down.
He felt that the world was going to be considerably more socialistic after
the war and that Mr. Churchill might find it difficult to adjust to new
conditions. A remark made to him by Mr. Stalin in one of their talks gave
him hope that there might be, after the war, more flexibility in Communism
than we actually have seen so far.

Franklin had been wondering aloud what would happen in their respective countries if anything happened to any of the three men. Stalin said:
"I have everything arranged in my country. I know exactly what will
happen." My husband said: "So much depends in the future on how we
learn to get along together. Do you think it will be possible for the United
States and the U.S.S.R. to see things in similar ways?" Mr. Stalin responded:
"You have come a long way in the United States from your original concept of government and its responsibilities, and your original way of life.
I think it is quite possible that we in the U.S.S.R., as our resources develop
and people can have an easier life, will find ourselves growing nearer to
some of your concepts and you may be finding yourselves accepting some
of ours."

This, of course, was casual conversation, and I give it as I remember
hearing my husband repeat it. It encouraged him to believe that confidence could be built between the leaders and that we might find a way to
live in the world together, each country developing along the lines that
seemed best for it.

My husband had great confidence in his own ability to understand others
and to make them understand our motives and the needs and realities of a

situation. One of his reasons for being willing to meet with the heads of other nations outside the country, when they were unwilling to come here, was his feeling that he could convince them better by personal contact than by letter or telephone. I think Franklin accepted what other men in high office said, and believed that if he kept his word they would keep theirs. But he was never prone to overlook a breach of contract.

I shall never cease to be grateful to Mr. Churchill for his leadership during the war; his speeches were a tonic to us here in the United States as well as to his own people. The real affection which he had for my husband, and which was reciprocated, he apparently never lost. It was a fortunate friendship. The war would have been harder to win without it, and the two men might not have gone through it so well if they had not had personal pleasure in meeting and confidence in each other's integrity and ability.

The day before Mr. Churchill left in June, 1942, young King Peter of Yugoslavia came to the White House and afterwards Franklin said to me: "That young man should forget that he is a king and go to work. In the long run, he would be better off." I think of that now when I see him with his wife and child. Waiting around for a throne is not really a satisfactory business.

That spring we had Crown Princess Marta and her children and household at Hyde Park. During the war she usually spent a week or more with us each spring and autumn on her way to some place for the summer or back to Washington for the winter. We came, for that reason, to know them all very well and I shall never forget some of the things I learned about the bringing up of royal children. Prince Harald seemed devoid of fear, and though he was frail when he first came, I can remember his swimming when the water was extremely cold. I thought he ought to come out and get warm, but I was told that the water in Norway was colder and that he must become accustomed to the cold.

The names of the people who came to see me that year recall a great many activities. One of the guests who gave my husband and me the greatest pleasure was John Golden, who always went to any amount of trouble to put on a performance or to find something he thought Franklin would enjoy. Franklin once told him that the first play he had ever seen was *The Black Crook*, which he had stolen away to see without the permission of his parents. John Golden found one of the original copies of the play and had it beautifully bound for him, which gave Franklin much real pleasure. He also did a tremendous amount of work for the servicemen, getting them free tickets for plays and movies, giving prizes for the best plays written by enlisted men, and putting on a show, the proceeds of which went to the Army and Navy Relief.

In August we had our first visit from Queen Wilhelmina of the Netherlands. My press conference ladies wanted to meet her, and she did attend one conference the morning after her arrival. During the course of the meeting she said something about the increase in tuberculosis in Holland under the Nazis, which she immediately afterwards regretted, fearing the Nazis would retaliate against her people. So I had to chase after the women and insist that everything the Queen had said about tuberculosis must be off the record.

This was Franklin's second meeting with the Queen of the Netherlands. The first had been when he called on her while she was staying with Princess Juliana in Massachusetts, not many miles from Hyde Park. Crown Princess Marta, who was staying with us at the time, went with him and she told with amusement how Franklin announced to the Queen that he had been nervous before meeting her because he had heard she was one of the most awesome of crowned heads. His respect for her increased with each meeting and both he and I came to have a warm affection for her.

The next event of real importance to me was my husband's decision that I should accept Queen Elizabeth's invitation to go to Great Britain to see the work the women were doing in the war and to visit our servicemen stationed there. I did not know that one of the reasons my husband was eager to have me go over was that those men would shortly be leaving for North Africa for the invasion.

Franklin had received some tentative inquiries about whether I would be interested in going over and seeing the role that the British women were playing in the war. Naturally the British looked upon my visit as providing an opportunity to get that story told in the United States, for the Queen, knowing I wrote a column and made speches fairly frequently, felt that I had access to the people here.

When my husband asked me how I would feel about going, I assured him that if he thought it might be helpful I should be delighted to go. Knowing that the North African invasion was coming off soon, he said that in addition to observing the work of the British women he wanted me to visit our servicemen and take them a message from him.

The trip to Great Britain seemed to offer me a chance to do something that might be useful. I asked Tommy if she would be willing to go with me, since I did not want to obligate her to make a trip that might entail some risk. She was entirely willing. I suppose the saving fact for all human beings at such times is that they never think anything is going to happen to them until it actually happens.

Before I left the United States, Harry Hopkins had told me not to pay too much attention to our ambassador, Mr. Winant, but to be sure to consult Averell Harriman on everything. I had known Mr. Winant for a long time and I had great respect and admiration for him, as did my husband. I made no answer to Harry's suggestion except to say that I had known Averell Harriman since he was a small boy because he had been an intimate friend and schoolmate of my brother's, so I certainly hoped to see him in London. I firmly determined, however, that I would consult Gilbert Winant and take his advice. I was sure that Averell Harriman would not have agreed with Harry, because he knew what a wonderful reputation Mr. Winant enjoyed with the British officials.

After Mr. Winant met us I was relieved of many anxieties. On the train we went over the proposed itinerary. I thought it was a bit strenuous, but later it was expanded to include much that I had never dreamed of doing. The itinerary had been gone over by the Queen and by Lady Reading, who was to take charge of me during a part of the visit. Mr. Winant would come for me the next morning; when we left the palace his apartment and maid would be at our disposal. I was not conscious of the need for protection, but both the prime minister and the ambassador felt I would be safer and have more privacy in his apartment than in a hotel.

I had been worried by the thought of having to visit Buckingham Palace, but I was determined to live each moment, aware of its special interest. Though certain situations might be unfamiliar and give me a feeling of inadequacy and of not knowing the proper way to behave, still I would do my best and not worry. Nevertheless, as we neared London I grew more and more nervous and wondered why on earth I had ever let myself be inveigled into coming on this trip.

Finally, we pulled into the station. The red carpet was unrolled and the stationmaster and the head guard on the train, both of them looking grand enough to be high officials of the government, told me that the moment to get off had arrived. There stood the King and Queen and all our high military officials. The only person in the whole group whom I felt I really knew was Stella Reading.

After the formal greetings, the King and Queen took me in their car, while Tommy was taken in hand by the lady in waiting and two gentlemen from the royal household, and we drove off to Buckingham Palace.

The King and Queen treated me with the greatest kindness. The feeling I had had about them during their visit to the United States, that they were simply a young and charming couple, who would have to undergo some very difficult experiences, began to come back to me, intensified by the realization that they now had been through these experiences and were anxious to tell me about them. In all my contacts with them I gained the greatest respect for both the King and the Queen. I did not always agree with the ideas expressed to me by the King on international subjects, but the fact that both of them were doing an extraordinarily outstanding job for their people in the most trying times stood out.

When we arrived at the palace they took me to my rooms, explaining that I could have only a small fire in my sitting room and one in the outer waiting room, and saying they hoped I would not be too cold. Through the windows they pointed out the shell holes. The windowpanes in my room had all been broken and replaced by wood and isinglass and one or two small panes of glass. Later the Queen showed me where a bomb had dropped right through the King's rooms, destroying both his rooms and hers. They explained the various layers of curtains which had to be kept closed when the lights were on; informed me that there would be a messenger outside my door to take me to the drawing room at the proper hour for dinner, and then left me to my own devices.

Buckingham Palace seemed perfectly enormous to me. The suite I had was so huge that when Elliott saw it he said that after this I would have to take the long corridor at the White House for my bedroom, because the one I had would never again seem adequate. The wardrobes were wonderful, the kind one longs for at home, but the 55-pound limit on baggage made my few clothes look pathetic hanging in those wardrobes. I wondered what the maid thought when she unpacked them. One evening dress, two day dresses, one suit and a few blouses, one pair of day shoes and one pair of evening shoes comprised my wardrobe for a visit to Buckingham Palace! One of the newspaperwomen, for want of something better to write about, later reported that I had worn the soles of my one pair of shoes through. The head usher at the White House read the story and thoughtfully sent me another pair.

Everything in Great Britain was done as one would expect it to be. The restrictions on heat and water and food were observed as carefully in the royal household as in any other home in England. There was a plainly marked black line in my bathtub above which I was not supposed to run the water. We were served on gold and silver plates, but our bread was the same kind of war bread every other family had to eat, and, except for the fact that occasionally game from one of the royal preserves appeared on the table, nothing was served in the way of food that was not served in any of the war canteens.

My visit to Great Britain was the beginning of a real friendship with Gil Winant. He was a shy person, but he had great intellectual integrity, a vivid imagination, which enabled him to understand situations that he had never experienced, and a sensitiveness to other people that enabled him to accomplish things many of his friends thought beyond his powers. He grew to love Great Britain and her people, and I think the statesmen who bore the brunt of the burdens during the war trusted and depended upon him.

I myself can never be grateful enough to him for the kindness with which he mapped out my trip and for the things he told me which helped me to carry out my task among the British people better than I might otherwise have done. He was a selfless person who gave little thought to his own comfort, but much thought to helping his friends. He made the time I spent in London both pleasant and comfortable. I shall always miss him, for he came to be one of the people that I looked forward to seeing from time to time. I cannot describe what it was he gave his friends. I do not even know that he considered me any more than an acquaintance, but I prized highly what he gave me; and I had a feeling that he shed light in dark places. He worked unceasingly in the hope of a better world for future generations.

With the King and Queen I had my first real look at the devastation— blocks upon blocks of rubble. Our first stop was at St. Paul's Cathedral, partly because the King and Queen wanted to give the faithful watchers who had saved the cathedral the satisfaction of a visit from them and partly so that I could stand on the steps and see what modern warfare could do to a great city.

I spent a weekend at Chequers, the country estate given by Lord Lee to the British government for the use of British prime ministers. There I watched Prime Minister Churchill playing a game on the floor with his grandson and noticed the extraordinary resemblance between the two. Mr. Churchill once remarked that his grandson didn't look like him, he just looked like all babies.

Mrs. Churchill was attractive and charming. One felt that being in public life she had to assume a role and that the role was now part of her. She was careful not to voice any opinions publicly or to be associated with any political organizations. Over the years, my admiration and affection for her have grown. She has had no easy role to play in life, but she has played it with dignity and charm.

For security reasons I had to have a code name, and someone with a sense of humor—I suspected my husband—had decided that "Rover" was appropriate. A hypothetical organization called "Rover's Rangers" had been organized by the young men at the United States embassy in London, with my husband as the "Starter."

After lunch one day we were scheduled to visit Elliott's unit at a place called Steeple Morden, but the chauffeur, who, for my protection, was a Scotland Yard man and not a regular driver, lost his way and we could not find the camp. No one who was asked would tell us how to get there— also for security reasons—so finally someone telephoned back to the United States embassy: "Rover has lost her pup" and asked for directions!

With Mrs. Churchill I went to visit a maternity hospital, and also to see how the women in the several branches of the military service were trained. During one of these visits, the air-raid warning sounded, but the girls went right on with what they were doing and paid no attention. I saw girls learning how to service every kind of truck and motorcar and to drive every type of vehicle; I even saw girls in gun crews, helping the men to load the guns. I visited factories in which women did every kind of work, and I visited one group of girls whose job it was to fly planes from one part of the country to another. Since it was unwise to keep a concentration of planes anywhere in Great Britain, these girls took over the plane when a pilot landed and flew it either to a place where it would be well camouflaged or to a repair shop.

At one time or another during this trip I visited Red Cross clubs of all types—our own American Red Cross, the British Red Cross, and St. John's Guild. At that time Harvey Gibson, the dynamic head of the Red Cross in Europe, was expanding its facilities in a remarkable manner, and though I occasionally heard that this or that particular club was doing something that my informant considered detrimental to the morale of the men or women, on the whole I thought the Red Cross was doing, in its recreation program at least, an outstanding job.

During this visit to England I started the practice, which I continued on subsequent trips, of collecting from the boys to whom I talked the names and addresses of their families, so that I could write to them on my return to the United States. I had quite a collection before I was through.

I also made a tour of the camps where our servicemen were stationed and ended it by spending one night with Queen Mary at Badminton. This was something that Franklin had particularly wanted me to do because King George V and Queen Mary had been kind to his mother when she visited England. He thought of Queen Mary as in some ways rather like his mother, and therefore made a point of my seeing her.

Here again I had the same sense of strain that I had felt before visiting Buckingham Palace. I was told that we must arrive at six o'clock—not five minutes before or five after, but at six sharp. To my surprise, Queen Mary met me at the door and took me to her sitting room, the only small room in that house, as far as I could see, and one which had a good fire. After a talk, she took me to my room, which, though cold and barnlike, was furnished grandly with Chinese Chippendale furniture. She showed me where the bathroom and the w.c. were, and they were cold too.

Tommy's room was as cold as mine. We dressed and went down to dinner, arriving in good time. At dinner I sat on the Queen's left, the princess royal on her right, the Duke and Duchess of Beaufort, the young relatives who owned Badminton, at either end of the table. General Knox, who seemed to manage the household, Lord Hamilton, gentleman in waiting to the Queen, and a lady in waiting completed the party.

After dinner, which was not a hilarious meal and during which I made valiant efforts at conversation, we went into the drawing room and stood for fifteen minutes. Queen Mary looked regal and every inch a queen, with many ropes of pearls and many sparkling bracelets and rings. She wore a black velvet evening gown and an ermine jacket. Then she asked me to her sitting room and also asked the princess royal if she wished to accompany us. Tommy was left with the others and soon escaped. I looked in on her when I was politely dismissed to go to bed, and found her already in bed because it was the only way to keep warm. However, I really enjoyed my visit and had a great admiration and real affection for Queen Mary after that.

She gave me, to bring back to Franklin, a photograph of herself, fully dressed with hat, veil and gloves, sawing a dead limb off a tree, with one of her dispatch riders, a young Australian, at the other end of the saw. She told me to tell my husband that she cared as much about the conservation of trees as he did and was sending him this photograph to prove it. Nothing I brought him from that trip gave him more pleasure than the photograph and the message, and he always felt that Queen Mary was a grand person.

Under Stella Reading's guidance I visited universities and innumerable factories, stayed on estates where the grounds were now being used for agricultural purposes and in country houses whose owners, now living in one small part of them, had turned them into nurseries for evacuated or wounded children. I saw the way the Women's Voluntary Services had organized to perform innumerable duties, from moving into a town which had just been bombed and needed everything from food to laundry service, to looking after the billeting of workers who had been moved from one factory to another.

Our days usually began at eight o'clock and ended at midnight, but I was so interested that at the time I did not even realize how weary I was gradually becoming. We wrote the column every day at whatever time we could fit it in, and sometimes in rooms so cold that Tommy's fingers would hardly work.

This was a nation at war, going through moments of great uncertainty and stress. But what I have often marveled at has been the people's stanchness and their ability to carry on during the years after the war and to accept the drabness of their lives.

One of the workers with whom I talked told me that the hardest thing was to keep on at your job when you knew the bombs were falling in the area of your home and you did not know whether you would find your home and family still there at the end of your day's or night's work. When we lunched with some of the women who were daily feeding the dockworkers, they told me: "We used to look down on the dockworkers as the roughest element in our community. We were a little afraid of them; but now we have come to know them well and will never feel that way again."

Women from many different backgrounds, who had never worked together before, were working side by side, just as the men were fighting side by side. These British Isles, which we always regarded as class-conscious, as a place where people were so nearly frozen in their classes that they rarely moved from one to another, became welded together by the war into a closely knit community in which many of the old distinctions lost their point and from which new values emerged.

When I visited a center where bombed-out people were getting clothes and furniture and other supplies, one young woman with a child in her arms and another dragging at her skirt said to me very cheerfully: "Oh, yes, this is the third time we have been bombed out, but the government gives us a bit of help and you people in America send us clothes. We get along and none of us was hurt and that's the main thing."

Back in London I had dinner with Prime Minister and Mrs. Churchill. During the dinner I had a slight difference of opinion with Prime Minister Churchill on the subject of Loyalist Spain. The prime minister asked Henry Morgenthau whether we, the United States, were sending "enough" to Spain and whether it was reaching there safely. Henry Morgenthau told him that he hoped we were, and I said I thought it was a little too late, that we should have done something to help the Loyalists during their civil war. Mr. Churchill said he had been for the Franco government until Germany and Italy went into Spain to help Franco. I remarked that I could not see why the Loyalist government could not have been helped, and the prime minister replied that he and I would have been the first to lose our heads if the Loyalists had won—the feeling against people like us would have spread. I said that losing my head was unimportant, whereupon he said: "I don't want you to lose your head and neither do I want to lose mine." Then Mrs. Churchill leaned across the table and said: "I think perhaps Mrs. Roosevelt is right." The prime minister was quite annoyed by this time and said: "I have held certain beliefs for sixty years and I'm not going to change now." Mrs. Churchill then got up as a signal that dinner was over.

Before I left for home my aunt, Maude Gray, Tommy and I drove out one day to Windsor Castle, for I wanted to report to Queen Elizabeth on my trip. While we were talking in her sitting room, the King, who had spent the day visiting our air force troops, came in with the children. Both the King and I had rather bad colds, which necessitated a good deal of attention to our noses. As we drove away from Windsor Castle my aunt said to me in shocked tones: "Darling, I never was so humiliated in my life. Your using those nasty little tissues and wadding them in your hand while the King used such lovely sheer linen handkerchiefs! What could they have thought!"

As the time for my return trip approached, my husband and Ambassador Winant and the prime minister discussed how I should travel. Tommy and I had our return passage on an American Export Lines plane. Both Ambassador Winant and the prime minister pointed out that, while I might not be concerned personally with the possibility of the Germans' discovering I was on a plane bound for Lisbon, I would be jeopardizing the other passengers. Finally, after many conversations over the transatlantic telephone, my husband, who did not want me to travel on a military plane, gave in and said: "I don't care how you send her home, just send her."

Twenty-four

Getting on with the War: 1943

AFTER WE HAD been back from London a few days a Washington columnist wrote for his paper a story asserting that Miss Thompson had asked me for a few days off to go to see her mother, who was ill. I was alleged to have said: "Why, Timothy, I didn't know you had a mother, but I am afraid we are much too busy for you to be away now."

It was so ridiculous that neither of us was annoyed. Miss Thompson wrote to the gentleman as follows:

"Your column quoting my request for a few days' holiday and Mrs. Roosevelt's alleged reply has just been brought to my attention.

"For your information, my mother died in 1928 and in order that there be no confusion about which parent I wanted to visit, my father died in 1932. Nothing could give me more satisfaction than to be able to visit either or both of my parents and get back to my job. If you, in your omnipotence, can tell me how to accomplish this, I shall be most grateful."

Needless to say, there was no answer to this letter and no correction in the column.

The day I arrived home we had a large dinner for the President of Ecuador, who was to be an overnight guest. I should have liked at least one evening to catch up on my family, for I had been away several weeks, but this is a pleasure a public person cannot always count on.

Very soon I began to realize that there would shortly be other trips about which I had better know very little. On January 9, 1943, Franklin left for Miami, Florida, and took off on the 12th for Casablanca. It was his first long trip by air across the water and I had hoped he would be won over to flying, but instead he disliked it more than ever.

Admittedly, a flight like this in time of war entailed some personal

247

danger, but that was something Franklin never gave a thought to. Long ago, when Mayor Cermak was killed, Franklin and I had talked it over and decided that that kind of danger was something you could do nothing about. You cannot be protected from a person who does not care whether he is caught or not. The only possible course is to put the thought of danger out of your mind and go ahead with your job as you feel you must, regardless of what might be called its occupational risks. In the case of the Casablanca trip there was also the fact that Franklin was doing an unprecedented thing, and he knew there would be criticism. That again was a consideration he could not let weigh with him. All the arrangements for the trip were made through the Secret Service; his departure was as secret as possible; the flag which indicates that the President is in residence was never taken down from the White House, and I went on with my daily routine exactly as though he were there.

When Franklin returned he was full of stories. He loved particularly to tell us how he had made Mr. Churchill unhappy by teasing him about his "bad boy," General de Gaulle. Mr. Churchill, of course, was responsible for General de Gaulle and the general had proved difficult about going to the meeting. Back of Franklin's teasing, however, there had been a serious purpose because he had felt that if Mr. Churchill put the screws on, General de Gaulle would have to come to Casablanca, since Great Britain was providing him with the money necessary to carry on his activities at the time. When the general did go, it was not altogether a happy meeting.

Afterwards when I questioned him about the meeting, Franklin said, "General de Gaulle is a soldier, patriotic, yes, devoted to his country; but, on the other hand, he is a politician and a fanatic and there are, I think, in him almost the makings of a dictator."

Another thing Franklin talked much about was the horrible conditions of the natives in the places he had stopped. He never minced words in telling Mr. Churchill that he did not think the British had done enough in any one of the colonial areas he had seen on this trip to improve the lot of the native peoples. He agreed with me that the United States, too, had a serious responsibility in Liberia, which we had never lived up to, and I was particularly happy when Edward Stettinius later went ahead with the plans for Liberia which he discussed with Franklin at that time. He formed a company to develop the natural resources of the country—a project that was only a dream when he talked with my husband after his return from Casablanca.

In early February I made a trip to Portland, Maine, where Cary Bok met me and took me to Camden to visit his shipyard, where he was building wooden vessels. This was something in which Franklin was greatly interested.

Later in the month I flew to Des Moines, Iowa, with Colonel Oveta Hobby, head of the WAC, to inspect their main training station. While I was there I took a side trip to speak at a college in Columbia, Missouri, and was back in the White House in plenty of time to greet Madame Chiang when she first arrived in this country. At that time she was in the Medical Center in New York City for treatment.

Madame Chiang seemed so small and delicate as she lay in her hospital bed that I had a desire to help her and take care of her as if she had been my own daughter. Occasionally I took someone to see her because I felt she would tire of seeing only me, and many people were anxious to meet her.

When it came time for her to leave the hospital we offered her our house in Hyde Park for a few days before she came to Washington. She spent several days there and then, accompanied by two nurses and her nephew and niece, Mr. and Miss Kung, who acted as her secretaries, she came to the White House and stayed until the 28th of the month. She should have been an invalid with no cares; but she felt she had work to do, that she must see important people in our government and in the armed services who could be helpful to China, and that she must fulfill certain official obligations.

I shall never forget the day I went with her when she addressed the House of Representatives, after meeting the senators. A little, slim figure in Chinese dress, she made a dramatic entrance as she walked down the aisle, surrounded by tall men. She knew it, for she had a keen sense of the dramatic. Her speech, beautifully delivered, was a remarkable expression of her own conception of democracy.

I saw another side of Madame Chiang while she was in the White House, and I was much amused by the reactions of the men with whom she talked. They found her charming, intelligent, and fascinating, but they were all a little afraid of her, because she could be a coolheaded statesman when she was fighting for something she deemed necessary to China and to her husband's regime; the little velvet hand and the low, gentle voice disguised a determination that could be as hard as steel.

A certain casualness about cruelty emerged sometimes in her conversations with the men, though never with me. I had painted for Franklin such a sweet, gentle and pathetic figure that, as he came to recognize the other side of the lady, it gave him keen pleasure to tease me about my lack of perception. I remember an incident at a dinner party during one of her visits which gave him particular entertainment. John L. Lewis was acting up at the time, and Franklin turned to Madame Chiang and asked: "What would you do in China with a labor leader like John Lewis?" She never said a word, but the beautiful, small hand came up and slid across her throat, a most expressive gesture. Franklin looked across at me to make sure I had seen, and went right on talking. He enjoyed being able to say to me afterwards: "Well, how about your gentle and sweet character?"

Her two young secretaries created a slight confusion when they first arrived in the White House, because her niece, Miss Kung, insisted on dressing like a man, and the valets, thinking I had made a mistake in assigning the rooms, unpacked Miss Kung under the impression that she was Mr. Kung. Then they went to the ushers' office and reported that I had made a mistake, only to learn much to their confusion that they had unpacked a lady. Franklin was also confused by her type of dress and when she came into the study where we all met before dinner, he greeted her as "my boy." Harry Hopkins quickly wrote a note saying: "This is Miss Kung." Franklin tried to cover up by saying blandly: "I always call all young things 'my boy'"; but everyone knew quite well that her clothes had completely fooled him. I do not believe she was offended by his mistake, for that was the impression she was trying to give. She hated being a girl—I suppose in protest against the inferior position sometimes assigned to women in China.

After Madame Chiang left us, she made a long trip by special train throughout the United States, out to the West Coast and back. It must have been a strenuous and difficult trip for her, and after her return she questioned Tommy carefully. Tommy and I had taken practically the same trip, following in her footsteps, a few days behind her, and heard about her everywhere. What mystified Madame Chiang was how it was possible for us to travel alone while she had forty people, yet never enough to do the things she needed to have done.

She asked Tommy who packed our bags, and Tommy said she packed hers and I packed mine. She then asked who answered the telephone, and Tommy said that whichever one of us was nearer it answered. She also asked who took care of the mail and telegrams and was told that we did it jointly. Her next question was, who looked after our clothes, and Tommy told her that if a dress needed pressing, we asked the hotel valet to do it. Finally she asked about my safety. Tommy explained that we did not consider "protection" necessary, since everyone was good to us, but that, of course, in various cities people would sometimes be assigned to meet us at the train and see us off and motor us about if we were going to be in large crowds; that this, however, was entirely dependent upon how the local authorities felt.

I have never asked for or wanted protection and in all the miles I have traveled and the many places I have visited I never have had an unpleasant incident. People might become a bit too enthusiastic; but it was all kindly meant and I felt it was because they loved my husband. I have had a tail pulled off my fur scarf as a souvenir, but nothing worse than that has ever happened.

During the month of April I went on a short trip with Franklin to inspect some war plants in Mexico and to meet the President and spend a few hours in Monterrey. It was an interesting trip to me, because it was the first time I had been in that country. My impression of the city is rather vague, for we drove fast and were watching the crowds rather than the city itself; however, Mexican hospitality, as expressed at the dinner we all attended and in the kindness of everyone with whom we came in contact, made a deep impression on the whole party. We traveled back with a feeling that Mexico was a close neighbor in spirit. My husband already felt close and friendly to the Mexican people, but to many of us this was a new experience.

I imagine every mother felt as I did when I said good-by to the children during the war. I had a feeling that I might be saying good-by for the last time. It was a sort of precursor of what it would be like if your children were killed. Life had to go on and you had to do what was required of you, but something inside of you quietly died.

At the time of World War I, I felt keenly that I wanted to do everything possible to prevent future war, but I never felt it in the same way that I did during World War II. During this second war period I identified myself with all the other women who were going through the same slow death, and I kept praying that I might be able to prevent a repetition of the stupidity called war.

I have tried, ever since, in everything I have done, to keep that promise I made to myself, but the progress that the world is making toward peace seems like the crawling of a little child, halting and slow.

May was a busy month in 1943. The President of Bolivia and his foreign minister stayed at the White House on two separate occasions. President Benes of Czechoslovakia and Prime Minister Mackenzie King each spent a night with us, and later the President and the President-elect of Liberia came. Their visit was a direct result of my husband's visit to Liberia on his way back from Casablanca.

Early one morning in July I was called on the telephone and guardedly told that there had been an engagement in which Franklin Junior's ship had been bombed. They thought it was getting into Palermo safely. That was all. It was long before I heard the details. After the ship had been bombed, it was taken into Palermo, where it continued to be shelled at intervals. It was tied to another ship, and men were injured on both of them. Franklin Junior had the good luck to be able to save one boy's life by carrying him down to the other ship's doctor. At the time he did not notice that he himself was hit in the shoulder, but to this day little pieces of shrapnel are there to remind him of it.

Eventually Franklin Junior's ship went to Malta for repairs and was still at Malta when he got word that he was to meet his father, who was on his way to Cairo. He was delighted at the chance of seeing him, but when Franklin told him he would like him on the trip as his aide, young Franklin's joy changed to determination that nothing of the kind was going to happen. After the repairs on his ship were completed, it would have to get home, and he knew it would be an anxious trip because the ship would not really be in top-notch condition. He felt he could not let the ship go back without him, after all he and his shipmates had been through together.

Franklin Junior and his father had quite an argument about where his first duty lay. The ship won in the end and his father gave him a letter of orders to return to it. Young Franklin realized that he could never show those orders to anyone, because security demanded that no one know his father was in the area. He had a difficult time getting back to Malta with no orders that he could show to get priority for the return trip.

Twenty-five

Visit to the Pacific

I DO NOT REMEMBER when my husband first suggested that it would be a good idea for me to take a good-will trip to the Pacific, though I do remember the suggestion came because he felt that Australia and New Zealand, being so far away, had been rather neglected in the matter of visitors. Both countries were exposed to attack and the people were under constant strain and anxiety. We had had to send a great number of our servicemen out there, an influx which had added considerably to the strain and which had been, for people whose own men were fighting in Africa and Italy, a disrupting even though reassuring occurrence.

Another reason for the trip was that I had received a number of letters from the women of New Zealand and Australia suggesting that, since I had seen the work of the women of Great Britain, I might be interested in coming out to see what was being done in their far-off countries.

At once I put up a strong plea to be allowed to see our men on Guadalcanal and other islands. I had done considerable visiting in the West Coast hospitals to which the early wounded from Guadalcanal and some from the 1st Marine Raider group (with which Jimmy served) were being returned; and I told my husband that it would be hard to go on doing it if, when I was to be in the Pacific area anyway, I were not permitted to visit the places where these men had left their health or received their injuries. He finally broke down and gave me letters to the commanding generals and to Admiral Halsey, saying that he was willing to have me go to Guadalcanal "if it did not interfere with the conduct of the war."

Franklin was going to the conference at Quebec on the 17th, the same day I was to leave for San Francisco, but we had a little time together at Hyde Park first. It was decided that my visit should be kept secret, so I

253

went on about my daily business as usual. Prime Minister Churchill, who was staying with us, still speaks occasionally of how surprised he was when I casually mentioned at dinner one night that I was leaving the next day for the Southwest Pacific.

He looked aghast. "What have you done about your trip?" I said all the plans had been made and the itinerary worked out. He asked who was going with me, and I said no one, because, having been subjected to much criticism on my return from Great Britain, I thought I would avoid some of it on this trip by taking up as little room as possible. I later found to my regret that some columnists were none too kind anyway, and that I might just as well have taken several people. Nothing more disagreeable could have been said. Mr. Churchill insisted on cabling to all his people in the Pacific, and they were most kind wherever I met them. I have always been grateful to him for his thoughtfulness.

I had gone to see Norman Davis, chairman of the American Red Cross, as soon as the trip had been decided on, and had asked if it would be of any assistance to him if I went to look over the various Red Cross installations and trouble spots. I hoped in this way to show that I was doing a serious job and not just running around the war area causing trouble. He said that I could be most useful, because he had been planning to send someone out there to inspect the Red Cross work. He asked me if I would be willing to wear a Red Cross uniform and make a report to him on my return.

I talked this suggestion over with my husband, since it seemed to offer a number of advantages. In the first place, uniforms meant less luggage, an advantage when traveling by air; in the second place, in a familiar uniform I would feel easier visiting hospitals and meeting servicemen. Franklin decided it would be a good idea, so I bought at my own expense the thinnest uniforms I could find, also a heavy one with a warm top coat, because I knew I would encounter extremes of weather. I conscientiously inspected every Red Cross activity in every area I visited and I hope that my reports were some compensation to Mr. Davis for the criticism heaped upon him for permitting me to go in uniform as a Red Cross representative.

Because Franklin felt that, since I was traveling on a military plane, I should not keep any of the money that accrued from my column while I was on this trip, I arranged for half of my earnings to go to the Red Cross and half to the American Friends Service Committee, also dividing between them what I earned for articles written after my return. Later I discovered that certain of the Republican members of Mr. Davis' board were afraid that if it were known I had given this money to the Red Cross some of the large donors who were strongly opposed to my husband politically would withdraw their contributions. Consequently, we never explained how I happened to go in uniform or what the financial arrangements were; however, I think it is now quite safe to give the facts.

On Christmas Island I had my first encounter with tropical bugs. When I walked into the room after supper and, putting on the light, found my floor completely covered with little red bugs, I nearly disgraced myself by screaming. Remembering that I was the only woman on the island, and that a scream would undoubtedly raise an alarm, I stamped my foot and all the little bugs scurried down through the cracks in the floor.

I saw everything the men were doing on that island, as I did on all the others I visited. Right from the beginning I followed my sons' advice, which was none too self-flattering, considering that they were officers. They had said: "Mummy, don't take every meal with the brass. See that you have a meal with the noncommissioned officers and get a noncommissioned officer to drive you around, and get one meal with the enlisted men themselves." The only way to accomplish the last was to get up and eat breakfast with the men before six o'clock.

I used to wonder how the pilots ever found the little dots of coral islands in that vast expanse of ocean. Having to come down so close to the water to land was a curious sensation at first, but I became accustomed to it.

Having no one with me as a secretary, I had to write my column either at night or during flights in the daytime. I am such a slow typist that this meant an extra two hours' work for me almost every day. However, when I had a long flight I could often write enough for two or three columns, which helped when I had an overcrowded schedule at some stop. I lost thirty pounds and when I got home I realized I was more tired than I had ever been in all my life. But I was not ill and the work got done—nothing else mattered.

When I reached Noumea and met Admiral Halsey, I presented my letters from my husband. The admiral has told his own story of how much he dreaded my coming. He did not dread it any more than I did, but I determined to do as well as I could, and if it was possible to get up to Guadalcanal. The admiral refused to give me the slightest inkling of what he had decided about that and told me in no uncertain terms that I would have to go to New Zealand and Australia first and that he would make his decision on my return. I thought I noticed a slight change in his attitude before I left; perhaps some good reports were coming to him from the hospitals and the various places I had already visited.

Wherever I went I met people I had seen before. That the many trips I had made in the United States during the depression years had an unforeseen by-product was evident as I walked through the hospital wards. Occasionally when I spoke to a boy, he would say he had seen me last when I spoke at his commencement or on some other occasion; then if I recalled something about his home town his whole face would light up, and I would feel that the endless miles I walked every day were worthwhile.

I stayed with the governor general and his wife while I was in the capital of New Zealand, and again with the governor general and his wife on Fiji, invitations I owed to Mr. Churchill's thoughtfulness. Both visits were pleasant though, of course, I had to follow my usual routine. In New Zealand especially, I tried to see something of the people of the country and what they were doing, as well as of our own men.

By that time we had only rest camps and hospitals in New Zealand, but I could see the effects of the tremendous influx of our men who had gone from there, first to Guadalcanal and later to other parts of the Pacific. By the time I got there some of the New Zealand men were coming back and I got one amusing letter asking me if I would not see that our men left their girls alone. When I spoke of the letter to some New Zealand people I was told a story to illustrate the difference between the approach of the average American GI and the New Zealand soldier. A GI was on a bus one day and found himself sitting behind a lovely-looking girl with fair hair. He leaned forward and said: "Angel, what heaven did you drop from?" As an opening gambit, that speech probably would never have occurred to a New Zealand man.

In the Red Cross clubs there one of the girls told me: "There is a boy here who says he does not want to speak to you or even be in the same room with you, because he understands you advocate that all the marines who came to the Pacific be quarantined for six months after they return, before they are allowed to go home." Here was a story that I had heard before leaving home. In my talk with the boys that day I mentioned the story, adding that the families of some of the boys who had written back home about it had sent the letters on to me. I told them how surprised I had been, since I had never thought of saying anything of the kind. I had a son in the marines and he certainly would never allow me to have any such ideas. Much later, after I had tested it out and found that the story was known to the noncommissioned officers and the men, some of the older officers suggested that it might have been broadcast by Tokyo Rose. Heaven knows how it started, but it plagued me for a long time, and a similar story was told in all parts of the world. The paratroopers in Italy complained that I had said the same thing about them, and I heard it again when I went to the Caribbean. Quite evidently it was propaganda designed to detract from the value of any contacts I might make, whether at home in the hospitals or on various trips.

While I was in New Zealand I visited Rotorua, the home of the Maoris, who had shown our servicemen much hospitality. The head guide, Rangi, who showed me about, was a wonderful woman, brilliant, witty and dignified.

When I reached Australia I stayed for a while at Canberra with the governor general and his wife, Lord and Lady Gowrie, who were kindness itself; I shall never feel grateful enough to them for all they did to make my visit useful and pleasant. I spoke to vast audiences and visited many hospitals, rest homes for our nurses, and recreation centers for our men. Boy after boy told me how kindly he had been treated in Australian homes, and that was equally true in New Zealand; however, Australia had a greater number of our men in proportion to her population. Nevertheless, they stood up under the strain in a remarkable manner.

In a rest home for nurses I asked one young nurse what she objected to most. She said, "The rat that sits in the middle of my floor and will not move no matter how much noise I make." Rats, insects and snakes were things one had to contend with daily in the hospitals on the islands, and one girl told me of waking up to find a snake neatly coiled on the outside of her netting. She could not get up until someone came and did away with it.

Many of these girls were working in hospitals where water was sometimes almost impossible to get; one cupful to a patient a day had to do for drinking and washing. The mud was so deep at times that even with the GI boots and trousers tucked into the tops it was difficult to get around. But I never heard any of them really complain.

It was in Australia, in a Red Cross club, that I had an interesting talk with some young men. They were mostly air force boys, some of them from West Virginia, and the discussion turned to John Lewis and the coal strike. I told them of a boy in a hospital who had said: "I come from West

Virginia. I'm a miner. It isn't the miners who are wrong; they've got a real grievance and they don't understand about us. You know that."

I was glad I knew mining areas well enough to realize that it was not even entirely John Lewis' fault. It was the fault of all of us, who should have paid attention long ago to the conditions under which the miners worked and not have left it to John Lewis to get for them the only benefits they had received up to that time. But the boys who had been miners themselves, or whose fathers were miners, had a difficult time trying to explain to their companions that there was any justification for a coal strike in wartime.

Back at Noumea, I still did not know whether I was to be allowed to go to Guadalcanal or was starting homeward. The last evening, after I had spent the day doing all the things that had been arranged for me by Admiral Halsey, he announced that I was to be ready to leave the next morning at eight o'clock for Efate. I was not to mention the name of the island because the Japs had never bombed it and we had some of our biggest hospitals there. He hoped that they did not know we were established there. From Efate I would go to Espiritu Santo and then on to Guadalcanal.

My diary may be worthy quoting:

> By six a.m. we were on Guadalcanal where we had breakfast with the commanding officer on the airfield; he is a great friend of Admiral Halsey's. At one point he was lost and everyone turned out to find him, including the admiral himself.
>
> Then the army officers came to get me, and as we drove off the trucks with the men who were working on the field were just coming in. Coletta Ryan and I leaned out to wave. At first there was complete surprise on the faces of the men, and then one boy in stentorian tones said: "Gosh, there's Eleanor." I am never quite sure whether to take this as a compliment or to be a little ashamed of it, but they were so evidently pleased to see women, we had to laugh and go on waving. The commanding officer was plainly horrified to have me treated with such levity, so I tried to make believe I considered it a great compliment.
>
> I visited all the improvements which have been made since this part of the island came into our possession. There are thought to be some Japs still on the other side of the island and there are still air raids.

One of the things which I shall never forget on Guadalcanal is my visit to the cemetery. The little church there was built by the natives and given to the soldiers, they even made an altar and the altar vessels, carving them beautifully and decorating the church with symbols which have special meanings for them—fishes of various kind which mean long life, eternity, etc. It was very moving to walk among the graves and to realize how united these boys had been in spite of differences in religion and background. The boy's messkit or sometimes his helmet hung on the cross which some friend would have carved with the appropriate symbol of the Jewish or Catholic or Protestant faith. Words that came from the heart were carved on the base, such as "He was a grand guy"— "Best buddy ever."

At 5:30 I went to the dinner that had been arranged and then back to the hospital to finish the wards. There was an air-raid alert just as we were driving in, which meant that we had to take to the shelter in the hospital grounds, with all the patients who could walk. For a short time there was a rather tense atmosphere, but somebody started to sing and we all joined in. When the all-clear sounded I went through the wards I had not covered before. I was much interested to see what the effects of the alert would be on those who could not leave their beds and go to the shelter. I saw only two men who were badly affected. . . .

The return trip to Hawaii was again made by way of Christmas Island because an attack was being made on the route we originally planned to take and it was thought not safe for me to go that way. My time on Christmas Island was short and I visited only one boy, about whom the doctor was very much worried. At the hospital I made him promise that he would try to get well if I would try to see his mother on my return. I did see her, and fortunately he recovered and came to see me when he got back to the United States.

This time I stayed some days in Hawaii, where I saw the training given under actual fire—and was greatly impressed by it—visited a great number of hospitals, and a New York State regiment. Judith Anderson met me at luncheon at one of the hospitals. She and Maurice Evans were giving Shakespearean plays on the islands in this group—*Macbeth* at the time—and it was a wild success. She told me with satisfaction that some of the boys would wait outside and ask her "who this guy Shakespeare" was and tell her it was the first time they had seen a real play with living people in it, and ask to be allowed to come again the next night because they did not think they got everything there was in the play. They were audiences such as few actors and actresses ever meet and I think repaid fully everything which Miss Anderson and Mr. Evans put into their trip.

Finally I took off for home. I have a lasting recollection of landing in California and having to sit in the plane while all the outer air was shut off and we were squirted thoroughly with disinfectant.

I had been to Hawaii, Christmas Island, Penryhn Island, Bora Bora, Aitutaki, Tutuila, Samoa, Fiji, New Caledonia; Auckland, Wellington, and Rotorua in New Zealand; Sydney, Canberra, Melbourne, Rockhampton, Cairns, Brisbane in Australia; Efate, Espiritu Santo, Guadalcanal and Wallis.

War trip number two was over.

Twenty-six

Teheran and the Caribbean

HAVING TOLD the story of my two trips to parts of the world where actual war was going on and where, of necessity, one saw the results of the war in the hospitals, I think I should say something of the impressions these trips left with me.

At first I could hardly bear the hospitals. There was, of course, a certain amount of pure physical fatigue from walking miles of hospital wards day after day; but that was nothing in comparison with the horrible consciousness of waste and feeling of resentment that burned within me as I wondered why men could not sit down around a table and settle their differences before an infinite number of the youth of many nations had to suffer.

The most horrifying hospitals were those in which the men who had been mentally affected by the experiences they had been through were treated. I could tell myself, of course, that these men would probably have broken under other circumstances, that there must be something wrong with our civilization when our young people were so vulnerable to mental illness and that we must work to discover the reasons and try to change them; nevertheless, my horror at seeing people who had broken mentally and emotionally made me lie awake nights.

There were times in the other hospitals when it was hard to accept the gallantry of the men themselves without showing how deeply sorry I was for them. I knew that that was the last thing they wanted and that their brave front of casual cheerfulness was put on to prevent people from showing that they were sorry.

Many of the boys I saw in hospitals are now leading happy and useful lives, but they carry with them, day after day, the results of the war. If we do not achieve the ends for which they sacrificed—a peaceful world in which there exists freedom from fear of both aggression and want—we have failed. We shall not have paid our debt until these ends are achieved.

One development gives me great hope for the future. Women have always come to the fore in wartime, but I think in World War II they took responsibility in more fields than ever before—in factories, on the farms, in business, and in the military services. They were an indispensable part of the life of the country. This was true in Great Britain, in Australia, in New Zealand, in France, in all occupied countries in Europe, in Russia, and in the United States. Women have become conscious also of the need to take part in the political life of their country. In the European countries more women are today playing an active role in public life than would have been possible before the war; and I am sure we are going to see great developments in the Asiatic area too. This, to me, is a hopeful sign, for women will work for peace as hard as they worked for the war.

On November 9, 1943, forty-four nations signed the agreements for the United Nations Relief and Rehabilitation Administration. The first administrator was former Governor Herbert H. Lehman of New York. Mr. Lehman proved by the way he set up his organization and conducted the work that he was a good organizer and had the patience of Job.

On November 11 Franklin left for his second war trip. He was to meet the Generalissimo and Madame Chiang in Cairo. This would be his first meeting with the Generalissimo, and Madame Chiang was to act as interpreter. Mr. Churchill met Franklin in Cairo and the talks went well.

Because at that time the U.S.S.R. was not at war with Japan, Marshal Stalin was reluctant to meet with the head of the Chinese government; consequently, when the talks in Cairo were over, Mr. Churchill and Franklin went on to Teheran to meet Marshal Stalin. This was the first meeting between Marshal Stalin and my husband. Franklin went to it with the determination that, if possible, there was going to be good will and understanding between them. I knew he was going to exert himself to the utmost to win the confidence of Stalin and to establish a better relationship between our two governments.

After Franklin had been in Teheran for only a day, Stalin insisted that, because of the rumors of unrest among the native people of Iran, the president must move into the same area of the city that he was in. Mr. Churchill was next door and the Russian soldiers could more easily protect them all.

Afterwards my husband told me that he felt there was a great distrust on the part of Marshal Stalin when they first met, and he had no idea, on leaving, whether he had been able to dissipate any of it or not. He added that he intended to see that we kept our promises to the letter. He hoped that Great Britain would be able to also, and said he would do all he could to help them do it. He felt that by keeping our word we could build the confidence of this leader whose people, though fighting on our side, still did not trust us completely. The U.S.S.R. needed all the help that we, with our great power of production, could give, while we were more than grateful for the fact that fighting in the U.S.S.R. kept so many German divisions busy.

In 1933 my husband had recognized the U.S.S.R., which had been isolated since 1918, and I am sure that at Teheran he made Marshal Stalin feel that his good will was genuine. After this meeting the co-operation among the three men grew steadily closer.

Franklin returned to Washington on December 17, exhilarated by the trip, full of new interests and seemingly in better health. Because of his keen interest in everything he saw and everyone he met, each trip seemed to have this effect on him.

Back in Washington, in January, 1944, we welcomed John's wife, Anne, and Haven and the baby, Nina, for an indefinite visit. Johnny had gone off with his ship on her trial trip and wanted Anne to settle the children in the White House so she would feel free to join him wherever he might put into port, if only for a day.

This visit was the occasion of one of the stories that we always enjoyed in the family. Franklin liked it so much that he continued to embellish it every time he told it. Johnny called me one evening just before Anne and the children were to come. I was out, so he talked to his father. First he told him when Anne would arrive and then proceeded to tell him about the various things that must be ordered and prepared for their arrival. Finally he said, "Be sure to order the diaper service." Franklin, who had never heard of it, said, "What did you say?" Johnny replied, "The diaper service." This bewildered his father who asked, "Is there anything wrong with the baby? We always boiled ours."

In February Anna arrived for an indefinite stay with little Johnny because her husband expected to be stationed in Washington for a while. Her two older children were in boarding school. Anna's presence was the greatest possible help to my husband. She saw and talked to people whom

Franklin was too busy to see and then gave him a digest of the conversations. She also took over the supervision of his food. In fact, she helped him in innumerable ways. Everything she did was done capably and she brought to all her contacts a gaiety and buoyancy that made everybody feel happier because she was around.

On the 4th of March Tommy and I left for our 13,000-mile plane trip in the Caribbean area. My husband had insisted that I take this trip. Because the war had receded in that area, the men stationed there felt they were in a backwater and chafed to be where they could do what they considered a more important job. Nevertheless, we had to have men there to guard and watch for submarines, because there was so much traffic to Europe, Asia and Africa. Franklin wanted the men to realize that he knew and understood the whole picture and believed they were doing a vital job—that they were not forgotten, even though they were not on the front line.

I was getting a little weary of the criticism heaped on me for taking these trips, but because my husband insisted that my visit to the South Pacific had been a success in that it had accomplished what he had hoped for, I decided to make this tour. He mapped it out, and I took Miss Thompson with me. The entire trip, from March 4 to March 28, was by air, and in that period we visited Guantánamo, Cuba; Jamaica; Puerto Rico; Virgin Islands; Antigua; St. Lucia; Trinidad; Paramaribo; Belém, Natal and Recife in Brazil; La Guaira; Caracas; Curaçao; Aruba; Barranquilla; Canal Zone; Salinas; Galápagos Islands; Guatemala; Havana, Cuba. From Havana we flew straight home.

Puerto Rico was seething with activity and did not seem to me at all like the quiet, restful spot I had visited ten years previously. Rex Tugwell was the governor of the island at the time of my second visit, and he was trying out some of the ideas he had become interested in during his first survey; and Adrian Dornbush was doing research to develop new uses for Puerto Rican materials—bamboo, sugar cane, palms, and the like.

I was joined in Belém by the wives of some of the Brazilian government officials, who had been sent to meet me, and by our ambassador, Mr. Caffrey, and his wife. I enjoyed having them with me on my visit to Natal and Recife, where, as in Belém, I saw all the army aand navy activities and inspected the recreation facilities.

The airfield at Recife had a special fascination for me because it was from there the men were checked out to start their long trek across the ocean. I had a chat with a boy who was getting his last orders before leaving for India, where he would be flying the Hump—one of the most dangerous trips. He had just been home on leave, and he told me that when flying low over some of the midwestern country on his way back to a base near his home, he had looked down and said to himself: "I wish I could say to you people below me, 'Do you know how lucky you are? What wonderful lives you have? How rich is your security in comparison to the millions of people I have seen in India and China?'" He was one of the many boys who, in India, saw famine at firsthand; I doubt if any of them will ever forget it.

One place my husband allowed me to go that was not, strictly speaking, a service base was Venezuela. I was driven from the airport up a steep road to Caracas. Franklin had said it was one of the most beautiful roads he had ever seen, and I agreed with him after driving over it. We were told that the road was built entirely by hand by men and women who had worked on it for several years; it was a sort of WPA project. My visit was merely one of good will but while I was there I learned something of the awakening interest among women of the country in the better care and feeding of children.

After a brief stop in Colombia we flew to the Canal Zone, where I was able to get a good view of the Panama Canal from the air. General Brett and Admiral Train had mapped out quite an active tour there, and I was glad to be able to visit boys in lonely camps, to ride in a PT boat to inspect the base, and in general to see as much of our men as possible.

I had an unexpected pleasure in Panama. The U.S.S. *Wasp*, the ship on which my son John was assistant supply officer, was going through the day I arrived and since he had four hours shore leave, he came to see me. It was the last time I saw him until the end of the war.

On leaving the Canal Zone I paid a brief visit to Ecuador, where a few men were stationed, and then flew to the Galapagos Islands. Quite a number of people thought this was an unnecessary trip, and various USO entertainers had been persuaded not to go there, to the great disappointment of the men. However, it was one place where my husband insisted I go, because he knew the men there were probably having a duller and more trying time than men stationed anywhere else in the world. After visiting it, I realized that he was right. We were much amused at the sign over the door: "Women Invited." We were the only women who had ever been on this island!

The climate at the coast station in Guatemala was terrible; the men found the heat and the insects and reptiles hard to bear. Over the door of their recreation room they had a sign: "Home of the Forgotten Men." Guatemala City, however, had a delightful climate and had I been on a pleasure trip I should have liked to spend some time visiting the old capital and some of the Indian villages.

The President of Guatemala gave a formal reception for me in his palace; all were seated according to protocol and brought up to be presented to me in groups according to rank or position. The palace is luxurious. As I was entering the building to attend this reception, escorted by our military officers, a flashlight bulb exploded, and before I could take a breath Guatemalan soldiers seemed to spring up out of the floor, and our officers seized my arms and rushed me away. It had sounded like a shot and no one was taking any chances.

Since this trip was not within easy reach of the enemy, it was publicized before I left, and countless mothers, wives, sweethearts and sisters wrote to beg me to try to see their menfolk. When I left home, I took with me a file of cards with the names and identification numbers of the men I'd been asked to look up, and as I reached each place, I gave the cards of the men stationed there to one of the officers and asked, if possible, to see them. The young men would be told, without explanation, to be at a certain place—usually an officer's room—at a given time. They would arrive, nervous and apprehensive, and when I appeared would invariably look surprised and greatly relieved. On my return I had letters to write to hundreds of people, because during the trip many other boys I met asked me to write to their families back home.

On this trip, too, I managed to have meals with the enlisted men, the noncommissioned officers, and the officers. It meant breakfast at 5:55 A.M. and not 6:00, dinner at noon, and supper at 5:00 or 5:30 P.M. In one place some Puerto Rican soldiers brought Miss Thompson and me our coffee at breakfast time all prepared the way they like it—mostly sugar and canned milk.

Everywhere I went I was treated with the greatest courtesy and consideration, though some of the top-ranking officers were frank in telling me they had not anticipated my visit with pleasure. Nevertheless, Ambassador Caffrey and some of the generals and admirals were kind enough to write to Washington that my trip had been helpful, and I have always hoped that I was able to give the men some pleasure and encouragement, which had been my husband's thought in suggesting this tour.

We stopped at Havana on the way back, where, as in any foreign country I visited, I met the government officials or their deputies. This always gave me a welcome opportunity to learn something about the country itself and to express the good will of our people toward our neighbors to the south.

We landed back in Washington, after having covered 13,000 miles by air, and many, many miles on foot going through hospital wards, camps and so forth.

In two days both Tommy and I felt that the trip already lay far behind. The accumulated work demanded such concentration to catch up that we were back in the daily routine almost before we had an opportunity to report on what we had seen and done.

Twenty-seven

The Last Term: 1944-1945

ALL THROUGH the winter of 1943-44 my husband had run a low fever at intervals and we thought he had picked up a bug on the trip or perhaps had acquired undulant fever from our cows at Hyde Park. Franklin seemed to feel miserable, which was not astonishing, considering that he had been through so many years of strain. Finally, on April 9 he made up his mind that he would go down and stay with Bernard Baruch at his plantation, Hobcaw, in Georgetown, South Carolina. Mr. Baruch had offered to take in his whole entourage.

There were times when Mr. Baruch differed with my husband on policies. There were also times, as often happens to any president, when the people around him became jealous of outside advisers such as Mr. Baruch and made it difficult for cordial relations to exist. However, my husband was inclined to be impervious to stories or rumors about anyone who he felt could be helpful; and, since Mr. Baruch is one of the people who can ignore the past, he was always ready to be useful when called upon. The personal relationship remained unbroken through all the years Franklin and I knew him.

Hobcaw was just the right place for Franklin, who loved the country and the life there, and he stayed almost a month. One day Anna and I flew down for lunch, along with the prime minister of Australia and his wife, Mr. and Mrs. Curtis, and I came home feeling that it was the best move Franklin could have made. I have always been grateful to Mr. Baruch for providing him with that holiday.

June 6, 1944, was a red-letter day. We had known for a long time that invasion preparations were being made, but everything had been kept very secret. When the time came, Franklin went on the air to give his D-day

268

rs. Roosevelt joins
epal's King Tridhu-
vana and his two
Queens during a
hort visit to the
untain kingdom's
pital city of Kat-
mandu in March,
952. *Wide World*

Demonstrating a western folk dance at a reception in Lahore, Pakistan, March, 1952. *UPI*

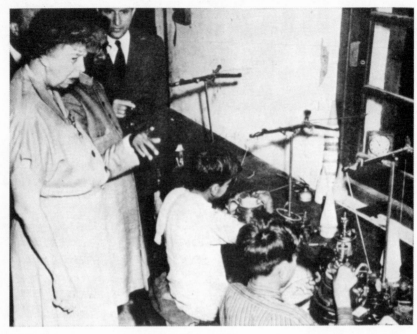

Watching boys at work in the hosiery section of the Faridabad Colony for displaced persons near Delhi, India, February, 1952. *Wide World*

Rehearsing for a reading of *Peter and the Wolf* with a Japanese symphony orchestra in Tokyo, Japan, May, 1953. *Franklin D. Roosevelt Library*

Mrs. Roosevelt with Leroy Collins at the Democratic National Convention, June, 1960, after she seconded the nomination of Adlai Stevenson. *Wide World*

With Senator Lyndon Johnson (right) and Anthony Akers (center) during the 1960 campaign. *Wide World*

Talking to President-elect John F. Kennedy in his suite at The Carlyle, New York, in January, 1961. *Wide World*

Talking with Alex Quaison-Sackey, Ghana Ambassador to the UN, and Wisconsin Governor Gaylord Nelson at the UN in May, 1961. *UPI*

Mrs. Roosevelt at the Roosevelt Day Dinner, February 2, 1961, at which Senator Herbert H. Lehman presented the 1961 Distinguished Award of the Americans for Democratic Action to the Reverend Martin Luther King. *UPI*

Ambassador Adlai Stevenson and Mrs. Roosevelt, a member of the U.S. delegation, listen to Ghana President Kwame Nkrumah address the General Assembly in New York, March, 1961. *UPI*

prayer, and for hours our hearts were with the men on the beaches. The news came in little by little. In spite of the sorrow our losses brought to many families, it was a great relief to know that permanent landings had been made and that the liberation of Europe had really begun.

Another election lay ahead in the fall of 1944. I knew without asking that as long as the war was on it was a foregone conclusion that Franklin, if he was well enough, would run again. A number of doctors were called in and he was given a thorough physical examination. Since to hand over to anyone else at that particular point would have been extremely difficult, it was decided that if he would agree to follow certain rules laid down by the doctors, he could stand going on with his work.

There appeared in a magazine an article written by a doctor who does not give his sources of information. This doctor states that my husband had three strokes while he was in the White House, one, at least, prior to this examination. I asked Dr. Ross T. McIntire whether my husband had had a stroke and he assured me that he had never had one. It would have been impossible for him to have had a stroke without some one of us, who were so constantly with him, noting that something was wrong. My husband would have been the last person to permit doctors to slur over anything which might have made him less able mentally to continue his work.

On July 7, while I was in Hyde Park, General de Gaulle lunched with Franklin in the White House. We wondered whether this visit would change his feeling about the general, but their meeting was evidently entirely formal though pleasant, and I saw no difference in Franklin's attitude.

From the 15th of July to the 17th of August Franklin was away on a trip to the Pacific. He had been in the European area a good deal; and he wanted to establish personal contact with the officers in the Pacific area and go over their plans for the war. Consequently, a meeting was arranged in Hawaii. From there he went to Alaska and the Aleutians. It was this trip that gave rise to the extraordinary tale that Fala had been left behind on one of the islands and a destroyer sent back for him. I have no idea where this story started, though I assumed it was with some bright young man in Republican headquarters.

In July I made a trip to Lake Junaluska in North Carolina to speak before a group of Methodist women. I had been hesitant about going anywhere in the South, because my conviction that the colored people should have full civil rights had, over the years, aroused a good deal of feeling there. This hostility found an outlet, particularly in election years, in a number of disagreeable letters and editorials and I felt my presence would not be helpful. However, this group was insistent and I was glad afterwards that I went.

I had great admiration for the courage of Mrs. M. E. Tilly of Atlanta, Georgia, who was the executive secretary of the Methodist women's organization. I was told that whenever a lynching occurred she went alone, or with a friend, as soon as she heard of it, in order to investigate the circumstances. Only a southern woman could have done this, but even for a southern woman it seemed to me to require great moral as well as physical courage. She was a Christian who believed in all Christ's teachings, including the concept that all men are brothers, and though she was a white southern woman she deeply resented the fact that white southern women are so often used as a pretext for lynching. Mrs. Tilly served with distinction on President Truman's Civil Rights Committee, and gained for herself the admiration of both Northerners and Southerners.

We were all saddened by the death of Marguerite LeHand on August 2. I was glad that I had been able to see her not long before when I went to Boston to visit the Chelsea Naval Hospital. She had worked for so many years with my husband and she had been so loyal and devoted, living with us practically as a member of the family, that I knew he would feel sad not to be able to pay a last tribute of respect by attending her funeral.

On September 10 we all left for Quebec for another war conference. Mrs. Churchill was to be there with her husband and Franklin had asked me to go. At first, Mr. and Mrs. Hull had planned to go, but Secretary Hull decided that he was not well enough. Later Franklin asked Henry Morgenthau, Jr., to come up to confer on a postwar plan for Germany.

Franklin was anxious that it should be made impossible for Germany again to start a war. I heard him discuss many plans, even the possibility of dividing Germany into its original principalities. He realized that the industrial power of Germany lay in the Ruhr, and he considered the possibility of international control of that region.

He undoubtedly discussed with Henry Morgenthau all of his ideas, including the possibility of reducing Germany to a country more dependent on agriculture than in the past, allowing her only such industry as was essential to a self-supporting state, and making sure that the economy of the rest of Europe would not again be so dependent on Germany for its prosperity.

Apparently there was a lack of co-ordination among even the highest levels of government thinking, both in our own country and in Great Britain. The net result of it all seems to have been that the President's intentions were not carried out—intentions which were shared by the Supreme Commander of the European Theater, General Eisenhower.

Franklin emphasized three points which he felt were important psychologically in Germany. I think they might well be remembered today:

"The first, that Germany should be allowed no aircraft of any kind, not even a glider.

"The second, that nobody should be allowed to wear a uniform.

"The third, that there should be no marching of any kind."

The prohibition of uniforms and parades, he thought, would do more than anything else to teach the Germans that they had been defeated.

At least a month before the Quebec conference my husband had received memoranda from Secretary Hull, Secretary Stimson and Secretary Morgenthau, members of the Cabinet committee he had set up to recommend a plan for the postwar treatment of Germany. All were carefully considered, so it is fair to surmise that Henry Morgenthau's plan more closely met the needs of the situation as Franklin saw it.

Henry Morgenthau himself told the story of his last interview with my husband the night before he died. He left him with the firm conviction that Franklin was still determined "not to allow any sentimental considerations to modify the conditions necessary to prevent Germany and the German people from becoming aggressive again." Henry Morgenthau felt that these views were embodied in the Potsdam Agreement. The trouble that arose later was not because of that agreement but because of the lack of further agreement. A careful analysis of much that happened would probably show that Mr. Churchill always favored a less harsh attitude toward Germany and, as fear of Russia increased, his feeling naturally intensified.

While we were at the Quebec conference, both Mrs. Churchill and I were asked to speak in French over the radio, and there were a number of entertainments which we attended. On the 18th Franklin returned to Hyde Park with Mr. and Mrs. Churchill. Their rest there was necessarily brief because the 1944 campaign was about to begin.

Franklin opened the campaign by speaking at the Teamsters' Union dinner in Washington, Daniel Tobin being an old and warm Democratic adherent. It was at this dinner that Franklin really laid the foundation for Mr. Dewey's defeat by the way in which he told the story of Fala's indignation over the Republican accusation that he had been left behind on an island, and retrieved only at the cost of untold sums of the taxpayers' money. By ridicule, Franklin turned this silly charge to his advantage.

After that dinner the campaign was on, but I was busy with a number of things which had nothing to do with it. A conference on rural education, organized largely through Mrs. Charles Ormond Williams' interest, was held in the White House on October 4 and 5.

Shortly after my birthday I went at the regular interval to donate blood to the Red Cross. The young lady at the desk was terribly embarrassed because I had passed the sixty mark in years and no one over sixty could be allowed to give blood. I was unable to see how in a few weeks my blood could have changed, but I felt I really entered old age on October 11, 1944.

At the end of the campaign Franklin and I drove through miles of New York City streets in one of the worst rainstorms I ever remember. We did everything that had been planned, but between times we stopped in a city garage so Franklin could change into dry clothes. Riding in an open car in that downpour, he was drenched to the skin. He ended up at the apartment, which I had been trying to get him to look at ever since we sold the 65th Street houses. He had told me to get an apartment in New York City in which we could stay occasionally after we left Washington, specifying that it should be in a place where he could work in peace with no steps anywhere.

He had every intention of spending the rest of his life, after leaving the White House, in Hyde Park and Warm Springs, but realized, since he planned to do some magazine work, that he must have some place in which to stay in New York City.

I was really worried about him that day, but instead of being exhausted he was exhilarated, after he had had a chance to change his clothes and get a little rest. The crowds had been warm and welcoming and the contact with them was good for him. People had seemed not to mind standing in the rain so long as they could get a glimpse of him as he waved at them. That must give anyone a very warm feeling. People love you when they believe you have done something really worthwhile for them, and there was no question but that the people of New York City had been telling him that day how much they cared. Men, women and children had stood for hours, and as far as I could tell it had made no difference that the sun was not shining.

Dr. McIntire had worried about the campaign, but I had told him early in the autumn that I thought Franklin drew strength from contact with people. On the day of our visit to New York City I felt that I had been right and that Franklin was better than he had been at the beginning of the campaign.

That night, October 21, Franklin spoke at the Foreign Policy Association dinner. I heard afterwards that some people thought he looked ill that night, but I was not surprised because, of course, he was extremely tired. We went to Hyde Park for the election. When the returns showed that his re-election was assured, he went out on the porch as usual to welcome our neighbors when they came down to greet and congratulate him.

Franklin went down to Warm Springs for Thanksgiving and had nearly three weeks there. I was always glad when he was able to go, because he got great satisfaction out of contact with the patients, especially the youngsters. I think he felt that Warm Springs represented something that he had really been able to do for people who suffered as he had suffered.

Again that year we went to Hyde Park for Christmas. Soon after, Franklin began to plan for his trip to Yalta. I remember that he was so busy it was well into January before he had time to open his Christmas presents. He would not let any of us do it for him, so little by little, as he had a few minutes before dinner, he had the pleasure of opening his gifts, every one of which he enjoyed.

Early in January, realizing this would certainly be his last inauguration, perhaps even having a premonition that he would not be with us long, Franklin insisted that every grandchild come to the White House for a few days over the 20th. I was reluctant to have thirteen grandchildren, ranging in age from three to sixteen, together, for fear of an epidemic of measles or chicken pox, but he was so insistent that I agreed.

After the inauguration it was clearer every day that Franklin was far from well. Nevertheless, he was determined to go to Yalta, and when he made up his mind that he wanted to do something he rarely gave up the idea.

Franklin had high hopes that at this conference he could make real progress in strengthening the personal relationship between himself and Marshal Stalin. He talked a good deal about the importance of this in the days of peace to come, since he realized that the problems which would arise then would be even more difficult than those of the war period. He also told me that he intended, if possible, to see some of the Arabs and try to find a peaceful solution to the Palestine situation.

On the way back, however, General Watson, who had wanted above all else to go on the trip, had a stroke, which I knew must be causing Franklin great anxiety. Before they were out of the Mediterranean he died. Harry Hopkins also was ill on the trip and got off at Marrakech for a holiday and rest. Altogether, dark clouds seemed to be settling over the ship and I was really worried.

Many things have been said about the "surrender" of the United States' interests in the agreements at Yalta. Edward Stettinius' book answers these accusations authoritatively and I hope it will be read by everyone who has for one minute thought that Franklin was not always first concerned with the good of the United States. However, that our welfare was inextricably linked with the welfare of other countries was something he believed deeply, and he also believed we needed the friendship of other countries.

Yalta was only a step towards the ultimate solution Franklin had in mind. He knew it was not the final step. He knew there had to be more negotiation, other meetings. He hoped for an era of peace and understanding, but he knew well that peace was not won in a day—that days upon days and years upon years lay before us in which we must keep the peace by constant effort.

Though Franklin had felt confident of being able to work with Stalin when he left for Yalta, not long after he got home he began to feel that the marshal was not keeping his promises. This was something he could not overlook, and I believe he wrote him a number of extremely stern messages. He still thought, however, that in the end he could make Stalin live up to his word, and that he, Stalin, and Churchill, having fought the war together, had gained enough understanding and respect for each other to be able to work things out.

In telling of his experiences on this trip Franklin always said that one of the most interesting and colorful episodes was his meeting with King Ibn Saud. The King arrived on a destroyer, sitting with all his entourage under a canopy on deck, the sheep which he had brought for food herded at the other end of the ship. Franklin said it was the strangest-looking destroyer he had ever seen. Beautiful rugs had been spread and everything done to make the King comfortable in fairly familiar surroundings. Franklin served coffee on their arrival and the King asked permission to have his own coffee-maker prepare the ceremonial coffee, which Franklin drank with him.

The purpose of this visit was to get some kind of agreement on Palestine; also, Franklin wanted to make some suggestions about the development of the Arab countries. He had always felt strongly that they should not turn over all their oil resources to the great nations of the world but should retain enough to use in pumping water to the surface to irrigate the desert for better agricultural development. He was sure that much of the desert land had underground rivers which would make irrigation possible. He also thought that much more could be done in the way of reforestation in these countries. He had mentioned this to the Sultan of Morocco when he and Mr. Churchill had dined with him during the Casablanca conference. Franklin said Mr. Churchill did not look too happy over the idea, but the Sultan seemed enthusiastic.

He tried talking on these subjects to King Ibn Saud only to be met by the statement that the King was a warrior and would continue to be as long as he lived. He said one of his sons—and he had a great many sons—was interested in agriculture and another was interested in conservation, but that he had no interest at all in anything except being a warrior and the King of his nomad people.

The King did not want his people changed and he felt that contact with Europeans would be bad for them. When it came to Palestine, Franklin got nowhere.

On the 1st of March, Franklin addressed the Congress, and I knew, when he consented to do this sitting down, that he had accepted a certain degree of invalidism. I found him less and less willing to see people for any length of time, needing a rest in the middle of the day. He was anxious to get away and I was pleased when he decided to go to Warm Springs, where he always gained in health and strength. He invited his cousins, Laura Delano and Margaret Buckley, to go down with him.

On April 12, in the afternoon, Laura Delano called me to say that Franklin had fainted while sitting for his portrait and had been carried to bed. I talked to Dr. McIntire, who was not alarmed, but we planned to go down to Warm Springs that evening. He told me, however, that he thought I had better go on with my afternoon engagements, since it would cause great comment if I canceled them at the last moment to go to Warm Springs.

I was at a benefit for the Thrift Shop at the Sulgrave Club in Washington when I was called to the telephone. Steve Early, very much upset, asked me to come home at once. I did not even ask why. I knew that something dreadful had happened. Nevertheless, the amenities had to be observed, so I went back to the party and said good-by, expressing my regrets that I could not stay longer because something had come up at home which called me away.

I got into the car and sat with clenched hands all the way to the White House. In my heart I knew what had happened, but one does not actually formulate these terrible thoughts until they are spoken. I went to my sitting room and Steve Early and Dr. McIntire came to tell me the news. Word had come to them through Dr. Bruenn in Warm Springs, first of the hemorrhage, and later of Franklin's death.

I sent at once for the vice-president, and I made arrangements for Dr. McIntire and Steve to go with me to Warm Springs by plane that evening. Somehow in emergencies one moves automatically.

When the vice-president came I could think of nothing to say except how sorry I was for him, how much we would all want to help him in any way we could, and how sorry I was for the people of the country, to have lost their leader and friend before the war was really won.

Then I cabled my sons: "Father slept away. He would expect you to carry on and finish your jobs."

Almost before we knew it we were on the plane and flew all through the night. The next day in Warm Springs was long and heartbreaking. Laura Delano and Margaret Buckley, Lizzie McDuffie, our White House maid, Daisy Bonner, the cook Franklin always had in Warm Springs, and Prettyman, the valet, were all stunned and sad but everyone was as self-controlled and calm as possible. Though this was a terrible blow, somehow one had no chance to think of it as a personal sorrow. It was the sorrow of all those to whom this man who now lay dead, and who happened to be my husband, had been a symbol of strength and fortitude.

Finally, the slow procession moved to the railroad station and we got on the train and started for Washington. The military guard surrounded the coffin in the back of the car where Franklin had sat so often. I lay in my berth with the window shade up, looking out at the countryside he had loved and watching the faces of the people at stations, and even at the crossroads, who came to pay their last tribute all through the night.

The plans for the funeral were as Franklin would have wanted them. We had talked often, when there had been a funeral at the Capitol in which a man had lain in state and the crowds had gone by the open coffin, of how much we disliked the practice; and we had made up our minds that we would never allow it. I asked that the coffin be opened once after it was placed in the East Room, so that I could go in alone to put a few flowers in it before it was closed finally. He wanted to be remembered as he was when he was alive.

It seemed to me that everyone in the world was in the East Room for the funeral services except three of my own sons. Elliott was the only one who, by luck, could get back; he had been asked to fly in the plane which brought Mr. Baruch and several others from London. Jimmy was able to come east but he did not reach New York City until after the funeral at Hyde Park, so he joined us on the train on our way back to Washington. Langdon Marvin, Jr., who was my husband's godchild, came with Jimmy. Franklin Junior and Johnny were out in the Pacific area.

Franklin wanted to be buried in the rose garden at Hyde Park and left exact directions in writing, but he had neglected to make the arrangements necessary for using private property, so we had to make those at the last minute.

After the funeral service in Washington we traveled to Hyde Park. Again no one could sleep, so we watched out of the windows of the train the crowds of people who stood in respect and sorrow all along the way. I was deeply touched by the number of our friends who had left their homes very early to drive to Hyde Park for the funeral, and especially by the kind thoughtfulness of Prime Minister Mackenzie King. My niece (Mrs. Edward P. Elliott) was living in Ottawa at the time and he had invited her to go to Hyde Park in his special train. After the burial I stayed in the house long enough to greet old personal friends and the officials who had come up from Washington, and then went back to Washington on the same train as President and Mrs. Truman.

They were both more than kind in urging me to take my time about moving out of the White House, but I felt I wanted to leave it as soon as possible. I had already started to prepare directions so that the accumulation of twelve years could be quickly packed and shipped. As always happens in life, something was coming to an end and something new was beginning. I went over many things in my mind as we traveled the familiar road back to Washington.

I am sure that Franklin accepted the thought of death as he accepted life. He had a strong religious feeling and his religion was a very personal one. I think he actually felt he could ask God for guidance and receive it. That was why he loved the 23rd Psalm, the Beatitudes, and the 13th chapter of First Corinthians. He never talked about his religion or his beliefs and never seemed to have any intellectual difficulties about what he believed. Once, in talking to him about some spiritualist conversations which had been sent in to me (people were always sending me their conversations with the dead), I expressed a somewhat cynical disbelief in them. He said simply: "I think it is unwise to say you do not believe in anything when you can't prove that it is either true or untrue. There is so much in the world which is always new in the way of discoveries that it is wiser to say that there may be spiritual things which we are simply unable to fathom. Therefore, I am interested and have respect for whatever people believe, even if I cannot understand their beliefs or share their experiences."

That seemed to me a natural attitude for him to take. He was always open-minded about anything that came to his attention, ready to look into it and study it, but his own beliefs were the beliefs of a child grown to manhood under certain simple influences. He still held to a fundamental feeling that religion was an anchor and a source of strength and guidance, so I am sure that he died looking into the future as calmly as he had looked at all the events of his life.

At a time of shock and sorrow the lesser emotions fade away. Any man in public life is bound to have had some close relationships that were later broken for one reason or another, and some relationships that were never close and which simply slipped away; but when Franklin died, many men who had felt bitterly toward him and who without question would feel so again, at that moment forgot and merged with the great mass of people in the country who felt that they had lost someone whom they needed. Harry Hopkins looked, the day of the funeral, as though he were just about to die. After his return from Marrakech, he had been practically confined to the house, and since both men were ill, it had been impossible for them to see much of each other. I do not think that they cared less for each other or that there was any break. I think the circumstances and their own health made it difficult for them to meet and consult more often.

As I look back now I realize that unwittingly Franklin's parents had prepared him well, through contact with themselves, travel abroad, and familiarity with the customs and peoples of many countries, to meet the various situations that he faced during his public life. They certainly never intended him to be in politics, but the training they gave him made him better able to accomplish his tasks.

The so-called New Deal was, of course, nothing more than an effort to preserve our economic system. Viewing the world today I wonder whether some of the other peoples might not have stood up better in World War II had something like the New Deal taken place in their countries long enough before to give them a sense of security and confidence in themselves. It was the rebuilding of those two qualities in the people of the United States as a whole that made it possible for us to produce as we did in the early days of the war and to go into the most terrible war in our history and win it. So the two crises that my husband faced were really closely tied together. If he had not successfully handled the one he could never have handled the other, because no leader can do anything unless the people are willing to follow him.

What brought this more clearly before me were the letters that came in such numbers after Franklin's death and which are now in the Franklin D. Roosevelt Library. Touchingly people told their stories and cited the plans and policies undertaken by my husband that had brought about improvement in their lives. In many cases he had saved them from complete despair.

All human beings have failings, all human beings have needs and temptations and stresses. Men and women who live together through long years get to know one another's failings; but they also come to know what is worthy of respect and admiration in those they live with and in themselves. If at the end one can say, "This man used to the limit the powers that God granted him; he was worthy of love and respect and of the sacrifices of many people, made in order that he might achieve what he deemed to be his task," then that life has been lived well and there are no regrets.

Before we went to Washington in 1933 I had frankly faced my own personal situation. In my early married years the pattern of my life had been largely my mother-in-law's pattern. Later it was the children and Franklin who made the pattern. When the last child went to boarding school, I began to want to do things on my own, to use my own mind and abilities for my own aims. When I went to Washington I felt sure that I would be able to use the opportunities which came to me to help Franklin gain the objectives he cared about—but the work would be his work and the pattern his pattern. He might have been happier with a wife who was completely uncritical. That I was never able to be, and he had to find it in other people. Nevertheless, I think I sometimes acted as a spur, even though the spurring was not always wanted or welcome. I was one of those who served his purposes.

One cannot live the life Franklin led in Washington and keep up many personal friendships. A man in high public office is neither husband nor father nor friend in the commonly accepted sense of the words; but I have come to believe that Franklin stands in the memory of people as a man who lived with a great sense of history and with a sense of his obligation to fulfill his part as he saw it.

On the whole, I think I lived those years very impersonally. It was almost as though I had erected someone outside myself who was the President's wife. I was lost somewhere deep down inside myself. That is the way I felt and worked until I left the White House.

One cannot say good-by to people with whom one has lived and who have served one well without deep emotion, but at last even that was over. I was now on my own.

PART III

On My Own

Twenty-eight

An End and a Beginning

I RODE DOWN in the old cagelike White House elevator that April morning of 1945 with a feeling of melancholy and something of uncertainty, because I was saying good-by to an unforgettable era and I had given little thought to the fact that from this day forward I would be on my own.

I realized that in the future there would be many important changes in my way of living but I had long since realized that life is made up of a series of adjustments. If you have been married for forty years and if your husband has been president of the United States for a dozen years, you have made personal readjustments many times, some superficial, some fundamental. My husband and I had come through the years with an acceptance of each other's faults and foibles, a deep understanding, warm affection, and agreement on essential values. We depended on each other. Because Franklin could not walk, I was accustomed to doing things that most wives would expect their husbands to do; the planning of the routine of living centered around his needs and he was so busy that I was obliged to meet the children's needs as well.

I had to face the future as countless other women have faced it without their husbands. No more children would be living at home. The readjustments to being alone, without someone else as a center of life and with no children about, would be difficult. Having Tommy with me made it easier at first, for Tommy, as she was called in the family, had long been my secretary and she made coming home to wherever it might be worthwhile. But there was still a big vacuum which nothing, not even the passage of years, would fill.

I had few definite plans but there were certain things I did not want

283

to do. I did not want to run an elaborate household again. I did not want to cease trying to be useful in some way. I did not want to feel old—and I seldom have. In the years since 1945 I have known the various phases of loneliness that are bound to occur when people no longer have a busy family life. But, without particularly planning it, I have made the necessary adjustments to a different way of living, and I have enjoyed almost every minute of it and almost everything about it.

It was not always easy. At first there was seemingly a greater adjustment to be made in my outer way of life than in my inner life. Ever since my husband had become president in 1933 I had lived in the White House, which meant a public existence. In earlier days he had held various public positions, but somehow our public and private lives had meshed more easily. Then came the years of his disabling illness. Later, beginning with the governorship of New York, we were back in public life on a changed basis. There was less of a family private life. Franklin was busy and there was at all times a public life that had to be planned and arranged with care.

As I look back now I think these latter-day readjustments in life have been made easier for me by the fact that I had become used to changes ever since Franklin's illness. I think I had long been preparing for the personal adjustments that came with his death. I had always been a good organizer and I could make decisions. In the long night's trip from Warm Springs, Georgia, before my husband's funeral in the White House I had made certain definite decisions. I did not want to live in the big house on the Roosevelt estate at Hyde Park. But what would the children feel? They loved the Hyde Park house. Their grandmother had made them feel it was their permanent home. How would it seem to have it swept out of their lives?

For myself, I knew I would live in the cottage that I had made out of my furniture factory on Val-Kill Creek, two miles back from the big house at Hyde Park. Tommy already had an apartment there. My cottage has a small apartment for the couple who work for me, two living rooms, a dining room, seven bedrooms, a dormitory for young people, two large porches downstairs and a sleeping porch upstairs. The cottage was an adjunct to our lives at Hyde Park but it was mine and I felt freer there than in the big house.

In his will Franklin left the place at Hyde Park to me and to our children throughout our lives if we desired to live there. At our deaths a certain acreage, including the big house, was to go to the government. But he left a private letter to me saying that he did not think we could afford to run the place and advising me to urge the children to give the house to the government at once. He wrote that his experience with the homes of other presidents had made it clear that visitors would make private life difficult. Characteristically, he remarked that he would hate to think of us taking refuge in the attic or the cellar in search of privacy.

I was happy when the children joined with me in deciding to turn the big house over to the government as soon as it could be arranged. I soon found that I had also better liquidate the farm at Hyde Park, since it was being run with doubtful efficiency. While I had my own daughter and three daughters-in-law and two sons with me, I arranged for the division of jewelry and furs, including all that had been designated for me from Franklin's mother's estate and everything else that I felt I would not need in my new way of life. Under the will I had first choice of silver, pictures, furniture, linen, china and other things, but I decided that I would take very little. I wanted a few things for sentiment—the Turner water colors my husband had given me, some of the linen and other objects that we had used for a long time. There were some things I would need that belonged to me. But, somehow, possessions seemed of little importance, and they have grown less important with the years.

My feeling that it is a mistake to hoard possessions was confirmed when I discovered under the eaves of the Hyde Park attic some bolts of Chinese silk. They probably had belonged to Mrs. Paul Forbes, my mother-in-law's sister, and had been literally "put under the plank," as she called it, many years earlier. When I found them hidden away under the eaves the beautiful silk had been hopelessly ruined by rain water.

After all the urgent matters had been taken care of as well as possible, and I had left the White House for the last time, I went to New York, where I had taken an apartment on Washington Square a year earlier. I had thought it would be just the right place for my husband and me when he left the Presidency. When I arrived there without him at ten o'clock on the evening of April 20, Lorena Hickok was arranging boxes of flowers and carefully gathering up the cards so we would know whom to thank.

Tommy was there, too, having traveled with me from Washington. The fact that she stayed on after Franklin's death made it seem at first as though he were on one of his trips and we were living the kind of life we would have lived in any case. That first summer of 1945 I did much physical work, clearing out cupboards in the big house at Hyde Park, unpacking boxes and barrels that had come from Washington.

President Truman sent to Hyde Park a chauffeur and automobile to help me through the first month. After the chauffeur left in the middle of May I discovered for the first time what the shortage of gasoline and automobiles meant to people generally. I had no car except the little Ford fitted with hand controls which my husband used to drive around Hyde Park. It was an open car and all right for summer. But when winter came we still had nothing else except a small work truck, and Tommy and I must often have been an odd sight when, wrapped in all the rugs we could find in order to keep ourselves from freezing, we drove between Hyde Park and New York City.

There were in the summer of 1945 a number of kind friends who worried about me. One day my long-time friend Major Henry Hooker, who had been close to Franklin, telephoned to ask if he and John Golden, the theatrical producer, could call at my apartment in New York. When they arived they were very serious-faced and asked me about my plans for the future.

"I've had a number of offers of various jobs that might interest me," I said.

"Now, Mrs. Roosevelt, we have come here to offer you our services," Mr. Golden said. "We have appointed ourselves as a kind of committee to help you. We would like to have you consult us in connection with the various things you have been asked or will be asked to do. Then we could pass on whether such proposals are a good idea. In other words, we would be a committee to consider how your life is to be planned."

Miss Thompson was sitting nearby and as he talked her mouth dropped open and she gave them both an unbelieving stare. "Did I hear you correctly? You want to plan her life?"

"Exactly," Mr. Golden replied. "As old friends of the family, we feel she should be careful to do only things that count. Now, our idea is that I will provide whatever showmanship is necessary and Major Hooker will pass legal judgment . . ."

I had either to interrupt them or to burst into laughter. "Look, my dears," I said, "I love both of you dearly. But you can't run my life. I would probably not like it at all."

They departed, still warmhearted, still a little worried and perhaps a little sad. "Remember," Major Hooker said, "we are still a committee and if you need us we'll always be ready to help."

As time went on, the fact that I kept myself well occupied made my loneliness less acute. I am not sure whether this was due to my own planning or simply to circumstances. But my philosophy has been that if you have work to do and do it to the best of your ability you will not have much time to think about yourself.

The first year after my husband's death was a busy one. Many persons—Princess Juliana of the Netherlands, Madame Chiang Kai-shek, Ambassador and Madame Andrei Gromyko of Russia, General and Mrs. Eisenhower—came to call at Hyde Park. And, particularly in the summer, my children and grandchildren, nieces, great-nephews and others were often there.

The real point at which outer readjustment seemed to culminate was on April 12, 1946, when we turned the big house over to the United States government at a ceremony attended by President Truman. In my speech I told how Franklin had pictured the estate, under federal auspices, as a place to which the people of our own country and even of the world might come to find rest and peace and strength, as he had. I said I had no regrets in turning it over to the government for safekeeping. It was better to pass the house on with its contents just as it had been left by my husband, so that it might not take on the personality of those who might have made the house their home after his death. "His spirit," I said, "will always live in this house, in the library and in the rose garden where he wished his grave to be."

Readjustments in one's inner life have to go on forever, I think, but my main decisions were made by the end of the first year. It was Fala, my husband's little dog, who never really adjusted. Once, in 1945, when General Eisenhower came to lay a wreath on Franklin's grave, the gates of the regular driveway were opened and his automobile approached the house accompanied by the wailing of the sirens of a police escort. When Fala heard the sirens, his legs straightened, his ears pricked up, and I knew that he expected to see his master coming down the drive as he had come so many times.

Later, when we were living in the cottage, Fala always lay near the dining-room door where he could watch both entrances just as he had when his master was there. Franklin would often decide suddenly to go somewhere and Fala had to watch both entrances in order to be ready to spring up and join the party on short notice. Fala accepted me after my husband's death, but I was just someone to put up with until the master should return. Many dogs eventually forget. Fala never really forgot. Whenever he heard the sirens he became alert and felt again he was an important being, as he had felt when he was traveling with Franklin. Fala is buried now in the rose garden at Hyde Park and I hope he is no longer troubled with the need for any readjustments.

I have led a busy life for many years and it has not seemed less busy since the death of my husband. In the years since 1945 my life has been complicated in some ways because my working hours are long. I travel a great deal and see many people. But in another way I live very simply, so simply that not a few visitors, especially those from some distant countries where servants are plentiful as well as inexpensive, are often surprised to find that I plan the meals, do part of the daily shopping, and serve dinner for a dozen guests with a "staff" consisting of a couple in the country, one maid in town.

In the years immediately after Franklin's death I discovered that financial matters could be rather nightmarish because I was not a trained businesswoman. At first I focused mainly on cutting down expenses and earning enough money to meet my regular bills. Franklin had been too busy during the last years to settle his mother's estate, which meant that now both estates had to be settled, and this took a long time. In 1933, when we first went to the White House, I had stopped sharing many of the expenses I had previously carried jointly with my husband. This had left me free to use most of my inherited income—about $8,000 a year— for clothes, which in Washington, and for almost the first time as far as I was concerned, were an important item. Then whatever I earned by writing and speaking could be used for my personal interests and charities.

But from the day of my husband's death it was clear that I would have to meet all the daily expenses of the apartment in New York and, for a short time, of the big place at Hyde Park, which had a considerable payroll. Luckily, my husband had left me two life insurance policies. I used their proceeds while awaiting settlement of the estate, which amounted to approximately a million dollars. Then I had to make another decision.

I could live on what my husband had left me and stop working. Or I could continue to work and pay most of what I earned to the government in taxes. I don't suppose that there was really much of a decision to make because, of course, I wanted to go on working. In my new position, however, because of the tax laws I could no longer give my earnings to people or organizations in which I was interested. I had to establish a charity fund into which I put all earnings from lectures, which amounts to about 20 to 30 per cent of my income. The laws permit me to give that much to tax-exempt charities, educational institutions, hospitals and churches.

I found in time that I could live on what I earned by writing, appearing on radio or television, and reading manuscripts at $100 a month for the Junior Literary Guild. Actually, these earnings total somewhat more than I spend on living expenses, and it is a good thing they do because all the income from my inheritance and more besides is required to pay my annual tax bills.

Although I have said that I live very simply, I do not mean that my life is always quiet or that things always go smoothly. It isn't and they don't. There was one day in 1957, for example, when I had a rather busy schedule, but I firmly announced that I was reserving "a few quiet minutes" before dinner for a chat with an old friend, Lady Reading, who had just arrived from England. The day was not far along, however, before another old friend, former Governor Adlai Stevenson of Illinois, called me on the telephone. He had just returned from a trip to Africa.

"I wondered if it would be all right if I dropped by and had just a few minutes' quiet talk with you before dinner," he said.

Of course, I told him I should be delighted to see him and he and Lady Reading arrived about the same time. We had hardly settled down in the living room when the doorbell rang.

There were two young men in the hallway. One of them was wearing a bathrobe—and obviously nothing else. He was staying in the apartment above mine while the owner was away and he had accidentally been locked out.

"Oh, I forgot! I left the water running in the bathtub and it will overflow and flood the floor."

Yes, I thought, and it will all come down through my apartment ceiling!

At that moment Governor Stevenson came to the door, saying that he could no longer stand the suspense and wanted to know what was wrong. When I explained, he rose to the emergency by dashing down to the basement and turning all the knobs he could find in an effort to shut off the water for the entire building. Meantime I sent around the corner to get a locksmith. By the time he arrived Governor Stevenson had acknowledged a certain lack of success as a plumber, but the locksmith was able to open the door of the boy's apartment before we were flooded out. It was all rather amusing but it did interfere with my "few quiet minutes" with my guests. In fact, by the time we sat down again it was so late that Dore Schary had arrived to be my guest at dinner and to read for all of us the new play he had written about Franklin's illness at Campobello.

I don't normally have many quiet minutes in the day. I get up around seven-thirty most mornings. At breakfast, I read the newspapers. Then I work out the menus for the day and write instructions in "the cook's book."

By nine o'clock my secretary, Maureen Corr, has arrived to start work with me on my daily newspaper column. I have three secretaries, but not all in the same place!

After my years of work with the UN I became a volunteer in charge of organization work for the American Association for the United Nations. On my lecture tours and other journeys, Miss Corr often goes along because I must find time to do my column and a monthly page for a magazine. I dictate the column, which Miss Corr takes down on the typewriter. Then I correct it and she puts it in final shape for the messenger who comes each day before two o'clock.

I usually try to arrive at my office at the A.A.U.N. by ten o'clock. In the early 1950's when I was a member of the United Nations delegation I often had to be present for a meeting as early as nine o'clock. At the A.A.U.N. office there is always some routine work in connection with organizing new chapters—we had thirty when I took the job in late 1953 but by 1960 we had about two hundred and fifty, and sometimes there is a meeting that I must attend in the afternoon.

I try to get back to my apartment for luncheon, if possible, and then in the afternoon I usually have engagements or errands to run or friends to see or perhaps a meeting of the board of some organization in which I am active. But, if not, I start work on the mail. I receive an average of about a hundred letters a day from relatives, friends and—mostly—from strangers. Virtually all of them are answered but obviously that is a task that requires sound organization. Miss Corr opens all except my personal letters and is able to draft answers to most of them because she is familiar with what I would say.

By the time my secretaries have drafted answers to these letters there are probably only a dozen or fifteen left for me to read and answer. I go through them at odd times, whenever I have the opportunity, and scribble a note indicating my reply. Then, usually in the late evenings, when all the answers have been typed, I read and sign them all. Many times, especially if I have guests or go out during the evening, I am still signing at one o'clock in the morning. I don't have to stamp the letters that are going to towns or cities in the United States because all wives of former presidents have the franking privilege, but I do have to buy stamps for the large number of letters that I send abroad.

Occasionally I do something on radio or television. One radio broadcast across the Atlantic I remember clearly. It was with Lise Meitner, who had helped to give us the secret of the atom bomb. She had worked on uranium research in Germany in the 1930's but had been expelled from that country under the Nazi regime because of her Jewish blood. In 1945 she was in Sweden and I, in New York, was asked to speak to her on a transatlantic broadcast. It was a strange experience. While I was in the National Broadcasting Company studio prior to the start of the program, the technicians hooked us up by telephone to the studio where Dr. Meitner was waiting in Sweden. When I spoke to her I found a very famous but very frightened lady on the other end of the telephone. We could hear the NBC man in Sweden coaxing her to open her mouth and speak. She almost wept. Finally I tried to reassure her, saying: "Don't be afraid. Listen carefully to what I say and then answer slowly, thinking exactly of what you want to say, and you will be good. You really speak English well." That was only one minute before we went on the air and I prayed that she would follow my advice. She did, and I believe the broadcast was successful.

Of course, I do not spend all my time in New York City. I cannot even guess at the number of miles I travel a year, but during the winter I am on the road perhaps one week and sometimes two weeks in every month, including fairly regular trips abroad. Many of these trips to deliver lectures (I give about 150 a year) or to work for the A.A.U.N. are quick ones, because whenever I have to speak at a luncheon or dinner I try to arrange it so I can go by plane, arriving just in time to keep my engagement, and return the same evening or at least early the next morning.

I do not grow weary of travel and I do not tire easily—not so easily as some younger people I know. Sometimes, it is true, my feet hurt. What I call my "White House feet" hurt largely because of a change in the bones in my instep caused by years of standing at receptions in the White House. I generally find pleasure in travel because it gives me an opportunity to catch up on my reading. In fact, I do most of my reading for pleasure on airplanes, since at home there seldom seems to be time to pick up the many books that interest me. Incidentally, if I have a complaint about the kind of life I lead, it is that I simply cannot find time to read as much as I wish.

Twenty-nine

Not Many Dull Minutes

MY MOTHER-IN-LAW once remarked that I liked to "keep a hotel" and I probably still do when I am at Hyde Park. There usually seems to be plenty of guests there and they may include almost anyone from the Emperor of Ethiopia to my newest great-grandchild. Sometimes there are so many guests that they arrive by the busload—perhaps a group of college students from various foreign countries who come for a few hours to sit under the trees and talk with me on any subject they please, or perhaps a crowd of seventy-five or so employees of the United Nations who have been invited for a picnic.

Each year I also have a picnic for about 150 youngsters from Wiltwyck School for delinquent boys. On that occasion I always try to enlist the help of my grandchildren, who wait on the guests and organize outdoor games. We feed the boys plenty and then they usually lie on the grass for a while and I read them a story such as Kipling's "Rikki-tikki-tavi" or "How the Elephant Got His Trunk." We also have a package of candy for each boy before they go home.

My picnic ground is a large one and in summers it is used perhaps once or twice a week by some school or social group and, if I am there, I always try to stop by to speak to them for a few minutes. Otherwise they have to take care of themselves. For that matter, my own guests at Hyde Park usually have to fend for themselves much of the time because there are certain periods every day when I have to be busy at my work. There are a pool where they can swim, a tennis court, a stream full of water lilies and a boat, and plenty of room for walking over the countryside—accompanied by my Scottie if he feels in the mood.

I drive my own car at Hyde Park, sometimes meet guests at the rail-

293

road station five miles from my cottage and do much of my own shopping at the roadside stands. During the summer months I keep the deep
freeze well stocked and always try to be prepared to feed any number up
to twenty—most of them unexpected—for luncheon.

A number of my visitors are friends or acquaintances connected with
my work for the American Association for the United Nations or with
my earlier life in the White House, while others are official visitors to
the grave of my husband. One of the most interesting was Emperor
Haile Selassie of Ethiopia, who came to Hyde Park while on an official
visit to the United States. He was a slight, bearded man with dignity and
strength of character and, I felt, a desire to foster freedom, peace and
progress in his country. It seemed to me that the Western clothes he
wore on his journey were less impressive on him than the robes and san-
dals of his own land, but he was a person I liked and admired.

The Department of State had, of course, made all arrangements for
his visit. A representative of the department advised me that there would
be nineteen persons in his entourage. He would arrive at noon and I was
to meet him at my husband's grave in the rose garden. He was to visit
the library, where the records of my husband's administration are kept.
He positively must get to the house by one o'clock because he wanted to
see a television broadcast of a film that he had made. Then, the State
Department representative added sternly, it was imperative that the Emperor have a half hour alone in his room before luncheon for rest and
contemplation.

I thought this a rather crowded schedule but I didn't try to argue with
the State Department protocol officer. I met the Emperor and accompanied him to the library. He was much interested in modernizing his
own country, and when he saw the excellent system for keeping records
in the library he became excited and ordered his staff to be assembled.

"Look," he exclaimed, "study this system. Here is how you do it—
here is how you keep history."

I barely managed to get him to the house on the stroke of one. He
found a low stool in the living room and seated himself in front of the
television set and seemed to forget everything else as the film of himself
came on the screen. I am not sure that he had ever seen television before.
The minutes passed and no sign that he was ready to retire to his room
for the scheduled half hour before luncheon. At last I approached him.

"Your Majesty, I believe you want to rest for half an hour alone."

"Oh, no, it is not necessary to be alone. I only wanted to take off my shoes for a while and you see my shoes are off."

Another distinguished visitor to Hyde Park was Prime Minister Nehru of India, who came to luncheon one day when a number of my grandchildren and their friends were there. A striking figure in his long, dark coat and white trousers bound tightly at the ankles, the prime minister seemed delighted to see the young people and after luncheon sat crosslegged in the middle of the living room and talked to them for a long time. He appeared to be just as interested in asking them questions as they were in hearing his views.

As I got to know the prime minister better, when I later visited India, I felt he was a man of great physical and moral courage. But I discovered that his remarkable intellectual abilities did not free him entirely from prejudice. In the dispute between India and Pakistan over Kashmir, Mr. Nehru was completely emotional because of his personal ties to Kashmir. I felt that he suffered a stoppage of all reason on that particular subject and contradicted the high ideals that he normally expressed in regard to the right of peoples to decide their own destiny.

It seems to me that Secretary of State John Foster Dulles' method of dealing with Prime Minister Nehru was unfortunate and unwise. In the 1950's India was newly independent and the Indians were highly sensitive in regard to their independence. Then, too, after the Communists came into power in Asia, India was the only large non-Communist nation in Asia. Mr. Nehru firmly expects India will remain non-Communist and this is of great importance to the West. Yet Secretary Dulles made several grave errors in dealing with India. While negotiating the Japanese treaties he did not go to India. Mr. Nehru felt this was an obvious slight. Then, when India and Pakistan were in conflict, we sent arms to Pakistan, theoretically at least for defense on her northern (Russian) borders. It created against us in India a bitterness that might well have been avoided by limiting our aid to Pakistan to the economic field. I cannot help feeling that Mr. Dulles failed to understand the feelings of many of the peoples with whom we deal.

After Franklin's death I did not plan to travel alone or purely for pleasure, but in recent years various circumstances have taken me on trips that covered a large part of the world. I do not want to tell about them in chronological order, like a secondhand Cook's tour, but I do want to say something here about the invitation I received in the spring of 1948 to visit England for the unveiling of the statue of my husband in Grosvenor Square, when I was also invited to spend a weekend at Windsor Castle.

The King and Queen were kindness itself. They showed me to my room and sitting room and told me that the King's mother, Queen Mary, was staying over at the castle in order to greet me. At dinner a Highland piper, dressed in kilts, came in to march once around the table, playing his bagpipes. There was, of course, much formality but I was impressed by the easy manner of the King, dressed during the day in tweed jacket and slacks like a country squire, and by the skill of the Queen in keeping their family life on a warm friendly level even in such a historical setting as Windsor Castle. Princess Margaret, for example, had some young friends in who promptly turned on the phonograph to listen to popular records. I was amused to notice that, like most fathers, the first thing the King said when we came into the room was: "Meg, the music is too loud. Will you please turn it down?"

On our first evening at the castle we were taken on a tour of the galleries after dinner. Like my mother-in-law at her Hyde Park home, Queen Mary knew where every painting and *objet d'art* was placed—or at least where she thought each one should be placed. She promptly observed with no particular pleasure that the King had changed the hanging of several paintings.

I was particularly struck by the then Princess Elizabeth, still a young girl at the time of my visit but very serious-minded. She came to me after a dinner given by the Pilgrims and said: "I understand you have been to see some of the homes where we are trying to rehabilitate young women offenders against the law. I have not yet been to see them but could you give me your opinion?"

I told her I was favorably impressed by the experiment. The government had taken over some of the country's historic houses that the owners could no longer afford to maintain and had put them under the care of young women prisoners, who, with expert guidance and advice, had done the work of rehabilitating the houses and gardens to preserve them as national monuments. What struck me at the time was that this young princess was so interested in social problems and how they were being handled.

One evening during my visit at Windsor Castle, when Mr. Churchill was there, we played The Game—a form of charades. Queen Elizabeth acted as a kind of master of ceremonies and chose the words that the rest of us were called upon to act out. She puzzled for some time over various words and occasionally turned to Mr. Churchill for assistance, but without success. The former prime minister, with a decoration on the bosom of his stiff white shirt and a cigar in his hand, sat glumly aside and would have nothing to do with The Game.

When Mr. Churchill, now Sir Winston, had been at the White House during the tense years of the war, he and Franklin would talk for hours after dinner. It had been a terrible strain on my husband to sit up until one or two o'clock and then have to be at his desk early the next day while his guest stayed in his room until eleven. I suppose I showed my concern about this at the time and the prime minister probably remembered it when on a later occasion in London he said, "You don't really approve of me, do you, Mrs. Roosevelt?"

Looking back on it, I don't suppose I really did—though the cigars and the various favorite drinks I had to remember had something to do with it.

I think I might interrupt my story here to say that I have seen Princess Elizabeth on several occasions since she became queen. Her loveliness does not change but she seems to me still more serious, as one might expect her to be under the burden of her duties.

On one occasion when I had been invited to the palace for a chat with her, a young secretary escorted me to my automobile.

"It must be terribly hard," I said, "for anyone so young to have so many official responsibilities and also carry on as a wife and mother."

He looked at me with what I thought was a surprised expression and said briskly, "Oh, no. Not at all. The Queen is very well departmentalized." How does one departmentalize one's heart? I thought.

There had been a warm behind-the-scenes controversy over the statue. Sir Campbell Stuart, head of the Pilgrims Association, which raised the money for the memorial, and the sculptor, Sir William Reid Dick, strongly felt that Franklin should be depicted standing, facing into the wind. But Winston Churchill, who was an artist himself, took issue. He argued that because Franklin could not walk the statue should show him in a sitting position.

The controversy was much in my mind after King George had spoken at the ceremony and then walked with me to the statue for the unveiling.

I pulled a cord and, as the covering dropped away, I found myself looking at a statue showing Franklin as he was some years before his death. The figure was standing, with one hand gripping a cane and with the familiar cape flowing back from his shoulders. It gave the impression of a young, vigorous man and I think that is the impression my husband would have liked to leave with the British people. I have never regretted that it was done as a standing figure.

The sculptured figure has two shallow pools on either side of it and around the pools are low marble seats where, as the landscape architect explained to me, people could come and sit and eat their lunches. Carved on the back of the four seats are the Four Freedom declarations. The architect said he felt Franklin had always liked to have the people close to him. "And here I have made this possible," he added.

Judging by what I observed when I visited Grosvenor Square in later years, the people agree with him. There are always people there and I have rarely seen the statue without at least one small home-made bouquet resting on the marble base.

Thirty

Learning the Ropes in the UN

NOW I WANT to turn back to late in 1945 when there began one of the most wonderful and worthwhile experiences in my life.

In December of 1945 I received a message from President Truman. He reminded me that the first or organizing meeting of the United Nations General Assembly would be held in London, starting in January, 1946, and he asked me if I would serve as a member of the United Nations delegation.

"Oh, no! It would be impossible!" was my first reaction. "How could I be a delegate to help organize the United Nations when I have no background or experience in international meetings?"

Miss Thompson urged me not to decline without giving the idea careful thought. I knew in a general way what had been done about organizing the United Nations. After the San Francisco meeting in 1945, when the Charter was written, it had been accepted by the various nations, including our own, through their constitutional procedures. I knew, too, that we had a group of people, headed by Adlai Stevenson, working with representatives of other member nations in London to prepare for the formal organizing meeting. I believed the United Nations to be the one hope for a peaceful world. I knew that my husband had placed great importance on the establishment of this world organization.

At last I accepted in fear and trembling. But I might not have done so if I had known at that time that President Truman could only nominate me as a delegate and that the nomination would have to be approved by the United States Senate, where certain senators would disapprove of me because of my attitude toward social problems and more especially youth problems. As it turned out, some senators did protest to the President against my nomination but only one, Senator Theodore G. Bilbo of Mississippi, actually voted against me. He had been critical of statements I had made previously in regard to discrimination against Negroes, but when some of the newspapermen in Washington asked him why he opposed my nomination he replied only that he had so many reasons he would have to write a book in order to cover them all. Anyway, my nomination was confirmed by the Senate, and I still marvel at it.

I might point out here that as a delegate to the United Nations and, later, as a member of the Commission on Human Rights I received a salary that would have amounted to about $14,300 a year, except that one is paid only for the days one actually works. My transportation and hotel room bills were paid by the government and I received around $12 a day for expenses when required to travel abroad. My actual expenses always exceeded these figures, but I never knew just how much I was out of pocket because I didn't keep a complete account of them. Therefore, the only sums I could deduct from my income tax were those that I recorded for official entertainment. I suppose my service as a delegate for seven years actually cost me a considerable sum.

I did not know that I was permitted to take a secretary with me to the meeting in London and when I said good-by to Tommy I was rather heavyhearted at the thought of crossing the Atlantic Ocean alone in January. Members of the delegation sailed on the *Queen Elizabeth* and the dock was swarming with reporters and news photographers who surrounded the senators and congressmen on the delegation to get last-minute statements and pictures. Everything had quieted down, however, when I drove in my own car to the dock and got aboard rather late and managed to find my way to my stateroom.

The first thing I noticed in my stateroom was a pile of blue sheets of paper on the table. These blue sheets turned out to be documents, most of them marked "secret," that apparently related to the work of delegates. I had no idea where they had come from but assumed they were meant for me so I looked through them. The language was complicated but they obviously contained background information on the work to be taken up by the General Assembly as well as statements of our government's position on various problems.

I promptly sat down and began reading—or trying to read. It was dull reading and very hard work. I had great difficulty in staying awake, but I knew my duty when I saw it and read them all. By the time I finished I supposed that the Department of State had no more secrets from me, but I would have found it hard to reveal anything because I was seldom really sure of the exact meaning of what was on the blue sheets.

At the time I feared this was because I couldn't understand plain English when it concerned State Department matters, but I changed my mind on this score because others seemed to have the same difficulty. I remember one occasion later when our secretary of state, General George C. Marshall, summoned all members of the delegation to a special meeting to discuss our position on an important point, which is not pertinent to this story. Because of some question I asked, he evidently felt I was not clear on the matter and he went over it again.

"Is that clear?" he asked.

"I'm sorry, sir," I replied, "but that is not the way I read it in the newspapers."

Somewhat irritated, the general said that I was mistaken and that he would send me a State Department paper covering the subject.

He did and I read it carefully. Then I read it twice. Still I didn't know what our position was. I sent the paper around to one of the department's best legal minds and asked him to explain it to me. He sent me a note in reply: "If this is what they send the President on the subject, God help the President!" Then I asked one of the delegation's most experienced advisers to come to my room and showed him the blue paper.

"You must be able to explain this," I said. "You must have had a part in writing this paper."

He studied it for a while and then said, "Yes, I had, but obviously it was not intended for you or anybody else to know what this paper meant."

But I am getting far ahead of my journey to London. One day, as I was walking down the passageway to my cabin, I encountered Senator Arthur H. Vandenberg, a Republican, and before the war a great champion of isolationism. He stopped me.

"Mrs. Roosevelt," he said in his deep voice, "we would like to know if you would serve on Committee Three."

I had two immediate and rather contradictory reactions to the question. First, I wondered who "we" might be. Was a Republican senator deciding who would serve where? And why, since I was a delegate, had I not been consulted about committee assignments? But my next reaction crowded these thoughts out of my mind. I realized that I had no more idea than the man in the moon what Committee Three might be. So I kept my thoughts to myself and humbly agreed to serve where I was asked to serve.

"But," I added quickly, "will you or someone kindly see that I get as much information as possible on Committee Three?"

The senator promised and I went on to my cabin. The truth was that at that time I did not know whom to ask for information and guidance. I had no idea where all those blue documents marked "secret" that kept appearing in my cabin came from; for all I knew, they might have originated in outer space instead of in the Department of State.

Later I discovered that there was at first some concern among the Democrats on the delegation whether Senator Vandenberg would "go along" on the United States plan in London or whether he might stir up a fuss. But their suspicions proved groundless.

"When the Charter meeting of the United Nations was held in San Francisco," the senator told me, "I didn't want to be a delegate. I didn't much believe in international organization along this line, but your husband urged me to go and insisted that I could vote exactly as I felt was right. On that basis I went."

Needless to say, Senator Vandenberg became one of the strongest supporters of the United Nations; it was he who worked hard to keep the budget moderate so that there would be no danger of driving out the smaller, weaker countries. His influence meant much in the early years when support was badly needed for this bold new concept of an organization that might be our only hope of avoiding future wars.

We stayed at Claridge's in London. Our offices were on Grosvenor Square about two blocks from the embassy. When I arrived there my adviser, Durward Sandifer, said that there were one or two members of the delegation's staff who would be available to discuss with me the problems of Committee Three.

As I learned more about my work I realized why I had been put on Committee Three, which dealt with humanitarian, educational and cultural questions. There were many committees dealing with the budgetary, legal, political and other questions, and I could just see the gentlemen of our delegation puzzling over the list and saying:

"Oh, no! We can't put Mrs. Roosevelt on the political committee. What would she do on the budget committee? Does she know anything about legal questions? Ah, here's the safe spot for her—Committee Three. She can't do much harm there!"

Oddly enough, I felt much the same way about it. On the ship coming over, however, State Department officials had held "briefings" for the delegates. We listened to experts on various subjects explain the problems that would be brought up, give the background on them, and then explain the general position of the United States on various controversial points. I attended all these sessions and, discovering there also were briefings for newspaper people aboard the ship, I went to all their meetings too. As a result of these briefings and of my talks with Mr. Sandifer and others, I began to realize that Committee Three might be much more important than had been expected. And, in time, this proved to be true.

One early incident in London gave me cold chills. Papers kept coming to my desk—and most of them marked "secret" or something of the sort. One morning when I walked into my office I found a notice to report at once to the security officer. I did not know where to find the security officer but, after numerous inquiries, I was directed to his office in the building. He confronted me with the fact that his staff, making their rounds at night, had found on my desk a paper that was marked "top secret." I recalled then that I had left my office at a time when my secretary was out and I had presumed that she would put all papers away when she returned and then lock up the office. Apparently she had not and I was guilty of a serious offense, which I never repeated. Thereafter I made certain that the papers were locked away in the file and that the office was locked. I also always carried personally the briefcase in which I took documents home for study, keeping it within reach or putting it in a safe place. I frequently noticed in later years, however, that information in papers marked "top secret" appeared in the newspapers even before it reached us. But that is one of the curious inconsistencies that you have to accept in government work.

Secretary of State James F. Byrnes had not accompanied the delegation, but he arrived by air soon after we reached London. He disliked delegation meetings and briefings and I never knew him to call one, except on one occasion, when the meeting was a kind of cocktail party at which we talked about our work in a desultory fashion. However, Mr. Byrnes stayed only a short time. Thereafter we had regular briefing sessions in which

State Department experts—or perhaps Edward R. Stettinius, who later succeeded Mr. Byrnes as head of the delegation—discussed each morning the important items on the day's program. These meetings were often held in a large room where around nine o'clock in the morning all the U.S. delegates and their advisers would gather, perhaps forty or fifty persons in all. Normally the head of the delegation would preside and outline the high points of the work to be done while the rest of us followed his remarks by reference to the printed or mimeographed documents that had been prepared for us by the experts before the meeting. Then, when certain complicated problems were to be discussed in detail, a State Department official with special knowledge of the subject would take over. If any points were not clear, the five delegates or their alternates would ask questions.

In this way all the delegates were able to keep up with what was going on in general—if they listened carefully and had time to read the prepared papers—and in addition each delegate and each alternate got detailed information about the particular committee or the special project on which he or she was working at the moment. These briefings became a regular part of my routine throughout the six years I was connected with the American delegation to the United Nations, regardless of whether we were in London, Paris, Geneva or New York.

I drove to the first session of the General Assembly in London with Mr. Stettinius, who was then assistant secretary of state, accompanied by Mr. Sandifer and two other young advisers. Each delegate had a desk and there were several seats behind him for his advisers. The gathering of so many representatives of the large and small nations was impressive.

The first business of the Assembly was concerned with organization and the election of the first president, Paul-Henri Spaak of Belgium, a wonderful diplomat, an eloquent orator and a statesman of stature who did much to help the United Nations get off to a good start. The first Secretary General of the United Nations was Trygve Lie, a Norwegian. He was an able man who strongly believed in the ideas behind the United Nations, which he served well. He was a positive personality, which possibly was a handicap in his position, for he eventually made enemies. It is important that the Secretary General not only should be a good negotiator but should be able to make practically everyone feel he is their friend—if such a thing is possible.

At the early sessions in London I got the strong impression that many of the old-timers in the field of diplomacy were skeptical of the new world organization. They had seen so many failures, they had been through the collapse of the League of Nations, and they seemed to doubt that we would achieve much. The newcomers were the ones who showed the most enthusiasm and determination. They were, in fact, often almost too anxious to make progress. It was fortunate that such men as Mr. Spaak and Mr. Lie were on hand and skillful enough to give the veterans new inspiration and to hold the newcomers in check when necessary.

During the entire London session of the Assembly I walked on eggs. I knew that as the only woman on the delegation I was not very welcome. Moreover, if I failed to be a useful member, it would not be considered merely that I as an individual had failed but that all women had failed, and there would be little chance for others to serve in the near future.

I tried to think of small ways in which I might be more helpful. There were not many women on the other delegations, and as soon as I got to know some of them I invited them all to tea in my sitting room at the hotel. About sixteen, most of them alternate delegates or advisers, accepted my invitation. Even the Russian woman came, bringing an interpreter with her. The talk was partly just social but as we became better acquainted we also talked about the problems on which we were working in the various committees. The party was so successful that I asked them again on other occasions. I discovered that in such informal sessions we sometimes made more progress in reaching an understanding on some question before the United Nations than we had been able to achieve in the formal work of our committees.

As a result, I established a custom, which I continued throughout the years I was connected with the United Nations, of trying to get together with other nations' representatives at luncheon or dinner or for a few hours in the evening. I found that often a few people of different nationalities, meeting on a semisocial basis, could talk together about a common problem with better results than when they were meeting officially as a committee.

As time went on, there were more and more women serving on various delegations, and ours usually had a woman alternate even while I was still a delegate. Helen Gahagan Douglas, Mrs. Ruth Bryan Rohde, and Edith Sampson all were extremely valuable on the United States delegation.

As a normal thing the important—and, I might say, the hard—work of any organization such as the United Nations is not done in the big public meetings of the General Assembly but in the small and almost continuous meetings of the various committees. In the committee meetings each nation is represented by one delegate or an alternate and two or three advisers.

The discussions and the compromises and the disagreements that occur in committee meetings are of utmost importance. At first I was not familiar with committee work and not sure of myself, but Mr. Sandifer was always seated just behind me to give me guidance. As time went on I got so I could tell merely by his reactions whether the discussion was going well or badly. If I could feel him breathing down my neck I knew that there was trouble coming, usually from the Russians.

There is a question many people have asked me about the responsibilities of a delegate to the United Nations. "You are representing your government, but do you do exactly what you are told to do or say? Do you have any latitude for self-expression or for personal judgment in voting?"

The answer is a little complicated. In the first committee meetings I attended in London I was in complete agreement with the position of the State Department on the question at issue: the right of war refugees to decide for themselves whether they would return to their countries of origin. I was uncertain about procedure, however, and often lagged behind when the chairman called for a vote. Finally, Mr. Sandifer said sternly:

"The United States is an important country. It should vote quickly because certain other countries may be waiting to follow its leadership."

After that I always tried to decide how I would vote before a show of hands was asked for and, as soon as it was, my hand went up with alacrity. In deciding how to vote, it is true that a delegate, as a representative of his government, is briefed in advance on his country's position in any controversy. In London, fortunately, I agreed with the State Department position. But later I learned that a delegate does have certain rights as an individual and on several occasions I exercised my right to take a position somewhat different from the official viewpoint.

Of course, a delegate cannot express his disagreement publicly unless he resigns, since obviously it would be impossible to have representatives of the same nation saying different things in the United Nations. But he may exercise his right to disagree during the private briefings. Before the start of a session we were told what subjects would be on the agenda. If you disagreed with the government's attitude you had the right to say so and to try to get the official attitude changed or modified. You could, if necessary, appeal to the President to intervene and you could, if there was no solution, resign in protest.

On one occasion I did object vigorously to our official decision to rescind, without explanation to our people, the position we had taken on recognizing the Franco government in Spain. I was joined by other delegates and the State Department put off action until it could explain the situation fully.

It was while working on Committee Three that I really began to understand the inner workings of the United Nations. It was ironical perhaps that one of the subjects that created the greatest political heat of the London sessions came up in this "unimportant" committee to which I had been assigned.

The issue arose from the fact that there were many displaced war refugees in Germany when the Armistice was signed—Ukrainians, Byelorussians, Poles, Czechoslovaks, Latvians, Lithuanians, Estonians, and others—a great number of whom were still living in temporary camps because they did not want to return to live under the Communist rule of their own countries. There were also the pitiful Jewish survivors of the German death camps.

The Yugoslav and, of course, the Soviet Union position, put forth by Leo Mates, was that any war refugee who did not wish to return to his country of origin was either a quisling or a traitor. He argued that the refugees in Germany should be forced to return home and to accept whatever punishment might be meted out to them.

The position of the Western countries, including the United States, was that large numbers of the refugees were neither quislings nor traitors, and that they must be guaranteed the right to choose whether or not they would return to their homes. I felt strongly on the subject, as did others, and we spent countless hours trying to frame some kind of resolution on which all could agree. We never did, and our chairman, Peter Fraser of New Zealand, had to present a majority report to the General Assembly, which was immediately challenged by the U.S.S.R.

In the Assembly the minority position was handled by Andrei Vishinsky, one of Russia's great legal minds, a skilled debater, a man with ability to use the weapons of wit and ridicule. Moscow considered the refugee question of such vital importance that he spoke twice before the Assembly in a determined effort to win over the delegates to the Communist point of view. The British representative on our committee spoke in favor of the majority report. By this time an odd situation had developed. Someone would have to speak for the United States. The question threw our delegation into a dither. There was a hurried and rather uncomfortable consultation among the male members and when the huddle broke up John Foster Dulles approached me rather uncertainly.

"Mrs. Roosevelt," he began lamely, "the United States must speak in the debate. Since you are the one who has carried on the controversy in the committee, do you think you could say a few words in the Assembly? Nobody else is really familiar with the subject."

I said I would do my best. I was badly frightened. I trembled at the thought of speaking against the famous Mr. Vishinsky. Well, I did my best. The hour was late and we knew the Russians would delay a vote as long as possible on the theory that some of our allies would get tired and leave. I knew we must hold our South American colleagues until the vote was taken because their votes might be decisive. So I talked about Simón Bolívar and his stand for the freedom of the people of Latin America. The South American representatives stayed with us to the end and, when the vote was taken, we won.

This vote meant that the Western nations would have to worry about the ultimate fate of the refugees for a long, long time but the principle of the right of an individual to make his own decisions was a victory well worthwhile.

Toward the end of the sessions we worked until late at night. The final night the vote on Committee Three's report was taken so late that I did not get back to the hotel until about one o'clock. I was very tired, and as I walked wearily up the stairs at the hotel I heard two voices behind me. Turning around, I saw Senator Vandenberg and Mr. Dulles.

"Mrs. Roosevelt," one of them said, "we must tell you that we did all we could to keep you off the United Nations delegation. We begged the President not to nominate you. But now we feel we must acknowledge that we have worked with you gladly and found you good to work with. And we will be happy to do so again."

I don't think anything could have made the weariness drop from my shoulders as did those words. I shall always be grateful for the encouragement they gave me.

Thirty-one

I Learn about Soviet Tactics

THE CONTROVERSY with the Communist-dominated countries over the fate of refugees in Germany aroused in me a desire to see for myself what had happened. I discussed my idea with Ambassador John Winant, who said he would arrange for me to visit Germany, with the aid of the Army, which was then in control of everything in occupied areas.

I was stunned and appalled by what I saw when we circled the ruins of Cologne and Frankfurt and other places that I remembered as great and crowded cities. Later when we circled Munich and looked down on the rubble of Berlin I felt that nobody would have imagined such utter, horrible destruction. Nothing could better illustrate the sickening waste and destructiveness and futility of war than what I was seeing.

Later I was to see the effects of the first atomic bomb on Hiroshima. The bombing of Germany had continued over a period of months and months. The bombing of Hiroshima was over in a few seconds. But the results were the same.

We landed first at Frankfurt, where there were a number of refugee camps, including one for Jews in Zilcheim and others for refugees from Estonia, Poland, Latvia and other countries that were now under Soviet domination.

At Zilcheim I was greeted by leaders of the Jewish refugee group. They had built a small hill with steps leading to the top where they had erected a stone monument inscribed: "To the Memory of all Jews who died in Germany." In all the Jewish camps there were signs of the terrible events through which these people had passed and of the hardships they continued to suffer, but they also showed with what courage and steadfast hope they could meet disaster.

In the mud of Zilcheim I remember an old woman whose family had been driven from home by war madness and brutality. I had no idea who she was and we could not speak each other's language, but she knelt in the muddy road and threw her arms around my knees.

"Israel," she murmured, over and over. "Israel! Israel!"

As I looked at her weather-beaten face and heard her old voice, I knew for the first time what that small land meant to so many, many people.

I went from Frankfurt to Berlin. With the help of American officials I managed to cover considerable ground. On a trip eleven years later I observed many differences between East Berlin and West Berlin; for instance, the brilliant lights of the Western sector and the almost complete darkness of the Eastern sector; but in 1946 I was conscious only of mass destruction and human misery.

We drove past the smashed Chancellery where Hitler had ruled and the bunker where he died and the pockmarked Brandenburg Gate that had been a symbol of Germany's greatness. Now there was desolation and the sordid, degrading sight of men and women and children dealing in the black market. Here in the shadow of the Brandenburg memorial and close to the ornate temple of Nazi imperialism all the degradation of war had come home to roost.

I also visited the quarters of refugees who had made their way from areas formerly occupied by the Germans, like the Sudetenland, to the Western sector. The people were crowded into unsanitary and ramshackle underground shelters without proper heat or water or food.

The whole journey had been a good one for me. I had grown and matured and gained confidence. After we landed in New York I wrote my thanks to the President and to the secretary of state for an unforgettable experience, and thought my work with the United Nations was over.

Not long after I returned to New York I received notice that the Economic and Social Council, which had been set up by the United Nations in London, had created a committee, the Nuclear Commission on Human Rights, to make recommendations on matters pertaining to the functioning of the UN Human Rights Commission. It was to meet in New York in the spring of 1946 and the members were named as individuals rather than as representatives of their various governments. I was asked on President Truman's invitation to be a delegate to the General Assembly.

We began work in temporary quarters at Hunter College in New York and carried on at Geneva and the United Nations headquarters at Lake Success, on Long Island, for the next two years. But during the same period I was again nominated and confirmed as a member of the United Nations delegation to the General Assembly and continued as a delegate until 1953. At the same time I was also the United States representative on the Human Rights Commission.

Thus, over the years, in one capacity or another, I saw a great deal of the Russian delegates and not infrequently felt I saw and heard too much of them, because they were usually the center of opposition to our ideas.

Perhaps Maxim Litvinov, whose wife was English, was the most skillful Russian diplomat in getting along with Western government officials. V. M. Molotov, who had been so rigid as foreign minister and who helped make *niet* such a famous word at the United Nations, was always correct and polite. But, although I saw him frequently and sometimes sat next to him at dinners, I never felt it was possible to know him well. In fact, it was difficult to know any Russian well and I suppose the Kremlin planned it that way. It was really impossible to have a private and frank talk with Russian officials.

One of the Russian delegates over a period of years was a big, dramatic man with flowing white hair and a bristling black beard, Dr. Alexei P. Pavlov, a nephew of the physiologist Ivan Petrovich Pavlov, famous for his studies of conditioned reflexes. His nephew was an able delegate but he seemed to feel the need of proving that he was a faithful Communist. He was a brilliant talker and he often gave me a difficult time in committee meetings.

More than once Dr. Pavlov arose with a flourish, shook his white locks angrily, and made a bitter attack on the United States on the basis of some report or even some rumor that had to do with discrimination against Negroes, particularly in our southern states. Of course, I always replied vigorously, pointing out that the United States had done a great deal to improve the social and economic status of the Negro.

On one occasion, when I was irritated to the point where I could no longer stand it, I interrupted him to say sternly, "Sir, I believe you are hitting below the belt." This may not have been elegant language for a diplomatic exchange but it expressed my feelings.

The Soviet delegates could be very thorough in seeking out American weaknesses or in distorting the picture of our country by citing some isolated fact to support their propaganda. Once the Russian delegate made much of what he said was a law in Mississippi forbidding any man to strike a woman with an ax handle more than two feet long. This was an example of American brutality.

"In my country," a French delegate mused, "the law forbids a man to strike a woman even with a rose, long stem or short stem."

Louis Hyde, a delegation adviser, telephoned our legal adviser in Washington to check on the allegation. The uncomfortable answer he received was that an old law something like that actually was on the books in Mississippi. In any event, we had no very strong reply.

The Russian delegates simply did not dare talk with a foreigner without taking the precaution of having a witness present, lest at some future time their superiors might accuse them of making traitorous statements. Not even brash, outspoken Dr. Pavlov, who so often berated me and attacked my stand at United Nations sessions, dared ignore this practice. One evening he and his colleague Alexander Borisov came to my apartment with several other guests. I had invited a friend who is an excellent pianist.

Dr. Pavlov listened happily, his big shock of hair falling forward and his black beard touching his chest. As they were leaving, Mr. Borisov went into the other room for his hat, leaving me alone with Dr. Pavlov. Dr. Pavlov leaned toward me and in a conspiratorial whisper said, "You like the music of Tchaikovsky. So do I!" This was as close as I ever came to getting a frank expression of opinion from a Soviet official.

I certainly do not want to give the impression that the Russian officials or representatives are surly or even unfriendly, because they are often quite the opposite. It is in official negotiation or debate that they adopt such rigid attitudes and distort facts so irritatingly and display such stubborn unfriendliness toward Western ideas. Despite their difficult official attitude, I always felt that the Americans should refuse to show unfriendliness toward representatives of the Communist bloc. Some of our delegates would not even be photographed shaking hands or talking with a Communist representative when the reporters and news photographers clustered around at the opening of each session of the Assembly or on some similar occasion. Presumably our reluctant delegates were taking the position that the Russians were mortal enemies, or perhaps they felt it would do them no good politically.

The Russians, on the contrary, were eager to be photographed shaking hands with and smiling broadly at the delegates of other nations, particularly Americans, realizing that this gave the impression all over the world that they were trying to be friendly and co-operative.

It is possible that Westerners never fully understand the complexity of the Russian character, but I constantly kept trying to do so throughout my service with the United Nations and later, because I know it is extremely important for us to learn all we can about our powerful international opposition.

I am not certain that there is any moral in these observations about my dealings with representatives of the Soviet Union. On second thought, there is, of course, a moral and a warning for those who love freedom, and it is probably best expressed by a kindly but tragic man who loved freedom very much indeed. His name was Jan Masaryk, the son of Thomas G. Masaryk, the first President and founder of the Republic of Czechoslovakia.

At meetings of the United Nations General Assembly it happened that the Czechoslovak delegation sat directly behind us. Jan Masaryk, as foreign minister of Czechoslovakia and head of the delegation, listened to the debates intently in the early days of the General Assembly, but when it came time for a vote he always followed the lead of the Russian delegation. This was not difficult to understand because the Russian armed forces practically surrounded Czechoslovakia. On one occasion he leaned forward and whispered:

"What can you do? What else can you do when you've got them right in your front yard?"

He found that what he did made no difference to the Russians. In February of 1948 the Communists seized power in Czechoslovakia by a *coup d'état* and a few days later it was announced that Jan Masaryk had died by leaping from a window.

Thirty-two

The Human Rights Commission

DURING MY YEARS at the UN it was my work on the Human Rights Commission that I considered my most important task, though as I have explained I was also a delegate to the General Assembly, which, at times when the two jobs more or less fused, caused some confusion.

Now to get back to the commission that made recommendations on the definite composition of the Human Rights Commission at Hunter College in the spring of 1946. The work in this perod was an intensive education for me in many things, including constitutional law, and I would not have been able to do much but for the able advisers who worked with me. I was more than grateful for the fact that Marjorie Whiteman, who has written a legal work on American treaties, sat behind me at almost every meeting and explained what we could or could not do for constitutional reasons. My first adviser at this time, James Pomeroy Hendrick, always remains in my mind, with Mr. Sandifer, as an ideal guide, philosopher and friend. Urbane and soft-spoken, with a quiet sense of humor, he was tireless and devoted. He never spared himself and so he made me work hard.

After I had been elected chairman of the commission I tried to push our work along as rapidly as possible. I might point out here that eventually we decided that our main task was to write an International Bill of Rights. This was to consist of three parts. First, there was to be a Declaration, which would be adopted as a resolution of the General Assembly and would name and define all the human rights, not only the traditionally recognized political and civil rights but also the more recently recognized social, economic and cultural rights. Since the General Assembly is not a world parliament, its resolutions are not legally binding on member

314

states. We therefore decided that the Declaration would be followed by a Covenant (or covenants) which would take the form of a treaty and would be legally binding on the countries that accepted them. Finally, there was to be a system for the implementation or enforcement of the rights.

We also finally recommended that the Human Rights Commission be composed of eighteen members, each of whom would represent one of the United Nations governments, and that they should be chosen on a rotating basis with due regard for geographical distribution, except for the representatives of the five great powers—the United States, Soviet Russia, the United Kingdom, France and China. As was customary, it was agreed that these five powers should be elected automatically to the new commission as members, leaving thirteen seats to be rotated among other members of the United Nations. These recommendations, however, came later. At the Hunter College sessions we were just getting started.

When we called for a formal vote on presenting our proposals to the Economic and Social Council, the Soviet Union merely recorded its "objections and dissent" to certain agreements and thus did not join in the recommendations of the preparatory commission. The Council accepted our recommendations and President Truman then nominated me as the United States representative on the commission. Being the first chairman of the commission, in addition to my duties as a delegate to the Assembly, kept me on United Nations work during five or six months of the year and I had to keep my daily schedule on a crowded timetable basis, with no minutes to spare.

I remember once when the Assembly was in session at Lake Success, Richard Winslow, who was manager of the office of the United States mission, told me that he had been urgently asked to arrange a time when I could talk to Tyler Wood, who was then assistant to Will Clayton, about a problem concerning the United Nations Relief and Rehabilitation Administration.

"Well," I replied, handing him my calendar, "here's my schedule. You figure out when I shall see him—if you can!"

He worked on the calendar for a while and then said that he and Mr. Wood would meet me at a certain hour when I would be leaving a New York hotel. They did. We got into the automobile that was waiting for me and Mr. Wood began talking. He talked until we had driven pehaps twenty blocks to the CBS studios, where I got out while they remained in the car. I did a broadcast with Mr. Dulles on some United Nations matter, then returned to the car and resumed talking with Mr. Wood while we drove from Madison Avenue to Broadway and Fifty-ninth Street. There I got out again and went into the United Nations Information Center, which was just being formally opened at ceremonies that I had promised to attend. I returned to the automobile and resumed my conversation with Mr. Wood as we drove downtown to the Hotel Pennsylvania, where Mr. Wood and Mr. Winslow left me. I continued on to my apartment at Washington Square, some twenty blocks away, but I had an appointment with Senator Austin at the Hotel Pennsylvania not long afterward, so I returned there within a short time. Arriving in the offices we had at the hotel, I discovered I had five minutes before meeting the senator, so I sat down in a big easy chair and closed my eyes.

A few minutes later I was awakened by a startled exclamation and looked up to see Mr. Winslow and Mr. Wood standing in the doorway, staring.

"How did you get here! We left you on your way home. We walked across the street, had a quick hamburger and coffee and came directly here, and you're already on the scene!"

In those days my life went long at that pace for long periods at a time and I suppose I enjoyed it, because I like to keep busy. When the United Nations headquarters was at Lake Success my schedule was complicated by the fact that I always had duties to attend to in New York early in the day and then had to drive for forty minutes to reach Lake Success in time for the opening of the Assembly or some other meeting at eleven o'clock. This suited Mr. Sandifer or any adviser because he always knew that I would be starting out at twenty minutes after ten. He could climb into my automobile with the assurance that for the next forty minutes I would be his "captive audience" and that our discussion of the day's work would not be interrupted.

In the period that I presided as chairman of the Human Rights Commission we spent most of our time trying to write the Universal Declaration of Human Rights and the Covenants, and there were times when I was getting in over my head. The officers of the commission had been charged with the task of preparing the first draft of the Declaration, and I remember that on one occasion, thinking that our work might be helped by an informal atmosphere, I asked this small group to meet at my apartment for tea. One of the members was the Chinese representative, Dr.

P. C. Chang, who was a great joy to all of us because of his sense of humor, his philosophical observations, and his ability to quote some apt Chinese proverb to fit almost any occasion. Dr. John P. Humphrey, a Canadian who was the permanent head of the Division of Human Rights in the UN Secretariat, and Dr. Charles Malik of Lebanon, one of the very able diplomats at the United Nations, also were at this meeting.

As we settled down over the teacups, one of them made a remark with philosophic implications, and a heated discussion ensued. Dr. Chang was a pluralist and held forth in charming fashion on the proposition that there is more than one kind of ultimate reality. The Declaration, he said, should reflect more than Western ideas and Dr. Humphrey would have to be eclectic in his approach. His remark, though addressed to Dr. Humphrey, was really directed at Dr. Malik, from whom it drew a prompt retort as he expounded at length the philosophy of Thomas Aquinas. Dr. Humphrey joined enthusiastically in the discussion, and I remember that at one point Dr. Chang suggested that the Secretariat might well spend a few months studying the fundamentals of Confucianism! By that time I could not follow them, so lofty had the conversation become, so I simply filled the teacups again and sat back to be entertained by the talk of these learned gentlemen.

Early in the meetings of the commission we discovered that while it would be possible to reach some kind of agreement on the Declaration, we were going to be in for a great deal of controversy with the Russian representatives, particularly Dr. Pavlov, who attempted at every opportunity to write a bit of Communist philosophy into the document. For example, at the end of practically every article the Russian proposed to amend the Declaration to read: "This shall be enforced by the state."

When such an amendment was proposed I, or one of the other Western delegates, would argue against it on the ground that this was an international declaration by the United Nations and that we did not believe it should be imposed by the power of the individual governments. We would then ask for a vote and the amendment would be defeated. But as soon as the next article was completed the Soviet delegate would again propose the same amendment and we would have to go through the whole business again with the same result, the defeat of the Soviet proposal. This naturally became monotonous but the Russians never gave up trying.

The drafting of the articles continued over many months. During our early work on the Covenants and measures of implementation it became apparent that it was going to be exceedingly difficult to agree on articles that would, if accepted, be legally binding on the various nations. This was difficult enough in regard to civil and political rights that have become fairly well accepted throughout the civilized world, but when it came to economic and social rights it seemed to me at times that agreement would be all but impossible. These articles have, however, now been adopted by the majority of the committee.

The reason for this, in part at least, was the vast social and economic differences between the various countries; the social and economic conditions in the United States, for example, as contrasted to existing conditions in a country like India. The gap was so great that it was well-nigh impossible to phrase concepts acceptable to both countries. Let me give one example to explain these difficulties.

With the aid of various specialized United Nations agencies, we set out to write the best possible article aimed at the encouragement of universal education. We achieved a preliminary draft that stated that everyone had a right to primary, secondary and higher education, the first two to be compulsory but all of them eventually to be provided free by the individual governments concerned. This might read well to a citizen of the United States but it was quite a different matter in India.

"Our economy is strained," Madame Hansa Mehta, the Indian representative, explained, "and we are trying only to give all children a primary education. What would happen if we suddenly attempted to provide secondary and higher education, too? The article should be amended to read that the goal is to be accomplished gradually, with due consideration for the economy of each country."

"The trouble with that," I replied, "is that I do not believe the United States Senate would ever ratify a treaty so vaguely worded. The senators would ask: 'What does gradually mean—five years or ten years or a hundred years?' I just don't believe they would accept it."

But if the economic problems of underdeveloped countries provided one stumbling block, the political systems of other countries, particularly the United States, provided another. Our delegation had to insist on including a states' rights clause because we could act only in regard to matters that were under jurisdiction of the federal government. We had to explain that in other matters, which were under the control of the states, we had power only to "recommend" that the states take appropriate action.

Australia and Canada were the only other countries in a similar position.

Many of the other countries resented the fact that they were being asked to commit all their people to the instruments we were drafting, whereas on certain matters the United States delegation could commit only a limited number of the people and hope that the various state governments would accept our recommendations. I could understand their resentment and their opposition to our "states' rights" system, but we always fought to get our amendment in. So far, however, the draft Covenants still lack a federal states' rights clause. We made slow progress in drafting the legally binding Covenants and even slower progress in framing measures of implementation that would provide means to enforce the Covenants.

Late in 1947 it was decided that the next meeting of the Human Rights Commission would be in Geneva, so we left for that city early in December with the idea of completing our work in time to be home for Christmas. As chairman, I knew that it would require much hard work and long hours to be able to adjourn before Christmas but I was in a determined mood and I warned all the delegations of my plans.

I immediately laid out a schedule of work that, with night sessions, I believed would enable us to adjourn by eleven o'clock on the evening of December 17.

Nobody objected to my plans, at least not until later, and I must say that everybody worked hard. My own day started at eight o'clock, when I met with my advisers at breakfast and went over the work schedule and any difficult problems. Then I would go to the Palais des Nations Unies, where the sessions were held and get through my correspondence in time for the morning session of the commission. At luncheon we usually got several delegates together to continue our discussions informally and then returned to the afternoon meeting. At night we had an after-dinner session or a meeting of our delegation. Later Mr. Hendrick and I would talk for perhaps an hour about the next day's plans, and after he had gone to bed Mrs. Hendrick would come in with a pile of personal letters on which we worked until after midnight. By the time I had dictated my daily newspaper column I was ready for bed.

This was a grueling schedule for everybody and within a few days I was being denounced—mostly in fun, I hope—as a merciless slave driver. But I must say we got through a great deal of work and kept to our schedule, for which I was very grateful to all the delegations.

We did end our work at eleven o'clock on the evening I had originally designated.

Our efforts to write a Charter or International Bill of Human Rights reached a kind of climax at the Paris sessions of the General Assembly in 1948. After our Geneva meeting we made steady progress on the Declara-tion, despite many controversies with the delegates from Communist countries.

Dr. Pavlov was a member of the commission and delivered many long propaganda harangues that appeared to be more for the purpose of pub-licizing the Communist point of view than in the hope of making changes in the Declaration. He was an orator of great power; his words rolled out of his black beard like a river, and stopping him was difficult. Usually, we had to sit and listen, but on one occasion it seemed to me that the rash accusations he brought against the United States and Great Britain were proving a real detriment to our work. Dr. Pavlov knew that most of us were getting tired of listening, but toward the end of one week when we were preparing to recess he began speaking again. He seemed likely to go on forever, but I watched him closely until he had to pause for breath. Then I banged the gavel so hard that the other delegates jumped in surprise and, before he could continue, I got in a few words of my own.

"We are here," I said, "to devise ways of safeguarding human rights. We are not here to attack each other's governments, and I hope when we return on Monday the delegate of the Soviet Union will remember that!" I banged the gavel again. "Meeting adjourned!"

Eventually we completed a draft of the Universal Declaration of Human Rights that we foolishly felt would be quickly accepted by the General Assembly, which was meeting in Paris in the autumn of 1948.

"I believe," General Marshall, who had become secretary of state, said before we left for Paris, "that this session of the General Assembly will be remembered as the human rights session."

As the session opened I was full of confidence that we could quickly get the Declaration through the formal hearings before Committee Three and have it approved by the Assembly. My confidence was soon gone. We worked for two months, often until late at night, debating every single word of that draft Declaration over and over again before Committee Three would approve its transmission to the General Assembly.

During this time I made a trip to Germany, at the request of General Lucius Clay, who asked me to address a group of German women doctors at Stuttgart. This was not an easy assignment. There had been, during the conflict with Hitler, a considerable campaign of hatred in Germany directed against me personally because I had spoken out as strongly as I could against most of the things represented by nazism, including the persecution of Jewish people. Furthermore, any occupation force, whether good or bad, just or unjust, is detested by the people it rules, and I have never had reason to believe that an exception is made of American troops. General Clay, however, was trying with considerable success to carry out a difficult assignment in Germany and he told me he believed it might be helpful if I spoke to the women in Stuttgart. So, of course, I agreed to do so.

There was a large crowd at the Stuttgart meeting, and, as I had feared, the women were cool and reserved if not bitter toward me when I arrived at the dinner. I had no intention of letting their coldness prevent me from saying certain things I had in my mind, so I began with a denunciation of the Nazi philosophy and actions. I made it as strong as I could and I expressed the opinion that the German people must bear their share of the blame. I had not expected my audience to be pleased by such remarks and they were not. The atmosphere became cooler.

Then I talked to them more approvingly. At that time the Russians were blockading Berlin, cutting off all coal and other supplies that moved over the normal land routes and forcing the United States to organize a gigantic airlift to supply West Berlin. The purpose of the Soviets was to force the Western powers to move out of Berlin. In this crisis the German people had acted magnificently and I praised them for supporting the democracies and defying the Communist power. I talked about the future, the recovery of Germany under a democratic form of government, and the hope that the United Nations would mean the end of international wars. Slowly the audience warmed up and I could feel a change of attitude as I concluded: "And now I extend to you the hand of friendship and co-operation."

On this trip I lunched with the women doctors and they told me about their problems with their own German refugees, who had to live on the German economy because they were German citizens but could not at that time of hardship find work. They were existing under miserable and dangerous conditions. I was also told of the difficulties of tracing children taken by Hitler from conquered Poland and other lands, under his plan of destroying their nationality. As the records were found, an effort was being made to restore the children to their families. Many of them did not even know they were not of German birth.

I stayed only a little more than a day in Stuttgart but the visit taught me much and I returned with zest to the work of the Third Committee of the General Assembly.

In the final vote in Committee Three, on presenting the Declaration to the Assembly, the delegates from four Moslem countries abstained, explaining that they believed the article on religious freedom was contrary to the Koran. We consulted Sir Zafrulla Khan, the foreign minister of Pakistan, the largest Moslem nation.

"It is my opinion," he declared, "that our Pakistan delegate has misinterpreted the Koran. I understand the Koran to say: 'He who can believe shall believe; he who cannot believe shall disbelieve; the only unforgiveable sin is to be a hypocrite.' I shall vote for acceptance of the Universal Declaration of Human Rights."

In the end there was no vote cast against the Declaration in the General Assembly, but there were some disappointing abstentions. The Soviet Union and its satellite countries abstained, since the Russian delegate contended that the Declaration put emphasis mainly on "eighteenth-century rights" and not enough on economic, social and cultural rights. The delegate from Saudi Arabia abstained, saying he was quite sure King Ibn Saud would not agree to the interpretation of the Koran. South Africa also abstained, I was sad to note; its delegate said that they hoped to give their people basic human rights, but that the Declaration went too far. Two small countries were absent. The Declaration was finally accepted by the General Assembly on December 10, 1948.

After the Declaration was accepted, it seemed to me that the United States had held the chairmanship of the Commission on Human Rights long enough. So at the 1951 meeting of the commission in Geneva, I nominated Charles Malik of Lebanon, with the consent of my government. He was elected and from then on I was just a member but a most interested member, for I believed the Human Rights Commission was one of the important parts of the foundation on which the United Nations might build a peaceful world.

The commission continued to work on drafting the Covenants, but this was so difficult that the United States group finally decided that it would be possible to progress only if we moved forward a step at a time. We proposed that there be two Covenants, one covering legally binding agreements on social and economic rights and another covering political and civil rights. This plan was vigorously opposed by some delegations, including the Soviets, on the ground that the economic and social rights were the most important and that they probably would not be accepted for years if they were in a separate covenant. But it seemed to our delegation that it was better to try to get what we could at that time. The civil and political rights already were a part of the law in many countries and were not so difficult to phrase in legal language that would be generally acceptable, although we knew that even this first step would be exceedingly difficult.

We finally won our point by only four votes, but taking the first step turned out to be even harder than we had expected. Progress had been made, but the Covenants were not well drafted, nor is the drafting yet complete, and I doubt whether they are likely to be accepted in their present form. Looking back over the work that has been done, I now believe it would be best to start anew by putting into the Covenant on civil and political rights only a few basic rights on which all could agree and to provide for adding other rights as it becomes possible to have them generally accepted.

The last session of the General Assembly that I attended in Paris was in the autumn of 1951, a session that continued after a brief Christmas holiday into February of 1952. Toward the end of this session Ambassador Austin became ill and for a short time I presided over the United States delegations. The heads of other delegations expressed affection for Senator Austin personally.

"We have not always agreed with the policies of the United States," most of them said in one way or another. "But if Ambassador Austin told us something was true, we knew it was true."

I served during the autumn of 1952, but at the end of each session all delegates automatically resign to permit the President to have a free hand in choosing his representatives. In the 1952 elections, a Republican administration came into power and all of us who were Democrats knew that our services with the United Nations had come to an end. But my interest in the United Nations had grown steadily during six years, and later I volunteered to work with the American Association for the United Nations so that I would not be out of touch with the work of the one organization that has the machinery to bring together all nations in an effort to maintain world peace.

Thirty-three

Foreign Travels

ALTHOUGH I HAD been bustling back and forth across the Atlantic Ocean rather like a harassed commuter for six years, my really extensive foreign travels did not begin until 1952 after the General Assembly in Paris.

The end of my duties as a delegate later that year meant that I no longer had to adjust my life to a schedule of meetings of the Assembly or the Human Rights Commission in various cities at frequent intervals. Though it was necessary for me to spend a certain amount of time traveling in connection with my work for the American Association for the United Nations, I had much greater flexibility in my schedule and was able to take longer trips abroad, always as a newspaperwoman and sometimes also as a representative of the A.A.U.N.

I had received a number of invitations to visit various countries. One was extended by Prime Minister Nehru. The invitation stuck in my mind and, as the Assembly was ending its sessions in Paris early in 1952, I decided the time might be right. "Instead of going back to New York as usual," I remarked to my secretary, "why not go home the long way— around the world. We've already got a good start."

So Mr. Nehru renewed his invitation and our ambassador to India, Chester Bowles, seemed pleased with the idea. Another thing that influenced me was that I had long wanted to visit Israel, particularly since I had seen the Jewish refugee camps in Germany and learned more of the eagerness of most of the refugees to migrate to Israel. As soon as I began making arrangements to stop in Israel on the way to India, I was approached by Charles Malik of Lebanon, whom I had come to know well on the Human Rights Commission.

"I know that you're going to stop in Israel on the way to India," he

324

said. "I really don't think you should stop there without visiting some
of the Arab countries. You should see more than one country in the Middle East."

A little later he made arrangements for me and my secretary, Miss
Corr, and we flew directly from Paris to Beirut, Lebanon, where we arrived late one evening. Beirut was a beautiful and peaceful-looking city
even at night, with the Mediterranean breaking softly on its beaches.
Next morning when I went out to get into the car, I discovered I was
to be escorted by a lorry filled with soldiers.

I had wondered a bit about the attitude of the people toward me because I had always been outspoken in my support of the state of Israel,
but everyone seemed friendly and I decided to ignore the presence of the
soldiers. When we halted to visit some historic site, the truck dashed up
and the soldiers leaped out to set up "lines of defense" around us. This
was an indication that the government was not at all certain about the
kind of reception I would be given by the people. At least the officials
were taking a rather alarmist view.

Actually, there were no signs of hostility and after a short time I became thoroughly irritated by what seemed to me intolerable nonsense.
I insisted that they get rid of the soldiers at once. They did so but I was
certain that throughout my visit there was always a guard of some kind
nearby.

I found my visit to the Arab countries extremely interesting. Lebanon
is perhaps the most Westernized of the Arab countries. We had planned
to drive to Syria, but there was so much snow in the mountain passes
that we went by air to Damascus, an amazing city with narrow streets
and bazaars.

The newspapermen to whom I talked in Syria were particularly difficult. They were bitterly nationalistic and bitterly opposed to Israel and
they badgered me with questions about why I should support the Israeli
cause.

"The Balfour resolution for establishment of a Jewish homeland was
accepted by the United States and Great Britain after the First World
War," I usually replied. "This action encouraged the buying of land by
the Jews on the assurance that a homeland would be created for them in
Palestine. I feel that it practically committed our government to assist
in the creation of a government there eventually, because there cannot
be a homeland without a government."

From Damascus I drove to Amman, Jordan, but our time was short and I had a chance to meet only two or three government officials. They were greatly concerned with the problem of the Palestinian refugees who had moved out of Israeli territory during the warfare between Israel and the Arab states and had been put into camps in Jordan. I visited many of these camps during my trips and found them distressing beyond words.

I had seen various refugees camps in Europe and had been impressed by the way the inmates kept their hopes alive and tried to make their temporary quarters into "homes" even under the most difficult conditions. I had been particularly impressed by the burning desire of many Jewish refugees to get to Israel. Now, in the Arab countries, I learned something of the grave problem of refugees from Israel.

The Arab refugee camps were the least hopeful I had ever seen. One of the principal reasons for this, I believe, was that nothing had been done to preserve the skills of the people. They seemed to have little or nothing to look forward to and nothing to do. Under such conditions the adults are likely to lose their skills and the children grow up uninstructed.

"Why," I asked my official guide, "are these people not given something to do? They might be making things to go on the market or helping to produce food. If they lose their skills they will be worthless citizens in any country they may finally settle in."

The guide gave a kind of helpless shrug. "There is unemployment in most of the Arab countries, and we cannot permit these people to seek work that would put them in competition with the citizens of the country."

The standard of living in the camps we visited was low and the housing was inadequate. I visited one tent where a woman showed us her small baby, who was ill. "The baby was bitten by a snake yesterday," the woman explained, as she put it back on the floor of the tent. There was nothing to prevent snakes from entering, and babies lying on the floor were an easy prey.

The refugees were fed on a budget of three cents per day per person. That would seem to be a pitifully small sum even for countries with a low standard of living but it represented more food than was available to some of the nomads living in the desert.

Going from the Arab countries through the Mandelbaum Gate into Israel was, to me, like breathing the air of the United States again. The

Mandelbaum Gate is nothing much, a movable barrier, with soldiers on guard. But once I was through the barrier I felt that I was among people with a purpose, people dedicated to fulfilling a purpose.

I spent seven days in Israel, the same number I had spent in the Arab countries. The health program is a monumental work. Much had been done in the past by Hadassah, which built and ran hospitals made possible by general private donations of persons in many countries.

I was greatly impressed by what the Israelis had done to reclaim the desert and make it productive, to develop the country industrially and to accept as permanent citizens hundreds of thousands of refugees from war and persecution in Europe and elsewhere. But I was even more impressed when I returned to Israel three years later and saw how much had been done in that short time.

Of course, no one should imagine that everything is perfect in Israel. The country has many large and small problems of all kinds to overcome, including the necessity for establishing a sound basis for its economic existence. A great deal has been done. The desert has been made to blossom, but there remain grave obstacles, such as the efficient use of water, to a peaceful and prosperous future. I believe that with reason and patience solutions can be found and they will greatly benefit not Israel alone but the entire area.

Not all of Israel's problems are economic. One issue that must be faced by the government is that of separation of church and state. At present the influence of the church is so great that it is often difficult to distinguish between it and the state. I was suprised to be told of a young man who had been refused the right to marry the girl with whom he was in love because she was an Orthodox Catholic. This is merely one example of the injustices that can grow out of such a situation, and the incidents will greatly increase in time. Apparently leaders of the state do not feel that their country is strong enough to undertake a solution to this problem because it would arouse bitter controversy, but someday it must be faced. When it is, I am confident there will be a separation of powers as there is in the United States.

We flew to Karachi, the capital of Pakistan, where I was to be the guest of the All Pakistan Women's Association, at the invitation of the Begum Liaquat Ali Khan.

Here, as earlier in Israel and later in India, I saw a country not only struggling with the problems that beset any young government but also suffering from the results of the partition that had accompanied the achievement of their long-sought independence. The division of this sub-continent into two independent states, one predominantly Hindu, the other predominantly Moslem, was economically painful to both parts. From the point of view of defense, too, the subcontinent is paying a ter-rible price for partition. The mountain ranges guarding its northern border made undivided India a single defense system. The Khyber Pass was one of the few breaks through which invasion was possible. But the sword of partition not only divided the land, cutting off crops from mar-kets and factories from raw materials, it also split up everything from debts and revenues to rolling stock and typewriters, including, of course, the army. So today, instead of a single strong united army deployed to meet possible aggression from without, two lesser separate armies must defend the frontiers of the subcontinent. And, instead of facing out-ward, these two armies now face each other across a line in Kashmir, over which India and Pakistan are at odds.

As in the case of the Israeli-Arab dispute, bitterness and fear of one's neighbor has resulted in spending for defense huge sums badly needed for health, housing, education, and other programs that would better the living standards of the people.

For Pakistan this division of the subcontinent had an added complica-tion. Not only was Pakistan itself separated from India, but its western portion was separated from its eastern portion by some eight hundred miles of Indian territory. Neither was it a clean cut, for no matter how the partition lines were drawn millions of Hindus and Sikhs still were left in Moslem territory and millions of Moslems in the areas that went to India.

It is against the background of these facts that we Americans must view the problems of Pakistan and India today if we are to understand the conditions that exist there and the importance of intelligent and effective help.

Some of the officials with whom I talked described to me the difficulties of those early days of independence when they were trying to get the gov-ernment set up. They worked in practically bare buildings. They had no desks, no pencils, no typewriters, no paper, few telephones. They sat on packing boxes, wrote on packing boxes, and occasionally made them into beds at night. There were no files, no statistics. More serious, there was—and still is—a grave lack of the kind of trained personnel without which it is almost impossible to carry on the business of government. A number of the members of the first Cabinet had never before held office. Nor were there bookkeepers or stenographers or clerks.

At the top there were and are, of course, some exceedingly able people who managed to get the government running; and many young people are now being trained intensively in various civil service jobs. Here the Ford Foundation is giving invaluable help, in India as well as in Pakistan.

I had met the Begum Liaquat Ali Khan at a meeting of the General Assembly in Paris and had found her delightful. After the assassination of her husband, which shocked the world, the begum had devoted herself to trying to carry out his plans for his people. It is because of her leadership and the example of the Begum Husain Malik, that the women of Pakistan have begun to free themselves of the restrictions imposed by tradition. The principal instrument through which they are acomplishing their really magnificent work is the All Pakistan Women's Association, which has set up medical clinics, established educational centers, diffused information about agricultural methods, developed skills and handicrafts.

Like all the Middle Eastern and Asian countries, Pakistan has been terribly handicapped by her lack of technical experts, people qualified to draw up, appraise and carry out the necessary development programs. To meet this need the Pakistan government, the United Nations Food and Agricultural Organization, the UN Economic Commission for Asia and the Far East, and the International Bank have wisely collaborated to set up in Pakistan a center where this kind of training is available. It seems to me to represent the best kind of international thinking and co-operation.

The spirit of the people of Pakistan is something one does not soon forget. There is courage and great vitality. They are determined to make their government succeed, and their nation a cohesive force. In talking to the men at the head of this government I was convinced that their devotion and intelligent approach, with the resolute support of the people, cannot fail to make Pakistan a great country.

We landed in New Delhi on February 27, and I was overwhelmed to find Prime Minister Nehru there to greet me, with a number of other officials and his sister, Madame Pandit, head of India's delegation to the UN. I was also extremely glad to see waiting for me Ambassador Chester Bowles and his wife. In them I was greeting good friends whom I had known for many years.

We drove directly to Government House, the official home of India's president, Rajendra Prasad, where, as protocol required, we were to spend our first night. The following day we were to move to the home of the prime minister and stay with him for the rest of our visit.

During the course of that first meeting I asked Prime Minister Nehru about a article on India's recent election, which I had read before leaving the United States. It described how people had spent days traveling through tiger-infested jungles in order to vote; how some of the primitive tribes had trekked miles across deserts, blowing little flutes, and announcing when they finally reached their destination that they had come to worship the god "Vote." Out of India's 360 million people, 90 million voted.

I told Prime Minister Nehru that I had been long enough an observer of political life to know that no great outpouring of voters occurs unless someone has done some remarkable campaigning. He beckoned me into his office and pointed to a map on the wall, which traced all his campaign trips before the election and showed how many miles he had traveled by air, train, boat and automobile—altogether 25,732. Not included, however, were the miles he traveled by bullock cart, on horseback and on foot. At the bottom of the map is a line reading: "The Prime Minister, it is estimated, talked personally to thirty million people in his audience."

The first two years of India's independence were complicated, as they were in Pakistan, by the staggering refugee resettlement problem. The country's needs were studied but there was much to be done, and everything needing to be done at once.

Nevertheless, though India has far to go, she has made an inspiring beginning. This new democracy seems to evoke the kind of passionate devotion among its leaders that our forefathers had for the democratic government they were establishing in America. Perhaps this is one of the greatest contributions the young democracies can make to the older ones. We have grown stale; we are inclined to take everything for granted. Perhaps we may draw from people who ford rivers and walk miles of jungle trails in order to vote a new sense of our responsibility and a revival of our forefathers' readiness to pledge "our lives, our sacred honor, and all our worldly goods" for the idea they believed would make this country a place worth living in.

What the leaders of India want and are determined to have is a democracy that is indigenous to their country, based on their own past and the character of their own people. It is in helping India to build in its own way and on its own strength that Ambassador Bowles has done such a remarkable job. In the less than half year he had been in India at that time he had made great strides in seeing that foreign aid was intelligently co-ordinated and applied. Perhaps even more important, he had given Indians an entirely new idea of American officialdom and a new confidence in our motives and our good will.

We must face the fact that in the years after the war our popularity took a terrible tumble in India, as it did throughout the Arab countries. Having shaken off the domination of one foreign power, they are understandably determined not to fall under the influence of any other. Even Nehru, it is said, was at first wary of Ambassador Bowles's suggestions for Point Four aid, lest they conceal some attempt at economic domination.

In addition, we have against us their feeling that because our skins are white we necessarily look down upon all peoples whose skins are yellow or black or brown. This thought is never out of their minds. They always asked me pointedly about our treatment of minorities in our country.

As I traveled about India during the next few weeks, the immensity of the task this new government faces became overwhelmingly apparent. India has two problems that seem to me particularly urgent: one is how to grow more food; the other is how to control the rising tide of her population.

With the food problem looming so large, India has had to put increased agricultural production ahead of everything else. Right now she spends $600 million a year and more importing food and cotton she could grow herself, simply to maintain the present inadequate level of diet and keep her textile mills running. She needs not so much to bring more land under cultivation as to get more from the farm land she already has. For instance, an Indian farmer gets only half as much wheat from an acre as an American farmer and only about one fifth as much cotton. To introduce modern methods to the farmers in the villages, India needs thousands of trained men: technical specialists of all kinds, agricultural chemists, experts in soil science, ecology and sanitation, mechanics who can repair implements, engineers to lay out irrigation and drainage works.

Water is another problem. India's great rivers contain more than enough for her needs but at present only a small part of the flow is being used. Only one fifth of her farm land is regularly watered.

International co-operation in many forms is giving magnificent impetus to improved food rations, technical assistance, health care. What can be done in these ways was vividly dramatized to me at Etawah, a district composed of some 700,000 people, scattered among many small mud villages.

The idea for this agricultural experiment was suggested by Albert Meyer, a New York architect, who is responsible for many of India's new buildings and is designing the new capital of the Punjab. Etawah is an Indian project. We furnish technical assistance and advice, and supplies that must be bought abroad, on the self-help principle that is the basis of all Point Four aid, but the plan is an Indian plan and what has been done has been done by the Indian people themselves.

For the first two years the project was headed by Horace Holmes, a Cornell-trained American agricultural expert from Tennessee. He had lived and worked with the farmers before he began to introduce any new ways. Then he induced a few of them to try something different as an experiment, perhaps imported seeds, different fertilizer, or a better tool. When they saw the difference these things could make they tried them on their own on a larger scale, and other farmers began to follow suit.

Already they had more than doubled their crop production; wheat which had grown about a foot high was now between five and six feet high. The cattle had improved and the cows gave more milk.

After our first two days in New Delhi we started by air on a trip that was to take us over a good part of India before we returned to the capital. That trip took us to Bombay and Trivandrum, the southwest tip of India, which has the highest literacy rate in India, 50 per cent as compared to an average of 10 per cent for the rest of the country. Now, as part of her Five Year Plan, India has drawn up a program to make education free and compulsory for all children between six and fourteen years of age. This means she will need about two million teachers and thousands of new schools.

From Trivandrum we flew to Mysore and from there on a sightseeing tour to Bangalore. The peak moment of all the sightseeing for me was the Taj. I will carry in my mind the beauty of it as long as I live. At last I know why my father felt it was the one unforgettable thing he had seen in India. He always said it was the one thing he wanted us to see together.

From Agra we flew to Jaipur and at length back to New Delhi, where we stayed at Government House with President Prasad, a gentle and quiet man with great strength of character.

It was at Allahabad, where I received an honorary degree, that I encountered the effect of Communist influence on the students. It is almost always difficult for us to realize why the Communist philosophy is easier for young Indians to accept than our own. We overlook the two major factors: they rarely know what we are talking about when we speak of freedom in the abstract; their most pressing problem, from birth to death, now as it has always been, is hunger. Freedom to eat is one of the most important freedoms; and it is what the Communists are promising the people of India.

From Benares to Nepal to Calcutta—so many crowded miles, so much want, so much ferment, so much blending of the timeless with the new. So much human need—and so little human communication, at least between Americans and Indians. One of these lacks of communication comes in our sense of values. Paul Hoffman, who asked me to lunch with him and his colleagues of the Ford Foundation in Los Angeles on my way home, crystallized this point. The American dream of the Horatio Alger success story is completely meaningless to the Indian. To him it is simply an indication of a struggle for material values. What we have failed to take to him is our spiritual values. An understanding of our own spiritual foundations may be one of the bridges we need to better understanding of the East and its people. We must show by our behavior that we believe in equality and in justice and that our religion teaches faith and love and charity to our fellow men. Here is where each of us has a job to do that must be done at home, because we can lose the battle on the soil of the United States just as surely as we can lose it in any one of the other countries in the world.

In the spring of 1953 I returned from a short trip to find bad news waiting for me. Miss Thompson was in the hospital. For several days I spent most of the time there. On April 12, on the anniversary of my husband's death, I went to Hyde Park. On my return I walked into the hospital just as dear Tommy died. There had been no sudden change. She just died.

Tommy had been with me for thirty years. In many ways she not only made my life easier but she gave me a reason for living. In almost anything I did, she was a help but she was also a stern critic. No one can ever take the place of such a person nor does one cease missing her, but I am sure she would not have wanted to live to suffer the torture of being an invalid.

Though my work for the American Association for the United Nations began in the spring of 1953, it did not become intensive until autumn. Consequently, I accepted an invitation that spring to be one of a group of exchange people going from the United States to Japan. The trip was under the auspices of Columbia University, which acted as host in this country for the Japanese who came here. Our hosts in Japan were Shigeharu Matsumoto and Dr. Yasaki Takagi, who represented the International House of Japan and the Committee for Cultural Exchange.

The reason the Japanese invited me was that their women were just coming into the responsibilities of functioning in a democracy after centuries in which feudalistic concepts had dominated their lives and customs. The attempt to change over to more or less democractic concepts in a short time naturally created many problems both of a political nature and in regard to family life. Some of the Japanese leaders hoped that an American woman, talking to groups of the Japanese women and men, would be able to explain to them the meaning of democracy and the manner in which a democratic government functions.

The fact was that after World War II the United States had rather arbitrarily insisted on giving the Japanese a democratic constitution, telling them that now they were going to be a democratic country. But this did not automatically change the old customs or turn feudalism into democracy. There were various articles in the new Japanese constitution that had been taken almost verbatim from Western documents, and some of these meant nothing to the Japanese or merely confused them because of the great differences between their social and economic background and the social and economic concepts of, say, the United States or France. So a period of education obviously was necessary, and I was happy to have a chance to do whatever I could to help spread the idea of democracy.

One of the first persons I encountered in the lobby of the Imperial Hotel in Tokyo was Marian Anderson, who had been singing with great success all over Japan. Later I held a press conference. I had always heard that the Japanese were avid photographers, but I never expected to see so many news photographers as greeted us in Tokyo. I was told that Adlai Stevenson gazed in wonder at them during his trip to Japan and exclaimed: "This is a photographic dictatorship!"

I will not attempt to describe our experiences in Japan in any chronological order because we covered so much ground in the five weeks we were there, but there were some highlights that stand out in my mind. A few days after our arrival we visited Princess Chichibu, the widow of the Emperor's brother. The princess had gone to the Friests School in Washington when her father was ambassador there. After her marriage she had kept in much closer touch with the people of Japan than other members of the royal family. Her former friends came to see her regularly to talk over problems of farming and she kept busy working with the Girl Guides, similar to our Girl Scout organizations, and with Four-H clubs, which have been active in Japan since the war in an effort to help young farmers learn modern methods of production.

The next day I had an interesting meeting at the Ministry of Labor with the people who run bureaus for women in industry, for improvement of rural life, child welfare and the like. These government bureaus bear the stamp of American organization but that does not mean they operate the way they do in the United States. The organization was imposed on Japan by the occupation authorities and American methods were not entirely suited to the facts of life in Japan: the place of women in the industrial system, the necessity for children to contribute to the family income, the ability of the economy to support such public service. In order to make these organizations practical, they had to be adjusted to fit conditions in Japan, and that has been a complicated task.

There is also the important question whether such services are welcomed by the public. As I was leaving the ministry a group of Communist party women, led by an American who is married to a Japanese, were waiting outside. The American woman stared at me and seemed to be highly strung to the point of fanaticism. As I stepped out the door the group began shouting anti-American slogans.

"Go home to America! We women who went through the war do not want any more war!"

The obvious answer was, of course, that neither did I want war. It is groups such as this one that keep the fear of war constantly alive in the peoples of the free world. I made numerous inquiries about Communist activities and strength in Japan. On one occasion I met with a number of college presidents in Nara and made a point of asking them about the attitude of students and professors.

"I doubt that more than a few are really convinced Communists," one said. "However, a few can make a good deal of noise because they know what they really believe in, while the others are divided and groping to find their way."

I was inclined to believe there was more real acceptance of Marxism among the students in Japan than these college presidents were willing to acknowledge to me. They did say that democracy was not making headway among the students and that it was not being well taught.

I talked to countless groups of women in many cities of Japan and there were certain broad themes that ran through all our discussions. One was the attitude of young people toward their elders and the attitude of the elders toward the young. Since the Japanese had been urged to accept the democratic idea of free discussion, there had developed a great deal of criticism between the two groups and this antagonism was increased by the fact that the young people blamed their elders for telling them that Japan could not lose the war. Much of the authority of the elders was undermined when the Japanese armies were defeated and the Emperor was declared to be a man rather than a god. The young people became cynical and disillusioned.

There were also many questions, particularly from the students, that I answered as best I could. Sometimes I was asked why the United States used the atom bomb and how I felt about it. I tried to explain the urgent reasons that prompted our leaders to make the decision in an effort to end the war quickly, but at the same time I expressed my feeling of horror about any kind of warfare. Another question was, "Do the people of the United States understand that the young people of Japan dislike rearmament and that, in order to rearm as urged by Washington, we have to change our constitution which was adopted at the request of the United States in the first place?"

Of course, world conditions had changed since they adopted the constitution that renounced war forever, but it was not so easy to see the threat of Soviet expansion through Japanese eyes as it was through American eyes. I don't suppose my explanations of the danger to the democracies were satisfactory to people who had never experienced democratic life.

These sessions were often exhausting, particularly if there were a large number of students in the audience, but what was most tiring to me was that everything had to be translated.

I remember one charming and rather sophisticated Japanese newspaper-woman who was beautiful in her native costume yet seemed to be familiar with Western customs. She told me that her greatest difficulty at home was with the "system of the pouch."

"What is that?" I asked.

"My mother-in-law," she said, "is old-fashioned. She has a large leather pouch and each week she puts into it all the family earnings. Then all of us become dependent on her ideas of how much we should spend or whether we should spend anything. In fact, she can practically tell us how to run our lives."

I found that this custom was practiced in many places. A woman who worked in a factory told me she went home on weekends to the farm where her family lived and that she always placed her earnings on the household shrine the night she arrived. The next morning they were in the mother-in-law's pouch. I found that most of the Japanese mothers in the working class look forward to the day when they will be mothers-in-law and can tyrannize over their daughters-in-law. Slowly these outdated customs are changing under the present government but it will be a long time before they are entirely gone.

I have had many experiences in my life, but I could not help feeling a twinge of anxiety as I prepared for my interview with Emperor Hirohito, the 124th of his line, and Empress Nagako. Knowing that old habits and customs were changing, especially for the women of Japan, I felt it would be interesting to know whether the Empress was able or desired to give some leadership in these changes.

The more I talked with groups of women in Japan the more I was convinced that, while the women were a force in their homes behind the scenes, they had not gained direct equality with men as provided in their new constitution, despite the fact that there were thirty women members of the Diet, or parliament.

There were certainly some intellectuals among the prominent women in the field of labor, in farm organizations and in social work, but they could not be called the most influential in Japan from the standpoint of social prestige. They were not, if I except Princess Chichibu, finding out how the girls in the factories lived or how the farm women worked in their fields or their homes.

There was a good deal of protocol attached to this meeting with the Emperor and Empress, in which I was guided by our ambassador, John M. Allison. After we were seated in the palace the Emperor and his wife arrived. The Empress wore a kimono. As I looked at her sitting calmly with her hands in her lap, with her face unlined and impassive, I could not help wondering what lay behind that placid surface. She must be a woman of extensive education. Her husband is a student of the sciences and has written several books. The Empress had always taken an interest in child education.

We talked about conditions generally and at one point the Emperor said he had always regretted that we had gone to war in spite of his vigorous efforts to prevent it. Now he hoped we were embarked on an era of friendship and peace.

Under the new constitution his position is changed but the Emperor can be an important figure. I think he was sincere in saying that he had tried to prevent the war and I decided that, if we behaved with tact and caution, we could count on him to help us build friendly relations with the Asian world. Even at that time he was hoping that Japan would become a member of the United Nations, as it later did, and that we could all work together for harmonious international relations.

I am afraid that during this interview I did not observe the rule that one should speak only when spoken to. I asked a few questions, or rather I made some remarks intended to draw out the ideas of the Empress.

"When I visited Pakistan and India," I said, "many changes were taking place, particularly in the status and activities of women. It seemed to me that women of all classes were drawing closer together and gaining in strength because of their greater knowledge of each other."

I looked at the calm face of the Empress, waiting for her to comment. She said nothing for a few moments and then replied: "We need more education." The Emperor broke in with some comment, and I thought perhaps that would be all the response I would get from the Empress, but she seemed to be thinking over my remarks, for in a few minutes she said: "There are great changes coming about in the life of our women. We have always been trained in the past to a life of service, and I am afraid that as these new changes come about there may be a loss of real values. What is your impression, Mrs. Roosevelt?"

"In all eras of change," I said, "there is a real danger that the old values will be lost. But it seems to me much less dangerous when the intelligent and broad-minded women who have had an opportunity to become educated take the lead to bring about the necessary changes."

"Our customs are different, Mrs. Roosevelt," the Emperor broke in. "We have government bureaus to lead in our reforms. We serve as an example to our people in the way we live and it is our lives that have influence over them."

That seemed to be the final word on how far the imperial family might go in assuming leadership in the new era in Japan. But I cannot help believing that, since the older women have been such an important influence in the home in the past, the future may see greater leadership exerted by the women of high social status, including members of the entourage of the imperial family.

As I look back on my visit to Japan, many incidents stood out as illustrative of the problems of establishing a democratic form of government in the Far East, and especially of educating women to take an active part in public affairs. One day in Tokyo I attended a round-table conference at the national Young Women's Christian Association with perhaps the most representative women leaders in the country. They were gravely concerned about progress in the new era of freedom. They made me see more clearly the difficulties created by an army of occupation or even by the presence of many American boys stationed at military bases in Japan. Unfortunately, we do not train our youngsters carefully enough before sending them throughout the world. They do not always remember that they are not merely soldiers but ambassadors, representing all that their own country stands for and all that democracy means to the rest of the world. The women were particularly concerned about the spread of prostitution and believed it could be controlled only by the closest co-operation between Japan and the United States.

The education of Japanese in democratic ways also was made more difficult at times by news from the United States telling of racial discrimination, of instances in Los Angeles and Texas where the work of UNESCO was attacked as communistic, and of the methods employed by the late Senator Joseph McCarthy in his Congressional investigations. Again and again Japanese told me they were confused and bewildered by these news dispatches, which were displayed prominently in the newspapers. "Will you please explain these attitudes?" one leading Japanese businessman asked me. "Japan hopes one day to be a member of the United Nations and to work loyally with that organization. But we are unable to understand why these things happen in a great democratic nation like the United States."

On another occasion a young man showed me a news dispatch from the United States saying that the Japanese government's victory in a recent election was because the majority of Japanese were accepting the policy of gradual rearmament which had been urged on the Tokyo government by our State Department.

"Do people in the United States really believe that?" he demanded. "Everybody knows that the government in Japan has been careful to say practically nothing on the subject of rearmament. Don't you realize that there is deep resentment here because many Japanese feel the United States used economic pressure at the time of the election in order to put into office people who favor the U.S. State Department's policies? For that reason, many feel that the United States is trying to make Japan economically a slave."

These are some of the suspicions and some of the grave problems that must be overcome—and, I feel sure, will be overcome—if our relations with the Far East are to be secure. Progress has been made toward this goal, but there are constantly arising new causes of misunderstanding, so that the road is a long and rough one. Perhaps our best hope is that the Japanese as well as ourselves want peace above all. This was impressed upon me strongly at the tragic city of Hiroshima.

To arrive in Hiroshima is an emotional experience. Here is where the first atom bomb ever to be dropped on human beings was actually used. The people of the United States believe that our leaders thought long and carefully before they used this dread weapon. We know that they thought first of the welfare of our own people, that they believed the bomb might end the war quickly with less loss of life everywhere than if it had not been dropped.

In spite of this conviction, one cannot see a city and be shown the area that was destroyed by blast and fire and be told of the people who died or were injured without deep sadness. To see the home where orphans were being cared for was to wish with one's whole heart that men could learn from this that we know too well how to destroy and must learn instead how to prevent such destruction. It is useless to say that Germany started the war and even started the research that led to the atomic bomb. It is useless to remember, as I did, the feelings of my husband and of the people of the United States when he heard the shocking news of the Japanese attack on Pearl Harbor. Pearl Harbor was only the climax of years of mounting misunderstandings and antipathies throughout the world. And out of all this came Hiroshima.

But it was not just here in this sad Japanese city that men and women and children suffered. All the world suffered. So it seems to me that the only helpful thing we can do, as we contemplate man's adventure into the realm of outer space, is to pledge ourselves to work to eliminate the causes of war through action that is possible only by using the machinery of the United Nations. If we do, then the peoples may understand each other a little better; they may have a better chance to be heard.

Contemplating the fate of Hiroshima, one can only say: "God grant to men greater wisdom in the future."

Thirty-four

The Long Way Home

MISS CORR and I continued on a western route around the world, stopping first at Hong Kong, which has become a fascinating crossroads of the free world in Asia. I was kindly received at Government House by Governor General Grantham and by American diplomatic officials stationed at this sensitive spot adjoining Communist China.

"Would you like to see the border of Communist China?" the governor general asked me.

"Indeed I would," I replied, "if that is possible."

As it turned out, it was no problem at all. The British general in charge of the border patrol called for me at my hotel the next morning and we drove over the hills to a little stream that separates Hong Kong from China. To my surprise, the "line" between the free world and the Communist world at this point is only a single strand of barbed wire and there is a bridge, guarded by police, over which a considerable number of Chinese go back and forth every day. These Chinese live on the Communist side but they own land on the Hong Kong side of the border stream and are permitted to cross each morning, often driving cows or pigs and carrying their farm tools, to work the land. Then in the evening they return across the bridge to the Communist side.

There did not seem to be many guards on either side of the border, but it was patrolled regularly. Nevertheless, a number of Chinese continued to flee across the frontier to Hong Kong every day or so.

"They were storekeepers, people with small means, who would have remained at their homes," the head of the border police told me, "but they said the Communist officials kept calling them up for questioning and

342

bedeviling them until they finally decided they would stand it no longer."

Talking with other officials and with refugees I got the impression that many of those who had fled to Hong Kong were neither Communist nor anti-Communist. They just wanted to be let alone and to be given a chance to earn a living. If the government did not try to tax them too heavily, they did not really care who ran it or whether it was corrupt; they just wanted to be left in peace.

The next day I met two gentlemen who had come from Taipei (Formosa). They represented the United States Committee to Help Chinese Refugees and were also busy trying to counteract the flood of Communist propaganda literature which comes into the Hong Kong area. This propaganda was largely cheap little books with pictures that misrepresent everything done by the United States or the United Nations as bringing death and destruction. Such propaganda was circulated widely among even the poorest Chinese and, so far as I could discover, little was being done by the democracies to offset these false stories.

I could not go to Taipei and not see Madame Chiang. But I knew that if I saw her I would have to tell her I did not think her dream of regaining China was possible. I felt that Chiang Kai-shek had had his chance and had not used the right methods to unify the country, and I did not believe that he any longer had any chance to do so. So I did not visit Taipei.

I might mention here that in 1955 I made a second visit to Hong Kong and found that there was more traffic across the little bridge leading to Communist China than when I had been there the first time. There were Chinese soldiers with rifles on the other side of the border and one of them had a camera with which he took a picture of our party. Dr. Gurewitsch, who was with me on the second trip, quickly adjusted his camera and took a picture of the Chinese guards, but before he could snap the shutter all the Communist soldiers lowered their rifles and more or less concealed them behind their backs. I suppose they were acting in accordance with their instructions to avoid giving an appearance of stern military rule on the Communist side of the barrier. No one spoke, however, and we were told that there was no fraternization between the soldiers on either side of the line.

At five o'clock on a beautiful day in late June Miss Corr and I skimmed over the brown fields of Turkey and caught a first glimpse of the wonderful greens and blues of the Mediterranean just before landing at Istanbul. I had not expected anyone to meet us at that hour of the morning but, to my horror, there stood our consul general, Mr. Macatee.

"You should not have come!" I exclaimed.

"Oh, yes," he replied, always the perfect diplomat. "It is so rare for me to get up at this time of morning that I am grateful to you for the opportunity to see the world when it is so beautiful."

I could well imagine that he would have much preferred to go back to bed instead of escorting us to the Blue Mosque, Hagia Sophia, the Byzantine Wall and the Bosporus. The early-morning light made the minarets and the domes beautiful.

Much too quickly it was time to return to the airport and catch the plane to Athens. We found upon our arrival that it was a holiday. We zigzagged through narrow, twisting streets, getting our first glimpse of the Acropolis. I was pleased to learn that Governor Adlai Stevenson was in Athens and would come to tea that afternoon. We arranged to visit the Acropolis and to see some of the excavations being made in Athens under our American group.

On some of our trips we saw many signs of American influence in Greece. Near Delphi there was a huge threshing machine near the road, well labeled to show that it had come from the United States as part of the Marshall Plan. We stopped to talk with the people running the machine and they told us that it quickly did work that would have taken days with slow-moving animals and men using old-fashioned implements. It was obvious in many places that America was having an influence on the Greeks as well as on other parts of the world. But whether this was bringing us friends I did not know.

While in Athens I had the good fortune to go out to luncheon in the country with King Paul and Queen Frederika. Our embassy had handled the arrangements and, as usual, they sent a dignified but slow-moving limousine to take me from my hotel to the palace. I started out about half past eleven, rolling sedately out of the city and up into the hills to the summer palace. It was cooler there and as we were rolling happily along there was a roar of a high-powered motor behind us and a racy sports car zipped around us and went bowling along the road at high speed.

I got a quick look at the occupants and realized that the King was driving and the Queen was beside him. They were dashing along the road as if they were racing drivers out for a morning's test spin, and making the most of it. They went so fast, in fact, that before we reached the palace we caught up with two automobiles which had passed us in pursuit of the

King's car, but had broken down later.

"Those are the men who guard the King," my driver said with a chuckle.

I found the Queen to be charming, warm and intelligent. The King's personality is not so warm, but he is an able man and greatly interested in the young people of his country, where there are so many orphans from war and disaster and where so many are hungry. I believe that I receive more letters asking for help from Greece than from any other country. At luncheon the Queen told me of her efforts to alleviate this poverty.

She told me that she hoped to visit the United States to study our rehabilitation hospitals where great progress has been made in helping handicapped or crippled children. Later she and the King did make the trip. I noticed that they reserved five days at the end of their official trip for unofficial visits in New York, and I wrote the Queen a note, asking whether she had been able to see the things she wanted to see.

She replied that she had not seen any of the things she really wanted to see, so I arranged a short tour for her. We guided her to several institutions in New York City that I thought she would want to visit. We went to the new hospital on the East Side where Dr. Howard Rusk has done so much to help the recovery of crippled children. The Queen was wonderful with the patients. One little boy who had had polio attempted to show her how he had learned to walk again, but in his eagerness he slipped and fell. It was the Queen who got to him before anyone else and picked him up.

"Never mind," she said. "Many of us fall when we try to show what we can do. But I'll help you and you show me again."

Later, as we were walking in a sedate little procession, we passed a city firehouse. Looking through the big open door, the Queen saw the brass fire pole and paused.

"Do you think they would mind if I went in?"

"I'm sure they would be delighted," I said. I went in and found a fireman on duty and introduced him to the Queen. She was much interested in the equipment and asked many questions.

"Perhaps it would be possible for you to demonstrate how the men answer an alarm," I remarked to the fireman.

He said that would be simple, and rang the bell. An instant later the men began sliding down the brass pole from the second floor and quickly jumped onto their trucks. Then, last of all, their big cat came sliding down the pole. The Queen laughed and clapped her hands in delight. Then she thanked the firemen, said good-by, and we rejoined our little procession.

We left Athens by airplane on July 6, 1953, for Yugoslavia. Flying over Macedonia, in Yugoslavia, I was impressed by the fact that it looked like good farming country, in contrast to the arid appearance of the land in so many parts of Greece, particularly in the mountains.

"One reason for the difference is that the Yugoslav government has made a determined effort to reduce the number of herds of goats," a Yugoslav told me. "Goats have been almost completely forbidden in some places. I can't say this program has been entirely successful, but at least they no longer eat every blade of grass down to the roots as they often do in Greece. Why, they even eat the trees and I have actually seen them climbing up into the branches of trees to feed."

We landed in Belgrade, where I was greeted by a number of old friends from the United Nations meetings.

My main purpose in visiting Yugoslavia was to interview President Tito (or Josip Broz, to give him his real name) but I was greatly interested in learning all I could about the country and its governmental system. I wanted to make my own observations of this man who had successfully fought the German army of occupation in Yugoslavia, who had established a government closely harmonized with Communist Russia after the war and had finally broken with the Comintern, declaring his independence of the dictates of Moscow.

I had been informed correctly that Yugoslavia was very different from Russia, where for generations peasants had been accustomed to living under the strict Czarist regime, to being attached to large family estates and to doing what they were told to do. It had always been difficult to tell the Yugoslavs anything. They fought foreign invaders and they fought each other for racial and religious reasons and sometimes perhaps for no reason at all. The Montenegrins, for instance, were never really conquered through the centuries of Balkan warfare. If an invader fought his way into the country, they retired to the mountains and defied anybody to come after them. The men were such traditional warriors that the women did, and continue to do, practically all the hard, everyday work.

At a luncheon with several government officials on my first full day in Yugoslavia, one of the undersecretaries of state told of changes that were being made in industrial management. "The state," he said, "will not run the industries. They will be operated by councils of workers, and this system, where it is being tried out, already has improved production. Workers quickly find out that good management is necessary, that all must do their best and the deadwood must be eliminated if an industry is to pay."

It was obvious that the Yugoslavs were experimenting in an effort to find government theories that would permit limited individual freedom within a Socialist framework.

In the next few days the people I talked with, including American officials and newspapermen, seemed to agree that there had been great changes in the government in the past year. Decentralization of governmental power had been encouraged, which I thought was quite remarkable in a dictatorship, where the leader or leaders usually want more instead of less power. Certain supervision and a measure of ultimate control by the central government would be continued, but it was evident that many more decisions were being left to the people's committees even in the smaller village groups.

One thing that I observed almost immediately in Yugoslavia was that the people were neither worried nor afraid. I did not hear a single Yugoslav say anything about the danger of war, although their old enemy Germany was rapidly gaining strength on one side of them and they had broken with the Soviet Union and its satellites, which lie on the other side. Perhaps if you have always lived with danger you can't afford to think with fear, or perhaps the people were too busy.

Later I made a trip to Sarajevo and on the way drove to Zenica, a good coal and iron ore center which was busily trying to become the Pittsburgh of Yugoslavia. The plants had been rebuilt and enlarged after the war and were already producing three times as much as they had before.

I asked many questions about how the plants were run and cleared up some of the theories that had been explained to me in Belgrade. For example, the theory is that the plants will be run by workers' councils. But, while that is technically true, the fact is that the councils sensibly employ technical experts to operate the plants and the experts report to and are responsible to the councils. I met two American engineers employed by one plant to direct operations.

I kept finding out more about the changing industrial system. At Zagreb we visited the Rade Koncar factory, named for a factory worker who was a guerrilla leader during the war and was killed by Italian troops. The plant was making electrical transformers and other machinery needed for the development of power plants. Like others I had visited, it was operated by a workers' council and technical experts.

"Our experts are new at this kind of thing and they have made some mistakes," the manager told me. "But last year we ran at a profit."

"A profit?" I said.

"Oh, yes, that is one of the incentives for high production. After taxes have been deducted, the workers' council divides the profits, half going to pay interest and amortization on borrowed money or to improve the plant. The other half of the profits is divided among all the workers."

"Do you think that arrangement has increased production?" I asked.

The manager looked at the head of the workers' council and smiled. "Of course it has," he said.

The head of the council expressed his appreciation for the aid that had been received from the United States since the Yugoslav break with the Comintern. In fact, almost everywhere I went in the country I saw signs of the benefits of American aid and was told many times that the people were grateful.

Speaking in a general way, I found Yugoslavia a delightful place to visit and an interesting country in which to study the changing industrial, social and political system. The people were well fed, but their diet is mainly meat, fish, fats and bread. It was like asking for the moon to ask for a glass of orange juice or a lemon for your tea—unless you were at the American embassy. The prices in the shops I visited seemed high. Friends later explained that both wool and cotton have to be imported and paid for in foreign currency, which was difficult for the government to arrange, so that the prices for these goods naturally were higher than one might expect. The price of foodstuffs seemed reasonable, but I could not understand why there was so little variety. Here was a country in which 70 per cent of the population was engaged in agriculture, yet there were only a few vegetables and fruits in the markets. Officials estimated that the average family had to spend from 50 to 80 per cent of its budget on food.

I talked to a number of farmers and decided that they were the least satisfied people in Yugoslavia. This was partly because the Tito regime originally followed the Soviet pattern of collective farms. After a few years this system was not a success and it was gradually changed to permit small private farms and to encourage co-operative farming. Some collective farms continued, however, in the best farming areas. The government provided all farmers with certain tools and with fertilizers and made available machinery such as they had never had before. But of all people, the farmers the world over are the most individualistic, and the Yugoslav farmers have been slow to accept new ways.

Industrially the country has certainly made progress and important social security measures have been instituted. Medical care is provided on a universal basis and the hospitals I visited were equipped with modern laboratory and research facilities, most of which came from the United Nations or the United States. Typhoid and malaria have been largely wiped out except in a few rural areas. Generally the medical services are better than one would expect in a country that calls itself as yet underdeveloped. There are unemployment benefits and old-age pensions under the social security system, as well as payments for all children. Considering the economy of the country, these payments are generous and make a great difference in the life of the people.

Changes have also been made in the school system, and in rural areas four years of school, from the age of seven to eleven, are obligatory. Then the child can go to technical school or to a factory school for several years. In the cities high school training is free and so is instruction at the universities, which are crowded.

These are important changes in the basic structure of the country and are in considerable contrast to conditions that existed before the war. The greatest difference in postwar Yugoslavia, however, probably is at the head of the government and I was eager to talk to President Tito.

Our trip from Zagreb to Brioni to call on President Tito was one of the most delightful days I spent in Yugoslavia.

We took the plane at Zagreb in midmorning and within a few minutes, it seemed to me, we had landed and were driving by automobile into Rijeka with Mayor Eda Jardas. Later we drove on down the Istrian coast and through lovely mountain country to a point opposite the island of Brioni, where the President's boat was waiting for us.

The trip across about two miles of water to Brioni was quickly completed and we were on a wonderfully wooded island which made a perfect summer residence for a busy president. There was a hotel for guests and villas to which the marshal invited special guests. We—Miss Corr, Dr. David Gurewitsch and I—were driven in an old-fashioned victoria from the landing stage to a guest villa on the water, with a fine view of the sea. There are no powered vehicles on the island except jeeps used by the military or police units guarding the President, and the absence of noisy motors and gas fumes added to the feeling of peaceful quiet all around us.

Next morning I arrived at the President's villa alone promptly at ten o'clock, riding in a victoria. There were no obvious signs of guards or police near the villa, although no doubt the marshal is protected in an unobtrusive way, as our White House is protected by the Secret Service men. I was ushered into a large room that the marshal uses as an office. At the door I could see Mr. Vilfan and another man at a desk far across the room and it made me think of the accounts of the office of Premier Benito Mussolini in Rome, where visitors had to walk across a huge, bare space of floor to reach the desk behind which stood the stern-faced Italian dictator.

As I entered, a young-looking man came across the room to greet me. For a few moments I could not believe that this was Marshal Tito because he seemed far too youthful. It was only after he had greeted me warmly and I had seated myself on a sofa beside him that I was able to observe that his hair was graying and there were deep lines of experience in his strongly molded face. He has great charm and a strong personality. His jaw juts out and he speaks in the manner of a man who gives orders and expects them to be obeyed. But he had a sense of humor, he was pleasant to me, and he conveyed the impression of speaking frankly and honestly.

Tito spoke a little English and some German, but most of the time we spoke through our translator, Mr. Vilfan, in order to be sure that there was no misunderstanding.

Later we all went down to the dock where we got into a speedboat to go to a small island that Marshal Tito uses as a retreat when he wishes to be alone. The marshal himself piloted one speedboat, taking me with him, and seemed to get a great deal of fun out of it.

Still later in the afternoon we took a short trip on the state yacht in the Adriatic. The security officers surrounding Marshal Tito were obviously nervous about the possibility of kidnaping, and the ship was accompanied by armed vessels while military airplanes were constantly overhead or nearby.

After dinner that night I talked to the minister of interior, who was one of the guests, about the number of political prisoners.

"There are not really many political prisoners," he asserted.

"Well, how many?" I persisted. "Would you say that as many as twenty-five political prisoners were arrested in a month? Or fifty? Or seventy-five?"

"Less than seventy-five," he finally replied.

"What is the reason for most of the arrests?"

"The major reason," he replied, "is for infiltrating Soviet ideas into Yugoslavia."

This answer struck me as amusing, because that seemed to be the main thing feared by anti-Communist investigators in the United States!

Like many men who have acquired power, the President evidently loves it and has a certain vanity. But he is intelligent enough to recognize that in Yugoslavia he can have power in the long run only if the people give it to him voluntarily. As a result, I believe, he is concerned with providing a government that benefits the people, or at least enough of the people to maintain him in power.

"Do you believe the people are contented under your Socialist form of government?" I asked him.

He lit a cigarette and looked at me questioningly. "If you owned property and the government nationalized it, would you be contented?"

I said that I would not be happy about it.

"Then I will say that I don't think everybody in Yugoslavia is content. But I believe the people realize that we are doing the things that will be best for our country in the long run."

I asked him about the working of Communism in Yugoslavia, where practically everything is nationalized, although citizens have the right to own private property such as a house or a small farm of not more than twenty acres.

"We have been rather disappointed," he replied, "that many of the workers' councils have not allocated their surpluses for the good of the community as a whole but have merely divided the funds among the workers."

I asked if he considered that his country was practicing Communism.

"Communism," he answered, "exists nowhere, least of all in the Soviet Union. Communism is an ideal that can be achieved only when people cease to be selfish and greedy and when everyone receives according to his needs from communal production. But that is a long way off."

He said that Yugoslavia was developing a Socialist state that was one step toward the distant aim of Communism. "I suppose," he added, "that I might call myself a Social Democrat." Marshal Tito does not want what is being developed in Yugoslavia to be called Communism, and he also objects to the use of the term "Titoism." Every country should develop according to its own needs, he continued, and he does not want Yugoslavia to be held up as an example for others, since Yugoslavia's system might not meet the needs of any other country.

"I am not a dictator," he insisted. "We have a group—all of us were Partisans during the war—that works closely together and prepares for each step to be taken." When a law has been prepared it is published in the newspapers; then various organizations, especially the trade unions, send the government letters containing criticisms and suggestions for changes. These criticisms are carefully analyzed, Tito said, and the law is redrafted and again published in the newspapers so that the people once more will have an opportunity to express themselves about it before it is sent to Parliament for consideration.

On the basis of our conversation, it seemed to me that the President conceived of the current government as a step forward in the education of the people. He was perhaps not sure what the final steps would be, but he hoped they would lead to development of a political body along socialistic lines with a social conscience that responds to the needs of the country rather than to individual needs. I concluded that he had a concept of self-government by the people quite different from ours, because there it comes from the top rather than from the bottom. But it did not seem impossible for our type of political philosophy to live and co-operate with the system that appeared to be developing in Yugoslavia.

I commented on the American aid that had come to Yugoslavia. "I have been favorably impressed by the appreciation and gratitude of the people here for that assistance," I said. "But mere gratitude, important as it is, does not convince us that the government will not swing back to the Russian system when it has reached a point where American help is no longer needed or no longer important."

"I am ready to repeat what I told your ambassador," he said. "Regardless of whether the United States gives us help or not, the attitude of Yugoslavia toward the United States will not change."

I doubt that many people will agree when Marshal Tito describes himself as a Social Democrat. He acknowledges that the use of force by the government was necessary in his country. I felt, too, that as yet there were inconsistencies in the development of his theories of government. But I left him with the opinion that this was a powerful leader and an honest one, with some kind of long-range concept of self-government by the people. And I thought that much of the future would depend on the United States and how well we could prove that our democracy is concerned about and benefits the people as a whole.

Thirty-five

Campaigning for Stevenson

MY PARTICIPATION in political campaigns was interrupted after Franklin's death in 1945, partly because I became a member of the delegation to the United Nations and took great pains not to mix political affairs with my official duties. I believed that the questions we were dealing with at the United Nations were of the greatest importance to our country's position in the world and that they should not be approached from a partisan point of view.

In 1952 it was my opinion that Governor Stevenson would probably make one of the best presidents we had ever had, but I also believed that it was practically impossible for the Democrats to win the election because of the hero worship surrounding General Eisenhower. I did make a speech on the United Nations at the Democratic National Convention that year at the request of President Truman, and I came out for Governor Stevenson, but I did not intend to be active in that campaign and I was not.

Why, then, did I re-enter politics in 1956? I was out of the United Nations delegation at that time, and I believed as strongly as before that Adlai Stevenson would make a good president. For another thing, I had not been much impressed by the progress of what President Eisenhower called Modern Republicanism.

The Eisenhower brand of Republicanism seemed to me to be an acceptance of certain social advances that some of the younger Republicans regarded as important to the party's status in our changing domestic picture. These things usually had their origin in the New Deal days but had become so much a part of the people's thinking that Republicans who had not solidified in the old mold were willing to accept them and had

353

more or less persuaded the President to think along the same lines. President Eisenhower had seen much of the international scene and was aware of the vital importance of our role in world affairs, but the net result of his administration had not been impressive, because there were enough old-line Republicans in powerful positions to keep the party, on the whole, a conservative, businessmen's party.

Of course, the Democratic party had many conservatives in powerful positions, too, but in general it was more progressive. Some of us have long hoped for a political realignment that would result in major parties that more truly represent the conservative and progressive thinking of the people. But it is difficult to say whether that will ever be possible.

Still another thing that influenced me in getting back into politics as the 1956 campaign approached was Governor Stevenson's high standing among statesmen of other countries which are our allies or which we want to have on our side in the world struggle against Communism. After his defeat in 1952 Governor Stevenson had taken a trip around the world to study conditions in other countries and, during my own world travels, I had been greatly interested in the impression he had made on foreign statesmen. Again and again they told me that Mr. Stevenson was the kind of man who listened, who wanted to learn all the facts.

After Governor Stevenson had traveled around the world and had made a special journey to study African problems, he came to call on me one day to talk about whether he should again seek the Democratic nomination for president. He is a very intelligent man but he is also a humble man, and there were questions he was trying to resolve in his own mind.

"Don't you feel," he asked, "that there are others who would do better than I as leader of the party?"

"I cannot think of anyone else," I replied, "who has the ability to do the job you could do in meeting the most vital needs of the day."

Though I urged Governor Stevenson to run, I did not expect to take an important part in the campaign and decided to go to Europe with my two grandsons at the time of the Democratic National Convention. To my surprise, this horrified some of my friends. "If you fail to attend the convention," one of them said, "everybody will think you have changed your mind about supporting Adlai."

So finally I sent my grandsons off alone on the boat and arranged to spend a couple of days at the Chicago convention before flying to

Europe. When I arrived at the Chicago airport I was received by several supporters of Governor Stevenson. While I was en route to Chicago, former President Truman, who had begged Mr. Stevenson to run in 1952, had come out in favor of the nomination of Governor Averell Harriman of New York.

I certainly was not thrilled by this news, for various reasons. President Truman had always been especially considerate toward me. I had reported to him personally after the various meetings of the United Nations and had learned that he had a remarkable understanding of the office and duties of the President. I felt that he had had to make more than his share of big decisions as president and that he had made few mistakes in times of crisis. The mistakes he made were human mistakes in smaller things.

That morning in Chicago I was thinking of President Truman's great ability as a campaigner, and I was dismayed by the idea of pitting my political judgment against his.

I was told that I was going not to my hotel but to a press conference. When we drove to the hotel where the newspaper people were waiting I had to face more reporters and more cameras than I had ever seen before. I was fearful of the ordeal of justifying my judgment in opposition to President Truman but actually it turned out to be no ordeal at all. I said as simply and frankly as possible what I believed, and it was no more difficult than an ordinary press conference.

The reporters, of course, made as much as possible of my opposition to President Truman because it is more interesting to write about disagreements than about routine agreement. But they hadn't counted on the fact that I had previously asked President and Mrs. Truman to luncheon that day. Mrs. Truman could not come but, immediately after my press conference, I met the former President in the grillroom of my hotel. The reporters scented another story. Were we going to make a deal? In no time at all, newspapermen had taken over a large table about three feet from my elbow and were more intent on my conversation with President Truman than they were on their food.

They didn't get much to write, even if they had keen ears. We talked about everything except the convention until we had finished luncheon and then our differences were mentioned only indirectly.

"I hope you will understand that whatever action I take is because I think I am doing the right thing," President Truman said.

"Of course," I replied. "I know you will act as you believe is right and I know you will realize that I must do the same."

President Truman nodded and grinned. "What I want to do is to make this convention do some real thinking about issues," he said.

Later, when I had gone to my hotel room, I felt that I was a fish out of water and that I really had nothing to do at this convention. But I did attend a reception Governor Stevenson gave in my honor and I accompanied him on visits to various state delegations to seek their support. I saw many persons in my room, attended a luncheon for women delegates, and went before the Platform Committee twice to speak on civil rights and education.

Paul Butler, the Democratic national chairman, also asked me to speak briefly in the convention. When I got there the pandemonium was so great that I don't believe any speaker could have been heard with the possible exception of Governor Frank Clement of Tennessee, whose keynote address proved that he had a strong voice. However, what I said could be heard over radio and television, and later many persons were kind enough to say that my words gained considerable attention in the contest for delegates. In any event, I was pleased when Governor Stevenson won the nomination.

During the lively contest for the vice-presidential nomination between Senator Estes Kefauver and Senator John Kennedy, a friend of Senator Kennedy came to me with a request for support. I replied that I did not feel I could support him because he had avoided taking a position during the controversy over Senator Joseph McCarthy's methods of investigation. Senator Kennedy was in the hospital when the Senate voted censure of Senator McCarthy and, of course, could not record his position, but later, when he returned to the Senate, reporters asked him how he would have voted and he failed to answer directly.

"Oh, that was a long time ago," the senator's friend told me. "He was unable to vote and it is all a thing of the past. It should not have anything to do with the present situation."

"I think McCarthyism is a question on which public officials must stand up and be counted," I replied. "I still have not heard Senator Kennedy express his convictions. And I cannot be sure of the political future of anyone who does not willingly state where he stands on that issue."

Senator Kennedy came to see me in Chicago and I told him exactly the same thing. He replied in about the words he had previously used in talking to reporters, saying that the McCarthy censure vote was "so long ago" that it did not enter the current situation. But he did not say where he stood on the issue and I did not support him.

I did not stay in Chicago for the balloting on the vice-presidential nominee but flew back to New York the day before my plane left for Europe. I felt a sense of great relief at leaving politics behind, and I expected to play only a very quiet role in the presidential campaign. It didn't work out that way. The two months after my return proved to be among the most hectic of my life, because I ended by doing far more than I had expected to do, and I had, at the same time, to keep my lecture dates.

I thought and still think that a good business executive does not make a good government administrator, nor does an administration of businessmen make for good government. A businessman needs certain qualities for success; a government official needs a wide variety of qualities and some quite different ones. He cannot be successful unless he has a knowledge of people and politics, and there is no doubt that a number of Eisenhower appointees had to learn this in a slow, difficult manner. Often businessmen go into government with the idea that they will be the men at the top and that their orders will be carried out. This is probably the correct approach in business, but in government it is necessary to persuade others that what they want to do is the best course. Unless Congress goes along with them, they can't get results. President Eisenhower evidently felt that he could establish an administration in the pattern of big business, but such an approach to the complexities of government is not necessarily either democratic or successful—as I believe he has discovered.

In the same way, I don't believe that because a man is a successful corporation lawyer he will necessarily be the best person to direct the Department of State. Outsiders like myself do not have all the facts at their command in regard to international affairs, but surely it was blundering that carried us into the mess in which we found ourselves in 1956 in the Middle East, and still find ourselves.

Secretary Dulles served in all but two of the United Nations Assemblies in which I served. I often observed that he was rarely inclined to take a stand, to say that this was right or wrong. He shied away from decisions because he didn't like to make himself responsible for a definite program.

This probably explains why he did not come to the defense of loyal public servants in his department when they were under bitter and unfair attack, which naturally led to low morale in the State Department.

I might add that I don't believe there is much question that Vice-President Richard Nixon will succeed Mr. Eisenhower as party leader, regardless of the opposition of some Republicans. I regard Mr. Nixon as a very able and dangerous opportunist, but since 1952 he has learned a great deal. He now knows the importance of gaining the confidence of the people and he has worked hard at it and made progress. This still does not make me believe that he has any strong convictions.

One of the important duties of the President—and one that the Republican administration neglects—is to be the educator of the public on national problems. Most people do not have the time or inclination to inform themselves fully on the complex and seemingly remote problems that must be settled by government. But if he knows the issues and explains them clearly, the President is in a position to make the people aware of what must be decided and to make them feel their responsibility as citizens in reaching a decision. Without such education of the people, democracy can become a dangerous kind of government because voters are called upon to make decisions or to support decisions without having sufficient knowledge of the factors involved.

To get back to the subject of that campaign, I had gone late in September to Oregon to do anything I could in behalf of Senator Wayne Morse's race for re-election to the Senate, this time as a Democrat instead of on the Republican ticket. I had to work my political appearances into a tight schedule so that I could also keep my lecture engagements, which were often in distant cities. That was a hectic period. I recall one occasion when I (speaking from Los Angeles) was to introduce Governor Stevenson over television for a speech he was making that night in Milwaukee, but I was also scheduled to speak at a luncheon, hold a news conference, attend a reception, and then go on to San Diego to appear on another television program. Because my plane was two hours late, the day was further confused. When I reached the studio where I was to introduce Governor Stevenson I had half an hour to spare. To the horror of the studio people, I insisted on having an office stenographer to whom I dictated two newspaper columns while the political managers stood by biting their fingernails.

There were a good many other days just as crowded. Later in West Virginia, in the mining area, I continued campaigning. I stopped at a mine when the shifts were changing and talked to some of the miners, something I had not done since the early days of the depression in the 1930's. The miners were better off than in those former days and I was happy to see the changes. I felt at home in this mining environment. It took me back to the depression period when I spent much time trying to see what could be done for the people, particularly the children, of this area.

On that campaign tour I traveled in all directions. I ran into Senator Alexander Wiley, the Republican incumbent, who was on his campaign tour. Senator Wiley was having his troubles because of the opposition of his Republican colleague from Wisconsin, Senator McCarthy. President Eisenhower had not come out strongly in Senator Wiley's support, although the Senator had been a staunch administration man in Congress. But I admired the way in which he had fought for a sound foreign policy and I greeted him warmly when I saw him in Marquette. I was later told that he felt this had done him no harm in his winning campaign.

As I moved rapidly from one area to another on a tight schedule I managed it only by taking every opportunity to snatch some sleep sitting in a plane or an automobile or resting a few minutes in a chair.

This kind of thing went on for weeks. I never fooled myself about the difficulties of defeating the incumbent administration at a time when there were no great and compelling reasons for the public to make a change. If the people are fairly comfortable and there is no great unrest, they prefer to let well enough alone, and it is seldom possible to stir them by pointing out that there are grave problems ahead—in this case, in the international field. You can't expect the voters generally to respond very strongly to such a situation. But in a campaign you have to feel that you may be able to overcome your handicaps, for otherwise you will not be able to give your speeches with any conviction. So I kept telling myself that we had a chance to win and that it was worthwhile to make the strongest possible fight.

I did, however, get awfully, awfully tired of motorcades. I have no idea how many times I rode through the streets of various cities in a procession of open-top automobiles carrying candidates for national and local office. Most of them were rather silly performances. There are only two people who really become well known to the people during a campaign. In this case, one was the President, whom they knew, and the other was the head of the opposition ticket, who was trying to become president. Of course, there are some local candidates for office whom they recognize, but as far as I was concerned the motorcade always seemed ridiculous because there was no reason for anyone to bother to come out on the street to look at me.

The last days of the campaign were really strenuous and I was getting mighty tired of the sound of my own voice. My final appearances were in Washington, where I was on a television program with Senator Margaret Chase Smith at five-thirty in the afternoon and in St. Louis the same evening, where I spoke in Kiel Auditorium. Early the next morning I took a plane back to New York and got to Hyde Park in time to cast my vote, which was the last if not least important thing I could do in behalf of Governor Stevenson.

The returns, of course, were unhappy from my point of view. I felt sad because I am a strong admirer of Governor Stevenson and I believed his abilities were needed to meet the problems that would arise in the next four years. But when it was over, I was glad to be out of politics.

Later my children told me I had tried to do too much. "You're going to have to slow down," they warned me. "You're going to have to stop working one of these days and you certainly should never get involved in another such job of campaigning."

Thirty-six

Bali and Morocco

MOST OF MY journeys abroad have been in connection with official or semi-official business of some kind, but I have been fortunate in being able to combine work with sightseeing and sometimes I have been able simply to take off on my own for a short time, as I did when I visited the famous island of Bali in 1955.

I had been asked to be a delegate to the World Federation of United Nations Associations, which was meeting that summer in Bangkok, the capital of Thailand, and I was happy to accept, partly because it would give me a chance for another look at the Far East en route. I did not feel that I was well acquainted with the problems and people of Indonesia, which was long in the Dutch colonial domain but is now a federation of independent republics. And I had always wanted to see Bali, which I had read so much about and which was usually pictured as the loveliest and most peaceful of the fabled South Sea Islands.

The Dutch, I knew, were not popular in the islands after the war and apparently were becoming still less popular. Yet I had known Queen Juliana for some years and felt that she had worked hard to further a better spiritual understanding among peoples. I should like to tell a little about the Queen, because before I went to Indonesia one of the royal families of Europe I enjoyed visiting was that of Holland. I had always admired the former Queen, Wilhelmina, for her staunch courage and her insistence upon being a good Dutch housewife as well as a capable ruler.

I have a very special feeling about Queen Juliana because, like Princess Marta of Norway, she came a number of times to stay with us at Hyde Park with her husband and children. Franklin was godfather to their third daughter. She and her husband have brought up their children in

361

a democratic way and part of the time they have attended the public schools. Once when two of the children and some small friends were walking home they passed an orchard where they picked up some apples that had fallen outside the fence but which, of course, did not belong to them. The owner called the police and a little later the police telephoned the palace and informed the then Princess Juliana that her children were more or less in custody.

"Very well," she replied, "you must deal with them just as with the others. Then telephone me again and we will come get them."

All the children were reprimanded by the police and at least a couple of them received additional punishment at the hands of their parents when they got back to the royal palace.

I was the guest of Juliana before she became queen at the time the University of Utrecht awarded me a degree of doctor of laws. It was a colorful ceremony and at the end of it the princess and I drove in a carriage drawn by four horses, with great pomp and ceremony, to the women's house of the university. The women were very proud because it was not often that a woman was given a degree, and on this occasion they not only participated in the ceremony but served as outriders accompanying our carriage. The princess was at the students' house with me, and I look back on that particular incident with great pleasure.

As queen, Juliana has worked vigorously to help develop understanding among Europeans. She has sought with other Continental powers to awaken the peoples of Europe to their responsibilities. Her government has been influential in the Council of Europe and she has led in the humanitarian efforts of her country to help refugees. The pages of history will record that she was a woman who loved her fellow human beings.

So, feeling as I did about the Queen, I decided in 1955 to take advantage of my journey to Bangkok and visit the islands that in past years had been so strongly under Dutch influence.

We spent a week in Japan. The standard of living was still poor when seen through Western eyes, but I felt that conditions were improving since I had been there in 1953 and that the people looked happier. One thing that had distressed me on my first trip was the number of difficult problems that would have to be overcome to establish democratic government firmly in that country. Yet when I returned there after two years I thought that the people were accepting more and more of the important aspects of democracy. They had gradually begun to want to take part and have a say in their government. Of course, the habits and customs developed during centuries of feudalism had not been eliminated overnight, but I thought a great change was taking place in the thinking of the people.

We flew from Japan to Hong Kong and then to Manila and touched down at Jakarta. It was almost dark when we arrived in Bali, and were met by Mrs. Bagoes Oka, the charming wife of an assistant to the governor of the province. The next day we drove to the village of Ubud through country that was green and seemed to have plenty of water. We stopped at a large compound with mud walls. There was an open market at the gate with all kinds of food and handwork on display.

"This is the local rajah's house," Mrs. Oka told me. "You will stay here in one of the guest houses." The rajah was a plump little man in a sacklike gown tied in the middle with a broad sash. For economic reasons, he had converted his compound into a kind of hotel. The guest houses each had one room with mud and wood walls and washing facilities were in a small separate room which one reached by going through an archway. There was little in the way of modern plumbing.

The basic food of the people is rice for every meal, usually with vegetables, but there is a feast about once a week when they eat chicken and pork and make up for the lack of variety in their daily diet. We did not have to eat rice all the time, but I must say that later when I moved to a little Dutch hotel overlooking the water the meals were good and I was so much more comfortable that it seemed like heaven.

By the time we left Bali for Jakarta and Bangkok I felt I had seen enough dancing to last me the rest of my life, but it was the kind of dancing that goes with the island and its people and we thoroughly enjoyed our visit.

The meeting of the World Federation of United Nations Associations in Bangkok was interesting but not particularly newsworthy. We were greeted upon arrival by the prime minister, Field Marshal P. Pibul Songgram, and his wife as well as people from the United States embassy. I found the city unusual and interesting despite the fact that it was the rainy season and sheets of water fell during the afternoons.

Thanks to a hospitable government, a number of us were able to make a trip to see Angkor Wat, the famous temple of the ancient Khmer Empire of Cambodia. We went by plane over a fertile valley where, in the rainy season, there was water everywhere. While still aloft we could see the temples at Angkor Thom and Angkor Wat. I thought they were the most impressive monuments I had ever seen.

There is another journey to a new and developing country which I want to describe before I come to what was to me the most important experience in recent years. But to do it I shall have to switch back to Hyde Park to a time not long after Morocco had achieved its independence from French colonial rule.

One day Archie Roosevelt, one of the State Department's experts on the Arab world, telephoned and asked if an old friend of his could come to my house for tea. I said I should be delighted, but I was amazed when a huge limousine arrived. A small girl got out, then an American woman, then a Moroccan woman, and finally two Moroccan men carrying a huge box of flowers.

I had not been expecting such a delegation but it turned out that one of the men was the chief adviser to Sultan Mohammed V of Morocco, who later became King Mohammed V. They had come to place flowers on my husband's grave and I had thought they were just coming for tea. They explained that they had expected to meet two officials from the State Department when they reached Hyde Park, but something had gone wrong and they did not show up until later.

After we had had tea, the adviser to the Sultan arose rather mysteriously and said, "Mrs. Roosevelt, I would like to speak to you alone."

After the others had left the room, he continued, "We Moroccans never forget a kindness. The Sultan asked me to say to you that he recalls your husband as one foreign head of state who gave him disinterested advice. He wants me to say that he believes there would have been no secret treaty between France and the United States in connection with the establishment of United States air bases in Morocco if your husband had lived. But we do not blame the United States for making the treaty and we will raise no difficulties now in the negotiations on the bases between your government and ours. The Sultan also extends an invitation for you to visit Morocco."

A few months later some friends of mine in New York told me that a problem had arisen in connection with a large group of Jews in Morocco who wanted to migrate to Israel. They had been granted visas by the French government and were prepared to go but, at the last minute, the Moroccan officials raised various obstacles to their departure.

"The French constabulary has been withdrawn and there is a good deal of Arab hostility toward the Jews," I was told. "They are now in temporary camps which are crowded and unsanitary and there is fear of an epidemic. We have tried to get something done to bring about their release but with no success and we have not been able to get any word from the Sultan. Do you think you might appeal to him?"

"I will write him a letter," I said. I wrote it at once, saying that the Jews apparently were in considerable danger and also that there was fear of an epidemic that might endanger everybody in that area. I said I knew that he was interested in all people and I hoped he could do something to relieve the situation. I did not receive any reply to my letter, but not long afterward I learned that the necessary permission for the Jewish group to leave Morocco had been issued and that they had gone to Israel about two weeks after I wrote to the Sultan.

In 1957 the crown prince of Morocco and his sister visited the United States and the crown princess came to call on me. She was accompanied by the wife of the Moroccan ambassador and several other ladies, and by the Moroccan minister to the United Nations. As they were leaving, the princess spoke briefly to the minister and he turned to me.

"My princess says that her father, the Sultan, extends an invitation for you to visit our country."

Later in the winter of 1957 Dr. Gurewitsch told me that he was planning to take his daughter Grania to North Africa for a vacation, and we decided to go as a party and visit Morocco. My son Elliott and his wife joined us.

The white-robed governor of Casablanca and a representative of the Sultan were at the airport to greet us. With them was Kenneth Pendar, whom Elliott and Dr. Gurewitsch greeted joyfully. Elliott had been in Morocco with the Air Force during the war and was assigned to his father when Franklin and Winston Churchill held their historic conference in Casablanca, so he knew the area well. We spent only a day at Casablanca, before driving to the capital, Rabat.

I was much interested in the country we drove through and in the people. I have never felt that the French were the best colonizers in the world, but, for that matter, no country can give another everything that it needs. The French had left in Morocco good roads and hospitals. Under Marshal Lyautey they had also kept something of the old flavor of the country; instead of permitting ancient Arab towns to be torn down for new buildings, they had seen to it that the new construction was outside the old sections. But the French residents of Morocco had almost a monopoly on power and irrigation and the Arab fields that we drove through were burned up by a severe drought. This naturally did not make the Arabs friendly toward the French colonizers. The Arab schools were poor and the country has a low literacy rate and, as usual, the masses have a very low standard of living. The Moroccans value their independence but the government had had to start almost from scratch and there was much to be done.

Generally speaking, I thought that it was remarkable that the Moroccan people, who for the most part live in great insecurity, had not been lured into Communism.

The Sultan had been in the hospital for an operation but only a couple of days afterward he invited our whole group to the palace. We drove there late in the afternoon and were immediately ushered into the large reception room. Chairs were placed around the room in a semi-circle. There were beautiful rugs on the floor. Mohammed V awaited us in a big chair on a raised platform. Despite his recent operation, he rose to greet me and I introduced the other members of our party to him. We were served refreshments as we chatted, and he politely asked the various members of the group about their interests and occupations. After a short time the others left but he asked Elliott and me to remain for a less formal talk.

The Sultan was young and handsome, with a sensitive and kindly face. There was humor in his eyes and his slender hands were expressive as he passed the usual string of beads through his fingers. He wore long white robes, white over some delicate color, and a small cap. His conversation made it clear that he was alert and deeply concerned about the welfare of the people, their need for economic security and for aid in developing social services. But he was also well aware of the international complications affecting the Arab world. From his remarks I felt that he hoped the three North African countries of Morocco, Tunisia and Algeria might become a kind of bridge between the East and the West, helping to ease the tensions created by extremist Arab nationalism in such countries as Egypt and Syria and to bring about a better understanding among nations.

I had felt since our arrival that there was on the part of the Moroccans a greater warmth toward the United States than in other Arab countries but I did not fully understand it until we had talked with the Sultan. This attitude of friendship went back to the time during World War II when Franklin and Prime Minister Winston Churchill met at Casablanca.

The French officials then ruling Morocco paid them a formal call, and when they departed Franklin said: "Now we must see the Sultan."

Mr. Churchill looked at him without much enthusiasm. "Why should we do that?" he asked. "We have seen the French."

"We must see the Sultan," my husband replied, "because this is his country."

The Sultan was thinking about that visit when he said my husband gave him disinterested advice that convinced him of the friendship of the United States. His attitude of helpfulness had become known everywhere in Morocco and many persons told me that the assurance of the friendship of the United States was a kind of milestone in the Moroccan campaign for independence.

A few days after our talk with the Sultan I witnessed another and unusual demonstration of the friendship of the people when we visited Marrakech and the area in the foothills of the Atlas Mountains. Shortly before noon one day we started out from Marrakech in three automobiles. The countryside was parched and dusty and the roads were sometimes mere tracks of dirt. We passed a great assemblage of perhaps two hundred camels as we left the city and later came upon a well where a bullock walked slowly around and around in a circle, drawing water for irrigation of the desert fields. As we bounced across the hills we came upon a wonderful view of the little village of Demnat, which lay on a hilltop beyond a dry, brown plain with the mountains rising up behind.

There were a few travelers on the road, some driving little flocks of sheep through swirling clouds of dust as we drove to the residence of the caid, some distance from Demnat. The leading officials of the town were there to greet us and the caid had prepared the usual Arab feast, great platters of rice and mutton and sweets that must be eaten with the fingers.

After the feast the officials of Demnat accompanied us across the plain to their ancient walled town, one of the oldest in Morocco, dating back to the tenth century. The road was a rough dirt track and the dust was thick and the sun was hot, but a large and enthusiastic crowd had gathered outside the main gate of the town.

"Welcome!" they shouted as our automobile drew up. "Welcome!"

Even more impressive to me was the fact that they had made a crude American flag, which was hung over the gate, and a sign saying, "We always remember President Roosevelt!"

The more I traveled throughout the world the more I realized how important it is for Americans to see with understanding eyes the other peoples of the world whom modern means of communication and transportation are constantly making closer neighbors. Yet the more I traveled the happier I was that I happened to have been born in the United States, where there exist the concept of freedom and opportunities of advancement for individuals of every status. I felt, too, the great responsibility that has come to us as a people. The world is looking to us for leadership in almost every phase of development of the life of peoples everywhere.

But leadership is a stern, demanding role and no person or state can lead without earning that right. On my visit to the Soviet Union in 1957 I was strongly impressed—I was almost frightened—by many things that showed how hard we must strive if we are to maintain our position of world leadership.

Thirty-seven

In the Land of the Soviets

I HAVE WRITTEN frequently about my enjoyment from visiting many delightful places around the world, including the police-run state of Yugoslavia. I would not want to live in Yugoslavia, nor would anyone who values personal freedom. But I think I should die if I had to live in Soviet Russia. I traveled there extensively for almost a month in 1957. When I went to Moscow, the Stalinist dictatorship had been replaced by the less fearful—in theory, at least—dictatorship of Nikita S. Khrushchev, but the people still existed under a system of surveillance that must cause anxiety and the power over them still seemed to me a hand of steel.

My trip to the Soviet Union was one of the most important, the most interesting and the most informative that I have ever made. I tried to understand what was happening in Russia by looking at the country through Russian eyes, and unless all of us in the free world approach the Soviet Union from that point of view we are going to deceive ourselves in a catastrophic manner. I remembered that only forty years ago this great mass of people was largely made up of peasants living in houses with mud floors and, perhaps, with a farm animal or two in the kitchen in wintry months. They were illiterate. They were oppressed. They were frightened of conquest by the Germans, and for many years they were bound together by a readiness to defend their homeland no matter how hard their lives might be.

We must never forget these things when we look at what Russia is today. I looked and was frightened. My fear was not of the Communist power or philosophy, not of awesome missiles or hydrogen bombs. What I feared was that we would not understand the nature of the Russian Revolution that is still going on, and what it means to the world. If we

369

fail to understand, then we shall fail to protect world democracy no matter what missiles or earth satellites or atomic warships we produce. So I want to explain carefully why I am frightened.

I must start my explanation back in the spring of 1957 when Dorothy Schiff, the publisher and owner of the New York *Post*, invited me to luncheon and posed a question. "Would you like to go to China and write a series of articles for the *Post?*"

"I certainly would," I replied.

"You make your application to the State Department for a visa and I will make the other arrangements."

I applied to the State Department and was refused a visa. I was irritated at the time. Later some of my irritation waned. The department has a responsibility to stand behind its visas and to afford protection to citizens traveling abroad on its passports, so I felt they had a right to point out that it was impossible to provide any protection for our citizens traveling in Communist China. However, it seemed to me that the department could say that if newspapermen wanted to go to China under those conditions they were free to go, provided the Chinese government would permit them entry. In any event, I did not get a visa to China and Mrs. Schiff asked me if I would go to Russia instead.

"Yes," I replied, "but I can't go until September, and I would want to take my secretary, Miss Corr, and Dr. Gurewitsch. He can speak Russian and his medical knowledge would also be of great importance in connection with my investigation of conditions."

It took three months to get our visas approved by the Russians. At the end of August the three of us flew to Frankfurt and Berlin, where I was surprised to see how much building had been done since my last visit and how rapid the German recovery had been. From Berlin we flew to Copenhagen early in the morning and there shifted to the Scandinavian airline to Moscow. The plane was so crowded, mostly with American and British tourists, but there were also some Central Europeans from the Soviet satellite countries. We stopped at Riga for passport examination and luncheon but were not allowed to leave the airport. That afternoon we flew on across Russia. I was surprised that so much of the country we passed over was wooded, for I had always thought of Russia as treeless steppes. It was getting dark as we approached Moscow but we could see that much new construction was in progress in the city; in many places the cranes and skeletons of buildings stuck up against the skyline. There were a surprising number of airplanes, most of them two-engine craft, on the ground at the Moscow airport, about the number one would see upon landing at Idlewild or LaGuardia in New York.

Two young men from the United States embassy met us at the airport, and we were also greeted by representatives of Intourist, the Soviet travel bureau, which was arranging my schedule of travel. I was not a guest of the government but was traveling as a reporter. My interpreter was Anna Lavrova, a charming and intelligent young woman who had been my husband's interpreter when he met with Premier Stalin and Prime Minister Churchill at Yalta in 1945.

My first impression of Moscow was that there was building going up everywhere. We drove past the lower side of the Kremlin on the way to the National Hotel, and it was very impressive with its many lights and high walls.

At the hotel Mrs. Lavrova accompanied me to my apartment, a sitting room, bedroom and bath. The furnishings were ornate and heavy, yellow damask, carved table legs and a generally old-fashioned atmosphere, and the plumbing, while all right, was far from modern.

The food was generally good at the hotel and we ate almost no place else, because prices were extremely high in the few restaurants that we might have patronized. There was borscht with big pieces of meat and much cabbage in it, chicken, and, of course, tea and caviar and cakes and lots of ice cream.

The Russians generally do not dress well. The government has discouraged any display in dressing because it is not important to the economic welfare of the country. Prices of clothes are high by American standards and there is little to be said for quality or variety. As a result, the people, whether on the street or in offices or working at manual labor, are dressed warmly but monotonously, usually in dark clothes and without distinction. About the only word to be used about the dress of the people was "drab."

The day after our arrival I called at our embassy and then went to the Intourist offices, where I talked with the head of the bureau. We went over my travel plans in detail.

"I want to get as far away from Moscow as possible," I said, "because I want to see all aspects of the country. I have always been fascinated by Tashkent and Samarkand. Perhaps I could go there unless it is too far off the beaten path."

The bureau director smiled. "We have a commercial jet airplane service to Tashkent every day. The flight takes four hours."

So he put Tashkent on the schedule, and Stalingrad, and a boat trip on the Volga, and the Black Sea and Leningrad and Kiev. But once I started traveling I didn't stick closely to the schedule—much to the dismay of Intourist—and in the end I had to cancel some of the trips because of lack of time. Whenever I decided that I needed more time in some place and changed the schedule, the Intourist people went into a polite tizzy. Most Russian travelers go where they are told to go when they are told to go.

I had made requests for interviews with a number of government officials as soon as I arrived in Moscow but it proved difficult to get specific dates confirmed. When the appointments were made, however, I was received with graciousness and friendliness and was given every assistance, including permission to visit many institutes and projects under the various ministries.

After a few days of seeing the ballet, visiting museums and attending a good one-ring circus, Miss Corr and I were driven to a state farm about twenty miles from Moscow. There are two kinds of farms in the Soviet Union, state farms owned by the government, which hires and pays the workers, who have no personal interest in production; and collective farms, where the land is owned, worked collectively and managed by private owners who elect one of the group as their head. Both types of farm are under state supervision.

Workers on the farms are given a house and a small plot of land which they may cultivate for themselves. Of course, the workers on a state farm do not take the risks that a collective farmer does. The collective farmer is in difficulties in a poor year when the crops fail; in a good year, however, he is able to raise his income considerably.

The state farm I visited was called Lesnie Poljana, meaning Prairie among the Forest. The state-appointed manager told me that they had two thousand acres under cultivation and that they had a breed of milk cows, called Holmogor, for which they raised food.

"There are 550 pedigreed cattle on the farm," he said, "and 226 of them are milk producers. The milk is all shipped in cans to institutions in Moscow."

Some 230 persons worked on the farm throughout the year and about 20 others were hired in the busy summer season. Women do what we think of as men's work all over Russia, street-cleaning and section-hand work on the railroads, and they did much of the work in the cow barns at this farm. There were some milking machines but most of the milking was done by hand. The beef cattle did not look particularly well fattened and throughout Russia I found that the meat is not so tender as ours, apparently because it is not hung so long. Chickens are usually not tender, so that one rarely had roast chicken. It usually was boiled or minced in croquettes or used in soup.

Not long after visiting the state farm we took the jet airliner for Tashkent, where I had a chance to visit a collective farm. Less than four hours after we left Moscow we came down at Tashkent, some two thousand miles away.

There was more desert here than I had expected and the green areas were confined to the source of water or to irrigated sections. Part of Tashkent dates back to the twelfth century, and this old section was being slowly torn down, the streets were being widened and new, modern apartment houses were being built.

The collective farm that we visited was owned by an organization of farmers. Out of the over-all income of the farm, 7 per cent goes to the government in taxes. Another 16 per cent goes for capital reserve, 1 per cent to amortization and the like. Thirteen per cent goes into the operation of services, of which there are many, and the remaining cash is divided among members of the collective. We were told that a man might get about 8,000 rubles a year in cash on this basis, plus shelter, services, food and so on, which meant that he is fairly well off. If the crops fail, of course, he is in trouble.

Cotton was the main crop, but the farmers also raised cattle for meat and milk. There were 1,160 houses and 1,700 able workers, representing a dozen different nationalities brought together in this ancient area of Central Asia. Each farmer annually received about 30 pounds of meat, a considerable quantity of grain, and 150 pounds of potatoes, in addition to which he might raise food for himself in his garden plot and keep a cow, for which the collective provided food.

We walked around part of the farm. There was no running water in any of the houses but they all had electricity and I frequently saw a one-burner electric plate on top of an old wood range. Toilet and bathing facilities were old-fashioned—usually a privy and a bathhouse.

Every inch of land seemed to be in use. Even where small fruit trees had been planted there were growing crops. The farm had a maternity hospital and a baby clinic but, in case of serious illness, the farm people went to hospitals in Tashkent. There was a nursery, a kindergarten and a school. Children were taken care of at these institutions while their parents worked in the fields, but nursing mothers could leave their work and go to the nursery at stated hours when feedings were given.

The manager of the farm said that there had been a steady increase in production in recent years, but this collective also had increased in size and it was difficult to know whether it was operating more efficiently and getting a greater yield from the land or had just acquired more acreage. Later, in Moscow, I talked about farm production with Senator Allen J. Ellender of Louisiana, who was making his third visit to Russia. He was interested in Russian agriculture and had been in the new area in Soviet Asia where a large region was being plowed up or the first time.

The senator felt that there was serious danger that the new land might turn into a dust bowl as happened in parts of our Southwest after the protective grass had been stripped from the plains. He said he had written a letter to Mr. Khrushchev warning him of this danger, but that the Communist party chief had not seemed to pay any attention. Later, talking to a deputy minister of agriculture, I asked him about this problem, but he said that a thorough investigation had been made before the land was plowed up and that the top soil was found to be more than three feet deep.

The Russians, incidentally, had imported some of the famous Santa Gertrudis beef cattle from the King Ranch in Texas for breeding purposes. They had been shipped to Russia several years earlier and I was told that they had disappeared. I was curious about them and eventually inquired at the Ministry of Agriculture about what had happened to them.

"Oh, they are the special pets of the minister," I was told. "They were shipped to the southern part of the Ukraine and they are still there and thriving. They have also had plenty of little ones!"

The College of Music and similar institutions illustrate how the Communists operate. Forty years ago there were no music schools in the area and the songs of the region were handed down from generation to generation. Then Moscow decided that it was important to preserve the culture of each of its republics and this was an example of how they were doing it. The college in Tashkent has 350 students and 150 teachers, who constantly watch for gifted young people so that they can become teachers or enter a musical career anywhere in the Soviet Union. The state provides 6 million rubles a year to operate the college, which also had sponsored some

30 theaters for students of drama in the Uzbek Republic.

On Sundays Tashkent was alive with music. There were little squares where singers gathered on platforms to entertain whoever happened to stroll by. There were dancers and musicians, too, and the crowds wandered about from one place to another, listening to the music.

We made a quick trip by air to Samarkand, and were met by two women, who were local officials, and a historian, who told us much about this capital city of Tamerlane. The government has spent heavily to restore some of the old buildings in the "blue city" and there are wonderful old tombs with colored inlays on their façades, including the tomb of the first wife of the Mongol conqueror and the tomb of Mohammed's cousin. Earthquakes had destroyed many of the buildings but there were still two domes of an extraordinary blue color. There is also a large hospital for bone tuberculosis, which we visited and where I was impressed by the docility of the children.

The most important things I learned about the Soviet Union—and the things that may be most difficult for democratic peoples everywhere to comprehend—came to a focus when I visited the city of Leningrad. I had been absorbing various ideas from the time I landed in Moscow and was gradually approaching certain conclusions on the basis of what I had seen and heard. But it was at the Leningrad medical school, which puts great emphasis on pediatrics, that I really saw what was happening in Russia and what this may mean in the world-wide struggle between Communism and democracy.

The influence of Dr. Ivan Petrovich Pavlov, a physiologist and experimental psychologist, on the Russians today is tremendous. I knew vaguely that, before his death in 1936, Dr. Pavlov had conducted many experiments and made extensive studies of conditioned reflexes and that the Soviet government had built a special laboratory for him. But I had not realized until I saw some of the results of his work at Leningrad and elsewhere that he may well prove to be far more famous in history as the father of a system that seems to be turning the masses of Russia into completely disciplined and amenable people.

I had told the Intourist people that I would like to go to the institute of medicine oriented toward pediatrics, where I could see their methods of handling children. At the institute they asked if I would like to see an experiment. Thirty-two children taken at birth from lying-in hospitals, whose parents had died or abandoned them, were being trained. The purpose of the training was to see whether they could develop in an institution and be as advanced, healthy and happy as in an ordinary home.

The nursery was well equipped. While the head teacher and several doctors watched with me, one of the nurses, a solid, friendly young woman in white uniform and cap, demonstrated the kind of training given the babies. It was here, I later realized, that the Pavlov theories were being put into practice. The same pattern is followed in all nurseries and also by mothers training their children at home.

A six-month-old baby was brought to the nurse for his daily conditioning. The routine was simple—to hold two rings out to the baby and persuade him to pull on them as the first step in the exercises. I noticed that the baby already knew what was coming and what he was supposed to do. He held out his hands to grasp the rings as soon as he saw the nurse. Then, after holding tightly to the rings throughout the exercise, he dropped them without being given any signal and shifted to the next exercise. This was using his legs and he went through the routine without any direction from the nurse. Then he lay rigid, waiting to be picked up by his heels and exercised on his head. After that the nurse picked him up and hugged and kissed him and spent some time playing with him as any mother might do with a small baby.

This attitude of affection and loving care was customary, I observed, with children of all ages at all the institutions that I visited. The next group I saw consisted of four children about a year and a half old, who went through a more complicated routine. They came in, like a drill team, took off their shoes, put them neatly in a row and pulled out a bench from the wall. One after the other, they crawled along the bench, then walked on it, then crawled under it. Then they climbed up on exercise bars. They knew exactly what to do and when to do it, like clockwork, and when they had finished the routine each one walked over and sat on the lap of a nurse. The nurse lowered them down backwards to the floor and pulled them up again in another exercise. Then the children put on their shoes, put the bench back in place and went out. This kind of training in behavior goes on year after year as the children grow up.

What, I asked myself, does this mean in ordinary life outside the nursery or schoolroom? And as I watched the children I knew that I had already seen some of the answers in the conduct of the Russian people, the generations that are growing up or have grown up since Dr. Pavlov conducted his experiments and drew his conclusions about the conditioning of reflex action.

Because of lifelong conditioning, the government can depend on the mass of the people—there will always be exceptions—to react in a certain way to certain stimuli. The Russians today are a disciplined, well-trained people; not a happy people, perhaps, but not likely to rise up against their rulers.

But more than this—much more—Americans should never forget that by controlling the entire economy the Soviet dictatorship can use this disciplined people to do things that are difficult if not impossible in our free economy. The Communist leaders are aware of this power and know how to use it. They put far more emphasis and far more money into scientific and research projects, for example, than we do. To take just one field of endeavor: in 1956 the Russian schools graduated about 26,000 doctors. In the United States, we graduated about 6,500.

In the Soviet Union free medical care appeared to be one of the things most highly valued by the people. The Health Ministry has agencies throughout the country but the rules are made in Moscow, with some adjustments for local conditions. To become a doctor one must attend school for ten years and then study at medical school for six years and then give three years of work to the state. The emphasis at first was placed on public-health doctors. After completing his work for the state a doctor may choose his specialty and have three more years of training. I was interested to discover that a doctor is not supposed to work more than a six-hour day.

The whole Soviet Union is divided into health districts. We visited one district center in Leningrad for the care of mothers and children. It deals only with healthy children. Those who are ill are sent to a hospital. The district has 19,000 children. There are three nurseries in the city and four outside where children are sent for a more healthful atmosphere. There are 18 kindergartens and 11 schools in the district. The district medical staff of 91 persons includes 51 doctors, each of whom spends two hours in the center and four hours making calls. They told us that only one child under a year old had died in the district in 1956 and only four children under sixteen had died. There was no venereal disease and no prostitution in the district. It is significant to note that there are more than 35 such centers in Leningrad alone, with 2,000 doctors devoting themselves purely to preventive medicine.

We later visited Sochi, far to the south on the Black Sea, where there are 50 sanitariums owned by government-run industries or by trade unions. If a doctor certifies the need for a worker to go to a sanitarium during his month's vacation, 70 per cent of the cost of his care is paid by the union. The worker pays for his transportation, at a specially low rate, and also pays 30 per cent of his expenses during this vacation period. In cases of serious illness, the time spent in a special hospital or sanitarium is not counted as vacation time.

At Sochi there is a remarkable arrangement that permits either men or women workers going to the sanitariums to take along their spouses, but at extra cost. I saw many husbands and wives enjoying the beautiful beach at Sochi, lying in the sun or swimming. The people spend much time and thought preparing for their holidays; in fact, I never realized how important vacations were until I heard them discussed so fervently in the Soviet Union.

I have written mostly about agriculture and medicine in Russia, but the government is just as keenly aware of the need for research and for generous financing in other scientific fields. There was in Moscow with us an American, Seth Jackson, who was a member of a United Nations delegation visiting Russia to study problems of forestry, particularly logging. He was a technical expert from our Department of Forestry, and it was his opinion that Russia was ahead in forestry research.

"The Soviet Union has surveyed all of its forests through the efforts of the Institutes for Research in Forestry," he said. "There are twelve such institutes in this country and they have steadily improved the machinery used for logging and other purposes. The United States hasn't ever mapped all of its forests."

There was another thing that interested me in regard to the Soviet encouragement of scientific progress. Able students have been given every opportunity to work freely, but I wondered what right they had been given to think. So I asked one scientist about it.

"Oh, we are encouraged to think freely just as we are given every encouragement to work," he replied, with a smile. "We are free to discuss, to challenge and to think whatever we please." But if you ask any of them a political question, they invariably reply, "We know nothing about politics."

Later in Moscow I had an interesting meeting with the Committee of Soviet Women, who were trying to arrange for an invitation to the United States. "Why is it so difficult," one of them asked, "for us to get visas to visit your country? We have been trying for two years to arrange a visit through the State Department but have failed miserably."

"Are you sure," I asked, "that your own government would give you permission to leave Russia?"

"Certainly," she said. "We have been given unequivocal assurances from our own government."

I told them that I would try to get a group from the National Council of Women of the United States to look into the problem and possibly take some action at the State Department. These women had a great desire to see America and I felt sure that it would benefit us to have a greater interchange between the Russian people and our own people. We have completely different backgrounds and our lives are completely different. But we have to see to understand. Possibly after seeing America they would prefer their own way of life but such interchanges might lead us to sufficient understanding to work out the kind of peaceful coexistence our leaders talk about but seem unable to achieve.

There was one other phase of the conditioning of the Russian people that I observed everywhere I went in the Soviet Union, and it is one of particular importance to Americans at present. The most familiar symbol in the country is the dove of peace. You see it wherever you go. I saw it painted on the sides of trucks on the streets; I looked down from the tower of Moscow University and saw a great white dove outlined in stone in the lawn. It was on posters in distant villages. The finale of a circus I attended featured the release of a flock of doves over the audience, following a patriotic speech.

The peace campaign was launched to remind the people that they must sacrifice and work because, despite Russia's desire for peace, their great enemy, the United States, is trying to bring about a war against Russia. The dove of peace symbolizes the efforts of the Soviet Union to protect the people from an aggressive war such as our government is alleged to be planning.

We Americans and the people of the free world must never forget or ignore this kind of distorted conditioning of the Russian people, this kind of indoctrination with ideas that are false but that by repetition can be drilled into the minds not only of the Russian people but of peoples in underdeveloped countries whom the Communists seek to turn against the United States.

A totalitarian regime regulates all the news—or almost all—that is available to the great mass of people. None but a Communist newspaper can be bought in the Soviet Union, so the people get only the slanted Communist point of view on what is happening in the world. They have no other interpretation of the position of the United States and little concept of world opinion other than that fed to them by the Kremlin.

For us merely to say that their beliefs are false is not enough, because they have been conditioned to believe that Washington is plotting a war and that Moscow is striving to protect them from our aggression; and they do believe it. Almost the only news about the United States that I saw in Russian newspapers was the story of school integration troubles at Little Rock, Arkansas. When I protested that the Russians were getting a completely distorted view of the United States and of the attitude of the American people, I was usually met with silence or obvious disbelief. Or, if the person I was talking with was educated and intelligent, his reply might be: "Oh, I know nothing about politics."

It may seem ironic to us that a dove of peace has become the symbol of an American plot to start a world war, but I was convinced that we are going to have to make far greater efforts than we have made in the past if we can hope to avoid the war that the Kremlin has told the people over and over and over again that we might start.

Thirty-eight

A Challenge for the West

AS SOON AS I arrived in Moscow I requested an interview with Nikita S. Khrushchev. I was told to write a letter in which I was to state the questions I would ask Mr. Khrushchev. I did so, saying that I wanted to record his answers.

As the days flew along I became discouraged about the possibility of seeing him, although that had been one of the main purposes of my visit to Russia. I was ready to admit failure. Then, three days before my scheduled departure, my interpreter said: "I forgot to tell you, but we go to Yalta early tomorrow morning."

The next morning we departed for Yalta. After our arrival we learned that Mr. Khrushchev would send his car for us the following day at nine-thirty.

Exactly at nine-thirty we drove downhill toward the Black Sea and finally came to a gate with a soldier on guard. We passed through the gate and, a few minutes later, through another similarly guarded gate, and then we approached a comfortable but not imposing house on a lovely site looking toward the city of Yalta. We had arrived exactly on the minute set for our appointment.

We were led through the yard and to a garden, where Mr. Khrushchev was talking with another gentleman. He came to greet us and bid us welcome, a short, stocky man with a bald head and a wide smile on his round, mobile face.

Dr. Gurewitsch, who had accompanied me, set up our portable tape recorder, so there would be no misinterpreting what we said, and we settled down to talk.

"I appreciate your coming here," he said, "and I want to speak of President Franklin Roosevelt. We respect him and remember his activities be-

381

cause he was the first to establish diplomatic relations between the United States and the Soviet Union. President Roosevelt understood perfectly well the necessity of such relations. He was a great man, a capable man who understood the interests of his own country and the interests of the Soviet Union. We had a common cause against Hitler and we appreciate very much that Franklin Roosevelt understood this task. I am happy to greet you in our land."

My first question concerned disarmament. I pointed out that after World War II we reduced our army from twelve million to one million men, but then, because of the Soviet Union's actions, we were forced to rearm. In such circumstances, I said, the American people wondered how the Soviet Union could expect us to agree on disarmament without inspection.

"We do not agree with your conception," he replied. "We consider that demobilization took place in the U.S. and in the U.S.S.R. In our country men and women were all mobilized. In our country perished roughly the number of persons you mention as making up the army of your country, almost the same number, Mrs. Roosevelt. I do not want to offend you, but if you compare the losses of your country with the losses of ours, your losses just equal our losses in one big campaign. You know what terrible ruins we got. We lost our cities. That is why our country was so eager to establish firm peace. No country wished it so eagerly."

But, we pointed out, the Soviet army was bigger than ours.

"I do not reject that our army was bigger. Take a map and look at the geographical situation of our country. It is a colossal territory. If you take Germany or France, small countries who keep their army to defend either their east or their west, that is easy; they may have a small army. But if we keep our army in the east it is difficult to reach the west because our territory is so vast."

I pointed out that after the war the Russians wanted a group of neutral countries between them and Germany, that Germany was no longer a military menace and that Great Britain could not be considered a military threat. Why, then, I asked, was it not possible to do without an offensive army in Russia, since it frightened the rest of the world?

"When we increase our arms," he said, "it means we are afraid of each other. Until the troops are drawn out of Europe and military bases liquidated, the disarmament will not succeed."

I told him that after World War II we had not been suspicious of Russia. I knew that my husband had hoped we would be able to come to an understanding. "But then," I went on, "we found the Russians did not strictly keep agreements made at Yalta and we became more and more suspicious."

The discussion continued. Mr. Khrushchev appeared to think that the Americans did not really want to liberate the European and Eastern countries. Instead, they had tried to destroy the will of the people. I countered with the suggestion that the acceptance of Communism did not, in our opinion, represent the will of the people. From that point on the discussion grew more heated. Did he, I asked, believe that a Communist world must be brought about?

"Communism will win in the whole world," he told me. "This is scientifically based on the writings of Karl Marx, Engels and Lenin." He went on to assure me blandly: "We are against any military attempt to introduce Communism or socialism into any country."

Much of our discussion is irrelevant now as conditions have changed in the world. Basically, there was no possibility of meeting in agreement on a single point. Except one, perhaps, equivocal as it seemed.

"Misunderstandings have grown between our countries," I said, "and there is fear on both sides. We will have to do things to create confidence. One thing is a broader exchange of people."

"I fully agree, Mrs. Roosevelt," he said in a calmer tone.

At the end of two and a half hours of conversation I felt fully convinced that Mr. Khrushchev knew the danger that any new war would bring to civilization. He was, I decided, convinced that war would be a disadvantage to the Soviet Union and to Communism because he believed that the wave of the future was socialism and that his cause would triumph without war. He believed it, I told myself, and he would try to make the future serve his purposes.

As I was leaving, Mr. Khrushchev wished me a pleasant trip and asked, "Can I tell our papers that we have had a friendly conversation?"

"You can say that we had a friendly conversation but that we differ."

He grinned broadly. "Now!" he exclaimed. "At least we didn't shoot at each other!"

For three weeks in the Soviet Union I had felt more than at any time in my life that I was cut off from all the outside world. For three weeks I do not believe I had heard anyone really laugh on the streets or in a crowd. I had been among hospitable people but they were people who worked hard, who lived under considerable strain, and who were tired. It was only after I had landed at Copenhagen and heard laughter and gay talk and saw faces that were unafraid that I realized how different were our two worlds. Suddenly I could breathe again!

But I was frightened too, and after I reached home my nagging fear continued. I was—I still am—afraid that Americans and the peoples of the rest of the free world will not understand the nature of the struggle against Communism as exemplified by the Soviet Union. It is urgently important for the sake of our country and people that we get rid of some of our great misunderstandings and that we see clearly the things that must be done.

We are in a great struggle between two vastly different ways of life. While we must have guns, atomic weapons and missiles for retaliation against aggression, they are not going to win this struggle or prevent a catastrophic world war. Nor is belief in the idea of democracy likely to have great effect in areas where democratic institutions are not established. To overemphasize the importance of military power or to propagate merely the abstract idea of democracy is to miss the point. There is much, much more to be done if Western leadership is to be accepted by the masses of the world's underdeveloped countries, if our way of life and our hard-won freedoms are to survive—or, perhaps, if anything is to survive in the atomic age—and flourish. We must provide leadership for free peoples, but we must never forget that in many countries, particularly in Asia and Africa, the freedom that is uppermost in the minds of the people is freedom to eat.

I think it is time for us Americans to take a good look at ourselves and our shortcomings. We should remember how we achieved the aims of freedom and democracy. We should look back in an effort to gauge how we can best influence the peoples of the world. Perhaps we made the greatest impression on underdeveloped countries in the 1930's when we ourselves were making a tremendous effort to fight our way out of a great economic depression. In that period we united behind bold ideas and vigorous programs, and, as they watched us, many people in far countries of the world began to realize that a government could be intensely interested in the welfare of the individual. They saw what was happening and it gave them hope that it could happen to them too. That was a generation ago, but again today it seems to me that it is essential for us to examine carefully our actions as a nation and try to develop a program for the welfare of the individual.

In this connection I was sometimes astonished during my visit to Russia to see what the Soviet government had brought about during four decades of Communist dictatorship. Illiteracy, which was once 90 per cent, has been reduced until it is now probably less than 10 per cent. The people have been educated in every field—crafts, arts, professions, sciences—and the government has used the educational system for political purposes, to shape the people to the will of the leadership.

Educators are sent where they are most important for the purposes of the government. Doctors are sent where they can be most useful. Workers are sent to distant areas of Asia because new fields must be plowed and crops planted. This is dictatorship and it is hateful; but the results achieved by the Soviet regime are obvious to anyone visiting Russia. The water is pure; the milk is clean; the food supply is increasing; industry has made mighty strides. The people are not free, but they are better off materially every year. They know little of other countries and they are willing to accept a hard life because of the insidious Communist propaganda that unites them in fear of aggression by the United States. Most of them are sustained by a belief in communistic aims.

The Russians recognize that there are vast masses of people in Asia, Africa and parts of Latin America who are closer to the economic conditions that existed forty years ago in Russia than they are to the conditions that have existed for many years in the United States. The leaders of the Soviets can say to them: "We know your conditions. Our people were once hungry, too; not only for food but for health and education, for knowledge and for hope for the future. Look at what we have done in forty years! Take heart. We can help you."

This is a challenge to democracy. This is the real challenge, and it cannot be met by mere words. We have to show the world by our actions that we live up to the ideals we profess and demonstrate that we can provide all the people in this country with the basic decencies of life, spiritually as well as materially. In the United States we are the showcase for the possibilities inherent in a free world, in democracy. If the lives of our people are not better in terms of basic satisfactions as well as in material ways than the lives of people anywhere in the world, then the uncommitted peoples we need on our side will look elsewhere for leadership.

We have spent a great deal in grants to our friends abroad but there is more than that to the struggle for the minds of men. For example, we have taken no trouble to invite delegations from other parts of the world to look at our system and see what we are doing under government auspices. If we are to be leaders we must offer needy countries technical know-how to help them achieve the freedom to eat, and practical help in developing, step by step, a democratic way of life. It is not enough to say that we do not like the Communist idea. We have to prove that our own idea is better and can accomplish more.

We *can* accomplish more. There is no reason for us to be frightened by the scientific achievements under direction of the Soviet government, which has concentrated money and manpower on sputniks and rockets for obvious propaganda reasons. We have been complacent and given as little money and as few men as possible for work that we should have pressed vigorously. We were more interested in our comforts, in making money, and in having all the luxuries possible in this comfortable world of ours. We have to change and we *will* change that approach. If we are to lead the free world we must become a mature people—or we may one day wake up to find that fear and laziness have reduced us from a strong, vital nation to a people unable to lead other nations in the only way to win the struggle against Communism, the way of the mind and the heart.

I can think of nothing more foolish than looking at the Russian scientific achievements and saying that we must rush to catch up with them by resorting to their methods. We have always said that our objectives were those that could be achieved only by a free people. Why should a free people slavishly follow a Communist lead? We must develop all our resources in our own way. We want our people to decide whether their children shall go to school, whether they shall be scientists or playwrights or mechanics. We don't want to be told what to do. What the world wants today is leadership in the true sense, and we had better decide what we want to achieve and then go ahead and do it as leaders and not as imitators.

The only thing that frightened me in Russia was that we might be apathetic and complacent in the face of this challenge. I can well understand why the Russian people welcome the good that has come to them. But I cannot understand or believe that anything that has to be preserved by fear will stand permanently against a system which offers love and trust among peoples and removes fear so that all feel free to think and express their ideas.

It seems to me that we must have the courage to face ourselves in this crisis. We must regain a vision of ourselves as leaders of the world. We must join in an effort to use all knowledge for the good of all human beings.

When we do that we shall have nothing to fear.

PART IV

The Search for Understanding

Thirty-nine

Second Visit to Russia

FOR SOME TIME my children and my friends have been warning me that I must slow down. They tell me that I am working too hard, seeing too many people, undertaking too many activities; that my interests seem to proliferate rather than to narrow. Which is certainly true.

I am willing to slow down but I just don't know how. Even when I am aware that people have used my time unjustifiably, I find myself interested in them. Even when a new project makes demands on my already crowded schedule, I find it difficult to reject it, so long as it serves a useful purpose. But I do feel that I am too old now to undertake any course of action or embark on foreign travel unless I am convinced that it will, in some way, be useful.

I had been much troubled by my first visit to Russia, where I had spent nearly a month visiting institutions of many sorts, and had concluded by having a three-hour interview with Mr. Khrushchev. The more I thought of that visit and the conclusions I had drawn from it the more troubled I was. What seemed most frightening about the conditions I found in Russia, the trends I discerned, the possibilities I envisioned, was that the people of the United States appeared not to have the slightest grasp of their meaning in terms of our own future.

Basic in all this was the impression I had gathered from watching the training—or rather the conditioning—of children in the Soviet Union into disciplined, amenable citizens, prepared to obey any orders given them and incapable of revolt. To return to the United States after that trip and hear people talk blithely of the possibility of the Russian people's rising up against their government (a situation made inconceivable by their conditioning from babyhood) or changing their attitude toward us (when every source of information is filtered through government hands) was more than disturbing. It was alarming. It meant that we were facing the greatest challenge our way of life has ever had to meet without any clear understanding of the facts.

There is in most people, at most times, a proneness to give more credence to pleasant news than to unpleasant, to hope that, somehow or other, things "will come out all right." But this was not the frame of mind that created the United States and made it not only a great nation but a symbol of a way of life that became the hope of the world. One can fight a danger only when one is armed with solid facts and spurred on by an unwavering faith and determination.

So, when Dr. Gurewitsch decided, a year after the first trip to Russia, that he would like to go back and see whether he could learn the answer to some questions in regard to physical medicine, I was eager to return to the Soviet Union and, on a second visit, without the distraction of strange first impressions, find out for myself whether my first conclusions had been sound.

Dr. Gurewitsch, his wife Edna, and I started our tour, in 1958, by attending a meeting of the United Nations Associations which was being held in Brussels because of the World's Fair.

The theme of the Brussels Exposition was "Better Living for the People Today," and on the whole I did not feel that it was as effective as it should have been. A great many people criticized our building, which annoyed me very much, as I thought it was beautiful and the layout of the landscaping was unusually fine. Inside, however, the exhibitions were not well arranged, and the mechanical displays were not working.

One of the most popular, though unplanned, features of our exhibit was the appearance there of Harry Belafonte. He had a great personal success, and his presence was most valuable as an answer to much of the criticism of the Americans on their attitude toward colored people.

The Russian exhibit was monumental. It can be summed up as marching, marching, marching, piled on marching. Pictures of young Russians marching to school, marching to factories, marching with the army, all looking young, healthy and vigorous. To most people from the Western countries that much marching is supremely dull. They had, I remember, a cyclorama which lasted for an hour and a half (with more marching, of course), but which was less interesting and less informative than the one produced by the Americans, which lasted only twenty minutes.

How much ultimate value this kind of exhibit had, either for the Russians or for us, I have no way of knowing. My own over-all impression was that the Russian exhibit gave an effect of enormous power and drive; but, though they displayed the best they had to offer to the best advantage, it was not good enough to match what we have. On the other hand, I felt that here again we had not used, in the best possible way, an opportunity to show the peoples of the world what the United States is all about.

One of the most pleasant episodes during my visit to Brussels was a luncheon with Queen Elizabeth of Belgium, whom I liked very much.

Queen Elizabeth is a musician and an artist. She paints, she does sculpture, she plays several instruments. In addition, she is a woman who plants gardens. But I think the loveliest thing about her is that she is really concerned about people. Of course, being a queen, she is cut off from people in many ways so that her approach is necessarily unrealistic, but she really wants to learn. She has a beautiful soul and a longing to be of service to humanity. She gives with great generosity, not only with her head but with her heart.

From Belgium we flew to the Soviet Union. The first five days of our visit were given up to the activities of the Soviet Association of the United Nations, which had invited all of our delegation to be its guests. This meant that we would have only a little over two weeks for the work we wanted to do and therefore we decided to concentrate on Moscow and Leningrad.

As soon as we ceased to be the guests of the United Nations, I was simply a private tourist visitor, but I had no trouble in making appointments with any department or in seeing anything I asked to see.

I did not try to see Mr. Khrushchev on this visit. I felt that he had had a great many American visitors and must have all the information he needed about us. Certainly, he had had plentiful opportunity to receive reports from those who had interviewed him.

My main object was to try to find out how many emotionally disturbed children there are in the Soviet Union and what treatment is being provided for them. The Russian answer to the problem of emotionally disturbed children lies, primarily, in their type of discipline, or conditioning of all children. They begin, as I have said before, when the child is two months old, and by the time he is seven years old the child is completely regimented. The Soviet children have little or no desire for freedom. Their conditioning and training has been carefully thought out to prevent deviation of any kind, on any level, from birth to death.

This conditioning provides, too, for the development of what one might call "safe leadership," that is, leadership within certain carefully prescribed limits.

For instance, each school class elects its president, at the age of seven years. The classes for this age group average about forty pupils. The little president marches his class into the schoolroom and tells when to get up and leave. He passes them on to two children from an older grade who see them safely out of the building. Then this little boy returns to help the teacher tidy up the schoolroom.

"How," I asked the teachers, over and over, "can you detect an emotionally disturbed child?"

They were disgusted. "Any deviation in behavior is reported immediately," they told me.

This uniformity in behavior and in response is, it seems to me, the factor which Americans fail almost entirely to understand, either in its essence or in its potentialities. This large-scale conditioning of human beings is something so new in the world that we cannot grasp it.

I should think that it would destroy initiative completely, but though I have frequently asked them, no psychologist can tell me what the results of this gigantic experiment with human beings will be.

On my first visit I had watched the training of small babies. On this trip I studied the older children, their training, their discipline, their complete absorption by the Communist system.

Whatever else a child's life in Russia may be, it is not easy. Indeed, life is easy for no one there. The children work in school from 8:45 until 1:45. If they have anyone at home, they return for a hot meal. Otherwise, this is provided by the school. For the next two hours, in the Pioneer Youth Home or room, they have exercises, supervised games, and are drilled in Marxism. Every child learns his Marxism backwards and forwards. By the time he leaves school he is prepared to take not only his skills but his political ideas with him wherever he may be sent, to whatever part of the world.

For another two hours there are outdoor games, also supervised. The Russian child is never alone. And when the school day ends he is assigned far more homework than falls to the lot of the American child.

As a part of the Pioneer Youth Movement, every big city provides a "children's palace," where the children go twice a week for two hours of various types of training and entertainment. This includes such diverse things as lectures on outer space, chess playing, storytelling, dancing and singing, and the development of handicrafts.

The one I visited was in Leningrad. The equipment was excellent and the shop equipment for training in manual arts was as good as or better than that in our own trade schools. And, of course, during the lectures or the games the training in Marxism is continued.

In the light of this standardized training, which is much the same whether one lives in Moscow or in a remote village, it is easier to understand why the teachers could tell me so promptly that "any deviation in behavior is reported immediately."

Madame Muravyeva, who was in charge of social service for the Soviet Union, told me that every schoolteacher is trained to watch for signs of physical, mental or emotional disturbance. Where such disturbances seem to be a result of home conditions, the social services work to improve these conditions. Where more drastic efforts are needed, the child is sent to a sanitarium, where, the minister of health told me, preventive therapy is used.

I was told that inadequate housing in the big cities, bad relations between parents, and undesirable conditions caused by heavy drinking could create emotional disturbances in the young.

After sitting through many classes in schools and visiting many more, I came back believing that the Russians have fewer emotionally disturbed children than we do and less of a problem with juvenile delinquency, particularly in the early years. Their problem comes primarily with those young people who go into the technicons, a type of technical school, at fourteen, because they are judged not capable of higher education. Therefore, at seventeen they are ready to take a job and suddenly, after having had every moment of the time planned and occupied, except for the hours when they work, they are free, their own masters, with their own money.

It is a heady thing to be given freedom all of a sudden, even the limited kind in the Soviet Union. So this, inevitably, creates a problem. These are the youngsters who, Mr. Khrushchev says, behave like our zoot-suit youngsters and create a problem by heavy drinking.

Those who attend technicons are much the biggest group of the young in Russia. As in any country, there is a large percentage which cannot profitably be educated beyond a certain point. In Russia, however, the search for talent, for the exceptionally bright, for the artistically endowed or the scientifically minded goes on constantly, and such exceptional youngsters are provided with every opportunity to improve their talents, increase their learning, and acquire as much education as they can absorb.

There is no fear of eggheads in Russia. They know that the speedy development of the country, which has already grown in forty years from one of the most backward to one of the most modern nations, can be achieved only by using every scrap of talent, every scrap of brains and ability they have.

I do not mean that these talented youngsters are indulged. Far from it. I visited an art school in Moscow where children talented in painting and in sculpture are given the best possible tools to work with and every opportunity to learn. But their life is Spartan. Their beds are probably completely hygienic but they are far from comfortable. Their food is sufficient to sustain life but drab as diet. The cold, even in September, in the building where they live and work, struck us as we thought of what the winters must be like. Yet these children range in age from only eight to seventeen.

The corridors were lined with examples of their work and I was much interested in inspecting them. I found that what the very young did was fresh and interesting. But it seemed to me that, as they grew older, they became more imitative under their training. This was particularly accentuated in the field of sculpture. When I went to the class for seventeen-year-old boys and girls I felt that both the concept and the execution of practically all their work was stereotyped, tied to the past of the classical tradition, but with little individual expression or feeling for modern forms of development.

Naturally, it is a great benefit to the talented young to be afforded every opportunity to develop their skills to their utmost. Russia is the only country which, next to its politicians and scientists, pays its highest salaries and gives its highest honor to its artists and its intellectuals.

But, while the salary may be higher and the recognition greater, in some basic ways the restrictions of life in Russia are the same, whether one is at the top or at the bottom of the scale. One rule seems to hold true: there is practically no privacy in Russia.

The number of rooms you are allowed to have in an apartment depends on the number of people who are to live in it. If there are four people, there are only two rooms. On the other hand, whether you are allotted six rooms or two rooms, your rent is still only 1 per cent of your income.

Before I left New York on this second trip to Russia, a letter appeared in the *New York Times*, written by a Russian woman who challenged the paper to publish it. She wrote that she wanted to hear from American women. Russia wanted peace, she said, and we did not. What were American women doing about it? She asked foreigners to come and see her, to discover for themselves how people lived in Russia.

At the request of the *New York Times* I answered her letter, and while we were in Leningrad we went to visit her. She lived in a new house on the outskirts of Leningrad, up five flights of stairs. There was an elevator but it never ran. She welcomed us, tremendously proud of her apartment, which, from her standpoint and that of most of her fellow countrymen, was palatial.

She had five children under twelve years of age, and the son went to a boarding school but came home for weekends. She was allowed three rooms, a bathroom, and a big kitchen. This meant that the smallest boy slept in the room with his mother and father, the two girls had a bedroom, and the two older boys slept in a room which served also as dining room and living room.

Her letter, I feel sure, had been supervised and approved by the government. To her delight it had brought her a number of answers, about three hundred, I think. Some of her other correspondents had come to see her, as we did.

We found her very friendly—indeed, most Russians are personally friendly to Americans—but nothing could shake her conviction that we, as a nation, threatened Russia and wanted war. Before the end of our visit, I think we had convinced her that we ourselves did not want war, but she still believed firmly that the United States did.

Why did our country have bases? she asked. We were ringing Russia round with bases. Which, of course, is true. But that Russia could conceivably constitute a warlike threat she brushed aside as nonsense, as hostile foreign propaganda.

When we left Leningrad we were touched to find that she had bothered to come to the train, in the middle of the night, to see us off.

The visit left us with a blank feeling of failure. There was no personal hostility between us. None at all. But there was an unshaken conviction that the United States not only threatens but actually desires and seeks war. Here we are, equipped with the best communications in the world, and yet we have not learned how to use them in a way that can reach people.

The friendliness of these people, always apart from the political bias in which they have been conditioned, is astonishing. I have noticed, over and over, when they come to the United States, even if they have met you only most briefly before, they greet you as though you were a long-lost friend, almost appealing for affection.

At one time the National Council of Women arranged, through the State Department, for two Russian women to visit the United States. A group of us raised the money for the trip, hoping that if they could see for themselves something of American life and the American temper it would give them something new to tell their people on their return.

These women lived here in private homes and were free of supervision by their own government, and, naturally, by ours, while they were in this country. I cannot believe that the visit was wasted. The more such visits are sponsored the better it will be for us because, if we continue to fail to tell our story convincingly abroad, at least the evidence is here at home without the telling.

All this is a digression from the problem of emotional disturbance. We visited the Pavlov Institute, and watched the training of various types of animals. The most interesting, of course, were the monkeys but we were warned not to get too close to the cage of the big ones, particularly if they did not happen to be good-tempered at the time. We also saw dogs being trained and being experimented with in many ways. It was not difficult to see how, out of this conditioning of animals, could come the theory of the conditioning of children. We also visited institutions where children who were handicapped by illness or some infirmity were spending the summer months, and where the care was excellent.

Then we went to a hospital where people are diagnosed. Anyone who thinks that he needs help can go to a clinic. If he can cope with his problem without going to a hospital, that is fine. Otherwise, he is treated in the hospital. This place cares for those threatened with mental and emotional disturbances and provides aftercare when they have returned to their normal lives.

The interesting thing is that there appeared to be no lack of man power for nursing in the Soviet Union. Here we are lucky if one nurse has only forty patients. In the Soviet Union one nurse had no more than four patients and a really disturbed person gets almost constant attention. This is possible because all the women in Russia are mobilized.

Of course, with the modern drugs the change in the mental hospitals is very great. We did see one room where patients were still given shock treatment, but this method of therapy is gradually disappearing.

There is a shortage of some of the new drugs in the Soviet Union. I do not know how serious this may be but, of course, it would make a difference in the treatment. In the particular hospital which I visited I saw very few badly disturbed people. I remember one young girl who had come in, thinking she had a monkey in her stomach. The nurse never left her for a minute.

I returned from Russia late in the fall of 1958 and attempted after my second visit to balance my impressions against those of my first one.

What stood out most sharply were the changes. The year before, there had been only trucks on the road. Now there were a large number of small cars and a considerable number of larger cars, all of them of Russian make.

The year before, my first impression as our plane circled Moscow, had been of the number of cranes where new building was going on. This time I found a number of new apartment houses had been built and the city was expanding. There were apartment buildings going up to house two million people.

The year before, the people had appeared to be uniformly drab. Clothing was not important in the economy, so the people had to do with what was provided. This time they were much better dressed. The expression on their faces when we saw them at the end of the day's work was happier, less anxious than it had been when they were closer to the Stalin regime.

On the whole, however, the second visit intensified the basic impressions of the first.

Today the Russian people are well disciplined, amenable to direction, healthy and determined to build a place in the sun for themselves and for their country. In our thinking about them we must remember how the situation looks from *their* point of view.

They have no freedom, we say. But they never had freedom, so they do not miss it. Forty years ago they not only had no freedom they had no education, they had no health care, they had no hope of bettering their condition.

For them what has happened has been, on the whole, of great value.

And farther on there is China, 600 million people who, in eight years, have come even faster along the road to modernization—and indoctrination—than the Soviets had done in the first eight years after the revolution. Yet the only way we have found to cope with this growing danger, this mushrooming threat, is to ignore their political existence, by which they lose face and feel bitterness; and to refuse to trade with them, by which we force them to build up their own ability to produce the very things they might buy from us, thus acting as a spur to their industrialization. Surely there is no framework for building world peace and understanding through these methods.

Today we are one of the oldest governments in existence; ours has been the position for leadership, for setting the pattern of behavior. And yet we are supinely putting ourselves in the position of leaving the leadership to the Russians, of following their ideas rather than our own. For instance, when the Russians set up a restriction on what visitors to the country may be allowed to see, we promptly do the same thing here, in retaliation. Whenever we behave in this manner we are copying the methods of dictatorship and making a hollow boast of our claim that this country loves freedom for all. We owe it to ourselves and to the world, to our own dignity and self-respect, to set our own standards of behavior, regardless of what other nations do.

I came back from that second trip to Russia convinced that any talk of an uprising of the people against their government was baseless nonsense. But I came back believing more profoundly than before that, by practicing what we preach, putting democracy to work up to the very hilt, showing the world that our way of life has the most to offer the men and women and children of all countries, we could regain our lost leadership. Against those mindless millions we can oppose the unleashed strength of free men, for only in freedom can a man function completely.

Forty

The American Dream

IF THAT SECOND trip to Russia aroused deep misgivings in my mind about the efficacy of the methods we have used in recent years in meeting the Soviet challenge, a journey which I made in 1958 to Morocco and another in the spring of 1959 to the Near East made me feel that we must think through once more our whole approach to world problems.

When I visited Morocco in 1958, the King kindly sent an aide with us and we were allowed to travel through the northern part of the country. This was the first opportunity I had had to see for myself the difficulties that arise in the transition stage between colonialism and independence. The troubles that Morocco was encountering were, it seemed to me, fairly typical of the basic difficulties of all young nations in transition.

As the French withdrew from the country, taking their nationals along, the villages found themselves stripped of teachers and doctors. Countless villages were without a single person trained to give medical assistance. The Moroccans were not yet prepared to replace the doctors, the teachers, and the service employees with their own men. It may be decades before they are ready to do so. Where, then, are the necessary people to come from? I'd like to go into this a little more thoroughly later on, because I feel in that answer lies the key, or one of the major keys, to the future.

As though this acute shortage of trained men were not enough, a severe drought had cut down the food supply drastically. The United States, through church organizations, had sent a considerable amount of food to alleviate the greatest need, but conditions were still bad.

Another, and unforeseen, difficulty was that the Moroccans had established markets, which are held on different days in different towns. With this new system they abolished the middleman, who was usually Jewish.

This meant that Morocco found itself with a number of people who had no longer any way of making a living.

The great problem seems to be that, while people may be able to fight successfully for freedom, they may not yet be prepared to set up a stable and functioning independent government. The French pulled out, but the Moroccans had no one to replace them. They were totally unprepared for self-government. They were, in fact, much worse off than they had been a year before.

Today this is happening in a more drastic form in the Congo with the withdrawal of the Belgians. The time for colonization has, perhaps, gone forever, but some intermediate transition system is essential if chaos is not to follow.

A recent Afro-Asian resolution in the UN reveals the difficulty of the position by these words: "Inadequacy of political, economic, social or cultural preparedness" shall not serve as a pretext for denying independence. Now, we cannot deny that such a pretext has often been used in denying the right of self-determination. But it cannot be denied, either, that without some basic qualifications, self-determination will lead to self-destruction.

The visit, which I made with my granddaughter Nina in the spring of 1959, was very brief: one week in Israel, two weeks in Iran, with stopovers in Paris and London.

In Soviet Russia one is in a country where a way of life, a political and economic philosophy, has crystallized. In the Near East the situation is different, the fluctuating and uncertain position of young countries which are in transition from the ways of the past to those of the future, with no certain path to tread and with the ultimate goal still obscure. That is becoming the situation of an increasing number of infant nations as they shake off the fetters of colonialism, or of ancient laws and customs, and grope for their own place in the sun. And what that goal is to be, what kind of place they are to occupy, what political philosophy they will choose in the long run, will depend in great part on how we, in this country, prepare to meet the challenge.

Is what we are doing good enough? Have the changes that have revealed themselves in recent years, particularly in Africa and the Near East and the Latin-American countries, shown overwhelming evidence that we are doing an intelligent job, an adequate job? I am afraid not. Genuinely afraid.

To me, the democratic system represents man's best and brightest hope of self-fulfillment, of a life rich in promise and free from fear; the one hope, perhaps, for the complete development of the whole man. But I know, and learn more clearly every day, that we cannot keep our system strong and free by neglect, by taking it for granted, by giving it our second-best attention. We must be prepared, like the suitor in *The Merchant of Venice* —and, I might point out, the successful suitor—to give and hazard all we have.

It was the season of Ramadan when we reached Shiraz, Iran, to visit my daughter Anna, whose husband was stationed there. Iran, of course, is not Arab, but many of its problems are similar to those of its neighbors in the Near East. The chief problem, it seemed to me, was poverty. The mass of the people have become poorer and poorer; their health has deteriorated; and so, in a disastrous way, have its natural resources. Or, more likely, the loss of natural resources has brought about the poverty. The mountains of Iran, once clothed with forests and covered with fertile soil, are bare now. The land is desert. And with this loss of the fertility of the soil, this loss of forests, has come an inevitable economic instability.

The health of the people is generally poor, with trachoma, tuberculosis and malnutrition the biggest medical problems. The country exists in a kind of flux. The tribes are unwilling to settle down into village life until they can be convinced that such a way of life offers more advantages. They want to be sure that there will be an opportunity to work gainfully, that health conditions will be better, that there will be educational advantages.

So far as the masses are concerned, this is still preponderantly an illiterate population. While there are schools in Shiraz and even in some of the villages, the compulsory education law is not enforced.

To add to the difficulty, so far as future improvement is concerned, the Iranian has no sense of community responsibility. The position of women is still inferior. All this militates against improved social conditions that might arise from the will of the people themselves, their desire and determination to better their own lot and that of their fellow countrymen.

In Shiraz we visited the Jewish community and found it grim indeed.

These people were living in one-room huts, without sanitation. There were not even doors or windows—just holes cut in the walls so that people could go in and out, and to admit a little light. As a rule, there was a little charcoal brazier in one corner for cooking and heating. Bedding was rolled up in the daytime and covered the floor at night.

From Iran we went on to Israel, where we spent Easter week. Since my return I have tried to analyze what makes the difference in atmosphere between Israel and its Arab neighbors and the great country of Iran.

I think the greatest difference lies in an atmosphere in Israel that one does not find in many other countries. Its young people may be chiefly responsible for it. They are excited by the dream of building a country and they work at it with gusto, with all their strength, with exhilaration and a kind of exaltation that cannot fail to impress the visitor. Difficult as conditions are, long and hard as the people labor, they do it in an atmosphere of faith and hope and conviction. It is the absence of these qualities in the other countries that is so disheartening. For men cannot live without hope. If it is not engendered by their own convictions and desires, it can easily be fired from without, and by the most meretricious and empty of promises.

I was much amused on my return from Israel to discover that wherever I lectured for the next few months people appeared to be less interested in world affairs than they were in the fate of a camel that Nina had bought in Israel but which we were unable to bring into the country, at the orders of the Department of Agriculture. Eventually, the camel was given to a poor Bedouin.

What I had learned on these two trips was much on my mind when I returned home. Why, I wondered, were we not more successful in helping the young nations and those in transition to become established along democratic lines? Why was it that the Russians were doing so much better? The answer can be oversimplified and an oversimplification is false and misleading. But part of the answer, and I thought a major part, was that Russia had trained its young people to go out into the world, to carry their services and skills to backward and underdeveloped countries, to replace the missing doctors and teachers, the scientists and technicians; above all, to fill the vacant civil service jobs, prepared not only by training for the job itself but by a complete briefing in the customs, habits, traditions and trend of thought of the people, to understand them and deal with them. Where they go, of course, they take with them their Marxist training, thinking and system.

And our young Americans? Were they being prepared to take their faith in democracy to the world along with their skills? Were they learning the language and the customs and the history of these new peoples? Did they understand how to deal with them, not according to their own ideas but according to the ideas of the people they must learn to know if they were to reach them at all? Had they acquired an ability to live and work among peoples of different religion and race and color, without arrogance and without prejudice?

Here, I believe, we have fallen down badly. In the past few years I have grasped at every opportunity to meet with the young, to talk with college students, to bring home as strongly as I can to even young children in the lower grades our responsibility for each other, our need to understand and respect each other. The future will be determined by the young and there is no more essential task today, it seems to me, than to bring before them once more, in all its brightness, in all its splendor and beauty, the American Dream, lest we let it fade, too concerned with ways of earning a living or impressing our neighbors or getting ahead or finding bigger and more potent ways of destroying the world and all that is in it.

No single individual, of course, and no single group has an exclusive claim to the American Dream. But we have all, I think, a single vision of what it is, not merely as a hope and an aspiration but as a way of life, which we can come ever closer to attaining in its ideal form if we keep shining and unsullied our purpose and our belief in its essential value.

That we have sometimes given our friends and our enemies abroad a shoddy impression of the Dream cannot be denied, much as we would like to deny it. *The Ugly American*, impressive as it was, struck me as being exaggerated. True, one of the first American ambassadors I ever met in an Eastern country was appallingly like the title character in the novel. There are doubtless many others, too many others; men who accept—and seek—the position of representative of their government abroad with no real interest or respect for the country they go to, and no real interest or respect for the image of their country which they present to other people.

Such men buy their position by gifts of money to their party or seek them because of the glamorous social life they may lead in exotic places.

"Oh, you must go there. You'll have a wonderful time. And the polo is top-notch."

They often do not know the language of the country; they are not familiar with its government or its officials; they are not interested in its customs
or its point of view.

The Russians—and I say it with shame—do this better. They are trained
in the language, history, customs and ways of life of a country before they
go to it. They do not confine themselves to official entertaining but make
a point of meeting and knowing and establishing friendly relations with
people of all sorts, in every class of society, in every part of the country.

When we look at the picture of Russian greed in swallowing one satellite
nation after another and contrast it with the picture of American generosity in giving food, clothing, supplies, technical and financial assistance,
with no ulterior motive in acquiring new territory, it is stupid and tragic
waste that the use of incompetent representatives should undo so much
useful work, so great an expense, so much in the way of materials of every
kind.

Of course, what the Russians have accomplished in training their young
people for important posts in the underdeveloped countries—which, I
must repeat, may affect the future course of these countries—has been
done by compulsion. That's the rub. For what we must do is to achieve the
same results on a voluntary basis. We do not say to our young people:
"You must go here and take such a job." But we can show them that
where we fail the Russians will win, by default. We can show them the
importance of acquiring the kind of training that will make them useful
and honorable representatives of their country wherever they may go
abroad.

Perhaps the new frontier today is something more than the new revolution in textiles and methods and speed and goods. It is the frontier of men's
minds. But we cannot cast an enduring light on other men's minds unless
the light in our own minds burns with a hard, unquenchable flame.

One form of communication we have failed abjectly in: the teaching of
languages. Most school children have several years of inadequate teaching
in one language or another. I say inadequate because the study of a
language, after all, is inadequate if one cannot learn to read and write it,
to speak and to understand it. During World War II the government
found a simplified and most effective method of teaching such difficult
languages as Japanese and Chinese to American GIs. In a matter of weeks
they had mastered more of the language than formerly they would have
acquired in the same number of years. And yet in our schools the old,

cumbersome, unproductive methods are still in use.

It seems to me so obvious that it should not need to be said that we must increase and improve the teaching of languages to our young people, who will otherwise find themselves crippled and sorely handicapped in dealing with people of foreign races and different cultures.

These are things our children should be told. These are the conditions they are going to have to meet. They ought to be made to understand exactly what competition they will encounter, why they must meet it, how they can meet it best. Yet I rarely find, in talking with them, that they have been given the slightest inkling of the meaning of the Soviet infiltration of other countries, or that the future the Soviets are helping to build is the one with which they will have to contend. I rarely find that anyone has suggested that our own young people should have any preparation whatsoever to cope with the problems that are impending.

That is why, in the course of the past several years, I have fitted into my schedule, wherever I could, occasions to talk with the young. Sometimes they come up to Hyde Park by the busload to ask questions or to discuss problems. Sometimes I talk at their schools or colleges.

Last year, in co-operation with Brandeis University, I experimented with a new idea. I agreed to do a series of nine television programs, which were then sold to education television stations throughout the country. It worked so well that this year I have agreed to do ten programs.

In addition to this, I lectured to a class given by Dr. Fuchs on international law and international organization at Brandeis. There were only thirteen in the class, all students who hoped to go into foreign service either for business or for the government, five of them students from foreign countries. I was a little staggered by this assignment, as I felt sure that many of these young people were better versed in questions of international organization than I was. But at least I could discuss with them the tangled problems of foreign politics.

This, of course, was a specialialized sort of lecture course, and I found it interesting and stimulating, as I have always found teaching. But what I would have preferred to say to these young people was something like the following:

Today our government and the governments of most of the world are primarily concerned—obsessed—by one idea: defense. But what is real defense and how is it obtained? Of course, a certain amount of military defense is necessary. But there comes a point where you must consider what can be done on an economic and cultural basis.

It seems to me that, in terms of atomic warfare, we should henceforth have a small professional army of men who have voluntarily chosen military service as an obligation to their country. But what then? What about the hundreds of thousands of young people who leave school every year, either from high school or from college? Are they, from now on, to have no participation in contributing to the welfare of their country?

Far from it. As matters stand, we draft young men into the service, train them until they are useful, and then let them go. This seems to me monstrous waste.

It has long been my personal conviction that every young person should be given some basic training that might, eventually, be useful to his country. As I thought about it, it seemed to me that this could be handled either in school or at college, and instead of calling all young men up for compulsory military service, we could offer an alternative along these lines:

Whether you finish college, or high school, you may, if you do not want to spend two years of compulsory military training, decide what country you would like to spend two years in. You will be given two years of basic training, either during school hours or in the evenings. If you want to go, say, to Africa or to other underdeveloped countries, you will, from the age of fifteen to seventeen, be taught the language, the history, the geography, the economic background of the country. You will be prepared to take with you a skill, or be trained for the most crying need in many transition nations, to fill the civil service jobs that Russia is now so rapidly filling. Or, if you are preparing for a profession, you may make use of that.

New industries are needed in these countries, there are technical needs in almost all areas. The economy has to be bolstered in countless ways. New techniques are required in agriculture. And nearly all of these countries need teachers badly.

I was greatly interested and pleased to hear that Chester Bowles's son turned down a scholarship at Oxford University to go to Nigeria, where he plans to teach in high school for two years.

What is saving Ghana today is that Sir Robert Jackson remained in the country after the withdrawal of Great Britain. He is using all his great experience and intelligence on behalf of the people as economic adviser to the Volta River Project. He is also being aided by his brilliant wife, the famous economist, Barbara Ward.

For people in young nations, which are still in a transition stage and setting up governments, such help could be more valuable than a large standing army or economic aid, particularly when in the new country there are few people capable of administering it effectively.

As I have said, this training and use of our young has been long in my mind. Wherever and whenever I could I have advocated it. Recently with the announcement of the Peace Corps, it appears that a similar plan will at least have a fair trial. Some of our young people will be given the opportunity to take up the slack in underdeveloped countries, and to bring our skills and our attitudes and our principles to them as free men. I am delighted that this has been done, and am hopeful that it may prove to be one of the most fruitful ways we have found of sharing our American Dream with others.

President Kennedy has initiated a Peace Corps through which he hopes the ideals of young, and perhaps not so young, Americans may be expressed to people throughout the world, particularly in the underdeveloped countries which need help at the present time. The methods of choosing people and arranging with the recipient governments are still being worked out. Colleges and universities that have programs for exchange will be aided where their programs seem to be worthwhile. This will be an educational job for Americans, giving them an opportunity to get a better idea of the world in which they live and at the same time will show a spirit of service which is prevalent in this generation of Americans but which has not had great opportunity so far for expression.

A suggestion has also been made for a younger U.S. group of older high-school age to work on forestry and soil conservation throughout the U.S. This would seem to me of great value but as yet this is not even in the active planning stage as far as I know, though I hope it will materialize before very long.

I have said that the Russians have accomplished by compulsion what we must accomplish voluntarily. But there is one element of this Russian training that I have neglected to mention. I don't see why I neglected it, because it is of paramount importance. They have taught their young to feel that they are needed, that they are important to the welfare of their country. I think that one of the strongest qualities in every human being is a need to feel needed, to feel essential, to feel important. Too often our own youngsters do not feel that they are really essential to their country, or to the scheme of things. We have not had enough imagination to show them how very much we need every one of them to make us the kind of country that we can be.

In Austria, a short time ago, Mr. Khrushchev said that he expected a Communist world in his lifetime. We have no time to waste.

All this, you may say, is far from the American Dream. Not at all. The American Dream can no more remain static than can the American nation. What I am trying to point out is that we cannot any longer take an old approach to world problems. They aren't the same problems. It isn't the same world. We must not adopt the methods of our ancestors; instead, we must emulate that pioneer quality in our ancestors that made them attempt new methods for a New World.

For instance, we are pioneers today in the field of automation. There is no possibility of holding back automation, but we can, at least, profit by the mistakes of the past in dealing with it. The industrial revolution, which began in Great Britain, put machinery into the mills and threw out the people to starve.

Eventually Great Britain was much better off as a result of the industrial revolution. But, because it was not prepared to cope with it at the time, a far-reaching and unexpected thing happened. Out of the industrial revolution and its abuses came Karl Marx.

With automation we have a new situation and on the way we cope with it will depend the attitude of the world. Here we are the undisputed leaders. But we cannot handle it without planning. We must learn to foresee results before we act. We cannot afford, today, to throw a lot of people out of work without making some provision for them. True, the conscience of the people is different now; we would no longer sit by and let people starve and die. But if we are going to cope successfully, if we are to make this new technique a blessing to society and not a disaster, we have to make plans. We cannot blunder along, hoping things "will come out all right." Government, industry, labor, all these must use their best brains, must be aware of and accept their full responsibility for the situation.

With decreased work hours there will come more leisure. What is to be done with it? Masses of people now working at machines, without any opportunity for self-improvement or bettering their condition, will be afforded new opportunities. But, unless we give them a background of education, they will not know how to make use of this opportunity for advancement. If they have no capacity for development, and no enterprise beyond sitting glued to a television screen, they will deteriorate as human beings, and we will have a great mass of citizens who are of no value to themselves or to their country or to the world.

It is a new industrial revolution that we are pioneering. The eyes of the world are on us. If we do it badly we will be criticized and our way of life downgraded. If we do it well we can become a beacon light for the future of the world.

And now, I see, my new concept of the American Dream is only the old one, after all. For, while those who started our government and fought for our right to be free may have thought in Old World terms to some extent, they, too, had a conception of the Dream being universal. The Thomas Jeffersons thought of education not for a handful, not even for their own country alone, but looked forward to the day when everyone, everywhere, would have the same opportunities. Today we have achieved so much more, in many ways, than our ancestors imagined that sometimes we forget that they dreamed not just for us but for mankind.

The American Dream is never entirely realized. If many of our young people have lost the excitement of the early settlers who had a country to explore and develop, it is because no one remembers to tell them that the world has never been so challenging, so exciting; the fields of adventure and new fields to conquer have never been so limitless. There is still unfinished business at home, but there is the most tremendous adventure in bringing the peoples of the world to an understanding of the American Dream. In this attempt to understand, to give a new concept of the relationships of mankind, there is open to our youngsters an infinite field of exciting adventure where the heart and the mind and the spirit can be engaged.

Perhaps the older generation is often to blame with its cautious warning: "Take a job that will give you security, not adventure." But I say to the young: "Do not stop thinking of life as an adventure. You have no security unless you can live bravely, excitingly, imaginatively; unless you can choose a challenge instead of a competence."

Milestones

IN OCTOBER of 1959 I reached my seventy-fifth birthday. It was a busy day, as most of mine are, with little time for introspection. Nonetheless, it was, in a way, a milestone, and I found myself looking back along the way I had come, trying to get a long-range view of the journey I had made and, if I could, to evaluate it. I wanted, if possible, to draw a kind of balance sheet, to formulate for myself the objectives I had had and to estimate how far I had achieved them.

This kind of introspection is one in which I rarely indulge. At times, of course, it is valuable in throwing light into dark places, but its danger is that one may easily tend to become self-absorbed in one's voyage of discovery and self-analysis.

People still ask me frequently how I planned my career and what over-all objective I had in mind. Actually I never planned a career, and what basic objective I had, for many years, was to grasp every opportunity to live and experience life as deeply, as fully, and as widely as I possibly could. It seemed to me stupid to have the gift of life and not use it to the utmost of one's ability.

I was not a gifted person but I was always deeply interested in every manifestation of life, good or bad. I never let slip an opportunity to increase my knowledge of people and conditions. Everything was grist to my mill: not only the things I saw but the people I met. Indeed, I could not express adequately the debt I owe to the friends who taught me so much about the world I live in. I had really only three assets: I was keenly interested, I accepted every challenge and every opportunity to learn more, and I had great energy and self-discipline.

As a result, I have never had to look for interests to fill my life. If you are

410

interested, things come to you, they seem to gravitate your way without your lifting a hand. One thing leads to another and another, and as you gain in knowledge and in experience new opportunities open up before you.

Before my seventy-fifth birthday something else had happened that forced me to turn back and look at my past life rather than to look ahead, as I prefer doing. Dore Schary wrote *Sunrise at Campobello*, a play that dealt with my husband's serious illness and his spiritual victory over being crippled. I can remember still the evening when the dramatist read his play to me. And I can remember the strange experience of seeing it performed.

I have been asked countless times how I felt about seeing myself, my children, my husband portrayed on the stage. Did I feel a sense of recognition? Did I say, "But it wasn't like that at all?" Did I feel that my privacy as a woman had been invaded?

The truth is that I watched the play with complete detachment. It is true that when I closed my eyes Ralph Bellamy evoked the very quality and cadence of Franklin's voice and I seemed to hear him speak. But, for the rest, it seemed quite impersonal; it was a play, so far as I personally was concerned, about someone else.

I think if the average person tries to look back he will be unable to remember what he was like, or how he looked, or even, except for major matters, what he did when he was young. He can remember only what he felt. Even in the case of my children I felt that I was watching the actions of quite fictitious characters. One of the best-drawn characters in that play, by the way, was Louis Howe. True, he was less untidy than the Louis I had known, but the lines were excellent and the portrayal was true of the man.

No, it was not by seeing the character of "Eleanor Roosevelt" on the stage that I could come any closer to an analysis of the woman who had now reached seventy-five years of age.

Looking back, I could see that the over-all objective of which many people spoke to me had no existence. It seems hardly human that anyone can plan his life clearly from the beginning, making no allowances for a changing or developing character or for circumstances.

I am sure that my objectives, during those early years at least, were constantly changing. In the beginning, because I felt, as only a young girl can feel it, all the pain of being an ugly duckling, I was not only timid,

I was afraid. Afraid of almost everything, I think: of mice, of the dark, of imaginary dangers, of my own inadequacy. My chief objective, as a girl, was to do my duty. This had been drilled into me as far back as I could remember. Not my duty as I saw it, but my duty as laid down for me by other people. It never occurred to me to revolt. Anyhow, my one over-whelming need in those days was to be approved, to be loved, and I did whatever was required of me, hoping it would bring me nearer to the approval and love I so much wanted.

As a young woman, my sense of duty remained as strict and rigid as it had been when I was a girl, but it had changed its focus. My husband and my children became the center of my life and their needs were my new duty. I am afraid now that I approached this new obligation much as I had my childhood duties. I was still timid, still afraid of doing something wrong, of making mistakes, of not living up to the standards required by my mother-in-law, of failing to do what was expected of me.

As a result, I was so hidebound by duty that I became too critical, too much of a disciplinarian. I was so concerned with bringing up my children properly that I was not wise enough just to love them. Now, looking back, I think I would rather spoil a child a little and have more fun out of it.

It was not until I reached middle age that I had the courage to develop interests of my own, outside of my duties to my family. In the beginning, it seems to me now, I had no goal beyond the interests themselves, in learning about people and conditions and the world outside our own United States. Almost at once I began to discover that interest leads to interest, knowledge leads to more knowledge, the capacity for understanding grows with the effort to understand.

From that time on, though I have had many problems, though I have known the grief and the loneliness that are the lot of most human beings, though I have had to make and still have to make endless adjustments, I have never been bored, never found the days long enough for the range of activities with which I wanted to fill them. And, having learned to stare down fear, I long ago reached the point where there is no living person whom I fear, and few challenges that I am not willing to face.

On that seventy-fifth birthday I knew that I had long since become aware of my over-all objective in life. It stemmed from those early impressions I had gathered when I saw war-torn Europe after World War I. I wanted, with all my heart, a peaceful world. And I knew it could never be achieved on a lasting basis without greater understanding between peoples. It is to these ends that I have, in the main, devoted the past years.

One curious thing is that I have always seen life personally; that is, my interest or sympathy or indignation is not aroused by an abstract cause but by the plight of a single person whom I have seen with my own eyes. It was the sight of a child dying of hunger that made the tragedy of hunger become of such overriding importance to me. Out of my response to an individual develops an awareness of a problem to the community, then to the country, and finally to the world. In each case my feeling of obligation to do something has stemmed from one individual and then widened and become applied to a broader area.

More and more, I think, people are coming to realize that what affects an individual affects mankind. To take an extreme example, one neglected case of smallpox can infect a whole community. This is equally true of the maladjusted child, who may wreak havoc in his neighborhood; of the impoverished, who become either economic burdens or social burdens, and, in any case, are wasted as human beings. Abuses anywhere, however isolated they may appear, can end by becoming abuses everywhere.

I learned, too, while I was groping for more and more effective ways of trying to cope with community and national and world problems, that you can accomplish a great deal more if you care deeply about what is happening to other people than if you say in apathy or discouragement, "Oh, what can I do? What use is one person? I might as well not bother."

Actually I suppose the caring comes from being able to put yourself in the position of the other person. If you cannot imagine, "This might happen to me," you are able to say to yourself with indifference, "Who cares?"

I think that one of the reasons it is so difficult for us, as a people, to understand other areas of the world is that we cannot put ourselves imaginatively in their place. We have no famine. But if we were actually to see people dying of starvation we would care quite a bit. We would be able to think, "These could be my people."

Because of our rather extraordinary advantages, it is difficult for us to understand the other peoples of the world. We started with tremendous national resources. Our very isolation, in those early years, forced us to develop them. Many of the people who settled here had escaped from poverty and want and oppression and lack of opportunity. They wanted to forget their background and they soon did, because the difficulty of travel made it hard for them to go back and refresh their memories. So we grew

out of the past and away from it. Now it would be valuable for us to remember the conditions of that Old World. It would help us to understand
what the poorer countries need and want today.

And this, I suppose, indicates what has happened to me in seventy-five
years. Though now as always it is through individuals that I see and understand human needs, I find that my over-all objectives go beyond individuals
to the fate of mankind. It is within that larger framework that one must
think today if mankind is to survive the threat that hangs, in a mushroom
cloud, over it.

So I come to the larger objective, not mine, except as I am an American,
but America's. It seems to me that America's objective today should be to
try to make herself the best possible mirror of democracy that she can.
The people of the world can see what happens here. They watch us to
see what we are going to do and how well we can do it. We are giving
them the only possible picture of democracy that we can: the picture as
it works in actual practice. This is the only way other peoples can see for
themselves how it works; and can determine for themselves whether this
thing is good in itself, whether it is better than what they have, better
than what other political and economic systems offer them.

Now, while we are a generous nation, giving with a free hand and with
an open heart wherever there is need or suffering (that we can understand,
at least), we have one weakness that, considering our political maturity as
a nation, is rather immature. We continue to expect the world to be grateful to us and to love us. We are hurt and indignant when we do not receive gratitude and love.

Gratitude and love are not to be had for the asking; they are not to
be bought. We should not want to think that they are for sale. What we
should seek, rather than gratitude or love, is the respect of the world. This
we can earn by enlightened justice. But it is rather naïve of us to think that
when we are helping people our action is entirely unselfish. It is not. It
is not unselfish when we vaccinate the public against smallpox. It is a
precautionary measure, but nonetheless good in itself.

Other nations are quite aware that when we try to bolster up their
economy and strengthen their governments and generally help them to
succeed there is a certain amount of self-interest involved. They are inevitably going to be on the lookout to see what we want in return. Consciously we do not want anything, but unconsciously almost anything we
do, as a nation or through the United Nations, is intended to benefit us

or our cause, directly or indirectly. So there is no reason for demanding either gratitude or love.

Our obligation to the world is, primarily, our obligation to our own future. Obviously we cannot develop beyond a certain point unless the other nations develop too. When our natural resources peter out, we must seek them in other countries. We cannot have trade if we are the only solvent nation. We need not only areas from which to buy but areas to which we can sell, and we cannot have this in underdeveloped areas.

We must, as a nation, begin to realize that we are the leaders of the non-Communist world, that our interests at some point all touch the interests of the world, and they must be examined in the context of the interests of the world. This is the price of leadership.

We cannot, indeed, continue to function in a narrow orbit or in a self-enclosed system. We cannot weigh or evaluate even our domestic problems in their own context alone. We no longer have merely domestic issues. Perhaps the best illustration of this is the question I am asked everywhere in the world:

"We hear you Americans pay to keep land out of production because there is too much to eat. Is there no better way to use your ability to produce food than to get rid of it?"

This is a home question; it is literally of vital moment to the millions of starving in the world who look to us. I do not see how we can retain world leadership and yet continue to handle our problems as though they concerned us alone; they concern the world. We feel that a surplus of food is only an embarrassment. We solve it as though only we were concerned. But think of the hungry people and their bitterness as the food that could save their lives is plowed under. To say they think it highly unfair is to put it mildly.

We have never put our best brains to work on the ways we can produce to the maximum, give our farmers a better income, and still employ our surpluses in a way to solve the pressing needs of the world, without upsetting our economy or that of friendly nations who might fear we were giving food to markets they are accustomed to selling to.

We have a great variety of climate, we can grow almost anything we want. Canada can grow only wheat. There need be no clash of interests here.

How have we tried to "solve" matters up to now? We cut our acreage and store the surplus or dump it; we pay our farmers too little to give them an income on a par with that of industrial workers, so we have a dwindling farm population. No one has ever sat down and said, "This is a problem you *must* work out."

It is in ways like these, using our intelligence and our good will and our vast capacity to produce, that we can meet and overcome the Communist threat and prove that democracy has more to give the world.

All this seems like a far cry from my seventy-fifth birthday and yet I find that, as I have grown older, my personal objectives have long since blended into my public objectives. I have, of course, realized that I cannot continue indefinitely the strenuous life I now lead, the constant traveling from state to state, from country to country.

What, then? Then, I thought, even if I must relinquish much of my traveling, perhaps there is a way in which I can still reach people with things that it seems important for them to hear. The most practical way of doing this is through a radio or television program. My radio and television agent shook his head.

"You are too controversial a figure," he told me. "The sponsors would be afraid of you. Some of them feel so strongly about you that they believe the public would not buy any product on whose program you might appear."

I remembered then that some years earlier the head of the Red Cross had been afraid to accept a donation for fear that my participation would drive away other subscribers!

It is startling to realize that one is so deeply, fanatically disliked by a number of people. And yet, while I weigh as honestly as I can their grounds for disapproval, when I feel that I am right in what I do, it seems to me that I cannot afford, as a self-respecting individual, to refuse to do a thing merely because it will make me disliked or bring down a storm of criticism on my head. I often feel that too many Americans today tend to reject the thing, however right they believe it to be, that they want to do because they fear they will be unpopular or will find themselves standing alone instead of in the comfortable anonymity of the herd.

As a result, when I believe, after weighing the evidence, that what I am doing is right I go ahead and try as hard as I can to dismiss from my mind the attitude of those who are hostile. I don't see how else one can live.

One day my radio agent appeared, looking very much surprised, to say that he had had an offer for me to do television commercials for an organization that sold margarine.

"I know this isn't the kind of thing you had in mind," he pointed out, "but if a conservative firm feels that you can sell their product I think you should at least try it. It may break the ice for you."

I thought it over. I had to face the fact that I would be bitterly criticized for doing commercials. On the other hand, if this was a field I wanted to open up I ought at least to see whether I could do it, no matter how disagreeable the reaction of many people might be.

So at length I agreed. The only stipulation I made was that, outside of selling the product, I should be allowed to say one thing of my own that I thought had value. So I reminded the audience that there were hungry people in the world.

There were, of course, as many disagreeable comments as I had expected, but the program went all right and the sponsors discovered that, after all, I did not prevent people from buying their product!

This year (1960-61) I am going to introduce a program of refugee stories, as my participation in the Refugee Year work of the United Nations.

The purpose of this refugee organization, now headed by Mr. Lint, is to try to reduce the population of the refugee camps in Europe; to wipe them out if that is humanly possible. Ten years is too long for these people to have lived in camps, stateless and with no solution in sight for their problem. There are children who have never known any other life.

Actually a good deal has been accomplished. The number of refugees has been greatly reduced. Where they still remain in camps, an effort has been made to provide permanent housing and to find them jobs. A number of countries have accepted what is called "hard-core cases," those who are blind or have other disabilities. Of course, I am referring now only to the refugee camps in Europe. There are between 800,000 and a million refugees in the Near East and no one knows how many in Hong Kong and in China.

The refugees of the world are a constant and painful reminder of the breakdown of civilization through the stupidity of war. They are its permanent victims. No time in history has known anything like the number of stateless people who have existed or survived the rigors of the past thirty years.

When we closed the work of the United Nations Relief Association in the United Nations we set up the present Commission for Refugees with headquarters in Geneva. No money, however, was set aside for this. Its function is to see that these people are given papers which will allow them to get work, to make life more possible for them, though they are still stateless.

Mr. Lint discovered that there were still many who needed financial help and he requested aid for a fund which he could use for this purpose. Every year he comes to the United States to get further funds to meet these needs.

In the American Association of the United Nations we were willed a considerable sum of money which was to be applied to alleviating the conditions of refugees. We had to set up a group to handle this, and, of course, we had to have the consent of the high commissioner to turn the money over to Mr. Lint for this purpose. Before long even this ugly scar of war may be healed.

Interspersed among my other activities, traveling and lecturing, work with the A.A.U.N., radio and television appearances, I continue to entertain a number of interesting people who visit Hyde Park from time to time, sometimes to leave flowers at my husband's grave or to visit the library, sometimes to come as guests to my cottage, either through arrangements made with the State Department or independently.

Perhaps the most confusing time was in September, 1959, when the visits of Princess Beatrice of Holland and Premier Khrushchev almost overlapped. The little princess came at the time of the Hudson-Champlain celebration. Like most foreign visitors she had been feted and had listened to speeches and had attended functions until she was exhausted.

When she reached my cottage she was very tired. There was an hour free before dinner, I told her, and she said wearily to her lady in waiting, "Please open my bed."

Young as she was, she had been living under the strictest protocol and had been entertained, for the most part, by much older people, dignified statesmen, and so forth.

There was, I assured her, going to be no protocol. I planned a buffet supper, with people waiting on themselves and seated at small tables, and my guests for her were some boys from Harvard and my granddaughter, who was about her own age.

Later my granddaughter told me of their conversation. The princess told them that she was going to college and how much she valued the time there. She had even regretted losing a month from college because of her trip to America. This was the last time in her life that she would be able to live naturally with other people.

She told them, too, what difficulties arose for young people in her position. There were so few people left whom they could marry.

She was a very gentle, simple person, very sweet and simply brought up.

On the morning of the day she left Mr. Khrushchev and his wife were to arrive on their first visit to the United States. The princess and her party—we had sixteen for breakfast—left at nine in the morning. We were to feed an unknown number of members of Mr. Khrushchev's party and tables were set up and ready for them, all managed by my faithful and capable couple.

Never, I think, have I seen anything like the number of state police who were called out by our anxious government to protect Mr. Khrushchev. When I reached the library, where I was to meet him, they were lined up, side by side, all the length of the driveway and parking place. When we returned to my cottage, the dirt road which leads from the highway to the house had men stationed every few feet all the way. They had even suggested the possibility of my trees hiding malefactors who could climb them to shoot at the Communist leader. But I put my foot down at having my trees destroyed.

Anyhow Mr. Khrushchev, his pleasant and simple wife, and his entourage arrived very late at the cottage, so late they had time for nothing but a glance around and a hasty bun, which Mr. Khrushchev snatched from a table to sustain him while they rushed back to New York for his speech at the United Nations.

No shots were fired, no unpleasantness of any kind occurred, and the piles of uneaten food were disposed of by the hordes of state police. It was all rather silly.

Before his arrival there had been much speculation about what Mr. Khrushchev would get out of his visit to the United States. I don't see how, in that hasty breathless fashion, any preconception could be altered. Perhaps if he had had any chance to speak to the farmers in Iowa at leisure, he could have obtained an effective, firsthand impression of the American people, of their independence, self-respect and self-reliance. But, being hurried along, he naturally could not be expected to get a very fair impression.

But even in that rushed, cursory visit, he must have realized that we are not ripe for revolution. He must have seen for himself that while we have great prosperity we are not entirely materialistic. At least, he *may* have seen these things. I don't know. I do think, however, that if foreign leaders could visit our country quietly and on their own, they would form a much sounder impression of it than through these exhausting official receptions, parades and endless speeches.

So an account of my seventy-fifth birthday ends, in spite of me, with a discussion of foreign affairs. There is such a big, muddled world, so much to be done, so much that *can* be done if we increase in depth of understanding, in learning to care, in thinking of hunger not as an abstraction but as one empty stomach, in having a hospitable mind, open like a window to currents of air and to light from all sides.

Forty-two

The Democratic Convention of 1960

AT THE END of the presidential campaign of 1956, in which I had worked
to the point of exhaustion for Adlai Stevenson, I determined that never
again would I take any personal part in a political campaign.

So much for my firm intentions! My involvement in the 1960 campaign
came about almost inadvertently. It grew out of a controversy in the
Democratic party in New York State, where boss rule was attempting to
replace the voice of the voters. The fact that my own party was involved
in this particular case did not absolve me from feeling that the situation
was intolerable. The morality of a party must grow out of the conscience
and the participation of the voters. We cannot condemn the bosses as
long as we sit back supinely and fail to wrest power from their hands and
restore it to the voters themselves. In order to function at all, democracy
depends upon the participation of the people in their government. It
cannot survive by boss rule.

I do not believe that the people of this country would submit passively
to boss rule and meekly abdicate their own rights and privileges if they
were clearly aware of the situation and understood the workings of the
machinery which makes bosses possible. Certainly the first step is to
start not at the top but at the bottom of the pyramid and curb the power
of the local city and state leaders of the political machine who, unchallenged, become the party bosses and, in a very real sense, our bosses.

The core of boss rule, naturally, is patronage. Many Americans have
little idea of how the machinery of politics is handled. They have too
little sense of responsibility in regard to its functioning. And yet boss rule
can exist only where there is widespread indifference.

"But what can we do about it?" people ask me. "I know it is disgrace

421

ful, but we're helpless to do anything."

The answer to that, of course, is that we are not in the least helpless. We can always do something if we care enough. It was in protest against the bosses of the Republican party machine—Hanna and Platt—that Theodore Roosevelt started his Bull Moose party.

One curious feature about political reform is that so many people feel it is "disloyal" to attempt to rectify the abuses in one's own party. And yet it is obvious that political morality is dependent upon the awakened conscience and private morality of the voters. Such "disloyalty" is simply an evidence of loyalty to principle.

Two years ago, at Buffalo, both the governor and the mayor of New York said they preferred a certain candidate for the U. S. Senate. Carmine De Sapio, the boss of the Democratic machinery in New York, calmly turned them down and took it upon himself to name his own candidate. The result was that he defeated the party's chance of victory by forcing ʋpon the voting public an unacceptable candidate.

Because of this highhanded action, in March, 1959, Senator Herbert Lehman, Thomas Finletter and I signed a statement backing reform groups in New York City. We declared that the people were weary of bossism.

The response of the people was swift. They set up a clamor to be heard as citizens with a right to a voice in their own government. Once started, the revolt began to grow and it is still growing and gaining strength. The result was that the regular party organization discovered it would go down in defeat unless the reform groups threw in their support and worked with it. But the reform groups made clear that, unless they were free of all control from the local organization, it would not have their support. The only way to get rid of one's chains is not by complaint or lamentation. It is by knocking them off.

Now, while I was determined to take no further part in presidential campaigns, I was stirred by reading a statement made by two of our leading historians, Henry Commager and Arthur Schlesinger, Jr., who declared that, while Adlai Stevenson was undoubtedly the best candidate for the Presidency, they did not think he could be nominated and consequently they were going to support John Kennedy.

It seemed absurd to accept anyone as second best until you had done all you could to get the best. For my part, I believed the best ticket would be Stevenson and Kennedy, with the strong chance that the latter would become president at a later time.

Having made this statement, I was immediately heralded by the Stevenson backers. Nonetheless, I did not intend to go to the Democratic convention. Three of my sons were strongly backing Senator Kennedy, and it seemed pointless for me to appear on the opposite side.

However, I did not agree with the people who said Mr. Stevenson could not be nominated because he had twice been defeated. His defeat, I felt, was a result of running against the hero worship of President Eisenhower, a factor which would not exist in this campaign. I felt, too, that there was no one who could serve us better in the present crisis of world affairs or who had earned higher regard and respect among other nations.

I was finally persuaded to go to the convention, where I was distressed to find that once again I was in opposition to Mr. Truman's political stand, and I made a seconding speech for Mr. Stevenson's nomination.

The result not only of the Democratic but of the Republican convention has been such that observers in both parties were left with an acute feeling of dismay. I am not concerned at this point with the merits of either candidate. What I found, and what numbers of Americans found, horrifying was the fact that the choice of a presidential candidate, the fundamental and basic right of every American citizen, was no longer a result of public thinking or an expression of the wishes of the majority of the people of the country; that, instead, it represented the decision of the party bosses.

This kind of thing, of course, should not be allowed to go on. Our political conventions, as they now function, are as obsolete as outmoded machinery. Our present need is to evolve a new method by which the voice of the people is heard and they again arrive at their own choice of the candidates who are to lead them and to carry out their wishes in government. We cannot again permit the political bosses to dictate who the nominees are to be.

The working of smooth political machines, such as we observed in the two recent conventions, is not new. It is only an intensification of a process that has been going on for years. But now that we have seen it clearly, the time has come to say, as many people are saying, "This is intolerable. We cannot permit it to go on."

How was it possible that in the 1960 conventions the choice of candidates was made without regard to the wishes of the American citizens? The answer lies in boss rule. The effect of local organizations on the choice of a presidential candidate is, unless checked, a strangle hold.

It works like this. The delegates to a convention are appointed by the state machinery. Generally a caucus is held of the delegates of each state and they are told that the leaders have decided they are to support a certain candidate. And why do the delegates supinely do as they are told? Because most of them hold some kind of public office and do not want to risk their positions. It is the rare delegate who, like Senator Lehman, can say, "I will not serve unless I am given complete freedom to vote as my conscience dictates."

Having been committed to the machine, the delegate can only carry out instructions. He remains deaf to the voice of his constituents. He may receive thousands of telegrams favoring another candidate but he disregards them. It is not the voice of the people but the voice of the machine boss that he heeds.

During the 1960 Democratic convention in Los Angeles, a large box of telegrams was handed to Mr. Prendergast. He opened one or two, saw they were in favor of Adlai Stevenson, and threw the box away.

It must be obvious to anyone who attended or watched either or both of the conventions of 1960 that if the delegates chosen cannot represent what they consider to be the majority opinion of the people of their district they might as well stay at home. The convention could, as efficiently, be attended solely by the two or three high-ranking bosses from each state.

All that would be lacking would be the demonstrations, which are, as a rule, artificial displays of enthusiasm arranged for by the machines or the candidates themselves. These demonstrations are largely controlled, in their extent, noise and length of time, by the National Committeemen, who allot to each candidate the number of tickets to which they feel he is entitled, according to his apparent strength. This choice rests upon the decision of a single man.

It was rumored at the 1960 Democratic convention that Mr. Kennedy's group, which was undoubtedly the strongest, received a far greater number of passes than those assigned to Mr. Stevenson's headquarters.

This situation, of course, was greatly simplified in the Republican convention at Chicago, for there the people were offered no choice of candidates for the Presidency; as, indeed, had been the case with Mr. Nixon's vice-presidency in 1956.

It has been many years since, in Baltimore, I attended my first political convention for the nomination of a president. At that time I felt, and I feel still, that to select the standard-bearer of a party in an atmosphere of noise, bands and balloons, to the accompaniment of the manufactured and synthetic excitement of parades, is to strip one of the most important features of our system of its dignity and meaning. The circus has almost overshadowed the serious purpose and far-reaching effect of these deliberations. One can imagine, in horror, the effect of accompanying debates in the Senate or in the House by interpolations of noise and music from the partisans of either side of the question.

The time has come to restore the choice of a presidential candidate to the people themselves. How can this be done? One possibility has occurred to me. Instead of continuing to leave the selection of the men who, in turn, select the candidate, in the hands of the city and state committees, we should elect the delegates ourselves. The simplest and most direct procedure would be, at the primary nearest the convention, to elect the delegates to attend that convention and to have the names of all the presidential aspirants listed on the ballot. Each voter could check the name of the candidate of his choice. The delegates to the convention would be required to vote for the candidate with the majority vote in that primary.

Of course, beyond the first ballot, it might not be practicable to hold the delegate to the original choice. An occasion might arise in which there would be a deadlock and it would be impossible to come to any definite conclusion.

The answer to this seems to me to lie in the caucus held by each state delegation. In the past this, too often, has resulted in the issuing of definite instructions. If the law required a secret ballot, so that the delegates could be free to vote, as all Americans are presumed free to vote, according to their consciences, it would be possible to achieve a system that would come much closer to reflecting the wishes of the people of the United States than our present one does.

This, of course, is only a suggestion. Certainly any method would require considerable elasticity because of the various state laws. The important thing is that the whole concept of the rules governing a convention system should come before the American people to be reassessed and discussed.

Another outmoded piece of machinery in the selection of the President is the presidential primary as it now functions. The chief trouble here is that the candidates spend their time running down their rivals in the same party. The net result is to furnish a large amount of ammunition to the opposition party in the campaign. An example is the Republican use, in 1960 campaign propaganda, of everything Senator Johnson had said about Senator Kennedy in the preconvention days.

I have been talking from the point of view of a Democrat, because I am more familiar with their tactics. But it would appear that the same tactics are used in both parties. In both cases, one had the feeling that the convention did not greatly matter. The votes had been sewed up beforehand.

There is time ahead to re-examine our machinery on state and city as well as national level, to find a method to ensure that each of us can make his voice heard as independent and responsible voters. We can do it if we want to.

As Adlai Stevenson said to some of his family and friends in his living room in Los Angeles, during the hush that followed the realization of his defeat at the Democratic convention, "Cheer up. All is not lost."

Looking back on that turbulent—but prearranged—convention, I am heartened by the memory of the warm spontaneous outburst of genuine feeling and tribute and love that greeted Mr. Stevenson when he entered the hall to take his seat. Even though the delegates had been committed in advance, there was no stifling this tribute to a great statesman and a magnificent citizen.

For him, modest as he is, lacking in vanity, so incapable of self-aggrandizement that he refused to lift his hand to seek the nomination, it must have been a heart-lifting moment.

One factor of the convention that I had cause to remember afterwards was that no one knows when a television camera is turned his way, as the cameras are constantly swinging around. Unless you are constantly aware that you are under scrutiny you are apt to be caught at unexpected and embarrassing moments.

Later I received many letters from people who said they sympathized with my tears after Adlai's defeat. As a matter of fact, it was not tears I was having wiped off my cheek but someone's lipstick.

Because the plain-clothes men were afraid that when I went up to second Adlai's nomination I would be caught in a mob, they circled me about. They were very nice and very solicitous and treated me as though I were made of Dresden china. In fact, they practically carried me, with the result that we moved so slowly I thought we would never cover the ground from one side of the arena to another.

The plain-clothes men held my elbows firmly at every step. Now, this happens to be one of the few things which indicate to me that I am supposed to be unable to navigate in the ordinary manner at my age and I resent it very much. Consequently, I kept trying to get away from and shake off their helpful hands. Presumably this showed up on television, because I received a number of letters from people who wrote to assure me that I had behaved in a most rude and disagreeable manner.

I was also criticized for coming in and receiving an ovation while Governor Collins was making his excellent speech, but, because of the noise, I was quite unaware of the fact that anyone was speaking. Sometimes, even now, I am still taken aback to discover how closely one's most trivial movements are followed in this day of television. It seems as though one can find privacy only within the silence of one's own mind.

Forty-three

Unfinished Business

"YOU REALLY must slow down." This is becoming the repeated refrain of my children and all of my friends. But how can I when the world is so challenging in its problems and so terribly interesting? I think I must have a good deal of my uncle Theodore Roosevelt in me because I enjoy a good fight and I could not, at any age, really be contented to take my place in a warm corner by the fireside and simply look on.

Early in July of 1960 I went to Washington for briefings at the State Department in preparation for the meeting in Warsaw, Poland, of the World Federation of United Nations Associations.

Of course, our American Association for the United Nations is not controlled by our government, but we always ask to be told of any situation that may exist in a country to which we are to send delegates. Such background information helps us to be better-equipped citizens and better able to carry on discussions with the other United Nations associations that may be present.

This trip, which I made in September, was my first to Poland and I was able to visit two cities, Warsaw, where the meeting was held, and Cracow. No cities could have been more dissimilar. Warsaw was probably one of the most completely destroyed cities in World War II. What the Germans failed to destroy by shelling they systematically burned. Almost nothing was left standing. The people were driven out into the woods and the city was demolished, stone by stone.

When the Russians finally liberated the area, there was some discussion about rebuilding. After all, there was nothing to start from. Perhaps it would be better to pick another location and begin from scratch, but at length it was decided to rebuild on the same site.

428

Because the mayor felt that the people should have roots, an attempt was made, as far as possible, to build a replica of the old city. An ancient square was reproduced almost exactly. They rebuilt the old church and put back the statues. Old stones were salvaged from the rubble to be used again. On the whole, it has been very well done, for while it is a modern city, the atmosphere of the old city has been re-created successfully. True, there is one horrible building, designed by a Russian architect, almost an exact copy of the hideous University of Moscow, though not quite so large.

Cracow, on the other hand, was left untouched by the war and has retained all its Old World charm, its typically Polish features, oddly but delightfully interspersed with traces of the influences brought there by Italian alliances. In contrast, near Cracow there is one of the new steel cities, on much the same pattern as the steel cities of Russia, signifying the opening up of a balanced economy, partly industrial, partly rural, and therefore a big step forward, as it brings the people of Poland the hope of greater prosperity.

Such hope is grasped eagerly, for it is evident on many sides that Poland is still a very poor country, and the cost of all this rebuilding has been a tremendous drain on the economy.

There are the inevitable shortages of goods. One Polish housewife told me that, while there are few things for which they have to queue up, still meat is always hard to find and is unprocurable on Mondays. Prices are high, on the whole, and I think it is safe to say in general that goods are of poor quality.

The biggest expense, in Poland as in Russia, is for shoes. Clothes are expensive and the material is so poor that wardrobes have constantly to be replaced. A young American woman, married to a Pole, said that her Polish friends simply could not believe her when she told them the suit she wore was six years old. Material like that was unobtainable in Poland at any price.

Nonetheless, one is conscious of the fact that the Polish people live with vitality and enthusiasm. Certainly, I could not have met with more hospitality and solicitude. One cannot help liking the Poles, whether ministers of state or casual workers whom one has an opportunity to meet and chat with.

It seemed to me, indeed, that Poland might well serve as a much-needed bridge of understanding between the Western and Eastern nations if—

and that is the stumbling block—if it succeeds in becoming a stable economic country. This, I believe, is possible if its borders are recognized by the Western European community and it is assured of nonaggression from any source. Certainly, such a bridge is going to be essential if we are to build up the beginnings of confidence between East and West. So, perhaps, Poland's own feeling of greater security—if it can be assured by the two opposing areas—may be the opening wedge to help the others to understanding.

However, it has not yet attained the kind of economic stability, let alone the prosperity, which its people hope for and long for. The people in Warsaw, which seems to epitomize Poland, assured me that the peasants were much better off than the city people because they not only had more to eat but did not have to keep up appearances and buy so many clothes and shoes as were necessary in the cities. But when I had an opportunity to drive out into the country and when I looked at the farms and the farm buildings I felt that the life of the peasant had not yet reached a very high level of comfort.

One thing that greatly interested me was that, while Poland is a Communist state on the Soviet pattern, the Polish people have not accepted as many state controls as the Russian people have. This is particularly true of the women. They are not obliged to take their children to nurseries at a certain age and leave them in the hands of the state. As a result, many of them prefer to stay at home and take care of their own children in their own way.

Another field in which compulsion is not so binding as in the Soviet Union is health care. While the pattern of universal medical care has been laid out in Poland, there is no compulsion to make use of it.

The chief thing one is conscious of in Poland is the fear of a possible change of the new boundaries, which might deprive the country of many of the minerals that make it possible to develop an industrial economy.

Remembering Poland's position on the map and her past history, it is easy to understand her uneasiness, but the people are going about their business and there is greater prosperity as the years go by. Even though they are a completely communistic dictatorship, there is a greater sense of freedom among the people than you find in the Soviet Union. In the new steel city there are one school, two kindergartens, and two nurseries per district. The architect told me the nurseries were almost empty. The women do not want to send their babies there for fear they will catch some contagious disease. The attitude that every woman must work is not being enforced in Poland.

But if the women have not supinely followed the communistic pattern, they are, from a long and tragic history, alert and uneasy about the course of events. They asked me over and over, "Do you think your government means to give Germany atomic weapons? We are afraid of Germany, of its growth once more in military strength."

On the whole, that trip to Poland was an interesting and a rewarding one, and it made me see that in these people we could build a bridge of understanding and good will.

In a way, it is, I suppose, ironical that I have visited many Communist-controlled countries without experiencing a single unpleasant incident or encountering one act of hostility or hearing one unfriendly word. Yet here in my own country, earlier in the year, the announcement of a public appearance I was to make in St. Petersburg, Florida, was followed by a telephoned threat that the meeting would be bombed. The threat was, of course, anonymous. Such people are almost invariably cowards.

I assume that the reason for this warning was the fact that I have always been outspoken on my position in regard to the race question, and the man without a name or a face had determined that I should not be heard. Nonetheless, I went. The meeting started and, in spite of the rumors, was very well attended. I was just about to speak when someone stepped to the microphone. The police of St. Petersburg had ordered everyone to leave the building and go some blocks away while a search was made for the bomb.

I assumed, after that, the people would go home, so I was pleased and surprised to find that they had all waited and came back when the building was declared safe. But what touched me most was the gallantry of a little southern woman who sat in the front row. The editor of a St. Petersburg paper told me, with pride, that she was his mother. When she was asked to leave she refused categorically to go home.

"If I am going to be blown up," she declared, "I can't think of any better company to be blown up with."

The meeting proceeded and I made a speech. We all left in peace and quiet, without incident. It confirmed my opinion that when people really mean business they don't notify you beforehand.

Some months later, during the heat of the political campaign, I was to address an audience of schoolteachers in Indianapolis. When I reached the city I was warned that there would be few people in the old tabernacle building where I was scheduled to speak because, several days earlier, a newspaper had printed an editorial urging the teachers to boycott my lecture. Apparently the paper felt that one votes more intelligently in a presidential election if one hears only one side of the story. As my talk, however, dealt with foreign affairs and America's position in world leadership, and did not touch on the campaign, its point did not seem particularly pertinent.

To my great pleasure, I addressed ten thousand teachers that morning. Not even standing room was available in the auditorium. A free citizenry, as I think these two incidents show, is not so easily coerced as a few people would like to believe.

Whether the editorial writer of the Indianapolis paper and the anonymous dealer in threats have learned this lesson I do not know. But it occurs to me that Mr. Khrushchev on his second and stormy visit to the United States must have realized that threats are often ineffective. During that visit he suffered two major defeats in the United Nations Assembly: one when the Asian and African resolution supporting Secretary-General Hammarskjöld's actions in the Congo was passed without the Soviet amendments; second, when the delegate from Ireland was elected to the presidency of the General Assembly instead of the delegate from Czechoslovakia.

I wonder if the people of this country as a whole realize how extraordinary that whole situation was. Mr. Khrushchev arrived in force, bringing with him the heads of the satellite nations, as though they were bogeys to frighten children. His only convert appears to have been Premier Fidel Castro of Cuba.

Mr. Khrushchev's objective was nothing less than the complete destruction of the United Nations, which he would have achieved if his suggestions that Mr. Hammarskjöld be ousted, that the UN be moved to another part of the world, and that a three-man governing board be set up, had been accepted. If he had been successful, the only machinery the world has through which it can work for peace would have been made impotent.

How great a loss, how disastrous a defeat for world peace and understanding and stability that would have been is evidenced these days in what is happening in the United Nations. More and more it is establishing itself as a place where reasonable decisions are being reached. In spite of Mr. Khrushchev's posturing and intemperate language, there does seem to be a gradual approach to an effort to settle international differences in the Congo. This would not have been possible if there had not existed a United Nations where all the representatives could get together to air their differences and find a *modus vivendi*. It is very important that we recognize this.

There was a time, at the outset, when people disillusioned by the League of Nations could scoff at the idea of another world organization designed to work for the peaceful settlement of international disputes. But that time has passed. Today we are seeing more and more clearly that it *can* work, that it *does* work, and it will be increasingly effective if we back it with all our strength. After all, it is because it is an effective organization that Mr. Khrushchev has been so determined to destroy it.

My estimate of Mr. Khrushchev's purpose has been challenged by Professor Golunsky, of the Soviet delegation to the UN. He says I have completely misunderstood Mr. Khrushchev. He points out that five major nations were able to agree on the establishment of the UN. Why, then, could not three heads be set up to carry it further? Obviously, this is ridiculous because, while Mr. Khrushchev's course could be represented by one of the three heads, since satellites are never allowed to differ, the Western countries have many differences and it would be impossible for one head to represent all the divergent opinions. The same thing holds true for the neutralists.

Clearly, colonialism is practically dead. In a very few places there has been some resistance on the part of colonial powers, but the great majority of the nations in Africa which are now becoming free have been granted this freedom by the colonial powers themselves.

If Mr. Khrushchev really believes in the self-determination of peoples, he should allow a free election under United Nations supervision in Estonia, Latvia, Lithuania, Albania, Hungary, Bulgaria, Czechoslovakia, Poland, East Germany—all Russian satellites.

One can well understand the desire of the emerging African states to remain free of the cold war in Europe, and one hopes that this will be possible. They have troubles enough of their own in setting up governments and in finding peaceful accommodations between their own tribes. Nkruma, head of the Ghana delegation, has suggested that an African agency, working under the UN, be responsible for the solutions of the

African situations which are probably going to arise pretty continuously for a long time. This may be a good suggestion, and I think it should be carefully discussed between the African groups themselves and the Secretary-General.

One result of Mr. Khrushchev's attack on the Secretary-General was the tremendous tribute paid to Dag Hammarskjöld in the vote of the UN special session. The adopted resolution passed 70 to 0 with a number of abstentions.

In passing the resolution the General Assembly called on all states to refrain from sending military aid to the Congo, except on request of the UN through the Secretary-General. This, of course, will only be done for a temporary period until the Congolese can work out their own difficulties and set up a central government. After that, it is hoped there will be no further need for UN military forces.

But, while Mr. Khrushchev was sternly rebuffed by the UN and endured a total defeat in his attempt to destroy the organization, one question troubled me then and still troubles me. For it was not all defeat. Mr. Khrushchev banged his shoe on the table, he shouted, he interrupted, he behaved hysterically and with gross bad manners. But this was not a pointless exhibition. There was method in it. By his clowning and his interruptions during Mr. Macmillan's excellent speech, he succeeded in forcing the newspapers to carry so much about his capers that the focus of interest was on him and therefore the impact of Mr. Macmillan's presentation was lessened.

What worried me most was that I did not feel that any one of the Western delegates succeeded in giving a real sense of inspiration about the ideals of democracy. No one said, with the force and the passionate conviction with which Mr. Khrushchev discusses Communism, what we are all about. And yet that is the one thing the Russians most fear, the one thing they cannot combat, the one thing they cannot compete with by production and more production, by space ships and space men. Indeed, it seems apparent to me that the focus has been deliberately thrown on outer space by the Russians to distract attention from our essential differences, to lead us cleverly to try to compete in outer space, to distract attention from the fact that, if people knew the true situation, knew what we stand for, what we live by, there could be no real competition at all.

Some leader must appear from the West who can put into words not the advantages of any form of economy, or any degree of production, but the inspiration of belief in the dignity of man and the value of the human individual. This is the basic difference; this is what we of the West must really fight for, and speak out about in ringing tones.

I would like to say, however, that I do not feel that we, as individuals or as a nation, gain either in dignity or in prestige by refusing to know the people who lead the great opposition to our way of life, by refusing to deal with them in friendship or at least with good manners when possible, or by refusing to learn to understand them as far as we can. To refuse to know or understand the opposition seems to me madness. It reminds me of one of the strangest attitudes during World War I when German was no longer taught in our schools, apparently on the theory that we could deal better with people with whom we could not communicate.

Because on his first visit to America Mr. Khrushchev had paid a most unsatisfactory and fleeting visit to Hyde Park and had been deprived of his lunch, I tried to make up for this situation by asking him to lunch or tea on his second visit. I got a prompt reply saying that he would be glad to come to tea.

On his arrival in this country, of course, he had proceeded to behave badly, trying to destroy the UN because he had not been able to get his own way and had been put out of the Congo just as we had been put out; trying, too, to exploit as far as possible the differences between Castro and the United States government. As a result of these antics, I had written several columns about his efforts to wreck the United Nations, so when the time for the tea arrived, I was rather dreading it.

The only other person I asked was Mrs. Kermit Roosevelt, who said she would pour. Mr. Khrushchev arrived, bringing Mr. Gromyko, Ambassador Mikhail Menshikov, and an interpreter. On the whole, our meeting was outwardly very friendly. He lost no time, however, in telling me about the growing economic strength of the Soviet Union, the increasing amount of iron ore, the fact that in twenty years they would be producing an astronomical amount of steel.

I remarked gently that if you produced that amount of steel you would have to have a market for it. That would require a rise in the standard of living in Russia and China, if they were to accomplish their objective.

As usual, within a couple of days after Mr. Khrushchev came to tea I began to receive letters that were more emotional than thoughtful and that took me to task sharply and bitterly for entertaining in my house the head of a great foreign power because his system of government happened to be different from our own. How, I wonder, do these people feel that we can learn to live together—as we must—if we cannot sit down over a cup of tea and quietly discuss our differences. At least, Mr. Khrushchev remarked at the end of our first long interview at Yalta, we didn't shoot at each other!

During all these years, of course, I have continued my regular newspaper column, which has run since 1935. After the Warsaw meeting I changed from a regular five-day column to a somewhat longer column which appears three times a week. I have continued, too, with my monthly magazine page, with my work for the A.A.U.N., with radio and television work, and with the lectures that take me far and wide.

And then, in spite of all my protestations that I would never again campaign actively, I did take part in John Kennedy's campaign for the Presidency, not so strenuously as I had worked four years earlier for Adlai Stevenson but as well as I could with the commitments I already had to carry out.

Having supported Adlai Stevenson during the convention, I was uncertain what I would do after the nomination. I withheld my decision to join Herbert Lehman as honorary chairman of the Democratic Citizens Committee of New York until I might have a chance to see and talk with the Democratic candidate and judge his qualities for myself.

When he came to see me at Hyde Park I found him a brilliant man with a quick mind, anxious to learn, hospitable to new ideas, hardheaded in his approach. Here, I thought, with an upsurge of hope and confidence, is a man who wants to leave behind him a record not only of having helped his countrymen but of having helped humanity as well. He was not simply ambitious to be president; he wanted, I felt convinced, to be a truly great president. He neither desired nor expected his task to be easy. He saw clearly the position of the United States in the world today as well as the shortcomings at home and was both too honorable and too courageous to color these unpalatable facts or distort them.

He believed that Americans could, as they have done in the past, meet and conquer the obstacles before them, but only if they knew what the obstacles were, what the conditions were, what must be done, by sacrifice, if necessary, by courage and conviction, certainly, to accomplish our ends.

And yet, because what happens in the next few years may well settle the future of the world for decades if not for longer, I waited, knowing what hinged on this election, for the first of the Great Debates. After that, I had no further hesitation. On the one side, I heard that all was for the best in the best of all possible worlds, that we lived in a country without unemployment or want, that our world leadership was unchallenged, and that it was, presumably, un-American to think differently. On the other side, I heard the less popular story, the one I had met face to face, over and over, in my travels around this country and around the world.

So I took part in the campaign. Unfortunately, I started out under a slight handicap as I picked up a virus and was far from feeling well, but I traveled to California by plane one afternoon and the next day was a fair example of what followed. In the morning, press conferences, television interviews, radio spots. A hasty bite of lunch. A long drive to a totally unimportant meeting. A long drive back. A brief rest at the home of my friend Mrs. Hershey Martin. A big meeting in a church, a meeting in a theater, a quick dinner, and a plane back to New York.

One day at home—and whenever I was at home I had meetings in various parts of the city—then a day in West Virginia, where we traveled 250 miles, stopping to shake hands and speak to outdoor crowds ten or eleven times. An hour's rest, a large rally, and back to New York by a small plane.

I campaigned in four states in the Middle West, two of which, I am glad to say, turned up in Mr. Kennedy's column. In the other two I felt I had not been very effective.

Again I say I am never going to campaign again. After all, next time I will be eighty and that would be absurd.

As the campaign advanced and I followed Mr. Kennedy's speeches, I came more and more to believe that he has the power to engender the sense of identification with him which is so important. If a man has this quality he can call out the best that is in people. Today the United States needs to be reminded of its greatness, and the greatness of a nation can never be more than the greatness of its people.

If my observation is correct, I have more hope for the solution of our problems than I have had for a long time. This does not mean that I am sure we can solve them all or that we will not make mistakes. But I do now have hope.

One feature of the campaign that dismayed and shamed me was the injection of the religious issue. It is a long time since I sat in my office and read the scurrilous literature that came into the Democratic headquarters during Alfred E. Smith's candidacy. Nothing quite so vicious happened during the 1960 campaign.

But the ugly feature was that it should arise at all. The question seems to me fairly simple. The Constitution gives us all religious freedom and we are not to be questioned about our religious beliefs. Some preposterous notions were set loose during the campaign: the Pope would dictate our form of government, our way of life, our education, our reading. The Catholic Church would dominate the nation politically as well as spiritually. This idea, of course, arises from the fact that in Spain, which is a Catholic country, the church does, for the most part, control the state. But Spain is not the United States and we have a Constitution which expressly provides for separation of church and state.

It is, I am afraid, true that frequently various religious groups endeavor to exert pressures and control over different legislative and educational fields. It is the job of all of us to be alert for such infringement of our prerogatives and prevent any such attempts from being successful. Like all our freedoms, this freedom from religious-group pressure must be constantly defended.

What seemed to me most deplorable was not the fact that so many people feared the strength of the Roman Catholic Church; it was that they had no faith in the strength of their own way of life and their own Constitution. Have we forgotten so quickly that our Founding Fathers came here for religious freedom—Protestants, Catholics, Quakers—for the right to worship God as they chose? This is our foundation stone. I, for one, believe in it with all my heart, and I reject, with shame and indignation, the fear, the lack of faith, the shaken confidence of those who would topple the stone on which we stand so proudly.

When the Great Debates had ended and another election was over, one could sit back, in a new quiet and calmness of spirit, to weigh what had happened. One thing I believe no one would challenge: the debates were a landmark in democratic procedure; they brought before the people of the whole country the candidates and their views. They stimulated a new interest in the issues, they emphasized the importance of the voting public's familiarizing itself with the issues at stake; they made the citizens, as they should be, a vital and participating element, with a stake in what happens to their country. The telling point, of course, is that, as a result of the debates, more people voted than have ever voted in the history of the country. And that was a victory for the democratic system.

And after the election—back to work. There is so much to do, so many engrossing challenges, so many heartbreaking and pressing needs, so much in every day that is profoundly interesting.

But, I suppose, I must slow down.

Index

Adamic, Louis, 232
Adamic, Mrs. Louis, 232
Adams, Henry, 84
Alassio, 30-31
Albany, N.Y., 64, 65-66, 146
Albert I of Belgium, 105
Allahabad, India, 332-333
"Allenswood," 20
Allison, John M., 337
All Pakistan Women's Association, 327, 329
American Association for the United Nations, 290, 294, 323, 324, 333, 418, 428
American Construction Council, 124
American Friends Service Committee, 136-137, 254
American Legion, 124
American Youth Congress, 193, 208-209
Anderson, Judith, 259-260
Anderson, Marian, 334
Aquinas, Thomas, 317
Arab refugees, 326
Atlantic Charter, 134, 222-223
Augusta, 222
Austin, Sen., 316, 323
Australia, 257
Austrian Tyrol, 28
Axel, Prince of Denmark, 96

Balfour, Mr., 87-88
Bali, 361-362, 363-364
Bankhead, William B., 203, 216
bank holiday, 164
Barker, Mrs., 93
Baruch, Bernard, 158, 179, 188, 268, 277

Beardall, Adm., 227
Beatrice, Princess of the Netherlands, 418-419
Beaufort, Duchess of, 243
Beaufort, Duke of, 243
Beirut, 325
Belafonte, Harry, 390
Bellamy, Ralph, 411
Belmont, Mrs. August, 69
Benes, Eduard, 252
Benham, Miss, 101
Bennett, Dr., 78, 115, 116
Berle, Adolf, 159
Berlin, 310, 321
Bernhard, Prince of the Netherlands, 221
Bertaux family, 25, 29
Bilbo, Theodore G., 300
Bingham, Robert, 131
Black, Van Lear, 114, 120
Black Crook, The, 237
Blair House, 173-174
Bleak House, 16
Boer War, 26
Bok, Cary, 249
Bok Foundation, 141
Bolívar, Simón, 308
Bonner, Daisy, 276
bonus march, 175-176
Borisov, Alexander, 312
Bourjaily, Monte, 197
Bowery Mission, 13
Bowles, Chester, 324, 329, 330-331, 406
Bowles, Mrs. Chester, 329
Boy-Ed, Capt., 86
Boy Scout Foundation, 124
Brandeis University, 405

443